The Jewish Response to
German Culture

The Jewish Response to German Culture

FROM THE ENLIGHTENMENT TO

THE SECOND WORLD WAR

EDITED BY

Jehuda Reinharz
Brandeis University

and

Walter Schatzberg
Clark University

PUBLISHED FOR CLARK UNIVERSITY
BY UNIVERSITY PRESS OF NEW ENGLAND
Hanover and London

UNIVERSITY PRESS OF NEW ENGLAND

Brandeis University   Dartmouth College
Brown University   University of New Hampshire
Clark University   University of Rhode Island
University of Connecticut   Tufts University
University of Vermont

Printed in the United States of America

LIBRARY OF CONGRESS CATALOGING IN PUBLICATION DATA
Main entry under title:

The Jewish response to German culture.

"Essays based on papers delivered at the International Conference on German Jews, held at Clark University, Worcester, Massachusetts, October 8–11, 1983."
Includes index.
1. Jews—Germany—Intellectual life—Congresses.
2. Judaism—Germany—History—Congresses. 3. Anti-semitism—Germany—Congresses. 4. Germany—Intellectual life—Congresses. 5. Germany—Ethnic relations—Con-gresses. I. Reinharz, Jehuda. II. Schatzberg, Walter.
III. International Conference on German Jews (1983 : Worcester, Mass.)
DS135.G33J47 1985   306'.089924043   85-14185
ISBN 0-87451-345-6

Cover illustrations, clockwise from left: Moses Mendelssohn; Synagogue at Ba-den-Baden, Kristallnacht, November 9, 1938; Oranienburger Strasse Syna-gogue in Berlin; nineteenth-century Jewish family in a Franconian village. *Back-ground illustration*: portion of a Memorbook from the eighteenth-century Palatinate, with water color and folk art patterns. All illustrations courtesy of the Leo Baeck Institute, New York.

5   4   3   2

To the Memory of Professor Uriel Tal

Contents

Preface

The following essays are based on papers delivered at the International Conference on German Jews held at Clark University, Worcester, Massachusetts, October 8–11, 1983. Scholars from England, Germany, Israel, and the United States examined the divergent but related paths followed by German Jews and non-Jews during the cultural, political, and socioeconomic transformations of Germany in the eighteenth, nineteenth, and twentieth centuries. Historians, philosophers, and literary scholars explored the interaction between a Jewish culture with its ancient heritage and a German culture in the process of modernization. The essays clarify the historical nature of the problematic relationship between Jews and Germans since the Enlightenment.

During the Enlightenment the ideological and legal foundations for the process of Jewish emancipation began. One of the first documents inspired by Enlightenment ideals and the exemplary figure of Moses Mendelssohn was Christian Wilhelm von Dohm's famous tract, *Über die bürgerliche Verbesserung der Juden* (1781), which called for equality of rights for Jews. Throughout their long history in German-speaking lands, the Jews' special position in a Christian society had been governed by edicts; emancipation, too, was granted through a series of edicts. In the Habsburg Empire, Joseph II issued a *Toleranzpatent* (Edict of Toleration) for Bohemia in 1781 and for Moravia in 1782. Within a framework of general reforms after Napoleon's victory over the Prussians, Chancellor Karl August von Hardenberg issued an Emancipation Edict in 1812, giving equal rights to the Jews of Prussia. That edict was extended in 1869 when the Prussian King Wilhelm I signed a law granting equality to all, regardless of religion, and abrogating all previous limitations on citizens' legal rights based on religious discrimination.

In his 1781 tract Dohm did much more than simply call for equal rights for Jews. He formulated an ideology that linked political freedom with character formation (*Bildung*). Speaking as an *Aufklärer,* Dohm called for the moral and political development of the Jews as people and as citizens. The essays in this volume examine the hopes, achievements, disappointments, and the ultimate tragic failure of the emancipation process.

George L. Mosse's essay provides the framework for this book. It traces the intellectual history of the concepts *Bildung* and *Sittlichkeit* (respectability) through which the German Jews expected to earn the social integration that was the promise of emancipation. He explains how the gradual narrowing of these concepts made them a threat to the very emancipation they were supposed to facilitate.

Alexander Altmann studies the far-reaching impact and implication of Moses Mendelssohn's archetypal role. Mendelssohn became the great model of Jewish educated citizenry in Germany and beyond. He sought to lead German Jews into a symbiosis of German language and culture on the one hand and Jewish tradition on the other.

Walter Röll's analysis of the Kassel "Ha-Meassef" is a case study of a Jewish community in Germany opening to the influence of secular European culture yet remaining closely identified with Jewish tradition.

Nathan Rotenstreich shows us Hermann Cohen as a philosopher within the German philosophic tradition. Cohen led the movement to return to Kant, and out of that return he developed a philosophy of Judaism. In this respect Rotenstreich places Cohen in a continuum with Moses Mendelssohn, with whom Cohen also shared the optimistic belief in the symbiosis of *Deutschtum* and *Judentum.*

Michael A. Meyer describes the German intellectual milieu in which the Jewish Reform movement emerged in the first half of the nineteenth century. He examines the work of three German-Jewish thinkers who developed theories of Judaism that responded to the dominant system of contemporary thought while at the same time agreeing with Jewish tradition. There was more opposition than adaptation in their ideas, but they made Judaism intellectually viable and thereby contributed to its deghettoization.

Jacob Katz takes a broad view of the participation of Jews in German culture as both producers and consumers. Through their active involvement in German culture, German Jews expected to accelerate the process of assimilation and integration. Katz maintains, however, that real integration into middle class German society eluded the Jews. Instead a subgroup developed, which conformed to some characteristics of the German middle class.

David Sorkin questions the extent to which acculturation and cultural production preserved or undermined the Jewish identity of German Jews. His case study of Berthold Auerbach shows us a Jewish writer who fully subscribed to emancipation ideology and yet remained a Jew both as a writer and as a man.

Lothar Kahn examines the generation of German-Jewish friends of Heinrich Heine who embraced the opportunities afforded by emancipation. They, too, became German writers. Whether they recognized their Jewish heritage and identity or not, they became increasingly aware of it with the resurgence of antisemitism in the post-Napoleonic era.

Harry Zohn describes the Jewish contribution to *fin-de-siècle* Vienna as an example of Jewish participation as producers of a secular culture with all the problems associated with the search for assimilation and symbiosis. Zohn chronicles the dominance of Jews in Vienna's literary and cultural life, many of whom sought salvation in ever-greater assimilation.

By contrast, Guy Stern looks at the relations between German-Jewish and Christian writers in exile during and after the apocalyptic events of Nazi Germany. He finds numerous examples of German-Jewish and Christian interaction and cooperation, the most notable example being the joint editorship of the *Weltbühne* by Karl von Ossietzki and Kurt Tucholsky, which was reminiscent of the Lessing-Mendelssohn relationship.

Werner E. Mosse examines the role played by Jews in Kaiser Wilhelm II's cultural matrix around the turn of the century. He sees essentially two antithetical cultures: the military, feudal, landowning, Lutheran proponents of the official culture, and a counterculture, heavily represented by Jews, that tended to be maritime, outward-looking, liberal, and broadly Anglophile. Mosse describes the relationships between the Kaiser and some of the more prominent Jews in this group, who have become known as *Kaiserjuden.*

Shulamit Volkov looks at the forces of dissimilation that drove Jews back together after 1890. The second and third generation of emancipated, liberal, Reform-minded Jews were frequently forced to acknowledge the limits of assimilation into German society. Both the rise of antisemitism and increasing contact with East European Jews at the turn of the century made German Jews more aware of their tradition and culture and led to a new assertion of Jewish identity.

Steven E. Aschheim explores the mythology of Jewish influence in the term *Verjudung*. He finds that this concept is related to the deep ambivalence Germans associated with the transformation of their country into a modern capitalist society. The success of Jewish acculturation and participation in the shaping of modern German culture became linked with German doubts about self and society in the new age, thereby reinforcing the emerging myth of *Verjudung*.

Marion Kaplan focuses on the relationship between German-Jewish women's organizations and the German-Gentile feminist movement. She describes the successes and failures of cooperation between the two groups and the survival strategies of Jewish women during the Nazi dictatorship.

Jehuda Reinharz traces the complicated Zionist response to antisemitism in the Weimar Republic. Believing that Palestine would solve the so-called Jewish Problem, Zionists for a long time left the defense against antisemitism to non-Zionist Jewish organizations. When more virulent antisemitism emerged in the last years of the Weimar Republic, the Zionist leadership increasingly turned its attention to the immediate dangers to Jews in Germany while at the same time continuing to work for a Jewish homeland in Palestine.

Kurt Düwell describes the efforts of Jewish cultural centers to maintain a cultural life in the face of Nazi restrictions during the early years of the dictatorship. The cultural centers provided Jews with the means of asserting and rediscovering their Jewish identity. At the same time, the cultural activities of these centers demonstrate how deeply German Jews were still attached to the German language and civilization.

In the final essay of this volume, Sybil H. Milton reminds us of the prodigious research that still needs to be done to tell the story of German Jewry. Her concern is with the documents that have survived the Holocaust but are scattered throughout the world in a variety of archives and the need to make these more accessible to the scholars working in the field of German-Jewish history.

These essays survey the dominant themes characterizing the German-Jewish experience during the two hundred years prior to the Holocaust. Research in the history of German Jews gives us the only picture we can have of a culture that has been destroyed.

May 1985   J.R., W.S.

Acknowledgments

For the initial inspiration and timely support for the International Conference on German Jews and for the publication of this volume, we wish to extend our appreciation to Henry J. Leir. We express our gratitude to the Goethe Institute of Boston, the Worcester Jewish Federation, and Clark University for their generous financial assistance. We are grateful to the German Consulate General in Boston for its encouragement and support.

We have dedicated this book to the late Professor Uriel Tal, who was a friend of many of the conference participants. He had taken an active part in planning the conference, but was unable to attend it.

We would like to express our special thanks to Professor Alexander Altmann, who accompanied the project from its earliest stage and has been helpful with advice and counsel throughout.

We would also like to thank Ann Hofstra Grogg for her superb editorial work and for preparing the index for the book.

The Jewish Response to
German Culture

GEORGE L. MOSSE

Jewish Emancipation
Between *Bildung* and Respectability

The history of German Jews was largely determined by the process of
Jewish emancipation. This process has often been explored by historians,
and yet several decisive aspects of Jewish emancipation in Germany remain to be discussed. The categories of legal, economic, and political history have been used to analyze the integration of Jews into German life,
while the history of ideas has served to clarify the place Jews held in
German thought. Factors not so readily assumed within traditional historical categories, however, also played an important part in the process
of Jewish emancipation. I will be concerned here with the ideal of self-
education or character formation and with those manners and morals
that constitute the idea of respectability. The course of Jewish emancipation took in all aspects of living—a way of life that Jews wanted to join
and Germans claimed as their own. Emancipated Jews did not merely
shed their old clothes in order to put on new, but attempted to become
radically changed men and women. Every aspect of this change was part
of the totality of the German-Jewish relationship.

The age into which a minority is emancipated will to a large extent
determine the priorities of its self-identification, not only at the time of
emancipation itself but into the future as well. Jewish emancipation in
Germany took place in the first decades of the nineteenth century, which,
for a relatively short period of time, saw many members of the middle
class and even some members of the aristocracy ready and willing to
transcend differences in background or religion. Jews were emancipated
into the autumn of the Enlightenment, when the ideals of rationalism,

pragmatism, and tolerance still retained their appeal. Jewish emancipation in Prussia—which will be my principal concern—was a result of defeat at the hands of Napoleon and the brief era of reform that followed during which it seemed as if the middle classes might break the monopoly of power held by the *Junker* caste. The annulment of bondage (serfdom in Prussia was abolished in 1807, four years before the emancipation of the Jews) and the upsurge of individualism promised well for the future. As part of this spirit of reform and liberality, the concept of *Bildung* was meant to open careers to talent and better citizenship through a process of self-cultivation based upon classical learning and the development of esthetic sensibilities.[1] Yet, at the very same time, society was also engaged in a search for stability and cohesion in the midst of social and political upheaval. Nationalism provided some of this cohesion and stability, but basic to the quest for social consolidation was the belief in a certain moral order expressed through the concept of respectability.

Both *Bildung* and respectability served to define the middle as over against the lower classes and the aristocracy. Jews were emancipated into *Bildung* and respectability, or, as it was expressed at the time, *Bildung* and *Sittlichkeit*—words much used by the German-Jewish press, in the sermons of rabbis, and in German-Jewish literature as well—exhorting Jews to acquire these entrance tickets to German society. To be sure, baptism was still the final certificate of acceptance; nevertheless, *Bildung* and *Sittlichkeit* played a less visible but almost equally important part in the acceptance of Jews by an ever more secular Gentile society. Jews, then, were emancipated into a society where *Bildung* promised equality and citizenship while respectability demanded a greater conformity in manners and morals than had existed earlier.

The importance of the ideal of *Bildung* as a key to German-Jewish emancipation has only recently received attention, and yet *Bildung* was considered the "knighthood of modernity," the possession of which signified membership in the bourgeoisie. *Bildung* meant considerably more than the difference between those who were educated and others who had little formal education; the concept combined the meaning carried by the word "education" with character formation. Man must grow like a plant, as Johann Gottfried von Herder put it, striving to unfold his personality until he becomes a harmonious, autonomous individual engaged in a

1. David Sorkin, "Wilhelm von Humboldt: The Theory and Practice of Self-Formation (*Bildung*), 1791–1810," *Journal of the History of Ideas* 44 (1983): 55–73.

continuous quest for knowledge.[2] Johann Wolfgang von Goethe's Wilhelm Meister (1795–96) always kept in mind "the cultivation of my individual self just as I am."[3] The tools used in furthering the process of self-education were the study of the Greek and Roman classics and the cultivation of esthetic sensibilities, once more exemplified by classical ideals of beauty. During his brief year as Prussian minister of education (1809–10), Wilhelm von Humboldt institutionalized the ideal of *Bildung* in the *Gymnasium* as well as in the university. Citizenship and *Bildung* were considered identical; after all it was one of the goals of Humboldt's educational reform to provide the Prussian state with better civil servants.

Bildung was readily embraced by Jews as helping to complete the process of emancipation. Berthold Auerbach, for example, wrote in 1846 that while "formerly the religious spirit proceeded from revelation, the present starts with *Bildung*."[4] Though most Jews sent their children to the more pragmatically oriented *Realgymnasium* rather than to Humboldt's humanistic *Gymnasium,* this was rationalized by *Sulamith,* for example, which reasoned in 1818 that Jews could not very well attend a "school for scholars" because they had to earn their living by trade. Nevertheless the *Realschule* taught "bourgeois vocations" while at the same time inculcating virtue and self-cultivation. Right thinking, so we are told, was taught through the study of mathematics, natural science, and history, a continuation of the Enlightenment approach to education that must have struck a responsive cord in German Jewry.[5]

Bildung was paired with *Sittlichkeit;* the open-endedness and individualism thought necessary for character formation were anchored in a restrictive moral order. The famous German dictionary by the brothers Grimm (begun in 1845 and not finished until 1931) defined *Sittlichkeit* as the proper moral comportment. Human actions based upon a moral imperative must express themselves through "decent" behavior and the "correct" attitudes toward the human body and its sexuality.[6] When, for example, *Sulamith,* a Jewish journal devoted to the cause of emancipation, examined in 1807 the state of *Sittlichkeit* among Frankfurt Jews, it

2. Hans Weil, *Die Entstehung des deutschen Bildungsprinzips* (Bonn, 1930), p. 47.
3. Johann Wolfgang von Goethe, *Wilhelm Meister's Apprenticeship,* trans. Thomas Carlyle (New York, 1962), p. 274.
4. Berthold Auerbach, *Schrift und Volk* (Leipzig, 1846), p. 323.
5. *Sulamith* 5, no. 2 (1818–19): 301–2.
6. Jacob Grimm and Wilhelm Grimm, *Deutsches Wörterbuch* (Leipzig, 1905), pp. 1266–72.

focused upon their cleanliness, sexual attitudes, and personal behavior. Decent and correct behavior was considered the outward sign of respectability.[7]

The concept of respectability was rather new in the age of Jewish emancipation, the result of the eighteenth-century pietistic and evangelical revivals, encouraged by the wars against "immoral France."[8] Respectability was not confined to the refinement of manners as part of the civilizing process that had begun with the change from feudal to court society, but set norms for all aspects of human life. These proved congenial to the upward mobility of the middle classes with their emphasis upon self-control, moderation, and quiet strength. Human passions and fantasies that might escape control were regarded as enemies of respectability, endangering social norms. Respectability provided social cohesion and set signposts that determined proper and improper behavior, the correct or incorrect attitudes toward the human body and its sexuality. Historians have barely begun to examine the concept of respectability, for it has been taken for granted, and yet it was a result of specific historical forces that met the needs of European society on the threshold of modernity.

Historians analyzing Jewish emancipation are beginning to refer to the concept of *Bildung* as aiding in the transformation of Jews into German Jews, but *Sittlichkeit* has been ignored, and this though Jews had to adjust their traditional ways to a new moral order of mostly Protestant inspiration. While some of the armor in the antisemitic arsenal consisted of the accusation that Jews were incapable of *Bildung,* a still more telling and long-lasting slander was that they undermined society through their uncontrolled sexual passions, their supposed slovenly looks and behavior—accusations that made *Sulamith* not only examine the comportment of Frankfurt Jews from the point of view of social respectability, as I mentioned, but also claim in its very first number that every people, including the Jews, is capable not only of *Bildung* but also of improving its "personal morality."[9]

To be sure, the quest for *Bildung* was in the forefront of those aiming at emancipation—*"Bildung* must be our principal business," asserted *Sula-*

7. "Betrachtungen in verschiedenen Hinsichten, über die Israeliten in Frankfurt am Main," *Sulamith* 1, no. 2 (1807): 153.

8. For the history of respectability, see George L. Mosse, *Nationalism and Sexuality: Respectability and Abnormal Sexuality in Modern Europe* (New York, 1985), chap. 1.

9. I. Wolf, "Inhalt, Zweck, und Titel dieser Zeitschrift," *Sulamith* 1, no. 1 (1806): 1.

mith[10]—but the need to teach respectable behavior and attitudes was recognized as well. The embourgeoisement of the Jews was crucial for their entry into German society at a time when middle-class social attitudes were making their mark, even though the *Junker* class retained political power. The embourgeoisement of the Jews must be seen as part of a more general trend—after all, the many lithographs that popularized Queen Luise of Prussia as a heroine of resistance against Napoleon no longer showed her in the midst of the royal court but surrounded by her husband and children, a middle-class family in royal dress.[11] Jews were judged by the standards of what was now considered decent, not only by Gentiles but by their own rabbis and press. The Frankfurt Jews, according to *Sulamith* in 1807, were passing through the childhood of culture; they lacked politesse, though their cleanliness was praiseworthy in spite of their crowded living conditions, while flirting and indecent sexual actions (*Unzucht*) had declined. They still did not know how to act with *Anstand*—according to decent and correct manners.[12] Many rabbinical sermons during the first decades of the nineteenth century repeat these concerns. Gotthold Salomon, for example, one of the most celebrated preachers of the time, called upon parents to teach children to enjoy pleasure only in moderation and to shun ill-concealed sensuousness encouraged by mixed dancing. "To be moderate in one's public amusements is part of . . . the refinement of manners."[13]

The "refinement of the Israelites" (*die Veredelung der Israeliten*) was forever on the lips of famous rabbis and filled the pages of *Sulamith*—the need for Jews to enter the process of *Bildung* and to show their devotion to social norms through their comportment—in short, the adjustment of Jews to the way of life of the middle classes. They must reactivate, we hear again and again, the urge to be virtuous, present in all men but lost to Jews during centuries of oppression. Men must get rid of their instinctual drives; to quote *Sulamith* once more, mere sensual pleasures must be rejected, "For what else is the meaning of virtue than the ruling of our passion through reason."[14] Jews were trying to escape their stereotype, in part encouraged by Gentiles and in part accompanied by taunts that Jews could never enter into respectability and become Germans.

10. Ibid., 5, no. 2 (1818–19): 47.
11. Mosse, *Nationalism and Sexuality,* p. 96.
12. "Betrachtungen in verschiedenen Hinsichten," p. 153.
13. Gotthold Salomon, *Twelve Sermons Delivered in the New Temple of the Israelites at Hamburg,* trans. Anna Maria Goldsmid (London, 1839), pp. 90, 92.
14. *Sulamith* 6, no. 2 (1822–24): 328.

The ghetto Jew was seen by the Gentile world as unproductive, earning his living through usury and by his wits, a *Schnorrer* incapable of
"honest work." The gospel of work was an article of faith in the age of
the industrial revolution, but for Jews it had a special significance if they
were to enter the German middle class. Working for a living, Jews were
repeatedly told, was the principal part of one's earthly vocation: "serving
the Divinity entails work as a sacred duty." This service demanded restraint and the rejection of pleasure. Self-control led to contentment, and
"no one who is idle attains happiness."[15] Just as the stereotype of the unproductive ghetto Jew was accepted in order to be exorcised, so the fear
of Jews perceived as unsteady and without roots pervades the sermons
and writings of men committed to Jewish emancipation. During the
1830s Gotthold Salomon inveighed against the danger presented by vac-
illating men who were described as effeminate and debauched. Like his
Protestant colleagues, he blamed such unsteadiness upon the fulfillment
of desire, just as gratification of sensuality must needs produce criminals.[16] But there is a tone of urgency here, an effort to stress the image of
masculinity so central to the concept of respectability as over against the
prevailing stereotype of the Jew.

Indeed, Jewish religious service itself had become a metaphor for
chaos and disorder in the Gentile world; the "Jew-school" seemed to exemplify irreverence and undignified behavior.[17] Leopold Zunz demanded
in the 1830s that "wailing must be banished from the temple."[18] Jewish
religious service had already been changed in order to conform to the
ideal of orderly and reverential behavior accepted by Christians as fitting
the occasion. While Jews proceeded to reform their own services, some
of the rulers of the German states decreed Jewish religious reform in order
to force the Jews to behave in a respectable manner, using Jewish worship to teach proper manners and morals. In 1823, for example, the
Grand Duke of Sachsen-Weimar-Eisenach promulgated rules for Jewish
religious service without, apparently, consulting rabbinical authority. Not
only were prayers to be said in the German language but all moving

15. Eduard Kley, *Predigten in dem neuen Israelitischen Tempel,* vol. 2 (Hamburg,
1826), pp. 69, 184.
16. Salomon, *Twelve Sermons,* pp. 92–93.
17. See, e.g., J. H. Campe's popular *Wörterbuch der deutschen Sprache,* vol. 2
(Braunschweig, 1808), p. 852.
18. Leopold Zunz, *Die gottesdienstlichen Vorträge der Juden, historisch entwickelt*
(Berlin, 1832), p. 479. For other examples, see George L. Mosse, "The Secularization
of Jewish Theology," in his *Masses and Man: Nationalist and Fascist Perceptions of
Reality* (New York, 1980), pp. 249–63.

around during services was strictly forbidden—as were all the noise and merriment that might take place inside the synagogue on Purim. Decent dress must be worn at all times, and the wearing of burial shrouds on Yom Kippur (customary among German Jews) was forbidden forthwith.[19]

The chief rabbi of the small duchy protested this decree, arguing that the state must not interfere with the life of individuals or individual organizations provided the moral fabric of society is upheld. Here the duke and the rabbi agreed, for the protest was directed only against having to say Hebrew prayers in German, while the chief rabbi himself saw the need for services to proceed in "true reverence, quiet and order"; for the rabbi as for the duke such reverential behavior symbolized the moral order. Small wonder that the rabbi's protest was ignored, though the new rules were enforced only in 1837 and choral singing introduced at the same time.[20]

Not only this chief rabbi, but most of the German-Jewish leadership understood only too well the importance of respectability for the cause of Jewish emancipation, and they were ready and eager to accept its dictates of conformity, the more so as respectability provided tangible signs as to how life should be lived in Gentile society. *Sulamith,* during the first decades of the nineteenth century, was filled with descriptions of Jewish schools dedicated to the teaching of virtue, emphasizing the duty of work as over against the temptations of idleness. Ludwig Philippson, rabbi and founder of the *Allgemeine Zeitung des Judentums,* writing on the Prussian king's birthday in 1837, stated with approval the basic presuppositions of respectability. "I am a Prussian," he began his tribute to the king, and he continued by asserting that the equality which the king grants to his subjects excludes sectarianism and divisiveness; instead, government must encourage order and quiet. When the majority wants to retain all that is decent and proper, Philippson concluded, one or two persons cannot be allowed to create a disturbance or to frustrate its will.[21]

Philippson linked civic equality to a respectable conformity. He assumed that this moral order corresponded to the wishes of the majority; patterns of thought and behavior that had not been generally accepted in the last century were now taken for granted. Philippson foreshadows a time toward the end of the nineteenth century when laws punishing so-

19. Cited in "Theologie," *Allgemeine Zeitung des Judentums* 1, no. 26 (July 2, 1837): 101–3.
20. "Theologie," ibid., no. 7 (May 16, 1837): 26–27.
21. "Zum dritten August," ibid., no. 45 (August 3, 1837): 177.

called abnormal behavior—the sodomy laws, for example, in England and Germany—no longer appealed to religious truth for their justification but to the people's sense of justice instead. The norms of society must prevail; they were a goal to be attained in the process of assimilation.

Jews brought into their process of emancipation attitudes crucial to respectability, and the usual stereotype of the rootless ghetto Jew did not correspond to realities, though both Gentiles and a large number of Jews accepted it as obvious truth. Above all, the traditional quality of Jewish family life could not be overlooked. Jews seemed to lead an exemplary family life even before the nuclear family was regarded as basic to the health of society and the state. After emancipation family bonds tended to take the place of rapidly loosening religious ties. "How much lack of order and confusion would rule in the world if God had not created this beneficent institution [the family] and elevated it into a sacred law." The well-being of all human society depends upon it, in the words of one rabbinical sermon, and the state has a stake in seeing to it that order and decency are preserved.[22] Once again, Jews offer their loyalty and collaboration to the state viewed as moral authority.

Jewish identity was linked to family pride, which was often the reason why German Jews refused baptism. When Moritz Oppenheim, one of the first German-Jewish painters, wanted to document Jewish patriotism in 1833–34, he painted a Jewish volunteer freshly returned from the German Wars of Liberation, admired by his entire family. Oppenheim painted many scenes from Jewish family life, projecting German middle-class values into his scenes of ghetto life as well. Here Jewish tradition was not merely compatible with the demands of citizenship, but both before and after emancipation exemplary of the middle-class way of life.[23]

Jews found it easy to enter into this aspect of respectability, for they had exemplified the bourgeois family before it was born, and perhaps because of this long tradition they were able to modernize their family structure more easily than the Gentiles. As Shulamit Volkov has shown, by the end of the nineteenth century German Jews not only had fewer children than other Germans but took better medical care of their in-

22. Marriage sermon of the district rabbi of Bamberg, reprinted in *Sulamith* 7, no. 2 (1833): 390.
23. Ismar Schorsch, "Art as Social History: Oppenheim and the German Jewish Vision of Emancipation," in *Moritz Oppenheim: The First Jewish Painter* (Israel Museum, Jerusalem, 1983), pp. 44, 51.

fants.[24] The Jewish family was a constant irritant to antisemites, as I hope to have shown elsewhere;[25] they were forced to argue that though Jews themselves lived the ideal bourgeois family life, this did not keep them from seducing Christian women and trafficking in white slavery. Indeed, the very success of Jewish embourgeoisement was turned by antisemites against the Jews, especially by racists like Richard Wagner, for whom the Jews not only exemplified the power of gold and a sterile legal order but also the undue restraint put upon human passions.[26]

Sittlichkeit narrowed the perspective of *Bildung* and tended to focus upon the finished product rather than upon the never-ending process of self-cultivation. Manners and morals were thought not subject to change but laid down for all time and place. The resulting way of life was described in Georg Hermann's novel *Jettchen Gebert* (1906), required reading for most German Jews. Jewishness in the novel is expressed through family pride, the "good name" of the Geberts, respected for their probity by Jews and Gentiles alike. The family business symbolized family worth, the visible proof that the Jew had become an honest bourgeois and respected citizen—a theme that is carried in German-Jewish literature from the Geberts to Lion Feuchtwanger's *Oppenheim,* written as the Nazis came to power, where the sale of the family business signaled the end of German Jewry. The older Geberts still lived in the world of the Enlightenment, but all of them wanted "a steady pace of life lived in the most perfect harmony." This pace of life was disrupted when Jettchen attempts to marry a penniless Christian writer. Jettchen's worldly, tolerant, and cultivated uncle gives two reasons why, despite the couple's love for each other, Jettchen cannot be allowed to marry, and both of them sum up widespread attitudes among German Jews. First of all, the writer does not belong to the bourgeoisie, while Jettchen cannot be torn from the middle classes; all her roots are there. Second, the writer is a Christian, and such a marriage would betray family pride, the Geberts having refused to trade their religion for advantage of position or title.[27] Opposition to intermarriage did constitute the bottom line of Jewish assimilation, while being regarded as a solid bourgeois was its

24. Shulamit Volkov, "Erfolgreiche Assimilation oder Erfolg und Assimilation: Die deutsch-jüdische Familie im Kaiserreich," *Jahrbuch, Wissenschaftskolleg zu Berlin* (1982–83), pp. 373–87.

25. Mosse, *Nationalism and Sexuality,* p. 142.

26. Paul Lawrence Rose, "The Noble Anti-Semitism of Richard Wagner," *Historical Journal* 25 (1982): 751–63.

27. Georg Hermann, *Jettchen Gebert* (Berlin, 1906), pp. 350, 259–61.

reward. When in 1933 Jews were expelled from active participation in German life and had to establish their own cultural organization, Georg Hermann's novel was still praised as recalling the finest tradition of the German-Jewish past.[28]

The contradiction between the openness and tolerance of *Bildung* and the restricted vision of respectability was not obvious to those living in the age of Jewish emancipation, though *Bildung* itself soon became a monopoly of a caste rather than accessible to anyone willing and able to participate in the process of self-cultivation. The alliance between academics and bureaucrats took control, guarding the concept from those without the proper humanistic education. *Bildung* was nationalized as well—an attribute of those who could boast Germanic roots and who alone could appreciate the good, the true, and the beautiful.[29] Not only *Bildung,* but respectability itself, contracted, elaborating the distinctions between those inside and those outside society. These narrowing visions were perhaps a greater menace to the continuing process of Jewish assimilation than the often crude and violent accusations of antisemites against the Jews. Here means of integration were cut off or made more difficult to use, not primarily because of unreasoning hatred against the Jews but because of the fear of social change, the attempt to find the solid ground in the midst of the chaos.

Those who were thought to lack respectability were branded as abnormal, hostile to the norms that society had established. Medicine came to the aid of respectability, defining normal or abnormal behavior as matters of sickness and health. The physician played a crucial part in elaborating the stereotype of the outsider, so different from that of the respectable citizen: unable to control his passions, his nerves shattered, weak of body and mind. Thus the stereotype of the insane and the antisemitic stereotype of the Jew shared the same "movable physiognomy."[30]

The medicalization of the outsider—those who did not fit society's image of itself, such as the insane, homosexuals, or habitual criminals—was accompanied by the medicalization of the Jew. Famous physicians at the turn of the nineteenth century, like Richard von Krafft-Ebing or J. M. Charcot, thought that Jews were inclined to nervousness because of weak

28. Account of lecture by Dr. Walter Perl, June 11, 1935, in Jüdischer Kulturbund, box III, Wiener Library, University of Tel Aviv.

29. George L. Mosse, *German Jews beyond Judaism* (Bloomington, Ind., 1985), chap. 1.

30. Sander L. Gilman, *Seeing the Insane* (New York, 1982), passim. For more on the medicalization of outsiders, see Mosse, *Nationalism and Sexuality,* esp. chap. 6.

nerves, the result of inbreeding.[31] Nervousness undermined that calm resolve respectability demanded. To be sure, these physicians believed that Jewish nervousness was a tendency that could be cured, while for the enemies of the Jews it became a racial characteristic that doomed them for all time. The alliance between medicine and respectability meant that health and sickness were to a large extent dependent upon the acceptance of the moral order. Those who stood outside the limits of respectability must be easily recognized through their looks and bodily posture as a warning to all normal persons. Superior health implies superior beauty, so the wisdom of both doctors and laymen ran; health and beauty always went together according to the Greek example.[32]

Strength and vigor were rewards for moral rectitude and proper comportment, the ideal of manliness that accompanied the rise of respectability. *Sulamith* cited Proverbs 31 as the justification for woman's passive role, in which learning to dance took the place that gymnastics and the toughening of the body held in male education. The toughening of the male body became an obsession at the end of the nineteenth century, though gymnastics had been practiced throughout the century in order to further the strength of the *Volk*. Jews had been members of gymnastic associations, though many local groups excluded them from membership. Toward the turn of the century Jews founded their own gymnastic associations. The cultivation of the body through sport was supposed to produce "muscle Jews," as Max Nordau told the Second Zionist Congress.[33] The *Jüdische Turnerzeitung* wrote in 1910 that sitting in cafés led to neurasthenia: Jews should feel ashamed for failing to steel their bodies.[34] Such Zionists believed that in the Diaspora some type of degenerative process had indeed taken place among Jews, mirrored in the appearance of neurasthenia. Not only Zionists but those, like Cesare Lombroso, committed to assimilation, shared these preconceptions.[35] They were based upon the need to repudiate the stereotype of the ghetto Jew of the past who through his appearance and behavior seemed to deny that ideal of manliness basic to respectability, and therefore to the pro-

31. Sander L. Gilman, "Jews and Mental Illness: Medical Metaphors, Anti-Semitism and the Jewish Response," *Journal of the History of the Behavioral Sciences* 20 (1984): 153.

32. Mosse, *Nationalism and Sexuality*, pp. 139, 140.

33. Max Nordau, *Zionistische Schriften* (Cologne and Leipzig, 1909), p. 379. The Second Zionist Congress met in Basel in 1898.

34. "Das Kaffeehaus-Judentum," *Jüdische Turnerzeitung* 11, nos. 5/6 (May–June 1910): 74.

35. Gilman, "Jews and Mental Illness," p. 154.

cess of Jewish assimilation. The same fear of rootless outsiderdom that
had haunted Gotthold Salomon at the actual time of emancipation remained to haunt German-Jewish history.

Jews who practiced sport or rode and climbed mountains are rare
in nineteenth- and even twentieth-century literature. Until the mid-
nineteenth century, for example, Jews on the German stage were usually
old men, lonely and without a family that would document their bourgeois status.[36] This image of old age was symbolic for lack of manly
vigor, and even when young Jews appeared in plays, they were usually
pictured as weak and puny. Small wonder, then, that some members of
the German Youth Movement stated that because of their weak bodies
Jews could never become Germans.[37] Adolf Hitler himself summed up
the thrust behind this accusation: the Jew drains from all races their energy and power, he tries to deprive them of all that might serve to steel
the muscles. The Jew turns healthy morals upside down, lacks hygiene,
and transforms night into day[38] (an example, by the way, that Hitler
himself seems to have followed). The outsider was the focus of all that
presented a danger to the norms of society, a menace to respectability.
Through his supposed bodily weakness the Jew menaced the ideal of
masculinity; as an unmanly man he threatened the clear and distinct division of roles between the sexes. I have shown elsewhere how racists accused the Jews of being feminine, an accusation based upon the stereotype of women as the antitype of manliness: passive, in need of protection,
not in control of their passions.[39] The sexual division of labor was at the
root of respectability, as important for social cohesion as the economic division of labor that G. W. F. Hegel and Karl Marx saw as essential for
the existence of capitalism.

Jews attempted to pass the test of their manhood and citizenship by
volunteering in the German Wars of Liberation, and in two versions of
the painting of the returned soldier, Moritz Oppenheim depicted him
either showing the Iron Cross, the highest decoration for valor, to his
family, or as bearing a wound home from battle. Thus Jews were emancipated not only into the age of *Bildung* and *Sittlichkeit* but also into the

36. Helmut Jenzsch, *Jüdische Figuren in deutschen Bühnentexten des 18. Jahrhunderts* (Hamburg, 1971), p. 151.
37. Ernst Michael Jovy, "Deutsche Jugendbewegung und Nationalsozialismus" (In-
augural diss., University of Cologne, 1952), p. 223.
38. *Hitler: Sämtliche Aufzeichnungen, 1905–1924,* ed. Eberhard Jäckel and Alex
Kuhn (Stuttgart, 1980), pp. 195–96.
39. Mosse, *Nationalism and Sexuality,* chap. 5.

Wars of Liberation against Napoleon. However well they performed in battle, the imputation of outsiderdom still lingered, and Jews passing the test of their manhood in war, side by side with their Christian comrades, were often accused of cowardice when it came to the point of danger. The antisemitic campaign against supposed Jewish shirkers in the First World War induced the high command to gather statistics on how many Jewish soldiers served in the front lines. Jews had to embrace the ideal of manliness and bodily strength as part of their embourgeoisement, but this imperative did not silence the suspicion of cowardice and bodily weakness that followed the emancipated Jew as a potential outsider.

Respectability itself was part of the narrowing vision of German society. Liberalism could remain alive even while respectability attempted to tighten the reigns, for political and economic freedoms were not supposed to entail freedom of manners and morals; rather the cohesion respectability provided was thought necessary to supply liberal freedoms with a stable base. The menace of potential outsiderdom threatened by respectability was not clearly perceived at the time. Liberalism seemed to provide a secure anchor for Jewish assimilation, despite the remaining obstacles to full citizenship. The harmonious life of the Geberts, with hardly a cloud on the horizon, was typical of many German-Jewish families before the First World War. The narrowing social vision seemed latent rather than operative, lying in wait until after the war when it found a mass base in its onslaught against Jewish emancipation. More research is needed on how *Sittlichkeit* both made Jewish emancipation easier and ultimately facilitated the image of the Jew as the outsider.

The concept of *Bildung,* once so promising for the process of assimilation, was detached from the idea of citizenship, increasingly devoted to a search for the good, the true, and the beautiful standing above the concerns of daily life. We have already seen *Bildung* substitute pedagogy for self-cultivation; now the product rather than the process counted. I have attempted to show elsewhere how Jews resisted the ever-narrowing concept of *Bildung* and sought to cling to its earlier humanistic ideal. At the start of a new wave of antisemitism, for example, in 1881 some leaders of the Jewish community called for subscriptions to a Lessing monument in order to remind Germans of the tradition of the Enlightenment and counter the growing fanaticism of the times. Just so, it has been calculated that most Goethe biographies were written by Jews in order to recall that Germany's cultural hero was committed to the humanistic ideals of *Bildung* and the Enlightenment.[40] Eventually even a writer like Berthold Litzmann, who in 1914 still pleaded for reconciliation with the French, took it for granted that "today, in contrast to the nineteenth century, intellectual independence and individuality can only flourish if they are rooted in the nation."[41]

Jewish commitment to the humanistic ideal of *Bildung* was based on the correct perception that only through transcending a German past, which the Jews did not share, could Jew meet German on equal terms. Historical roots had played no part in Humboldt's concept of *Bildung*, and the classics upon whose knowledge the concept so largely depended were considered a universal heritage. Similarly, the concept of respectability was based upon a moral order and not dependent upon shared historical roots.

Emancipation meant not only a flight from the ghetto past but also from German history regarded as an obstacle to integration, for even if the national past was myth rather than reality, the Jews were, through no fault of their own, excluded from participating in the roots of the nation. The search for common ground transcending history was one reason why Jews as a group tended to support cultural and artistic innovation to a greater extent than did Gentiles. Jews provided a disproportionate share of support for the *avant garde* and for educational experiments as well.[42] This *avant garde* in arts and letters broke with past traditions but did not really menace respectability. Thus one could remain *sittlich* and support expressionist or impressionist painters, or the *avant-garde* theater, even if it presented nudity upon the stage and experimented with all forms of sexual expression. Supporting cultural innovation not only helped overcome the handicap of a separate past but also continued the impetus of *Bildung* as a process of self-cultivation. But then, *Bildung* had always concentrated upon culture and all but ignored politics and society.

Bildung furthered a cultural vision of the world. This facilitated the division between culture and other aspects of life that led many Germans to equate *Bildung* with a vague quest for "higher things," as we have seen, but it also made it easier to support cultural innovation while remaining traditionalist in politics and social life. Moreover, it blinded

40. For these and other examples, see Mosse, *German Jews beyond Judaism,* passim, esp. chap. 3.
41. Berthold Litzmann, speech of November 26, 1914, in his *Ernst von Wildenbruch und der nationale Gedanke* (Berlin, 1914), p. 10.
42. See Jacob Katz, "German Culture and the Jews," in this volume, pp. 85–99.

those committed to the primacy of humanistic culture to political realities. Jews tried to make contact with the masses of Germans, largely through literature,[43] but they were also suspicious of these masses as easily aroused and carried away by passion. Jews shared fully what James Sheehan has called the lingering doubt of liberals about the relationship between what they regarded as the real *Volk* of enlightened and liberal men and the masses of the German nation. They feared what Jacob Auerbach castigated at midcentury as the fanaticized and misled masses, and once again, not without reason.[44] The pressure of mass politics, the desire of the German masses for their political emancipation, introduced an emotional and irrational factor into politics rather easily captured by the antisemitic German Right.

The necessity to transcend the past and the effort to continue the emancipatory ideal were common to most German Jews, whatever their political faith. Young Jewish socialists tried to concretize the ideal of a common humanity through the manner in which this transcendence must be accomplished. The final victory of socialism over present property relationships would issue in the triumph of humanity, the true unfolding of *Bildung* and the Enlightenment. The early Zionists, in turn, attempted to humanize their nationalism, regarding the nation as a stepping stone to a shared humanity.[45] However, all these young Jewish socialists or nationalists, despite their desire to transcend political liberalism, never sought to attack *Sittlichkeit*. Indeed the goal of the revolution or of the new Jewish nation was to strengthen *Bildung* and *Sittlichkeit*, not to abolish them. For assimilated German Jews, they provided the common ground upon which all Germans could meet, ignoring differences of religion or historical experience, and where, in the last resort, Germans could meet on terms of equality with the other members of the human race.

Bildung and *Sittlichkeit*, which had stood at the beginning of Jewish emancipation in Germany, accompanied German Jews to the end, blinding them, as many other Germans, to the menace of National Socialism. Though the Centralverein deutscher Staatsbürger jüdischen Glaubens waged a courageous fight against *völkisch* nationalism, it seemed incon-

43. Mosse, *German Jews beyond Judaism*, chap. 3.

44. James J. Sheehan, *German Liberalism in the Nineteenth Century* (Chicago, 1978), p. 107; Jacob Auerbach, "Lessing und Mendelssohn," in Sigismund Stern, *Einladungsschrift zu der öffentlichen Prüfung der Bürger und Real-Schule der Israelitischen Gemeinde* (Frankfurt a.M., 1967), p. 57.

45. Mosse, *German Jews beyond Judaism*, chap. 5.

ceivable that someone like Hitler, apparently without *Bildung* or the proper comportment, could occupy Otto von Bismarck's chair in the Reich's chancellery.

The embourgeoisement of the German Jews in all its hopes and frustration must be seen against the background of the embourgeoisement of German society as a whole. *Bildung* and respectability were two important aspects of the triumph of the middle classes, exemplified by the spread of decent and correct manners and morals—of a certain way of life—long before it was completed by the sharing of political power. The ideals of *Bildung* and respectability, once so promising, eventually proved dangerous to that process of emancipation which they had once encouraged. *Bildung* turned away from Humboldt's concept, falling into the hands of narrow-minded academics and bureaucrats. *Sittlichkeit* as respectability played a more complex role through stigmatizing and identifying those supposedly outside social norms, presenting a potential danger to Jews as new arrivals. Emancipation made all aspects of German life relevant to the Jewish situation in Germany, especially those social and cultural factors apt to be taken for granted as an integral part of a way of life that dated from the past and would never change.

The historical myths of nationalism both narrowed the base of this way of life and gave it a new dimension of immutability. Jews had to transcend this historical base even while attempting to maintain *Bildung* and respectability—ideals that in reality were not immutable but changing with the passage of time, just as they had triumphed only in the age of Jewish emancipation. Thus the process of emancipation reflected some basic demands of modern society that, for better or worse, both Jews and Germans were forced to fulfill. German Jews became *Bildungsbürger,* exemplifying until the end of their history the ideals current at the time of their emancipation.

ALEXANDER ALTMANN

Moses Mendelssohn as the Archetypal German Jew

The term "archetypal" as used in the title of this essay needs some clarification. It does not correspond to the way it was used by Carl Gustav Jung, who associated the archetypal with myth and the collective unconscious. The term as understood here implies nothing of the sort. It simply suggests that the image of Moses Mendelssohn served German Jewry as a model upon which to form itself, as a potent directive, and as an assuring symbol of what it stood for. In many ways Mendelssohn was the first modern German Jew, the prototype of what the world came to recognize as the specific character, for better or worse, of German Jewry. The uniqueness of that character can hardly be disputed.[1]

There is ample evidence of the fact that the Jews of Germany were acutely conscious of the role Mendelssohn's image played in their lives. A steady stream of literary production was devoted to an evaluation of his personality and the works he had left behind. The literature is permeated with a sense of Mendelssohn's relevance for the basic aspirations that animated German Jewry. The private correspondence of prominent Jews like Leopold Zunz and Moritz Lazarus contains frequent references to Mendelssohn; he was obviously much alive in their consciousness. Outstanding anniversaries of Mendelssohn's birth and death were cherished occasions for public commemoration and fresh spurts of literary activity

---

1. The question as to whether German Jewry faced problems different from those encountered by other European Jewries was discussed at a colloquium held in Jerusalem in 1970. See *Zur Geschichte der Juden in Deutschland im 19. und 20. Jahrhundert* (Jerusalem, 1971), pp. 20–34.

about him.[2] To all intents and purposes, he was the patron saint of German Jewry. The numerous anecdotes that circulated and the many witticisms—some in rhyme—that were attributed to him were often spurious, but, precisely on this account, they testify to the popularity and almost legendary status he had attained as the very incarnation of wisdom and virtue. There was a tendency among the rank and file to lose sight of the more strictly defined contours of the philosopher and writer by indulging in a purely sentimental approach à la Gartenlaube.[3] Yet the awareness of his truly historical accomplishments was never seriously in jeopardy.

These observations apply to the bulk of German Jewry, which was determined to uphold the Jewish heritage in one form or another. Those who chose the path of total assimilation were, naturally, at loggerheads with Mendelssohn. Karl Marx had only harsh, disparaging words to say about him. Heinrich Heine, on the other hand, was sufficiently imbued with Jewish values to feel a great respect for the man. Moses Hess, who, from Marxism, returned to the fold, gave the most concise expression to his view of Mendelssohn's significance by pointing out that Mendelssohn had shown how a modern intellectual may remain a Jew.[4]

The questions that this essay seeks to answer are, In what manner did the archetypal function of Mendelssohn's image operate? What are the specific areas in which it came to fruition? In reply, altogether four points may be elaborated.

I

First, Mendelssohn was the first Jew to identify himself with the cultural concerns of Germany and to make the German tongue the medium of his literary creativity. Although a master of biblical and rabbinic Hebrew and continuing, in some not inconsiderable measure, to use it for literary purposes, he confessed that his most personal thought could be adequately

2. Herrmann M. Z. Meyer, *Moses Mendelssohn Bibliographie* (Berlin, 1965), pp. 121–74 and passim.

3. Fritz Bamberger, "Die geistige Gestalt Moses Mendelssohns," *Monatsschrift für Geschichte und Wissenschaft des Judentums* 73, n.s. 37 (1929): 81; Henry Wassermann, "Jews and Judaism in the *Gartenlaube*," *Leo Baeck Institute Year Book* (hereafter *LBIYB*) 23 (1978): 60.

4. *Karl Marx–Friedrich Engels Briefwechsel*, Abt. 3, Bd. 4 of *Marx–Engels Gesamtausgabe* (Berlin, 1931), p. 340; *Karl Marx–Friedrich Engels Werke*, vol. 32 (Berlin, 1965), p. 686. On Heine, see S. S. Prawer, *Heine's Jewish Comedy: A Study of His Portraits of Jews and Judaism* (Oxford, 1983), pp. 56–57 and passim. For Moses Hess, see his *Rom und Jerusalem: Die letzte Nationalitätsfrage*, 2d ed. (Leipzig, 1899), p. 41, where Mendelssohn is listed with Saadia, Maimonides, and Baruch Spinoza, who, "despite their progressive intellectual development, did not become apostates."

expressed only in the German language. This may have been due partly to the stultified growth of Hebrew, but it is explained, above all, by his nearly total immersion, in his late adolescence, in the modalities of German language and literature. Already his anonymously published first work, the *Philosophical Dialogues* (1755), was sufficiently distinguished in its diction to be mistaken, by one of the reviewers, as a work by Gotthold Ephraim Lessing.[5] It is well known that Mendelssohn's contemporaries, including Immanuel Kant and Johann Wolfgang von Goethe, admired his style. Wilhelm Dilthey spoke of the new German prose created by Lessing, Mendelssohn, the young Goethe, and Justus Möser as a factor that made the writing of the great legislative enterprise of the age of Frederick II (1794) possible.[6] In November 1785, when Mendelssohn, in the anguish over the Jacobi affair, needed to hear some words of encouragement, August Hennings reminded him of some of the accomplishments he had to his credit: in his early metaphysical writings, he had been the first to present the depth of speculative thought in graceful fashion; in his contributions to *Literaturbriefe,* he had molded the literary taste of the Germans.[7] Mendelssohn was, no doubt, the archetypal figure of Jewish *literati* in Germany.

He was, at the same time, the spiritual ancestor of all those numberless Jews who cherished in the German language "the sweet sound of the mother tongue." The intimacy with German, for which Mendelssohn had to struggle hard, came naturally to generations of Jews after him. What a travesty of the truth it was when, on April 12, 1933, one of the "Twelve Statements of the German Student Body" said: "When a Jew writes German, he lies."[8] Robert Schumann would hardly have set poems by Heine to music had he felt them to be anything but German and authentically human. The authenticity of Mendelssohn's German prose remained the hallmark of the best of German-Jewish writers down to Karl Wolfskehl and Franz Kafka.

This leads us to the much-debated question as to whether one may speak of a German-Jewish symbiosis. Selma Stern-Taeubler concluded

5. Alexander Altmann, *Moses Mendelssohn: A Biographical Study* (University, Ala., 1973), pp. 39–40.

6. Wilhelm Dilthey, *Gesammelte Schriften,* 3d ed. (Stuttgart and Göttingen, 1964), 12:143.

7. August Hennings to Moses Mendelssohn, November 1785, in *Moses Mendelssohn Gesammelte Schriften Jubiläumsausgabe,* ed. Alexander Altmann (Berlin, 1929), 13:326.

8. Quoted by Ingrid Belke, *In den Katakomben,* special issue of *Marbacher Magazin* 25 (1983), Chronik 1933, p. 67.

the final chapter of the third volume of her great work, *The Prussian State and the Jews,* by quoting Martin Buber describing the dialogue between Lessing and Mendelssohn as "the earliest stage of the symbiosis between the German and the Jewish spirit." She added, "The dialogue ended in 1933, when the symbiosis had not been accomplished though it had been a 'real possibility.' "⁹ In other words, the friendship between Lessing and Mendelssohn was the first and last instance of a true dialogue or symbiosis between German and Jew. This bleak appraisal has to be qualified on two counts. First, Mendelssohn's relationship to Lessing was not the only exemplification of that "real possibility," though it undoubtedly was the one he most cherished. He had other close and intimate friends—Friedrich Nicolai, Thomas Abbt, Hennings, and, to a lesser extent, Dr. Johann Georg Zimmermann and Elise and Johann A. H. Reimarus. Second, during the nearly 150 years between Mendelssohn's death and 1933, many instances of friendship and true dialogue did occur, as Gershom Scholem, the most outspoken opponent of the symbiosis theory, readily admitted.¹⁰ Ingrid Belke's admirable edition of the correspondence between Heymann Steinthal and Gustav Glogau is an apt reminder of this fact.¹¹ Though severely limited in scope, the precedent set by Mendelssohn and his German friends did not remain without fruitful consequences.

The symbolic significance that German Jews increasingly attached to the friendship between Mendelssohn and Lessing was indicative of the disillusion they suffered in their efforts for social acceptance. Mendelssohn's image as linked to Lessing's represented an ideal that had eluded them. Recalling and celebrating that friendship between the "Dioscuri" was more of an incantation than anything else. The archetypal figure of Mendelssohn assumed here the aura of mythical rather than prototypical reality. This is equally true of the dream role he played as the model of the hero in Lessing's drama *Nathan the Wise.* When it first appeared in print (1779), it was at once taken for granted that the figure of Nathan portrayed none other than Mendelssohn.¹² German Jews eagerly adopted this interpretation. How firmly they clung to it may be gauged from the fact that *Nathan the Wise* was selected for the première of the Jewish

9. A condensed English version of the chapter appeared in Selma Stern-Taeubler, "The First Generation of Emancipated Jews," *LBIYB* 15 (1970): 40.

10. Gershom Scholem, *Judaica,* vol. 2 (Frankfurt a.M., 1970), p. 16.

11. Ingrid Belke, ed., *Moritz Lazarus and Heymann Steinthal: Die Begründer der Völkerpsychologie in ihren Briefen,* II, 1 (Tübingen, 1983), pp. 1–367.

12. Altmann, *Mendelssohn,* pp. 569–70.

Kulturbund theater in Berlin, on October 1, 1933—an occasion intended by the Nazis to mark the ghettoization of German Jewry.[13] The choice of this particular play was inspired, no doubt, by two considerations: first, by the Jews' desire to remind the German people of Lessing's idea of tolerance, and second, by their determination not to become ghettoized in spirit, no matter how narrowly they were otherwise confined. The performance of *Nathan* recalled the image of Mendelssohn who had led his people out of the ghetto. The legacy bequeathed by him, a wide-openness to culture, was to remain their treasured possession.

Mendelssohn had, indeed, become the great *Vorbild* of the Jewish educated citizenry (*Bildungsbürgertum*) in Germany and beyond. He epitomized all the virtues enshrined in the typically German term *Bildung,* for which there is no equivalent in any other language. To the early generations of "the Enlightened" (*maskilim*), Mendelssohn was an object of boundless admiration, a kind of new Moses.[14] He was enthusiastically hailed as the harbinger of a new dawn. Varying Alexander Pope's lines on Sir Isaac Newton, an anonymous contributor to *Ha-Meassef* wrote: "Truth and religion lay hid in night. / God said, Let Moses [Mendelssohn] be! And there was light."[15] During the last phase of German Jewry, the Weimar period, Franz Rosenzweig lamented the excess of *Bildung* and the paucity of Jewish substance,[16] but essentially he, too, continued to follow the Mendelssohnian pattern of deghettoization that had become the norm in Western Europe and was the envy of many an Eastern European Jew.[17]

II

There is a further dimension to Mendelssohn's archetypal role, and it relates to his image as a loyal Jew. I have already mentioned Moses Hess's somewhat simplistic, yet true and compelling, observation that Mendelssohn showed how one could remain a Jew even though one's intellectual pursuits had opened up vistas far away from Judaism. Mendelssohn had to face repeated challenges to his Jewish faith, but he never wavered in his allegiance. The forthrightness and elegance of his reply to Johann

13. Belke, *In den Katakomben,* p. 6.
14. See James H. Lehmann, "Maimonides, Mendelssohn and the Me'asfim," *LBIYB* 20 (1975): 87–108.
15. *Ha-Meassef* 3 (1786): 161, quoted in Altmann, *Mendelssohn,* p. 758.
16. Franz Rosenzweig, "Bildung und kein Ende," in his *Kleinere Schriften* (Berlin, 1937), pp. 79–93.
17. See Baruch B. Kurzweil, "The Image of the Western Jew in Modern Hebrew Literature," *LBIYB* 6 (1961): 171–72 and passim.

Caspar Lavater earned him increased respect and gave delight to many. What enabled him to remain steadfast was, in the first place, his deep-rootedness in the Jewish tradition. Yet there was more to it. In his answer to the Swiss evangelist he declared:

> I may say that not only yesterday did I start to investigate my religion. I recognized at a very early time the duty to examine my opinions and actions, and if, from my early youth on, I devoted my hours of leisure and recreation to philosophy and *belles lettres,* I did so solely for the purpose of getting ready for that urgent examination. . . . Had the result of my research of many years not been a decision in favor of *my* religion, it would necessarily have been imperative for me to announce it through public action. I fail to see what could have tied me to a religion so overtly strict in appearance and held in such contempt by the general public, had I not been persuaded, in my heart, of its truth.[18]

This statement indicates an attitude of inner freedom, a sense of interior distance *vis-à-vis* the tradition and its impact. Mendelssohn remained a Jew not because he was an heir to the tradition and/or motivated by respect for authority, but from a free inner choice. True, he was immersed in the rich world of Hebrew literature and participated in what, with Ludwig Wittgenstein, we may call the "language-game" of his native religion, in a form of life inherited and well understood. Yet, according to his testimony repeated more than once, he managed to look at his inheritance with its powerful stock of images objectively and critically— from a distance. His continued loyalty was the fruit of a decision on his part. He was a Jew by conviction, not merely by birth. He proved that distance need not annul loyalty; on the contrary, it helped to confirm it. It is this sovereign attitude that prefigures, in an archetypal sense, the way in which many modern German Jews down to Hermann Cohen, Martin Buber, and Franz Rosenzweig came to embrace Judaism.

There is a certain affinity between Mendelssohn's approach to Judaism and the attitude characteristic of medieval Jewish philosophers in Spain, Provence, and Italy, who rejected mere reliance on authority (*taḳlid* in Arabic) and applied rational standards to the interpretation of biblical and rabbinic theology. In the case of Mendelssohn, the stance of objectivity is already manifest in his application of esthetic categories to the Scriptures, a type of evaluation that he took from Robert Lowth's famous *De sacra poesi Hebraeorum* (1753). In so doing, Mendelssohn intro-

---

18. Mendelssohn to Johann Caspar Lavater, December 12, 1769, *Mendelssohn Gesammelte Schriften Jubiläumsausgabe* 7:8–9.

duced a viewpoint that was totally absent from the medieval mind. His critical stance expresses itself, above all, in the freedom with which he discriminated between authentic and nonauthentic elements in Judaism, identifying the latter with the kabbalistic tradition, especially its demonological and magical aspects. As an exponent of *Aufklärung,* Mendelssohn sought to discredit the mystical elements of the tradition, and he thereby became the prototype of an outlook that dominated German Jewry until Gershom Scholem began to rehabilitate the Kabbala in the late 1920s. Mendelssohn's antikabbalistic attitude was not entirely new. It had been anticipated by Italian-Jewish rationalists like Elijah del Medigo and Leone Modena. Yet it derived added force from the intellectual climate of the Enlightenment. Mendelssohn also felt free to criticize the method of excessive dialectics (*pilpul*) frequently employed in the study of the Talmud. Here he stood on more solid ground, for some outstanding rabbinic authorities had done likewise.

In the aggregate, all this tends to show that Mendelssohn's attachment to Judaism was tantamount to a free and discriminating loyalty. It was the stance of a Jew who claims the right and the duty to look upon tradition not as something monolithic, undifferentiated, but as an entity composed of various layers, not all of which were of the same validity. Well versed in the tradition, Mendelssohn discovered possibilities of molding its future course. He discarded the long-ingrained perspective that saw all phases of the past as unified by a mystical synchronicity, as it were.[19] Although, as a child of the Enlightenment, he had not yet developed a truly historical sense, he was enough of a scholar to realize that Judaism had to be comprehended in historical terms, and he drew the consequences. In his *Jerusalem* (1783) he presented a picture of what he considered to be the "true," "authentic" Judaism, shorn of accretions he disapproved of. In this respect he became the forerunner of many German-Jewish interpreters of the faith down to Leo Baeck, who viewed tradition sympathetically but with critical eyes. Mendelssohn was no reformer, nor was he the "Luther of the Jews," as he was erroneously dubbed by a contemporary Christian writer.[20] There was no "Luther of the Jews." German Jewry went through a series of attempts at reform, not through a Reformation. Mendelssohn could be called, with more

19. On the traditional stance, see Max Wiener, *Jüdische Religion im Zeitalter der Emanzipation* (Berlin, 1933), pp. 38–39.
20. See Altmann, *Mendelssohn,* p. 9.

justification, the founding father of the objective-critical approach that came to fruition in *Wissenschaft des Judentums,* when Leopold Zunz and his friends embraced the philological-historical method initiated by the German school of classical studies (*Altertumswissenschaft*).

The linkage of Jewish loyalty and inner freedom that Mendelssohn bequeathed to German Jewry is a corollary and, in a sense, an expression of his notion that religion, if it is truly to be religion, must be noncoercive. Whereas the state has the right of coercion and exists by virtue of the social contract that empowers it to enforce obedience to the laws, religion consists in man's relationship with God and lives by the power of inner persuasion. It simply cannot be enforced without losing its character. This thesis is the burden of the first part of Mendelssohn's *Jerusalem.* With this emphasis on freedom *in* religion, he coupled a political demand for liberty *of* religion, but from an inner Jewish perspective his great concern was for abandoning all semblance of coercion in religious matters. In his preface to Menasseh ben Israel's *Vindiciae Judaeorum* (1782), he appealed to the rabbis and elders of his nation to forgo the use of excommunication (*herem*) as a means of enforcing religious conformity.

Mendelssohn must have been aware of the fact that, from late antiquity down to the threshold of the modern age, the functioning of Jewish life in exile (*galut*) depended, to a large extent, on the exercise of communal controls; that the Jewish community had no choice but to form a kind of "state within the state." Yet envisioning as he did a new order of things as a result of emancipation, he wished to see Judaism assume the character of a pure religion, free of all attributes of power. The model he advocated was to become the blueprint of Jewish life in the period of emancipation.

III

My third point concerns Mendelssohn's archetypal role as the first philosopher of Judaism in modern times. I shall not deal with Mendelssohn the philosopher of the Enlightenment who earned the epithet the "German Socrates," was one of the pioneers in German esthetics, and made a valiant effort to uphold the metaphysics of pure reason even in the face of Kant's critique of it. His place in eighteenth-century German philosophy was one of distinction, and his fame suffered eclipse only when Kant overtook him and gave philosophy a new direction. Today, when much attention is being paid to the eighteenth century as the cradle of modernity, Mendelssohn is a figure of renewed interest.[21] Yet all this is not my concern here. My object is confined to an elucidation of Mendelssohn's significance as a pioneer in modern Jewish thought.[22]

In Mendelssohn's interpretation of Judaism, reason as understood by the Enlightenment is written large. In his view, the eternal truths, which are necessary truths of reason and form the content of natural religion open to all men, are also the truths of the Jewish religion. They relate to God's existence, His providence, and the future life in which reward and punishment are meted out. Mendelssohn lived at a time in which one could still believe that these propositions were capable of demonstrative proof and certainty. The tradition of René Descartes's, John Locke's, and Gottfried Wilhelm Leibniz's rational faith in their "necessity" was still potent among the moderate deists, and Mendelssohn could feel on safe ground in affirming them. In a sense he was far more radical in his reliance on reason alone than those Christian philosophers who were ready to admit the validity of revelation as an additional source of religious truth of a superrational kind. As Mendelssohn pointed out, there was no need for a divine revelation to assure man of the truths the knowledge of which made for his felicity in this world and the next. Nor, he suggested, would it have befitted God's universal love for all mankind to single out a particular nation as the beneficiary of a special revelation concerning those truths. Judaism did not claim to possess knowledge about God in excess of what man was able to obtain by his own unaided reason. Where Judaism differed was not in matters of doctrine but of law, commandments, and ways of serving God. It was solely its legislation that was revealed at Sinai, and that legislation—the realm of *Halakhah*—was not, as Baruch Spinoza had declared, a device for the furtherance of purely political, mundane goals but itself closely linked to the eternal verities of Judaism, which were identical with the truths of natural, universal religion. For the commandments were meant to be constant reminders of God's existence, providence, and justice, while some of them were to recall the historical experiences surrounding the act of revelation.

The dichotomy thus established between Judaism as a "religion of reason" and Judaism as a "revealed legislation" was hardly commensurate

21. Michael Albrecht, "Moses Mendelssohn: Ein Forschungsbericht, 1965–1980," *Deutsche Vierteljahrsschrift für Literaturwissenschaft und Geistesgeschichte* 57 (1983): 64–166.

22. For a more elaborate treatment, see Alexander Altmann, "Reflections on Mendelssohn's Concept of Judaism," *Jewish Thought in the Eighteenth Century: Harvard Judaica Texts and Studies,* forthcoming.

with the organic character of the Torah as an indivisible unity of doctrine and law, belief and action. On the other hand, Mendelssohn's emphasis on the rationality of the Jewish religion and his rejection of superrational mysteries such as were characteristic of Christianity reflected a stance that had been much in vogue in medieval Jewish philosophy as far as it had to engage in polemics.[23] Mendelssohn was the first modern Jew to adumbrate the notion of a definite superiority, in rational terms, of Judaism over Christianity, and the stand he took became paradigmatic for the Jewish Hegelians and neo-Kantians. His trust in reason led him to the assertion that Judaism made no demands on faith, except in the sphere of historical truths. Here, again, a polemical attitude is evident. It is directed, in particular, against Friedrich Heinrich Jacobi's philosophy of faith, which regards rationalism as the road to atheism and feels itself in deep accord with the Christian idea of faith as the *refugium* of the truly religious soul. It may be recalled that Friedrich W. J. Schelling, too, took issue with Jacobi and, though affirming faith as the necessary last stage in man's endeavor to comprehend God, insisted on the use of dialectic as the initial method of approach. Mendelssohn's denial of the requirement of faith—he recommended rational conviction instead—did not correspond to authentic Jewish religiosity, but, as a philosopher of religion, he was entitled to seek the road to God through reason, and in this respect his precedent set the stage for other German-Jewish thinkers to follow. The way in which reason was understood by the idealist philosophers and, later, by the neo-Kantians, changed conspicuously,[24] yet all Jewish philosophers down to Hermann Cohen followed Mendelssohn in presenting Judaism as the "religion of reason."

It would be a misreading of Mendelssohn to assume that in equating Judaism, as a body of beliefs, with natural religion, he lost sight of the historical dimension. Whereas the deists and Kant were bent upon the elimination of the historical element from religion, Mendelssohn was keen to preserve it. Indeed his profoundest consideration stemmed from the prophetic view of history. He saw the messianic goal of history in the triumph of pure, unadulterated monotheism over degenerate beliefs (idolatry, paganism) and unbelief (atheism), and he assigned to the "ceremonial" law the function of ensuring the continuing existence of the Jewish people as the torchbearer of the true religion. This historical per-

---

23. Daniel J. Lasker, *Jewish Philosophical Polemics against Christianity in the Middle Ages* (New York, 1977).
24. The static reason of the Enlightenment philosophy became dialectical.

spective concerning the function of the ritual is something distinctly modern. Medieval Jewish theologians had sought to define the "reasons of the commandments" (*ta'amey ha-mitsvot*) in either rational or mystical terms. Mendelssohn did not presume to "enter into the Sanctuary," as he called this particular enterprise, but, instead, he viewed the law as a whole as having a messianic purpose in mind. It is this historical (or metahistorical) viewpoint that enabled him to affirm the continued validity of the revealed law until such time as God would abrogate it as solemnly and publicly as He had proclaimed it. Kant remarked *apropos* this utterance that it betrayed a certain callousness, a disregard for the hopes for an alleviation of the "burdens pressing upon the people."[25] Wilhelm von Humboldt showed greater understanding when he interpreted Mendelssohn's loyalty to the ritual law as flowing from a desire to prevent the "national spirit" (*Nationalgeist*) of the Jewish people from perishing, a desire "worthy of a sagacious mind."[26]

What Humboldt failed to see was the messianic perspective that informed Mendelssohn and gave spiritual depth to his concern for the preservation of the Jewish people through adherence to the Torah. In Mendelssohn's view, the survival of Israel as a separate nation was a matter of religious concern. It was bound up with an ideal to be achieved. It had an ultimate purpose beyond the natural instinct for self-preservation, national identity, or sentimental considerations. It was an idea that compelled Jews to remain Jews. At the very end of his *Jerusalem*, Mendelssohn declared that if abandonment of our separateness as a nation were the price to be paid for the granting of emancipation, we would have to reject the offer. This proud statement was not lost on subsequent generations of German Jews. It is reechoed in Hermann Cohen's discussion of "The Law" in his *Religion of Reason from the Sources of Judaism* (1919). After praising Mendelssohn's "great messianic tendency," Cohen pleads for the recognition of the need for maintaining a measure of separateness, even "isolation," in cultural respects, seeing that, ultimately, the future of pure monotheism was at stake.[27]

25. Moses Mendelssohn, *Jerusalem*, trans. Allan Arkush, introd. and commentary Alexander Altmann (Hanover, N.H., 1983), pp. 123, 236.

26. Hans Liebeschütz, "Judentum und deutsche Umwelt im Zeitalter der Restauration," in *Das Judentum in der deutschen Umwelt, 1800–1850,* ed. Hans Liebeschütz and Arnold Paucker (Tübingen, 1977), pp. 5–6.

27. Hermann Cohen, *Religion der Vernunft aus den Quellen des Judentums* (Leipzig, 1919), pp. 421–23, 430–32.

IV

Finally, Mendelssohn represents the archetypal fighter for Jewish civil rights. Throughout his life he had been the spokesman for the downtrodden and persecuted of his people. In numerous instances he had exerted his personal influence on their behalf. He had been the force behind Christian Wilhelm von Dohm's epoch-making treatise *On the Civil Improvement of the Jews* (1781). When Joseph II proclaimed the Edict of Toleration (1781–82), Mendelssohn considered the time propitious for open action on his part, and in his preface to Menasseh ben Israel's historic apologia and, above all, in his *Jerusalem,* he broke a lance for civil equality. What he sought to achieve was a political rather than a social solution to what was later called the Jewish Problem. He advocated a secular state on the, broadly speaking, Lockean pattern (which he somewhat revised) such as was being instituted in the United States. Indeed, at the very time he wrote *Jerusalem,* Thomas Jefferson was writing his *Notes on Virginia* (1782), which took a similar direction. It was Count Mirabeau who, in a book published in 1787, put Mendelssohn on the same pedestal with the framers of the American Constitution and with A. R. J. Turgot, the French liberal theorist. The analogy had not occurred to any one of the many German reviewers of *Jerusalem.*

What Mendelssohn envisaged was a secular state in which there was no longer any civil discrimination on grounds of religion. Such a state would secure Jewish rights of redress in cases of injustice, allow for active participation by Jews in the political process, and, as a result, confer dignity on the Jew. This agenda was adopted by German-Jewish leadership when the struggle for emancipation entered into a more acute phase in the nineteenth century. Gabriel Riesser made this platform his own. It was thwarted by the rising tide of German nationalism, which would not tolerate an alien element in its midst. Germany was not America. Her tragedy was that she never produced an Abraham Lincoln who said, "I don't want to be a slave, neither do I want to be a master." The masterrace complex was too deeply ingrained in the German psyche to permit noble sentiments of this sort. The response of many German Jews was flight into assimilation and conversion rather than political struggle and preservation of their Jewish identity. What caused anxiety was, in the first place, social ostracism. The denial of political equality was considered to be of secondary importance. The proud and upright stance that Mendelssohn had assumed was the very opposite to the self-denying atti-

tude of those who sought to conceal or negate their Jewish identity. Instead of accepting prejudice as a seemingly ineradicable disease, they tried
to overcome it by the pretense of being no less German than the Germans,
an attitude that merely aggravated the problem.[28] Fortunately, this is not
the whole picture. There were others—and they formed the nucleus of
Jewish survival—who followed in Mendelssohn's footsteps.

Mendelssohn considered antisemitism to be a phenomenon resulting
from prejudice. He saw in it nothing more than a survival of medieval
Jew-hate produced and nurtured by the Christian church, which stigmatized the Jewish nation as the Christ-killers. With the progress of enlightenment, he hoped, this inherited prejudice would fade away. Although he realized that in the modern period antisemitism had changed
its color, he did not hesitate to identify it with the old, "superannuated"
prejudice, the roots of which were difficult to extirpate. In our time Jacob
Katz has put forward a similar theory.[29] Mendelssohn's view may be described as typical of the Enlightenment mentality, which was fond of
diagnosing manifestations of crass irrationality as "prejudices." The Kantian philosopher Johann G. C. C. Kiesewetter defined the Enlightenment
itself as "a critique of prejudices."[30] Mendelssohn simply applied that
current mode of explanation to antisemitism. He might have pondered
the fact that Jew-hate goes back to Greco-Roman antiquity and is also
found in the Islamic world, where it is unrelated to Christian theology.
Whatever the ultimate reasons of this disturbing phenomenon may be,
he clung to the prejudice theory because it offered the comforting pros-
pect of an eventual remedy. Prejudice is bound to give way, in the long
run, to a more enlightened opinion. In this optimism subsequent generations of German Jews found solace and hope. Again, Mendelssohn provided an archetypal pattern that guided the type of defense (*Abwehr*)
aimed at spreading enlightenment.[31] Strangely enough, this utterly in-

---

28. Hannah Arendt's critique of Mendelssohn in her consideration of German-
Jewish leadership in the nineteenth century is misapplied. See Leon Botstein, "Liberating
the Pariah: Politics, the Jews, and Hannah Arendt," *Salmagundi: Politics and the
Social Contract,* Spring-Summer 1983, no. 60, pp. 78–81.

29. Jacob Katz, *From Prejudice to Destruction: Anti-Semitism, 1700–1933* (Cambridge, Mass., 1980).

30. Werner Schneiders, *Aufklärung und Vorurteilskritik: Studien zur Geschichte
der Vorurteilstheorie* (Stuttgart–Bad Canstatt, 1983), pp. 312–13.

31. Barbara Suchy, "The Verein zur Abwehr des Antisemitismus," pt. 1, *LBIYB*
28 (1983): 205–39. See also Eleonore Sterling, "Jewish Reaction to Jew-Hatred in the
First Half of the 19th Century," ibid., 3 (1958), 103–21; and Marjorie Lamberti, "Liberals, Socialists and the Defence against Antisemitism in the Wilhelminian Period,"
ibid., 25 (1980): 147–62.

effective method was still tried in the 1920s, when the storm signals of virulent racism should have been unmistakable.

I conclude my analysis with a brief reference to the limitations that Mendelssohn's archetypal function suffered in the very last phase of German Jewry. The rise of Zionism on the one hand and the emergence of religious existentialism on the other tended to render the Mendelssohnian pattern in its political and religious complexion obsolete. Politically, the old blueprint for accommodation in the *galut* came under severe attack by Zionist ideology, and the rationalistic trend in Jewish philosophy gave way to new ways of thinking as represented by Buber and Rosenzweig. There is symbolic significance in the fact that in the Buber-Rosenzweig translation of the Bible the rendition of the Name of God as "The Eternal" (*der Ewige*) was changed into "HE" [IS PRESENT] (*ER [IST DA]*). "The Eternal" reflects a philosophical approach, a concern with the eternal truths of reason. "HE" has a religious connotation. It points to the presentness of God and, at the same time, to the unapproachable mystery of His being. Mendelssohn's translation of the Bible had sought to lead the German Jews into a symbiosis with German language and culture. Buber and Rosenzweig endeavored to recapture, through their mode of translation, the very character of the Hebrew original. The direction they took was the reverse of Mendelssohn's.[32]

The transformation that was taking shape in both political and theological thinking was well described by Leo Baeck, the most representative figure in the last phase of German Jewry. In a series of lectures he gave in 1956, he spoke of Moses Hess, the pioneer of Zionism, as a legitimate rival of Mendelssohn's leadership, and he acknowledged Franz Rosenzweig as the new star on the horizon of German-Jewish theology.[33] Yet such awareness had in no way diminished German Jewry's sense of indebtedness to Mendelssohn's legacy. On the eve of the catastrophe, in 1929, the two-hundredth anniversary of his birth was made the occasion

32. Wera Lewin, "Die Bedeutung des Stefan George-Kreises für die deutsch-jüdische Geistesgeschichte," ibid., 8 (1963): 187. See also Rosenzweig to Martin Buber, December 29, 1925, quoting Julius Blau, who made precisely this point: "This [the new Bible translation] answered the need of contemporary German Jews; it represented Mendelssohn's endeavor a century ago, only in reverse direction: at that time they had to learn German, now Hebrew [*jüdisch*]." Rosenzweig, *Briefe und Tagebücher*, vol. 2 (The Hague, 1979), p. 1072.

33. See Leo Baeck, *Von Moses Mendelssohn zu Franz Rosenzweig: Typen jüdischen Selbstverständnisses in den letzten beiden Jahrhunderten* (Stuttgart, 1958). An excerpt relating to Moses Hess had appeared in *LBIYB* 2 (1957): 38–44.

for starting a new edition of his collected works in a form commensurate with the highest standards of modern scholarship. This Jubilee Edition, which is now nearing completion, stands as a document of the role Mendelssohn played in the consciousness of what was once German Jewry.

The Kassel "Ha-Meassef" of 1799

An Unknown Contribution to the Haskalah

Every attempt to understand the great innovations in the life and culture of the Jews of Central Europe during the second half of the eighteenth century starts with Moses Mendelssohn.[1] I begin my essay with the following generation. In the early 1780s some of the new ideas of the century had taken hold among groups of young Jews, and a movement began that was a Jewish analogy to the German Enlightenment. The Haskalah and its first important periodical, *Ha-Meassef* (The Collector),[2] cannot be understood without consideration of their roots in the European Enlightenment and especially in its Prussian variety. The model for *Ha-Meassef* was the *Berlinische Monatsschrift,* "the most important forum for the German Enlightenment in its last and highest phase."[3] But even before the first issue of the *Berlinische Monatsschrift* appeared, a group of young Jews in Königsberg, Prussia, took the first step toward the pub-

1. A new *Forschungsbericht* has been recently published. Michael Albrecht, "Moses Mendelssohn: Ein Forschungsbericht, 1965–1980," *Deutsche Vierteljahrsschrift für Literaturwissenschaft und Geistesgeschichte* 57 (1983): 64–66.
2. For concise information about *Ha-Meassef,* see Moritz Steinschneider, *Catalogus Librorum Hebraeorum in Bibliotheca Bodleiana* (Berlin, 1852–60; reprint, Hildesheim, 1964), cols. 575–79; Tsemah Tsamriyon, in *Encyclopaedia Judaica* (Jerusalem, 1971), vol. 11, cols. 1161–62; Israel Zinberg, *A History of Jewish Literature,* trans. and ed. Bernard Martin (Cincinnati, 1976), vol. 8, pt. 9, "The Berlin Haskalah," pp. 75–87, and bibliographical notes, pp. 231–32; Günter Stemberger, *Geschichte der jüdischen Literatur: Eine Einführung* (Munich, 1977), pp. 177–78.
3. Werner Krauss, "Über die Konstellation der deutschen Aufklärung," in his *Studien zur deutschen und französischen Aufklärung,* Neue Beiträge zur Literaturwissenschaft, no. 16 (Berlin, 1963), p. 350.

lication of their journal.[4] In December 1782 they formed the Society of Friends of the Hebrew Language. To understand the way in which *Ha-Meassef* was conceived by its founders, it is therefore fitting to compare it to the manner in which the editors of the *Berlinische Monatsschrift* described the subjects to be treated in their new journal:

1. news from the entire range of sciences, especially concerning recent discoveries, insofar as they are of general interest;

2. descriptions of peoples and their customs and institutes, preferably of those from countries nearby;

3. observations concerning everything that is human and that can contribute to our knowledge of ourselves and our fellowmen;

4. biographical reports about interesting men, especially about those whose accomplishments have not yet brought them the fame they justly deserve;

5. contributions to the development and study of German language and literature, both contemporary and historical;

6. translations of important masterpieces from antiquity that have not yet been given the attention they deserve;

7. extracts from unknown texts from abroad that are worthy of note;

8. miscellaneous essays of various kinds that are appropriate to the orientation of our journal.[5]

These guidelines give an indication of the spirit of mind that generated so much enthusiasm among the group of young Jews in Königsberg. Their *Meassef* was to become "the most important organ for Haskalah writers."[6] In a letter to Naphtali Wessely, these young *maskilim* explained that some of them were "Torah scholars and some commanded foreign languages—Greek and Latin, as well as modern," and went on to say that "their entire goal and wish is to spread our holy language

4. Plans for the appearance of the *Berlinische Monatsschrift* were twice advertised in other journals, so Moses Mendelssohn and his friends of course knew about them. David Friedländer, devoted to the new ideas and, like Mendelssohn, a wealthy owner of a silk factory in Berlin, came from Königsberg. The plan for the new Society of the Friends of the Hebrew Language was conceived by members of the Friedländer family. Two of David's brothers, Simeon and Zanvil, and Isaac Euchel, a teacher in the Friedländer household, were those young men in Königsberg who, together with Mendel Breslau, signed the prospectus (*Naḥal Ha-Besor*) for the new Hebrew journal. See Michael Graetz, in *Encyclopaedia Judaica,* vol. 7, col. 177; and Zinberg, *History of Jewish Literature,* vol. 8, pt. 9, p. 76. Zinberg was wrong in writing that they followed the pattern of the "then very popular *Berlinische Monatsschrift.*"

5. The prospectus of the *Berlinische Monatsschrift* is reprinted in Norbert Hinske, ed., *Was ist Aufklärung? Beiträge aus der "Berlinischen Monatsschrift"* (Darmstadt, 1973), pp. 1–2.

6. Stemberger, *Geschichte der jüdischen Literatur,* p. 177. See also Zinberg, *History of Jewish Literature,* vol. 8, pt. 9, p. 77.

among our people as much as possible and to demonstrate its beauty to all nations."[7]

Only a few months later, at the end of the prospectus of the new journal, the authors spoke poignantly of the "demands of the new time, the time of education and enlightenment. . . . See how all people strive after knowledge. . . . How can we sit calmly with folded hands? Behold, men of great knowledge have arisen among us. They wish to lead us in the paths of Torah and wisdom." In conclusion the prospectus informed the public that *Ha-Meassef* will consist of the following five divisions:

1. poems and poetic articles;
2. treatises on philology, exegesis, and other sciences, as well as on moral and physical education;
3. biographies of great men of "our nation";
4. news of events in Jewish life in various lands;
5. reports about new books that appeared.[8]

Of course there were differences between the intentions of the two periodicals. *Ha-Meassef* had a different audience from that of the *Berlinische Monatsschrift,* and even key words like "knowledge" did not mean the same in both journals. One of the most impressive results of the Haskalah was, for example, that Jewish boys and even girls finally had the opportunity to learn such subjects as arithmetic and geography at school. The editors of the *Berlinische Monatsschrift* had a broader understanding of "knowledge." They announced their intention of presenting descriptions of various peoples and their customs and institutions, as well as biographical reports about interesting individuals. *Ha-Meassef,* however, carried the typical restriction to Jewish affairs—to news of events in Jewish life in various countries and to biographies of great men in the Jewish world.

Ha-Meassef soon became the main forum for Haskalah writers, but it also had a considerable influence on the public in general. There exists a very good source of information about the latter, for lists of subscribers are published in volumes 2–4. Here are a few details. For a Hebrew periodical, the number of subscribers to the second volume was large. We know of 213, including commission agents. But this is far less than the number of copies ordinarily sold by a German periodical of that time,

---

7. Quoted in Zinberg, *History of Jewish Literature,* vol. 8, pt. 9, p. 75. This letter was written before April 1783, since Naphtali Wessely's answer, printed in *Ha-Meassef,* is dated Nissan 13 [April 15].

8. Quoted in Zinberg, *History of Jewish Literature,* vol. 8, pt. 9, p. 76.

roughly 400 copies.[9] In the following two years the editors published the names of, respectively, 19 and 72 new subscribers, but we do not know how many cancellations occurred at the same time. One may conclude that in the beginning there were roughly 200 to 250 paying readers; most of the copies were naturally read by an entire circle of acquaintances.[10] One finds, moreover, well-known Christian men of learning among the subscribers: Hofrat Ritter (Johann David) Michaelis (1717–91) and Hofrat (Johann Gottfried) Eichhorn (1752–1827), both of Göttingen, and Professor (Johann Gottfried) Hasse (1759–1806) of Königsberg.[11] Other Christian subscribers were Kammerherr von Suhm of Copenhagen and Kirchenrat P. Geiser of Kiel. Only one library subscribed to *Ha-Meassef:* the Stadtbibliothek Danzig. Most of the 17 subscribers from Vienna are called *Herr;* apparently they were baptized Jews. This is also true of Dr. med. Christian Julius Frederik de Meza of Copenhagen.[12] The famous Mme. Fanny Arnstein also lived in Vienna. She was a daughter of Daniel Itzig, *Oberlandesältester* of the Jews of Prussia, and the only woman in the lists.[13]

As the lists of subscribers always indicate where they lived, we know where they were concentrated.

The most important facts about the circulation of *Ha-Meassef* can be summarized as follows: First, even at the very beginning, in the years from 1783 to 1787, the journal circulated as far as Amsterdam, Metz,

9. It seems that at that time a German weekly was profitable if it sold more than 500 copies. See Wolfgang Martens, *Die Botschaft der Tugend: Die Aufklärung im Spiegel der deutschen Moralischen Wochenschriften* (Stuttgart, 1971), p. 112. The first edition of Mendelssohn's Bible translation of 1778–83 had 515 subscribers. Steven M. Lowenstein, "The Readership of Mendelssohn's Bible Translation," *Hebrew Union College Annual* 53 (1982): 180.

10. In 1797, at the end of the last issue (p. 399), the editors added a note in Judeo-German (German printed in Hebrew letters) in which they discussed the possibility of editing a further issue of *Ha-Meassef.* They told the public that the number of subscribers had diminished from 150 to less than 120; under these conditions the journal could no longer be published. For the sake of the journal's aims, they would continue their work with one more issue at a price of 12 *groschen.* As soon as the number of subscribers reached 250, each number would be sold for 8 *groschen,* and if the number of subscribers rose to 350, each number for 6 *groschen.* We learn from this that the number of subscribers in 1797 was in fact 120 and that the editors did not believe it could rise to 350.

11. For Johann David Michaelis, see the entry in Johann Georg Meusel, *Lexikon der vom Jahr 1750 bis 1800 verstorbenen teutschen Schriftsteller,* vol. 9 (Leipzig, 1809); for Johann Gottfried Eichhorn and Johann Gottfried Hasse, see the entries in George Christoph Hamberger and Johann Georg Meusel, *Das gelehrte Deutschland oder Lexikon der Jetzt lebenden teutschen Schriftsteller,* vol. 2 (Lemgo, 1796), and successive editions.

12. Gordon Norrie, in *Dansk biografisk Leksikon* (Copenhagen, 1938), 15:569.

13. Lowenstein, "Readership of Mendelssohn's Bible Translation," p. 183.

Towns Mentioned in the Lists of Subscribers
of *Ha-Meassef*, 1784–86

Vol. 2		*Vol. 3*	
Amsterdam	19	Bonn	1
Berlin	49	Frankfurt a.M.	2
Bielefeld*	1	Gradiske*	1
Breslau	5	Königsberg	2
Buhn*	1	Mainz*	1
Copenhagen	19	Metz*	1
Danzig*	1	Nancy*	1
Dessau	1	Prague	7
Frankfurt a.M.	11	Stargard*	1
Glogau	3	Szklów	1
Göttingen*	2	Vienna	1
Hamburg	14		
Hanover	5	*Vol. 4*	
Hasenpoth/		Berlin	4
Aizpute	3	Brunswick	1
Kassel	3	Fürth	3
Kiel	1	Göttingen*	1
Königsberg	26	Hanover	?
Köslin*	1	Königsberg	1
Krefeld*	3	Köslin*	1
Nancy*	1	Lublin*	1
Potsdam	1	Metz*	10
Prague	11	Mulhouse*	1
Stargard*	1	Prague	20
Strasbourg	17	Stendal*	1
Szklów	4	Vienna	25
Vilna	4	Wusterhausen*	1
Warsaw*	1	Züllichau	2
Wesel	1		
Wieliczka*	4		

An asterisk indicates that there were no subscribers in that town to Mendelssohn's Bible translation. See Steven M. Lowenstein, "The Readership of Mendelssohn's Bible Translation," *Hebrew Union College Annual* 53 (1982): 194–95.

and Strasbourg in the West, Copenhagen in the North, Hasenpoth/ Aizpute, Vilna, and Szklów in the Northeast, and Lublin and Wieliczka in the Southeast. Second, there were, of course, a few cities where subscribers were concentrated. One of every five copies went to Berlin (49 in all); one out of eight stayed in Königsberg (26 in all). In the fourth volume many new subscribers from Vienna and Prague were listed; at that time approximately one-half of all the copies (142, or 47 percent) were sold in Berlin, Königsberg, Vienna, and Prague. Perhaps this, as well as the fact that many subscribers lived in Amsterdam, Hamburg, and Frankfurt am Main, is to be expected. Those who are familiar with Christian Wilhelm von Dohm's *Über die bürgerliche Verbesserung der Juden*[14] and its account of the situation of Jews in Alsace will not be surprised to find that 16 or 17 copies went to Strasbourg (but Cerf Beer was not among the subscribers).

Finally, the lists of subscribers to *Ha-Meassef* provide valuable hints regarding the spread of the Haskalah in the 1780s. Subscribers from Metz, Strasbourg, Hamburg, and Copenhagen suggest that by the mid-1780s the Haskalah had spread west of the Berlin-Prague line and that the new ideas of the time were playing a role in a large number of towns and cities.[15] Many towns had one to three subscribers: Wesel, Krefeld, Bonn, Bielefeld, Hanover, Brunswick, Stendal, Göttingen, Kassel, Fürth, and so on.

In these communities, many of them small, who, together with a friend or even alone, would have dared to subscribe to *Ha-Meassef,* an antitraditionalist journal? Why did they do so? What did they learn from it?

I have no answer to these questions. All I can do is discuss conditions in one of these communities and shift attention to a more particular subject: a hitherto unknown "Meassef" written in 1799. Therefore I take

14. Christian Wilhelm von Dohm, *Über die bürgerliche Verbesserung der Juden* (Berlin, 1781), French ed., *De la réforme politique des Juifs* (1782). See also Horst Möller, "Aufklärung, Judenemanzipation und Staat: Ursprung und Wirkung von Dohms Schrift 'Über die bürgerliche Verbesserung der Juden,'" in *Deutsche Aufklärung und Judenemanzipation,* ed. Walter Grab, *Jahrbuch des Instituts für deutsche Geschichte,* Beiheft 3 (Tel Aviv, 1980), pp. 119–49.

15. The map in H. H. Ben Sasson's *History of the Jewish People* (Tel Aviv, 1969), p. 319, shows that the Haskalah was concentrated in Amsterdam and Venice in 1750 and the following decades spread only to Frankfurt am Main, aside from Amsterdam, west of the Berlin-Prague line. By 1800 the movement had reached Leghorn, Berlin, Prague, Vienna, Trieste, Königsberg, Zamość, Lemberg, and Szklów. The map also appears in Azriel Shochat's article about the Haskalah in the *Encyclopaedia Judaica,* vol. 7, col. 1434. As a whole, my results concur with Lowenstein, "Readership of Mendelssohn's Bible Translation."

Kassel and its Jewish community as an example—perhaps not a representative example, but an instructive one.

Kassel had only one subscriber to *Ha-Meassef;* we know his name, Löb Po(u)pert, from the subscription list in volume 2 and from a list of agents for the journal in volume 4.[16] He ordered three copies—perhaps he was a commission agent. Who received these copies? The Kassel manuscript will at least indicate what kind of men in Kassel read this Haskalah journal fifteen years later, at the end of the century. But before speaking about them, it is useful to have a look at the historical setting in Hesse-Kassel and at the history of the Jewish community in Kassel.

When Napoleon advanced eastward against Prussia and won the famous battle of Jena, Hesse-Kassel became part of the new kingdom of Westphalia, whose king was Jerome Bonaparte, Napoleon's brother. Seven years later, in 1813, when an alliance of Russian, Prussian, and other armed forces succeeded in defeating Napoleon, Prince Elector Wilhelm I of Hesse-Kassel returned to his country and reinstituted a government that was very reactionary. All rights that had been granted by royal authorities to Jews and others were declared illegal; in other words, the *status ante* was reestablished as if the years 1806 to 1813 had never occurred.

Regarding the spread of Enlightenment ideas in Kassel we are fortunate to have a new study at our disposal.[17] Landgrave Friedrich II spent a great deal of money on two schools in Kassel, which was his residence, and he was especially interested in the reorganization of the Collegium Carolinum, which in 1766 became a universitylike institution. At least five recognized Enlightenment figures taught there between 1770 and 1780, but they had only about fifty students.[18] In 1773 there were at least three Jews in this group.[19] Besides the Hofbibliothek with its forty to fifty thousand volumes—only a few of which, however, were contemporary—there were three, and perhaps even more, bookstores with rental libraries. They were an enormous asset for modern-thinking people, and

16. There were two subscribers of Mendelssohn's Bible translation of 1778–83 in Kassel. Lowenstein, "Readership of Mendelssohn's Bible Translation," p. 195.

17. Hans Erich Bödeker, "Strukturen der Aufklärungsgesellschaft in der Residenzstadt Kassel," in *Mentalitäten und Lebensverhältnisse: Beispiele aus der Sozialgeschichte der Neuzeit. Rudolf Vierhaus zum 60. Geburtstag* (Göttingen, 1982), pp. 55–76.

18. Ibid., pp. 59–60; Karl-Hermann Wegner, "Bildungswesen," in *Aufklärung und Klassizismus in Hessen-Kassel unter Landgraf Friedrich II, 1760–1785,* ed. Peter Gercke and Friederike Naumann (Kassel, 1979), p. 152.

19. Bödeker, "Strukturen der Aufklärungsgesellschaft," p. 70.

we happen to know that they were used by modern-thinking Jews. Lucius Liffmann (1772–1803), the son of the *Vorsteher* of the Jewish community and later a medical doctor, confessed that in the years before 1790 he had read every book of value he could find in Kassel.[20] Unfortunately, as a logical consequence of a conflict between the aims of the proponents of Enlightenment and the reactionary Landgrave Wilhelm, "freedom of action for well-educated people in Kassel began to be narrowed even before the Revolution,"[21] and, for example, the Collegium Carolinum was shut down in 1786.[22] In 1799 censorship became more severe, and 139 books were confiscated from the town's rental libraries. It seems that at this time Kassel ceased to be even a secondary center of the Enlightenment.[23]

In the first three quarters of the eighteenth century, the Jewish community in Kassel was very small:[24] in 1744 only 18 families had permission to live there.[25] The importance of the city in Jewish life grew, however, when the landrabbinate was transferred from Witzenhausen, east of Kassel, to Kassel itself in 1772 (the *yeshivah* stayed nonetheless in Witzenhausen).[26] In the last decades of the eighteenth century the

20. P. F. Brede, "Biographie des Herrn Lucius Liffman, der Heilkunde Doktor in Cassel," *Sulamith* 3, no. 2 (1811): 222. See also *Reichs-Anzeiger*, October 15, 1795, quoted in Horst Möller, "Wie aufgeklärt war Preussen?" in *Preussen im Rückblick*, ed. H.-J. Puhle and H.-U. Wehler, *Geschichte und Gesellschaft*, Sonderheft 6 (Göttingen, 1980), p. 184.

21. Bödeker, "Strukturen der Aufklärungsgesellschaft," p. 75.

22. Wegner, "Bildungswesen," p. 153.

23. Bödeker, "Strukturen der Aufklärungsgesellschaft," pp. 75–76.

24. See Felix Lazarus, "Hessen-Kassel vor der Fremdherrschaft," in *Festschrift zum 75 jährigen Bestehen des jüdischen-theologischen Seminars Fraenckelscher Stiftung* (Breslau, 1929), 2:237–71; Rudolf Hallo, *Geschichte der jüdischen Gemeinde Kassel* (Kassel, 1931); Paul Arnsberg, *Die jüdischen Gemeinden in Hessen: Anfang, Untergang, Neubeginn* (Frankfurt a.M., 1971); Arnsberg, *Die jüdischen Gemeinden in Hessen: Bilder, Dokumente* (Darmstadt, 1973). In his "Hessen-Kassel nach der Fremdherrschaft," *Monatsschrift für Geschichte und Wissenschaft des Judentums* (hereafter *MGWJ*) 78 (1934): 588 n. 2, Felix Lazarus mentioned his unpublished "Geschichte der Synagogengemeinde Kassel"; I do not know whether the manuscript still exists.

25. See Lazarus, "Hessen-Kassel vor der Fremdherrschaft," p. 269, n. 1; Gerhard Hentsch, *Gewerbeordnung und Emanzipation der Juden im Kurfürstentum Hessen* (Wiesbaden, 1979), p. 17, following a "Bericht der Oberrentkammer vom 31. Dez. 1799 an den Landgrafen." The *Oberrentkammer* stated that "die Zahl der Judenfamilien von 18 im Jahre 1744 auf derzeit 99 Familien gestiegen sei." The same number for 1744 is given by the *Oberrentkammer* on August 16, 1802: "Weil nach Vorschrift der Verordnung die Zahl der Juden, wie solche in anno 1744 subsistirt hat, nicht überschritten werden soll, gleichwohl damahl in Cassel nur 18 Familien waren, und deren jezt 85 sind." Antrag J. S. Feldheim, Marburg, Hessisches Staatsarchiv, 5/2333. The population of Kassel was about twenty thousand during the second half of the eighteenth century. Bödeker, "Strukturen der Aufklärungsgesellschaft," p. 60.

26. Arnsberg, *Die jüdischen Gemeinden in Hessen*, 1:431.

number of Jews increased rapidly. Ten years after the establishment of the landrabbinate in Kassel, 48 families, or a total of more than 350 persons, lived as *Schutzjuden* in Kassel.[27] In 1799, the year in which "Ha-Meassef" was written, there were 99 families living as *Schutzjuden* in Kassel,[28] which is to say more than 700 Jews. In the following years the government succeeded in restricting the number of Jews in the capital. We know that in 1802, 14 families were either forced to leave Kassel or left it voluntarily.[29] In 1812 the number of families was nearly the same as in 1799—101.[30] There can be no doubt that the happiest days for Jews in Kassel were during the *Franzosenzeit* under Jerome, and it was probably at that time that the 9 Jewish families who in 1812 registered themselves as being from Alsace came to the town.[31] An opinion often expressed among Jews in the region was that the learned, the *lamdanim*, lived in Witzenhausen with its old *yeshivah*, whereas the rich, the *ketzinim*, lived in Kassel.[32] This saying can be validated with statistics: in 1808, 11 percent of the 920 Jewish families of the Département Fulda lived in Kassel, but they paid 16.7 percent of the property tax in 1810.[33]

In 1794 a rabbi from Bamberg, Arje Löb ben Abraham Meyer Berlin, became chief rabbi of Kassel.[34] He had been born in 1738 in Fürth, where he had his first position as a rabbi. In 1789 he became a *Landrabbiner* in Bamberg. He died in 1814 at the age of seventy-six. His elder brother, Noah Chaim Zwi Hirsch (1737–1802), was first a rabbi in Bayersdorf (near Erlangen), then later in Bayreuth, in Mainz, and in the so-called Three Communities (Hamburg-Altona-Wandsbeck).[35] Löb Meyer's wife was named Rechel, a daughter of Bermann Hamburger, the *Vorsteher* of the Jewish community in Fürth. They had four sons.[36] In 1805 their eldest (?) son Coppel was living in Hesse as a *Schutzjude*.

27. Antrag A. S. von Bastheim, Bericht der Kriegs- und Domainen-Cammer, October 24, 1782, Marburg, Hessisches Staatsarchiv 5/2350.

28. Lazarus, "Hessen-Kassel vor der Fremdherrschaft," p. 269, n. 1.

29. Ludwig Horwitz, *Die Israeliten unter dem Königreich Westfalen: Ein aktenmässiger Beitrag zur Geschichte der Regierung König Jérômes* (Berlin, 1900), p. 94.

30. Lazarus, "Hessen-Kassel vor der Fremdherrschaft," p. 269, n. 1.

31. Marburg, Hessisches Staatsarchiv, 76a/28, 11.

32. Arnsberg, *Die jüdischen Gemeinden in Hessen*, 2:409.

33. Horwitz, *Die Israeliten unter dem Königreich Westfalen*, pp. 78, 83, 94.

34. For information about Löb Meyer Berlin and his family, see Adolf Eckstein, *Geschichte der Juden im ehemaligen Fürstbistum Bamberg* (Bamberg, 1898), pp. 176–79; Eckstein, *Nachträge zur Geschichte der Juden im ehemaligen Fürstbistum Bamberg* (Bamberg, 1899), pp. 5–6, 42–43; Peter Wiernik, in *The Jewish Encyclopedia* (New York, 1901), 3:78; Marburg, Hessisches Staatsarchiv, 76a/28, 11.

35. Louis Ginzberg, in *Jewish Encyclopedia* 3:82.

36. Felix Lazarus, "Das Königlich Westphälische Konsistorium der Israeliten," *MGWJ* 58 (1914): 578.

Their youngest son Bendix, who had been a secretary to the rabbi in Altona—that is to say to his Uncle Noah Chaim—was living there, too, but
he was refused a working permit by the government in Kassel.[37] Rabbi
Löb Berlin seems to have been a reformist since his youth in Fürth,[38]
and later during his years in Kassel he decided that "it is permissible to
use pulse, tea, and sugar on Passover."[39] During the reign of Jerome, Löb
Berlin became a *Consistorialrat*. He was important and beloved in his
time, and there exist two portraits of him.[40]

In the second half of the eighteenth century the growing prosperity
among the Jews in Kassel created new problems. The Jewish community
began to expand, and the Christian tradesmen as well as the authorities
were startled by these developments. It was under such circumstances
that the Jews in Kassel faced the task of finding a successor to Rabbi Joseph Michael Kugelmann.[41] We can be sure that in deciding to choose
Löb Meyer Berlin they were very well informed about his knowledge of
the Talmud, his abilities as a judge, and his attitude toward the Haskalah,
since they chose him in spite of trouble he had experienced in Bamberg.
A suit had been filed against him as a result of one of his juridic decisions, and he had to wait in Bamberg for months before the *Fürstbischof*
granted him permission to leave. Löb Meyer Berlin decided to go to Kassel as a man of fifty-six, certainly with the intention of staying there for
the rest of his life—as, in fact, he did. We may surmise that he left Bamberg not only because of troubles in that community but also because he
felt that Kassel would be a proper place for a man with his ideas. Christian Wilhelm von Dohm had lived in Kassel for three years, from 1776
to 1779, as a professor of finance and statistics at the Collegium Carolinum,

---

37. Lazarus, in "Hessen-Kassel vor der Fremdherrschaft," and in "Hessen-Kassel
nach der Fremdherrschaft," pp. 267–68, was wrong in assuming that Bendix was not
in Kassel at that time. In May 1805 a juryman in Kassel declared "als Herr Bendix
Berlin die sämtlichen Actuariatsgeschäffte, . . . schon mehrere Jahre hindurch verse-
hen," and Löb Meyer Berlin wrote on June 15, 1807, "Mein Sohn Bendix hat sich . . .
zuvörderst bey dem jüdischen Gerichte zu Altona und nun seit geraumer Zeit unter
meiner Leitung dergestalt zu qualificiren gesucht." Marburg, Hessisches Staatsarchiv,
17/2, 1199.

38. Neubürger, "Notiz," *MGWJ* 22 (1873): 192: "Er war vielmehr in Fürth
schon in frühem Mannesalter als 'neumodisch' bekannt und ist auch hier unter . . .
R. Salomon Cohn, mit dem Bann belegt worden." Lowenstein is wrong in assuming the
contrary. "Readership of Mendelssohn's Bible Translation," p. 188.

39. Wiernik, in *Jewish Encyclopedia*, 3:78.

40. See Hallo, *Geschichte der jüdischen Gemeinde Kassel*, reprinted in Arnsberg,
Die jüdischen Gemeinden in Hessen, and Adolf Kohut, *Geschichte der Juden in
Deutschland* (Berlin, 1898), p. 678.

41. In 1780 Josef Hess became rabbi of Kassel; about 1790, he was succeeded by
Joseph Michael Kugelmann. Aron Freimann, in *Jewish Encyclopedia*, 3:602.

and we know that a modern-minded, Hebrew-reading minority lived there. Since 1784, three copies of the printed *Meassef* had existed—and I think circulated—in Kassel's Jewish community. It seems that in 1794 a liberal, progressive rabbi came to a Jewish community that was itself not entirely traditionalist, a community with many members who had arrived there during the previous ten to thirty years.

Kassel was the capital of Hesse-Kassel, but it was situated in the far northern part of the state, and the border was only some five kilometers to the northeast. To the northwest, it was only one-day's walk (about thirty-five kilometers) across the border to another well-known Jewish community in Warburg. Warburg was a small town in the *Hochstift* Paderborn, which of course also became a part of the new kingdom of Westphalia in 1807. Twenty years earlier, in 1786, there were fifty-three Jewish families living there.[42] For more than thirty years, from 1774 to 1805, Shmuel Josef Steg had been Warburg's rabbi; he died in 1807.[43] He had been born in Steeg, a small village on the Rhine near Koblenz, and studied *gemara* in Bingen, Frankfurt am Main, and finally in the famous *yeshivah* in Prague. Like Löb Meyer Berlin and his brother Noah Chaim, Steg was an eminently learned man and an authority on the Talmud. He was also the father of at least three sons: Maier (b. 1776), Juda (b. 1780), and Manke (b. 1781).[44] I mention them because we shall encounter Manke Steg once again when examining the Kassel "Meassef."

Jerome's royal government was favorable to Jews, in fact the most favorable in Germany at that time. Jews became citizens like all others, and the progressive among them were allowed to establish a modern Jewish school system.[45] The Konsistorialschule was founded in Kassel in 1809, about thirty years after the foundation of the first modern school in the Jewish world, the Israelitische Freischule in Berlin (1778). Thirty years are a long time, but during that period only four other modern schools had opened their doors in Germany: the Königliche Wilhelmsschule and the Industrieschule für israelitische Mädchen in Breslau (1791 and 1801), the Franzschule in Dessau (1799), and the Philantropin in

42. Bernhard Brilling, "Zur Geschichte der Juden in Warburg: I. Die Familiennamen der Warburger Juden (1807–1812)," *Zeitschrift für die Geschichte der Juden* 10 (Tel Aviv, 1973): 56–57.

43. Emil Herz, *Denk ich an Deutschland in der Nacht: Die Geschichte des Hauses Steeg* (Berlin, 1951), pp. 40, 72, 75.

44. Brilling, "Zur Geschichte der Juden in Warburg," pp. 64–65.

45. Lazarus, "Das Königlich Westphälische Konsistorium der Israeliten," pp. 199–208, 326–58, 454–82, 542–61.

Frankfurt am Main (1804).[46] Jerome's Kassel must have been attractive
for a Jewish man of learning, for in 1808 David Fränkel (1779–1865),
the grandson of Mendelssohn's teacher, the headmaster of Dessau's flour-
ishing Franzschule, and the founder of the *Sulamith* journal,[47] agreed to
come to Kassel to found a school similar to that in Dessau. In 1810 the
Konsistorialschule had 71 pupils; later the number increased to 100 pupils with eight teachers, three of whom were full-time. We shall return
to them in a moment, when we examine the "Meassef" manuscript. In
that very year, 1810, the first seminary in the world that trained Jewish
teachers in a modern and progressive manner was founded in Kassel.[48]
For a short time at the beginning of the nineteenth century, Kassel became a center of modern Jewish education in the tradition of Moses Mendelssohn and the German Haskalah; not *lamdanim,* but rather *maskilim*
lived there besides the *ketzinim.* We do not know who was the first to
discuss these new ideas in Kassel, but we do have a few clues: *Ha-Meassef*
subscriptions and a remark by Lucius Liffmann about himself in the
1780s, the "Meassef" manuscript in 1799, and the founding of the Gesellschaft der Humanität in 1802 with Lucius Liffmann as its first president.[49]

The Kassel "Meassef" is a small Hebrew manuscript, a booklet in oc-
tavo of sixty-six pages, preserved among the treasures of the University
Library in Strasbourg.[50] It contains poetry and prose of various kinds,
some being translations of German poems and prose. The title page indicates that the contributions were written and collected in 5559 (1798–
99) in the Jewish community in Kassel. The collection has five parts,
each of which begins with *shirim* (poems). Only in the first two parts
are the sections labeled, namely:

46. Ibid., p. 197 n. 3. In Austria, Joseph II issued edicts in 1781–89 in which "the
Jews were ordered to establish 'normal' schools or to send their children to the state
schools. . . . As a result of these edicts, 42 schools were opened in Moravian communities by 1784, 25 in Bohemia by 1787, and about 30 in Hungary by the end of the
1780s. In Galicia 104 schools were established." Azriel Shochat, in *Encyclopaedia
Judaica,* vol. 7, col. 1441.
47. Wiernik, in *Jewish Encyclopedia,* 11:583.
48. Lazarus, "Das Königlich Westphälische Konsistorium der Israeliten," pp. 196–
99, 204, 507, 509, 201.
49. Hallo, *Geschichte der jüdischen Gemeinde Kassel,* p. 32.
50. "Ha-Meassef," Bibliothèque Nationale et Universitaire, Strasbourg, MS. 4040.
For a short description, see *Catalogue général des manuscrits des bibliothèques pu-
bliques de France: Départements,* vol. 47, *Strasbourg* (Paris, 1923), p. 707.

1. *shirim* (poems)
2. *mishle musar* (moral examples)
3. *mikhtavim shonim* (treatises of various kinds)
4. *teva* (nature)
5. *mine tiviim* (species of natural objects)
6. *korot ha-itim* (events of the times)

The fact that the later parts lack the clear structure of the beginning of the manuscript suggests that the enthusiasm of the writers may have diminished during the year. The scheme of division was adopted from the printed *Meassef* volumes; the first three sections can be found in the seventh and last printed volume of the first series, which was issued in 1797; *korot ha-itim* is to be found in the sixth volume (1790). The printed *Meassef* never contained *toldot minim ha-tiviim* (natural history), but the *meassefim* promised to publish articles on this subject in the volume to come, which was not published until 1809. The Kassel manuscript's scheme had thus been already developed by the authors before they wrote their texts. A proof of this is that in the first part of the manuscript the fourth section is lacking, and we find the notice *yipaked mekomo* (p. 8), just as sometimes in the printed *Meassef* volumes.

Eighteen contributions in verse or prose include a footnote in German and in Latin script, with Latin letters for the authors' names as was the custom in German at that time. These footnotes refer to a German source, in the same way as in the printed *Meassef* volumes. In addition one footnote in Hebrew refers to the *Maarikh Maarahot,* a Hebrew dictionary by Philippus Aquinas, printed in Paris in 1629. Ten of the originally German pieces are taken from Adam Olearius's *Persianischer Rosenthal,* a translation of Sheikh Sadi's Persian collection *Gulistan.* The *Persianischer Rosenthal* had been edited in the seventeenth century,[51] but the translators may have used one of the collections printed in the late eighteenth century. The other German texts are also contemporary ones, published during the twenty years prior to 1799: a fable by Daniel Holtzmann,[52] a fable by Christian Fürchtegott Gellert and another probably by a differ-

51. Adam Olearius, *Persianischer Rosenthal* (Schleswig, 1654, 2°; 1660, obl. 4°; Hamburg, 1696, 2°). It is likely that Johann Gottfried von Herder was the link between Olearius and the translators in Kassel. In his *Zerstreute Blätter: Vierte Sammlung* (Gotha, 1792), he published translations of some of Sadi's epigrams. *Herders sämtliche Werke,* ed. Bernhard Suphan, vol. 26 (Berlin, 1882; reprint, Hildesheim, [1968]), p. 309.

52. Daniel Holtzmann, "Das Krokodil und die Eidechse," in his *Fabeln nach D. Holtzmann herausgegeben von* [August Gottlieb] *Meissner* (Leipzig, 1782).

ent author,[53] a poem entitled "Lob der Faulheit" (Panegyric on Laziness) by Gotthold Ephraim Lessing,[54] a dialogue between the Greek philosopher Thales and a Milesian nobleman by August Gottlieb Meissner,[55] two passages from *Ein Unterhaltungsbuch zur Beförderung der Menschenkenntnisse* by Adam Friedrich Ernst Jacobi,[56] and a passage about the seal from a *Naturgeschichte für Kinder* by Georg Christian Raff.[57] Hebrew translations of works of Gellert and Raff had also been printed in the *Meassef* volumes; one also finds there Johann Jakob Dusch, Salomon Gessner, Friedrich von Hagedorn, Albrecht von Haller, Heinrich von Kleist, Moses Mendelssohn, Michaelis, and Karl Wilhelm Ramler. Now, in the latter decades of the eighteenth century, German literature reached a culmination in Weimarian classicism, and philosophy also entered the fascinating era of German idealism. It is strange, and significant, that the Jewish authors in Kassel did not translate a single passage from the works of Johann Wolfgang von Goethe, Friedrich von Schiller, Christoph Martin Wieland, or Immanuel Kant. An anacreontic poem of little merit and some fables represent German literature; passages from schoolbooks or popular writings represent philosophy and the natural sciences. This is not meant as a reproach to the Jewish authors; at that time the ordinary German reader was just beginning to discover the Weimarian Goethe and other authors like him. But it demonstrates, nonetheless, the gap that existed between progressive European culture and the Jewish world at the end of the eighteenth century.

What did the authors emphasize, and what can be said about their intentions? We find two hints on the title page. First, a printed vignette with a portrait of Thales is glued on in the middle. Thales is also to be found within the manuscript, in a dialogue translated from a German source. Thales, the philosopher who is said to have uttered the famous maxim "Know thyself," was concerned with the philosophy of nature,

53. Christian Fürchtegott Gellert, "Der Tanzbär," in his *Fabeln und Erzählungen* (Leipzig, 1746–48), other editions entitled *Auserlesene Fabeln* (Berlin, 1780, 1788; Leipzig, 1795). The other fable, "Die Eidechse und die Heuschrecke," seems to have been written by a different author.

54. Gotthold Ephraim Lessing's "Lob der Faulheit" was first published in 1747. For other editions, see *Gotthold Ephraim Lessings sämtliche Schriften*, ed. Karl Lachmann and Franz Muncker, vol. 1 (Stuttgart, 1886), pp. 59–60, 74.

55. August Gottlieb Meissner, "Bruchstück aus Thales Leben," in his *Skizzen: 11. und 12. Sammlung* (Tübingen, 1796), pp. 38–42.

56. Adam Friedrich Ernst Jacobi, *Ein Unterhaltungsbuch zur Beförderung der Menschenkenntnisse* (Eisenach, 1793–94).

57. Georg Christian Raff, *Naturgeschichte für Kinder*, Teil 20 of *Sammlung philosophischer Schriften* (Göttingen, 1778; Tübingen, 1788).

mathematics, and technical inventions, and Denis Diderot stated that "Thales had been the thinker who 'introduced the scientific method into philosophy, and the first to deserve the name of philosopher.' "[58] Meissner's dialogue between Thales and a Milesian nobleman, taken from Diogenes Laërtius, the famous Greek biographer, does not show Thales as he actually was.[59] It is a sequence of questions and answers, such as, What is the most beautiful thing? (the world), the largest? (the universe), and so forth. Here we read, What do you think is man's best feature? And Thales answered, Knowledge. Whatever the authors in Kassel knew about Thales, for a Haskalah journal to choose Thales was typical.

The second hint on the title page is a motto taken from Kohelet (Ecclesiastes): "Whatsoever thy hand findeth to do, do it with thy might; for there is no work, nor device, nor knowledge, nor wisdom, in the grave, whither thou goest" (9:10). It is a very active life that this quotation proposes, and we may presume that the men who adopted it as a motto were not content with the Jewish way of life of the time, which they thought poor and passive. The title page reveals the authors' intentions: it contains a summons to a life in the Jewish tradition but one that is active and open to the influence of European traditions, including the ideas of the Enlightenment, Thales and Kohelet—I think the *meassefim* of the 1780s would have agreed with these perspectives, and it was perhaps in the printed *Meassef* that Kassel writers' appreciation for them originated.

The authors of the Kassel "Meassef" signed their little contributions in the same way as the authors of the printed volumes—using initials, names, patronymica, toponymica, and so forth. From this information we can draw conclusions about how this "Meassef" was composed, which parts each author was responsible for, and what kind of contributions each made.

The most enthusiastic contributor was Isaac/Eisik ben ha-rav *morenu ha[rav]* Feist *nero yair* mi-Bamberg; the second most enthusiastic one was Manke ben Abraham Amsterdam me-Offenbach. Each of them wrote more than a quarter of the texts. Each of them also had a brother who contributed to "Ha-Meassef"; Löb Feist Bamberg was a younger brother of Isaac, and Aron Abraham Offenbach was a brother of Manke. A

58. Denis Diderot, "Grecs (philosophie des), in his *Oeuvres complètes,* ed. Jules Assézat, vol. 15 (Paris, 1876), p. 64, quoted by Peter Gay, *The Enlightenment: An Interpretation,* vol. 1, *The Rise of Modern Paganism* (London, 1967), pp. 72–73.

59. See Jürgen Mittelstrass, *Neuzeit und Aufklärung: Studien zur Entstehung der neuzeitlichen Wissenschaft und Philosophie* (Berlin, 1970), p. 19, n. 2.

fifth author was Simon Hechinger, a friend (*ḥaver*) of Isaac Feist.[60] The
latter three wrote rather less, together as much as Isaac Feist Bamberg
did alone. Finally, there were two others who contributed only one poem
each: they were probably guests in this circle of Jews, staying in Kassel
for only a short time. We have met one of them already, Manke *ben ha-
rav ha-gaon ha-gadol mo*[*renu*] *ha-*[*rav*] Shmuel Steg, born in 1781,
therefore eighteen years old in 1799, and the son of the rabbi in Warburg; the other was called Löb Halberstadt.

As regards the translations of German texts, the facts are the same:
more than half of them are signed by Isaac Feist Bamberg; his brother
Löb and Manke Abraham from Offenbach did the remaining ones.
Those who contributed the most original texts were therefore also the
ones who did the most translations. But who were these men? What can
be learned about them from documents and books?

Like Manke Steg, Isaac and Löb Feist Bamberg were sons of a rabbi.[61]
Rabbi Uri Feis(t) was a *dayan* in Bamberg and succeeded Rabbi Löb
Meyer Berlin in Bamberg when Löb Meyer became chief rabbi in Kassel
in 1794. For some time Löb Feist Bamberg was a teacher in Warburg:
we know of a *bar mitzvah drasha* in which a boy thanked his teacher Löb
Bamberg.[62] Later on Löb Feist was a freethinker; he committed suicide in
Bamberg in 1858. He may have been the Levi Bamberger, a teacher in
Gütersloh, roughly one hundred kilometers northwest of Kassel, who in
1826 applied for the rabbinate in Bielefeld, about eighteen kilometers
northeast of Gütersloh, but was refused because he was a freethinker.[63]
Löb Feist's brother Isaac became a medical doctor through the support of
Lucius Liffmann in Kassel.[64]

60. These are Simon Hechinger's own words in a comment on a *shir jedidus* (poem
of friendship) on p. 3.

61. Eckstein, *Geschichte der Juden im ehemaligen Fürstbistum Bamberg*, p. 179.

62. The *drasha* was written before 1824. Max Grunwald, "Altjüdisches Gemein-
deleben," *Mitteilungen zur Jüdischen Volkskunde* 16, no. 2 (1913): 27.

63. Arno Herzig, *Judentum und Emanzipation in Westfalen*, Veröffentlichungen des
Provinzialinstituts für westfälische Landes- und Volkskunde, Reihe 1, Bd. 17 (Mün-
ster, 1973), p. 45. Levi Bamberger wrote in his application: "Der Wunsch [ist], mein
ganzes Dasein der Aufklärung meiner Brüder in Israel zu weihen, allen nicht gesetz-
lichen Orientalismus zu entfernen und sie für die Fortschritte des Zeitgeistes empfäng-
licher zu bilden."

64. See Brede, "Lucius Liffmann," p. 230. Like Liffmann, Isaac Feist studied in
Göttingen. Götz von Selle, *Die Matrikel der Georg-August-Universität zu Göttingen,
1734–1837*, Veröffentlichungen der historischen Kommission für Hannover, vol. 9
(Hildesheim, 1937; reprint, Nendeln, 1980), no. 20450 (April 17, 1804). Isaac was in
Kassel when Liffmann died in 1803. *Sulamith* 3, no. 2 (1811): 237. Monika Richarz,
*Der Eintritt der Juden in die akademischen Berufe: Jüdische Studenten und Akademiker
in Deutschland 1678–1848*, Wissenschaftliche Abhandlungen des Leo Baeck Instituts,

Aron Abraham of Offenbach can also be identified if one is familiar with the way in which Jews in the kingdom of Westphalia acquired family names in 1812. They were free to choose with two restrictions, one of which was that names of towns and places in the kingdom itself were not allowed.[65] So Aron Abraham altered the name of his birthplace Offenbach to the family name Rosenbach, just as others altered Stadtberge to Stahlberg or Paderborn to Paderstein. This Aron Abraham Rosenbach is well known.[66] Born in 1772 in Offenbach, he was twenty-seven when the "Meassef" manuscript was written.[67] He lived in Kassel in 1799 and stayed there until his death. In 1804 and 1805 he applied for a *Toleranzschein* (work permit) for Kassel, which he ultimately received. He wanted to earn his living as a *Gesetz- und Zehngebotschreiber* (a writer of Torah scrolls), and the Jewish community's council confirmed that he was able to give lessons in talmudic studies, Jewish religion, and writing Hebrew.[68] In 1809 he became one of the first three teachers at the Konsistorialschule in Kassel. Rosenbach was regarded as a learned man with a good knowledge of Hebrew. In 1812 we find him being called a master and a rabbi. In 1816 and 1817 he published short Hebrew texts in the Jewish journals *Sulamith* and *Jedidja*. He edited Hebrew calendars for 5585 and 5586 (1824–25 and 1825–26), and he died in 1827. About his brother Manke, on the other hand, we know only that in 1812 he no longer lived in Kassel.

Regarding the other authors of the Kassel "Meassef," I have merely a few conjectures to make. It is unlikely that Simon Hechinger, or Hechingen, was born in the small community of Hechingen in Württemberg.[69] In Fürth, however, where rabbi Löb Meyer Berlin was born, the deputy of the Jewish community, Naphtali Jacob bar Abraham Hechingen, died in 1762,[70] and Simon Hechinger, called *ha-nehmad we ha-*

28 (Tübingen, 1974) did not mention Isaac's name, but referred to his brother Dr. iur. utr. Karl Feust (1798–1872) and to two other relatives—Dr. Philipp and Dr. med. Emmanuel Feust (pp. 148, 163, 206). Eckstein, *Geschichte der Juden im ehemaligen Fürstbistum Bamberg*, mentions neither Isaac nor Karl.

65. Brilling, "Zur Geschichte der Juden in Warburg," pp. 50–51.

66. For complete information about Rosenbach, see Lazarus, "Das Königlich Westphälische Konsistorium der Israeliten," pp. 326–29, 557, 559.

67. Marburg, Hessisches Staatsarchiv, 76a/28, 11: Cassel no. 141.

68. Ibid., 5/2340.

69. Paul Sauer, *Die jüdischen Gemeinden in Württemberg und Hohenzollern: Denkmale, Geschichte, Schicksal* (Stuttgart, 1966), p. 90, reports that in 1775, thirty-seven Jewish families lived in Hechingen. In "Ha-Meassef," Simon Hechinger is not called *from* Hechingen.

70. Leopold Löwenstein, "Memorbücher," *Zeitschrift für die Geschichte der Juden in Deutschland* 2 (1888): 88.

maskil kevod rabbi in the Kassel manuscript (p. 61), could be a grandson of this man.[71] Löb Halberstadt, about whom we know nothing definite, might have been a relative of rabbi Löb Meyer Berlin, whose grandfather was Rabbi Sanwel Halberstadt. The latter lived in Halberstadt, Berlin, and Strelitz, had eight children, and died in 1742.[72]

Let me now sum up what we know about the authors. We have two sons of the rabbi of Bamberg and a son of the rabbi of Warburg. Two— Löb Feist and Aron Abraham—became teachers, and one became a medical doctor. In 1799 one was twenty-seven, another eighteen, and another must have been a young man because he lived until 1858. So we may say that the Kassel manuscript was the work of a small group of young men who admired the printed *Meassef* that had ceased to be published and who wanted to create a faithful imitation of it. Since we have records regarding every adult male Jew living in Kassel in 1812, we know that only one of the contributors to "Ha-Meassef," Aron Abraham, still lived in Kassel at that time. So it seems very likely that most of the contributors were neither born in Kassel nor belonged to families that lived in Kassel. I conjecture that they were *talmidim,* pupils living with and learning from Rabbi Löb Meyer, and they were probably not his only students, for Löb Meyer was well known as a learned man.[73] And who else could have been the center of a group of five to seven mostly young authors writing Hebrew poetry and prose in Kassel in 1799? We cannot be sure whether or not they were all in fact physically present in Kassel when they wrote their contributions, but I believe they were.[74]

I have limited myself in this essay to considering how the "Meassef" manuscript could have been written in Kassel, why it took the form it

71. Simon Hechinger could also be Simon Höchheimer (b. ca. 1750, d. after 1822 in Fürth), physician and author. See Meyer Kayserling, in *Jewish Encyclopedia,* 6:433–34. As it seems, Simon was a brother of Moses ben Chaim Cohen Höchheimer (ca. 1750–1835 in Ansbach), *dayan* in Fürth, and later rabbi in Ansbach. Steinschneider, *Catalogus Librorum Hebraeorum,* no. 6448, and William Zeitlin, *Bibliotheca Hebraica Post-Mendelssohniana* (Leipzig, 1891–95), p. 137, called him Hechim (Hechingen). Simon Höchheimer lived an adventurous life in various towns and wrote, among other books, *Über Moses Mendelssohns Tod* (Vienna and Leipzig, 1786), which includes a Hebrew passage.

72. Eckstein, *Nachträge zur Geschichte der Juden,* p. 5.

73. In the contract of Tewele Scheuer, for example, rabbi in Bamberg from 1759 to 1767, the community confirmed that it would pay the living costs of eight students. Eckstein, *Geschichte der Juden im ehemaligen Fürstbistum Bamberg,* p. 14.

74. The manuscript itself indicates only that Manke Abraham and Simon Hechinger were actually in Kassel at that time. Manke Abraham signed a piece of prose beginning "Po be-ir Q . . . ascher be-H . . . ha-medino" (here in the town of Kassel in Hesse) (pp. 29–31). Hechinger once is called "Shimon Hechinger be-Kassel" (p. 61).

did, and what kind of people wrote it. I should be pleased if I have contributed an example of how, at a time when the German Enlightenment was waning in influence, the Haskalah influenced cultural life in a relatively large, secondary Jewish community, one that would later become a center of modern Jewish education. There were many different factors behind that development; the Kassel "Meassef" of 1799 attests to some of them.

Hermann Cohen

Judaism in the Context of German Philosophy

Three aspects of Hermann Cohen's opus call for an analysis: (1) Cohen's position in nineteenth- and twentieth-century philosophy in its relation to Immanuel Kant; (2) Cohen's harmonistic interpretation of the alleged symbiosis between Germany and the Jews or, more pointedly, the affinity between *Deutschtum* and *Judentum;* and (3) Cohen's philosophy of Judaism and some of its compounds.

I

Hermann Cohen's philosophical system must be understood in relation to the development of nineteenth-century German idealism and, more specifically, within the movement "back to Kant." In turn, this renaissance of Kant's philosophy has been understood as a critical response to the perceived failure of absolute idealism, particularly as manifested in G. W. F. Hegel's system. Chronologically, Cohen's approach cannot be detached from the successful completion of the return to Kant, though Cohen could not accept the cephalocentric interpretation of Kantian philosophy. Cohen tried to establish a system that in no way emphasizes subjectivity, and certainly not the organic human faculties such as *cephalos* or even the senses imbued with *a priori* forms. Otto Liebman, for example, a representative of the movement back to Kant, attempts to maintain time and space as the forms of sensibility and thus to ground them in what can be described as the human physiological equipment. In this context it is appropriate to refer to what Cohen says about the relation of intuition (*Anschauung*) to thinking and about the primacy attributed in

Kant's own system to intuition, namely that although according to Kant thinking has its beginning in something outside itself, for Cohen this view involves a weakness in Kant's philosophy. Herein lies the ground for the movement away from (*Abfall*) Kant. A significant point in this context is Cohen's critique of Kant's interpretation of the form of time and its position. There is in Kant, according to Cohen, an improper mixture of thinking and representation. Succession in time is understood as in the subject, and hence as psychological, as if the succession were given in and for itself rather than being interpreted, as it should be, as a matter for creation. In this latter sense, it could occupy the position of the paradigm of the object.[1] The central point is that forms are created (*erzeugbar*) and not merely presented as given or as identifiable within the framework of sensibility. Since they are created, forms are involved in a process of creation that is continuous and has its ground in the principle of origin (*Ursprung*) as an eternal principle of logic. Only that grounding safeguards the eternity of the task of logic.[2] I would emphasize at this point the reference both to the task and to eternity, since the issue is to consider the essence of the rational approach manifest in logic as a continuous task that never reaches its culmination. Hence the system is the highest goal or, in Cohen's formulation, *aufgegeben* and not *gegeben*.[3]

Because of that systematic attitude there is no room for invoking the concept of the "thing-in-itself." We move within the line of continuity of knowledge. The impressions (*Empfindungen*) need not surreptitiously invent the object; rather they become reactions to the stimuli (*Reize*). We remain within the interrelation between immanent factors present in the scope of cognition.

The presentness of the "thing-in-itself" within the horizon of consciousness is for Kant the ultimate guarantee for the givenness of data that as such cannot and will not be integrated in the process of knowledge. This is one of the main issues on which Cohen takes exception, referring to the prejudice of givenness that impairs the originality, self-sufficiency, and indeed the creative sovereignty of thinking.[4] Hence the datum occupies a tentative position until it is deciphered by creative thinking. The fact that thinking never reaches its end has its correlate in the givenness of data; but the data are not an ultimate fact to be encountered by thinking, but a relative component to be integrated in the struc-

1. Hermann Cohen, *Logik der reinen Erkenntnis* (1902), introd. Helmut Holzweig, vol. 6 of Cohen, *Werke* (New York, 1977), pp. 151–52.
2. Ibid., p. 37.   3. Ibid., pp. 397, 532.   4. Ibid., p. 28.

ture of knowledge. The relativization of the datum is an indication of the infinite process of knowledge. By the same token, its character and position are subject to change since, before the cognitive process deciphers the datum, it is a datum. But after the process has reached the stage of deciphering, the datum ceases to be a brute fact and becomes integrated in the structure of the cognitive profile.

Cohen's system can be described as pointing to a progressive conceptualization. That feature of the system has been characterized by a somewhat metaphoric description: the creation (*Erzeugung*) is itself the created (*das Erzeugnis*). Thinking itself is both the goal and the process of its activity. The Kantian view that the multitude of sensual data must be given from a source outside thinking has been replaced by the system of progressive conceptualization. Indeed, the progress indicated is a replacement of the centrality of synthesis in Kant, because in Kant synthesis is a unification of forms of thinking with forms of sensuality or of forms with material, whereas in Cohen thinking itself is of the character of synthesis.[5]

Cohen's neo-Kantianism had a bearing on his system of ethics. Because of the essential role of ethics in religion, I shall be concerned with Cohen's system as it appears within the context of the philosophy of religion.

Yet I must offer a remark on the impact that Cohen's systematic position had on the interpretation of Kant, since he dealt extensively with Kant's system in its various components. This remark will confine itself to the notion of transcendentality, which in Kant's system is related to the synthesis once transcendentality has been identified with *a priori* concepts valid for the data. It would be presumptuous to assume that Cohen changed the meaning of transcendentality when he interpreted Kant. Yet there are nuances in Cohen's rendering of it that go beyond Kant in the direction of a system of progressive conceptualization, for example, when the fundamental concepts of a transcendental character are understood as being the foundation of the phenomena (*Erscheinungen*) and their laws. Obviously, in Kant, too, transcendentality refers to laws, but the conjunction of laws and appearance (*Erscheinung*) implies a totality or a whole. In this sense transcendentality points to the construction of a whole and not to a stratum of forms applicable to data.[6] When a transcendental

5. Ibid., pp. 25–29.
6. Hermann Cohen, *Kant's Theorie der Erfahrung* (1889), 3d ed. (Berlin, 1918), p. 94.

condition is understood as a part and component (*Glied*) of a higher whole (*eines höheren Ganzen*),[7] we encounter what could be described as a partially holistic position. This is a position that does not represent a structure of syntheses, since such a structure presupposes a dichotomy of thinking and sensuality. To be sure, what has been described as a partial whole receives additional elucidation by reference to the idealism criticized by Cohen.

Cohen's reformulation of the core of Kant's system must be seen in relation to the trend of absolute idealism. I shall consider this by juxtaposing Cohen's system with Hegel's. By way of introduction let me say: (1) Cohen does not attempt to formulate an identity between reason and reality as Hegel did, though Hegel did assume that that identity, present in a latent way, can be, and is, progressively discerned. Cohen remains within the framework of Kant's distinction between the spontaneity of cognition and the data, though the border between the two poles or aspects is mobile. (2) Cohen maintains the view that philosophic exploration should limit itself to discerning the presuppositions of knowledge and science. He does not present a total system in which the various manifestations of knowledge and science are integrated, as does Hegel. Cohen's system presents different provinces of knowledge as coexisting and not as immersed in a progressive discernment of the identity between reason and reality that ends in the total identity of the two. (3) In this context we must understand Cohen's distinction between idealism and metaphysics: for idealism, the ultimate foundations of truth and science are cognitive processes, the "laying of foundations" (*Grundlegungen*); for metaphysics, there are foundations (*Grundlagen*). The active term *Grundlegungen* denotes the dynamic or progressive aspect of cognition, while the term *Grundlagen* signifies the ever-present reality of rational contents and structures.[8] Hypothesis (*Grundlegung*) in Cohen does not refer to mere hypotheses (*Hypothesen*).[9] (4) Philosophizing is bound to start with the presuppositions of science. We must be strict in attempting to grasp the meaning of a statement: I refer to philosophizing and not to philosophy. Thus we remain within the boundaries of Kant's approach, since the concern is with presuppositions of science and not with its integration into a philosophical system. Without scientific truth there is no veracity, and without veracity there is no truth.[10] The homogeneity (*Einheitlichkeit*) of the system demands a central point in the founda-

7. Ibid., p. 183.   8. Cohen, *Logik*, p. 303.   9. Ibid., p. 515.
10. Ibid., p. 604.

tion (*Fundament*) of logic. Cohen could not agree with Hegel's view that logic coincides with metaphysics as the science of things comprehended by thoughts capable of expressing the essences (*Wesenheiten*) of things.[11]

These considerations form the basis for Cohen's criticism of Hegel's notion of totality, which Hegel conceived as the totality of being (*des Seienden*) and not as the totality of conditions. It is evident that the emphasis on conditions has an inherently Kantian connotation.[12] According to Cohen, Hegel's central position in regard to contradiction is related to that distinction, since contradiction is meant to be the inner driving factor of the dynamic character of thinking; that is, it turns the progressive character of knowledge into the manifestation of the dialectic of knowledge and leads to the abyss.[13] Hegel remains within the orbit of an ontology according to which all being is the self-manifestation of the concept.[14] Here again we recognize the difference between Kant and Hegel as well as Cohen's adherence to the trend represented by Kant, namely, that there is no way to transform the structure of concepts into being. Concepts are presuppositions or instruments, not substances or the total substance exhibited step by step. Though the duality of concepts and data becomes fluid, it is not overcome by presenting contradictions as inherent in reason and by suggesting the ultimate unity of contradictions in and through the identity of reason and reality. We can assume that Cohen integrated in his system what can be described as the dynamic character of the distinction between concepts and data, but that he did not accept the notion of a dynamic ultimate synthesis between the two.

II

The relation to Kant is the central inspiring factor not only in the formulation of Cohen's philosophical system; it is also a pivotal issue in his evaluation of German culture and the position of the Jews and of Judaism *vis-à-vis* that culture. According to Cohen, the fundamental concept of Kant's ethics is mankind. That concept, however, appears not only in the system of Kant but is present in what Cohen calls *Deutschtum* and which, in turn, is based on an ethical notion. Cohen adds a comment that is meant to show the affinity between *Deutschtum* and humanity. Hatred, he says, is not a characteristic passion (*Affekt*) in the German soul.

11. G. W. F. Hegel, *Wissenschaft der Logik*, pt. 2, in *Sämtliche Werke*, ed. Hermann Glockner (Stuttgart, 1927–40), 5:24, 63.

12. Cohen, *Logik*, p. 329.   13. Ibid., p. 112.   14. Ibid., p. 416.

Hence the equality of rights granted to the Jews in Germany is based on a moral disposition more profound than anywhere else.[15] "Every German must know his Schiller and his Goethe and carry them in his heart with the intimacy of love. Yet this intimacy presupposes that he has won a rudimentary understanding also of his Kant."[16] Kant's impact on the essence of *Deutschtum* has its correlate, Cohen suggests, in the affinity between Kant's ethical system and Judaism—an affinity that is to be affirmed in spite of the severe criticism leveled by Kant against Judaism, describing it as a sum total of statutory laws and as not being a religion at all. Cohen points to the impact that the interpretations of Baruch Spinoza and Moses Mendelssohn had on Kant's evaluation of Judaism. Cohen says of Judaism that it is characterized by opposition to egotism and by a tendency to transcend the horizon of the individual. Opposition to selfishness, which is inherent in the essence of the law, is common to Judaism and Kant. In spite of Kant's concept of the autonomy of the moral law, Cohen affirms the affinity between Kant and Judaism by virtue of the notion that God is the originator and guarantor of the law of morality. The idea expressing this notion lies at the root of Judaism.[17]

The alleged affinity between the Jews and Judaism on the one hand and the German people and *Deutschtum* on the other invites some observations. We notice that Cohen embodies, as it were, the position he ascribes to the German people. He presupposes in *Deutschtum* not only a national spirit *qua* historical factor but also as an articulation of such a spirit in a formulated attitude and in principles that have become a common possession. Cohen says in another context that the primary origin is the national spirit, which in turn becomes the primal ground for the individual.[18]

Employing the concept of *Nationalgeist* leads Cohen to face the problem of nationalism; and from the history of that concept we know very

15. Hermann Cohen, "Deutschtum und Judentum" (1915), in his *Jüdische Schriften,* ed. Bruno Strauss, introd. Franz Rosenzweig (Berlin, 1924), vol. 2, *Zur jüdischen Zeitgeschichte,* pp. 279–80. The presentation of the topic is included under the sub-heading "Judentum und Staat."

16. Ibid., pp. 282–83.

17. Ibid., p. 293. Different aspects of the issues relevant for this part of the exposition are contained in *Reason and Hope: Selections from the Jewish Writings of Hermann Cohen,* trans. Eva Jospe (New York, 1971).

18. Hermann Cohen, *Religion der Vernunft aus den Quellen des Judentums* (Leipzig, 1919), p. 28. Subsequent citations to this book will appear in parentheses in the text. The English translation is by Simon Kaplan (New York, 1971), p. 24. On Cohen, see Nathan Rotenstreich, *Jewish Philosophy in Modern Times: From Mendelssohn to Rosenzweig* (New York, 1968), pp. 52–105.

well the interrelation between the two. Apparently Cohen thought that a solution of the problem that avoided Jewish nationalism, while assuming the presence and activity of the Jewish national spirit, was to be found in looking at monotheism as a creation of the Jewish national spirit. In monotheism lies the origin (*Ursprung*) of the history of man. We must emphasize the universal position of man and not the particular position of the Jew; the son of Israel is first the son of Noah and only then the son of Abraham. There exists, moreover, an inner relationship between monotheism and messianism (I may add that this view is significant for the assessment of Cohen's attitude toward German culture); it guided Johann Gottfried von Herder in his conception of the biblical spirit. The isolation of the Jewish community would seem to contradict the messianic avocation of Judaism. Yet, Cohen points out, in the modern period the image of the Messiah took on the features of the German spirit ("Jetzt aber erstand ihnen der Messias im deutschen Geiste wieder").[19] We may wonder whether that statement is meant to apply to the trend of German spirituality and culture as moving in the direction of *Humanität* or whether it represents mere praise for opening the gates for the Jews' entrance into German culture. Cohen traces the impact of the ideal of humanity on German culture and history as expressed, for example, in the granting of suffrage to the Jews. In any case, Cohen is translating the broad notion of messianism and humanity into the "small cash" of legal arrangements.

The inescapable dilemma which Cohen was bound to face is that of the *prima facie* contradiction between particularity inherent in the concept of national spirit and the universality or universalism of messianism. Cohen attempted to resolve that dilemma by suggesting the distinction between nation and nationality. "Nation" has a political meaning and thus is congruous with statehood, while "nationality" has a cultural or spiritual meaning. Nationality cannot be understood as implying a political entity and hence does not come into conflict with the state or the nation. Jewish nationality, for example, cannot be antagonistic to the German state and the German nation. Cohen rejected Zionism since Zionism retrogressively aspired toward a national state; it implied the isolation of the Jewish community and, by the same token, contradicted the messianic destiny of Judaism because isolation eventually takes the shape of a separate state (*Sonderstaat*) (p. 427). At this point it must be observed that Martin Buber took issue with Cohen on the essence of Zionism and

19. Cohen, "Deutschtum und Judentum," p. 267.

significantly shifted the focus of Zionism from political aspiration (state-hood) to the endeavor of overcoming the dispersion of the Jewish people by bringing its scattered parts together in the Land of Israel.[20] One has to wonder whether Cohen's response to Buber meets Buber's point. The Zionist, says Cohen, believes that Judaism can be preserved only through full and unlimited peoplehood (*Volkstum*). We entertain the opposite view; namely, that only universal, *Humanität*-oriented Judaism is able to preserve the Jewish religion.[21] Yet the concrete manifestation of that universality which expresses itself in hope and confidence is manifested in our love for *Deutschtum,* not only because Germany is our homeland or because we have found there our place like a bird its nest but because we draw from the treasures and wells of the German spirit. Cohen's is an idyllic presentation of the coexistence of the Jews with the German peo-ple along with an adherence to the original version of the reform trend in Judaism in the nineteenth century. On the issue of liturgical reform and the relation between the law (*Halakhah*) and religion, Cohen con-siders the Reform movement as truly religious (p. 433). One may ven-ture to say, not only retrospectively against the background of the Holo-caust but also in looking at Cohen's rhetoric to place it in his context, that Cohen is swept by a kind of exaltation and ceases to be guided by an analysis of concepts and situations.

III

The most prominent expression of Cohen's interpretation of Judaism is his posthumous work on religion. It is impossible to present here a full interpretation of Cohen's philosophy of Judaism, which sees in Judaism the source of the religion of reason. I shall confine myself to the presen-tation of a few aspects viewed against the background of Kant's inter-pretation of religion, since the attitude to Kant is the major concern of this exploration. It throws light also on Cohen's position within the intel-lectual history of Germany and on his position in the attempted symbiosis between *Deutschtum* and *Judentum.*

A reference to the respective titles of the two works is called for. Kant attempts to formulate a philosophy of religion that will place religion *"within the boundaries* of reason."[22] Hence there is an indication that

20. Martin Buber, *Völker, Staaten und Zion* (Vienna, 1917).
21. Hermann Cohen, "Antwort auf das offene Schreiben des Herrn Dr. Martin Buber an Hermann Cohen" (1916), in *Jüdische Schriften*, 2:336.
22. The notion of *innerhalb der Grenzen* apparently had an attraction for philoso-phers who were close to Kant's tradition. Thus Paul Natorp wrote a book entitled

here is no full identity between religion and the realm of reason. One of the manifestations of this reservation concerning the position of religion *vis-à-vis* reason is the conception that morality as the essence of religion and the common bond between itself and reason is self-sufficient. It does not stand in need of being *given* to man. On the contrary, only the self-sufficient moral imperative can be interpreted as connoting duties originating from God. To be sure, at one point we find in Kant a sort of mitigation of that position when he says that the interpreter of the revealed teachings is the God in us.[23] Thus, somehow, he is hinting at the position of reason as implying a kind of *imitatio dei,* adding that our own reason knows the divine character of the teaching bestowed on us.

Cohen takes a further step in posing revelation within the context of the religion of reason. Revelation must be seen in the framework of creation: creation implies being (*das Sein*) as the source of becoming, whereas revelation refers to the source of the being of man. The human reason is a special problem within the manifold of becoming. Thus the very presence of reason within the human realm is to be explained as creation directed toward man. Revelation in this sense is the continuation of creation insofar as it turns toward the creation of man as an entity endowed with reason. In this context of revelation morality becomes prominent. The underlying notion seems to be that reason has its highest manifestation in morality (p. 82). We may say that the special position of man is made possible by the creation of man as a selected entity. That selected entity has its most prominent expression in morality; and this would be Cohen's version of Kant's notion of the primacy of practical reason.

Revelation is described as a spiritual transmission (*Mitteilung*) (p. 88). Hence we may ask whether transmission denotes content or rather the very quality of reason or spirituality. Through reason both creation and revelation achieve their purpose (*Vollzug*) or perfection. Man reaches the stage of knowing God; he is not only a creature of God, but his reason makes him subjectively the discoverer of God (p. 103). Revelation is a truth of reason (p. 489), a characterization that does not imply the Leibnizian view. It means that in order to arrive at the position

Religion innerhalb der Grenzen der Humanität (Freiburg i.B. and Leipzig, 1894). The book's subtitle is *Ein Kapitel zur Grundlegung der Sozialpädagogik.* Humanity in the title and social pedagogy in the subtitle indicate the strong ethical orientation of the book.

23. Immanuel Kant, "Der Streit der Fakultäten," in *Kants Gesammelte Schriften,* Akademie Ausgabe (Berlin, 1907), 7:48.

of revelation, reason is a precondition, but, by the same token, in order to arrive at the position of reason, revelation is a precondition. Thus there is "correlation," a sort of circle or, to use the well-known metaphor of *Pirkei Avot,* "tongs are made by tongs."

The question must be raised whether this view of revelation obliterates the notion of *Ursprung* as the highest level of spontaneity as Cohen has conceived it in his system. The following observations are a tentative interpretation of the relation between *Ursprung* and revelation. In the first place, there is no mediation (*Logos*) between God and reality (p. 56). It follows that the positing of reason by revelation does not impose on reason any constraints in terms of the activity of reason as self-activity. As creation is the consequence of the uniqueness of God (p. 76), so also is revelation. The most essential meaning of the monotheistic concept of creation lies in ethics. Hence we may say that reason is the highest expression of creation, but it does not erase the spontaneous activity of reason. God is the original ground of activity, and this is the meaning of God as the creator (p. 74).

Man is a creature because he belongs to the universe at large, which is characterized as the realm of becoming, and because of his endowment with reason, which is posited by revelation. The position of the creator is identical with the position of being, which in turn is the explication of the position of uniqueness, and that position is the cause for the emergence of the realm of becoming (p. 74). Thus we have to distinguish between being and becoming, that is, between being as present and becoming as merely coming-to-exist. There are, as it were, two aspects to becoming: (1) it comes to be; (2) it comprises whatever comes to be.

Yet in spite of the dependent position of man (which indeed is grounded in the very conception of creation), there pertains a correlation between God and man or, seen from the opposite perspective, between man and God. To be sure, there exists also a correlation between nature and God, but that correlation is not immediate; rather, it is a correlation only through the mediation of man (p. 429). That correlation is grounded in reason which is the endowment of man *par excellence;* reason connotes the principle of good and thus it connects God and man, religion and morality (p. 339). Certainly that statement is to some extent enigmatic since religion may connote a universe of discourse and an attitude on the human end. God's entrance into relation with man (p. 82) is not religion since it is either creation or revelation, while religion must be understood as an acknowledgment of those acts or positions on the part of man. Yet Cohen formulated the correlation also as religion and morality. He did so in order to emphasize a kind of symmetry in the notion of correlation. The emphasis on correlation has a ring of polemics against pantheism seen as based on the notion of identity between man and God, whereas in monotheism, of which Judaism is the most prominent representative, God is the precondition of all becoming and therefore also for the moral aspect in man.[24]

Within that correlation the certainty of confidence in God and the assurance of His truth are to be placed. These attitudes give rise to a feeling of exaltation (*Hochgefühl*) that is but the faith in God (p. 264). The notion of correlation serves here as the ground for establishing the attitude of faith, which cannot be understood as that of mere morality (p. 208). The awe of God and the traditional expressions of that attitude are the ground of the commandments (p. 418) as well as of prayer, which is the link between religion and morality (p. 438). We notice that though correlation has its anchor in morality, it is also the ground for the emergence of the religious disposition proper, which is not identical with morality and cannot be immersed in it. We wonder to what extent the reference here is to the religion of reason or to religion against the background of reason, for such a description would differ from that of the boundaries of reason and would differ also from the pronounced notion of the religion of reason. In any case, the notion of correlation seems to serve for the identification of Judaism as monotheism proper. This excludes a move in the direction of pantheism, as if the latter would be the adequate manifestation of a rational attitude to the universe. The introduction of religious attitudes proper into the context of correlation implies a criticism of Kant. Prayer and commandments have their justification in correlation and cannot be viewed and rejected as statutory attitudes only.[25]

The transcending of the realm of ethics as formulated in Kant's system is present not only in the religious attitude as such but also in the position of the individual. I turn now to this topic. Here Cohen's conception is even more explicit than in his identification of religion and morality, which still carries the connotation of Kant's system of ethics.

Kant is the philosopher of morality who identified morality with rec-

24. On the various aspects of Cohen's concept of correlation, see Alexander Altmann, "Hermann Cohens Begriff der Korrelation," in *In Zwei Welten: Siegfried Moses zum Fünfundsiebzigsten Geburtstag*, ed. Hans Tramer (Tel Aviv, 1962), pp. 377–99.

25. Hermann Cohen, "Innere Beziehungen der Kantischen Philosophie zum Judentum" (1910), in *Jüdische Schriften*, vol. 1, *Ethische und religiöse Grundfragen*, pp. 284–305.

ognizing the dignity of man. Cohen says that the essence of morality lies in the correlation of God and man (p. 114); this essence also implies holiness. To be sure, Kant says that the humanity in our person is holy, but holiness consists in the full congruence of our will with the moral law. According to Cohen, it is the goodness and holiness of God that assure the morality of man as an I. The self-sanctification (*Selbstheiligung*) has the security of its success in the goodness of God (p. 251). Cohen's statement can be looked upon as echoing Kant's notion of the postulates, but one cannot avoid the impression that the dependence of man on God becomes stronger in Cohen's statement than it is in Kant's conception.

There is an additional element that calls for a new interpretation and evaluation, namely, the position of the individual as against the universality of mankind. Man encounters the Thou as a fellow man (pp. 116ff.). The discovery of the Thou leads to the discovery of the I or to the consciousness of the I, which amounts to the ethical knowledge of my I (p. 17). The individual presents a problem that constitutes the specific essence of religion in its difference from ethics. The dissolution of the individual in the whole is the characteristic feature of ethics, since ethics guides the individual in the direction of the whole and projects the whole as an ideal fulfillment (p. 208). This statement corroborates the suggestion that the ethical essence of religion cannot obliterate the difference between religion and ethics. Cohen underlines the specific essence of religion *vis-à-vis* ethics. That essence amounts to a different perspective on the position of the individual—ethics being characterized by the involvement of the individual in the whole of mankind, while religion has its specific character in its emphasis upon the irreducible position of the individual. This must be stressed in spite of Cohen's emphasis on the centrality of universal messianism in Judaism and, thus (at least by way of mediation), in the religion of reason.

Cohen faced the problem of what he called the discovery of the individual.[26] The reality of sin is the means of that discovery (p. 11). It is clear that the attempt to identify a means of discovery has a polemical innuendo; that is, the individual is not encountered empirically but must be conceived in his moral capacity or, rather, in the failure thereof. Sin is a concept imbued with a moral and, indeed, religious connotation. The

26. The problem of the fellow man (*der Nächste*) is explored in Cohen, "Die Nächstenliebe im Talmud" (1888), "Zum Prioritätsstreit über das Gebot der Nächstenliebe" (1894), and "Der Nächste" (1914), in *Jüdische Schriften*, 1:145–74, 175–81, 182–95.

individual as such is identified through his consciousness of having committed a sin. Sin thus becomes the foundation (*Grundlegung*), as it were, of the individual (p. 217). If we attempt to interpret Cohen's conception we may say that in sin—that is to say, in a mode of behavior that does not comply with the moral law—the agent withdraws into his own separate orbit. To be sure, this is only the initial position of the individual and is the means for the primary identification of the individual but is not the ultimate position of the individual. We may say that the relation of the individual to sin is not interpreted in a Kierkegaardian manner. Sin is the point of departure for the sake of a process in which the individual will turn in the direction of what might be described as the positive direction of his correlation with God. His ontological and thus ethical correlation with God will be realized not only in itself but also for itself, if we may apply the Hegelian terms to the context before us. In any case, since that positive turn is possible, Cohen cannot agree with Kant's version of sin as radical evil. As stated earlier, sin is only the point of departure and is not the manifestation of an inherent evil in man.

We may say that religion as a moral conception *vis-à-vis* ethics is related to the different conceptions of the position of the individual viewed either as an agent in himself or as the bridge toward universality. When Cohen refers to the religion of reason he refers therefore to a reason that cannot be merely the foundation of a universal network of relations under which the data are subsumed. Reason comprises also the irreducible position of individuals whose moral position has to be saved. We may wonder to what extent Cohen eventually presented a synthesis between that conception and the major trend of Kant's system to which he attempted to adhere and which he tried to reformulate.

In any case, without going into additional elements of Cohen's system and its problematic character, I shall conclude by emphasizing that Cohen's conception of philosophy, of culture, and of religion must be seen against his Kantian background, both historically and conceptually. He represented that background and tried to elaborate it.

Reform Jewish Thinkers and Their German Intellectual Context

The Reform movement in modern Jewry is often conceived narrowly, simply in terms of ritual changes and the ideologies that were conceived to justify them. Yet in a larger sense the task of religious reform required not only a rationalized program of liturgical change but also a theoretical conceptualization of Judaism. For apart from a response to the prevalent esthetic and ecclesiastical norms of religious practice, modernization also implied confronting Judaism as a system of belief with dominant currents in Christian theology and academic philosophy.

It will be my purpose here first to examine the intellectual context against which the early Reform movement was constrained to reassert Judaism and then to deal with the writings of three systematic thinkers who undertook that task in Germany during the first half of the nineteenth century. I hope to show that both with regard to the position it ascribed to historical Judaism and with regard to its compatibility with basic Jewish doctrines, the intellectual milieu in which the Reform movement emerged was thoroughly uncongenial to theoretical integration, that therefore the relationship which the systematic thinkers established was only indirectly one of adaptation and far more one of outright opposition.

To deal with the views of Judaism held by non-Jews in this period and with the Jewish thinkers of the time means necessarily to traverse ground well mapped out by scholars of Jewish philosophy. Yet in bringing together milieu and response I hope to reveal a bit more clearly the sharp lines of contrast contained in the composite picture.

THE INTELLECTUAL CONTEXT

It is ironic that the earliest and most fundamental modern challenge to Judaism should have arisen from its own midst. A product of the Sephardi community in Amsterdam, Baruch Spinoza (1632–77) moved rapidly beyond the traditional Jewish teachings upon which he was raised until he eventually developed a philosophical system that contradicted the most basic doctrines of Judaism. Excommunicated on account of his views, he bequeathed to subsequent generations a disagreeable but highly influential conception of his ancestral faith. Although for the most part modern Jewish thinkers took issue with Spinoza's ideas—whether or not they mentioned his name—there were certain elements in his thought that appealed to some of them.[1]

Spinoza's major work, the *Ethics,* undermined the foundations of Judaism and of Christianity alike. The transcendent creator God of the Bible was replaced by the purely immanent God equivalent to nature. In a deterministic system, free will—the basis of moral responsibility—no longer had its place and personal immortality became an illusion. Even the most radical Reformers of the following century rejected Spinoza's ontology—in the case of the Jewish philosopher, Hermann Cohen (1842–1918) most vociferously. In his *Theologico-Political Treatise,* Spinoza made Judaism out to be religiously superfluous. Reason was sufficient to determine the goodness and eternal divinity of God, and therefrom to deduce a morality. The Bible was necessary for the masses, but not at all for the philosopher. Nor were the prophets a unique treasure. Spinoza relativized their message: prophets, he noted, appear also in other nations; the prophetic gift was not peculiar to the Jews. No less problematic was the preference Spinoza expressed for Christianity over Judaism. Although he never converted, Spinoza assigned to Jesus a role in revelation far more elevated than that of the Hebrew prophets: "If Moses spoke with God face to face as a man speaks with his friend (i.e., by means of their two bodies) Christ communed with God mind to mind." At another point he says, "Christ was not so much a prophet as the mouthpiece of God." In Spinoza's clearly jaundiced view, Judaism was exclusivist and predominantly concerned with material needs, while Christianity alone was universalistic and spiritual. In fact, Judaism was actually a deleterious

---

1. The challenge of Baruch Spinoza and his influence on modern Jewish thought is especially stressed by Eliezer Schweid, *Toldot ha-hagut ha-yehudit ba-et ha-hadashah* (Jerusalem, 1977).

influence that, Spinoza suggested, may well have emasculated the minds of its adherents. If the Jews had nonetheless persisted to modern times, their survival was not on account of any innate virtues in their religion but because they had separated themselves from other nations, attracting universal hatred not only by their outward rites, which conflicted with those of other nations, but also by the sign of circumcision, which they scrupulously observed.[2]

These were views no Jewish religious thinker could allow. Yet other elements of Spinoza's biblical criticism were to a greater or lesser extent absorbed by Jewish writers for whom the commitment to historical analysis did not stop short even at the text of the Pentateuch. Spinoza had cast serious doubt upon the Mosaic authorship of the Torah; increasingly so did the Reformers, especially after the higher biblical criticism became more widely accepted in the second half of the nineteenth century. But Spinoza's most divisive legacy was his limitation of the Mosaic law's validity to the period when Jews possessed their own state and temple; it was, he argued, the constitution of their polity and had lost all binding force once the Jews went into exile.[3] Mendelssohn and most Jewish thinkers who followed him rejected this idea, but prominent radical Reformers, beginning with Samuel Holdheim, adopted it to justify abrogation of ceremonial observance.

In Germany, Spinoza's thought enjoyed considerable popularity beginning with the last decades of the eighteenth century. His view of Judaism corresponded easily with Christian prejudices and even influenced those who were favorably disposed toward individual Jews. Spinoza had written that "religion was imparted to the early Hebrews as a law written down, because they were at that time in the condition of children, but afterwards Moses and Jeremiah predicted a time coming when the Lord should write His law on their hearts."[4] This notion, that Judaism represented the faith of people who were spiritually children, was echoed by Gotthold Ephraim Lessing (1729–81) in his influential essay, *The Education of Humanity*.[5] Here the established Christian idea of the superses-

---

2. *The Chief Works of Benedict de Spinoza*, trans. R. H. M. Elwes, vol. 1 (New York, 1951), pp. 19, 49, 55–56, 68, 199. See also Isaac Franck, "Spinoza's Onslaught on Judaism," *Judaism* 28 (1979): 177–93; and Franck, "Was Spinoza a 'Jewish' Philosopher?" ibid., pp. 345–52.

3. *Chief Works of Benedict de Spinoza*, 1:72, 120–22.

4. Ibid., p. 165.

5. Gotthold Ephraim Lessing, *Die Erziehung des Menschengeschlechts* (Berlin, 1785). See also Michael Graetz, "*Die Erziehung des Menschengeschlechts* und jüdisches

sion of the older faith by the younger was clothed in a new, historical garment. Revelation and reason, in reciprocal relation, led upward as the human spirit progressed from stage to stage. For centuries religious progress characterized ancient Israel, but, during the Second Commonwealth, Judaism reached the end of its capacity for internal religious development. While its rabbis misguidedly and in vain sought to read more advanced ideas into the elementary textbook of the Hebrew Bible, a better pedagogue, Jesus, appeared and enabled humanity to advance further upon its path. Lessing thus made contemporary Judaism an anchronism. Jewish writers were forced to reject his relegation of Judaism to a primitive stage in a process that had gone beyond it. But ironically the thrust of Lessing's approach soon became essential for the theological enterprise of the Reformers. While Moses Mendelssohn had insisted on an unchanging Judaism whose eternal truths could never be supplanted or even substantively refined, Reform ideologists adopted Lessing's notion of religious advance during the course of history. For them, too, revelation became progressive as succeeding ages built upon the past. But they parted company with Lessing in insisting that Judaism had not ceased to be capable of progress. Far from being merely a stage in a universal process of religious development, it was itself the bearer of ever-richer insights into the nature of the divine and God's will for all humanity.

Among German philosophers Immanuel Kant (1724–1804) had by far the most widespread and lasting influence on modern Jewish thinkers. His rejection of Christian dogma, especially the innate corruption of man, together with his insistence that religious faith begins with action rather than atonement, made his thought highly conducive to a Judaism that stressed divine commandment rather than the salvation wrought by faith. Like Lessing, Kant presented a wholly unacceptable conception of Judaism.[6] But he also outlined the possibility of a rationally viable faith, challenging Jewish writers to reinterpret Judaism to fit his definition of an intellectually and morally respectable religion.

Eight years after *The Education of Humanity,* in 1793, Kant published

---

Selbstbewusstsein im 19. Jahrhundert," *Wolfenbütteler Studien zur Aufklärung* 4 (1977): 273–95.

6. On Immanuel Kant's and G. W. F. Hegel's conceptions of Judaism, see Nathan Rotenstreich, *The Recurring Pattern: Studies in Anti-Judaism in Modern Thought* (London, 1963), pp. 23–75. A wide range of views is presented in David Charles Smith, "Protestant Attitudes toward Jewish Emancipation in Prussia" (Ph.D. diss., Yale University, 1971).

his *Religion within the Limits of Reason Alone*. Under the influence of
Spinoza and Mendelssohn, but probably also of long-standing Christian
tradition, Kant here defined Judaism in its original form as "a collection
of mere statutory laws upon which was established a political organization." In fact, Judaism was "really not a religion at all," since it made
no claims upon conscience. Insofar as it possessed genuinely religious
characteristics, these were foreign imports derived from Greek wisdom.
Biblical Judaism stressed only external acts and outward observances,
lacked belief in a future life, and excluded all but ancient Israel from its
communion. Its God was a political autocrat, who merely desired obedience to commands and mechanical worship, not the moral being required
by religion. Christianity, since it was utterly different in all these respects, could not have arisen out of Judaism; it was rather the suddenly
created product of a revolution that for the first time produced a genuine
religious faith.[7] Much as Kant's conception of biblical Judaism represented a severe distortion, its articulation by the most highly regarded of
all German philosophers made it easier for Jews personally inclined to
reject their heritage to justify the step of conversion. Moreover, Kant's
influential idea that beyond all historical religions there was "a single,
unchanging, pure religious faith"[8] dwelling in the human conscience—in
essence the religion of the future—made indifference to all specific elements of Judaism religiously respectable. For if God required nothing
more than steadfast diligence in leading a morally good life, in fulfilling
one's duties to fellow human beings, then all ceremonial and symbolic
expressions were ultimately superfluous.

Rejection of the Kantian misconception of Judaism fell upon all who
sought to rescue its reputation. What singles out the Reformers' relation
to Kant is their adoption of so much that the Königsberg philosopher
pointed to as being not Jewish and stressing its centrality within their
own Jewish self-definition. The idea that pure religious faith is essentially
moral rapidly became the theoretical basis and the practical operative
principle of the Reform movement. Its influence dominates the writings
of Reform Jewish thinkers. No less is the primacy of morality reflected
in the prominent role given to the sermons that were delivered in the
new congregations—sermons that focused not on points of ceremonial
law but on virtuous conduct in business or family relationships. Kant had

7. Immanuel Kant, *Religion within the Limits of Reason Alone*, trans. Theodore M.
Greene and Hoyt H. Hudson (Chicago, 1934), pp. 116–20.
8. Ibid., p. 115.

declared that ceremonies to please God were morally indifferent and historically representative of paganism. A house of God was properly a "meeting place for the instruction and quickening of moral dispositions."[9] Thus, instead of being the religion of no morality—as Kant defined it— the Reformers sought to present Judaism as the religion most exclusively concerned with morality, and hence most worthy of the future. The Kantian idea of individual autonomy in religion likewise assumed centrality among the Reformers, where it was used to undermine the authority of tradition, forced consideration of how God could both command and allow for human moral responsibility, and militated against the Reformers' own sporadic attempts to impose varying degrees of religious conformity.

Kant recognized, moreover, that historical faiths were bound to sacred texts that did not necessarily reflect the highest morality. Where text and conscience were in conflict, Kant left no doubt as to which should be forced to yield. He agreed with Spinoza that the highest purpose of scriptural study was moral improvement. Consequently it sometimes became necessary—and wholly justifiable in his eyes—to utilize forced rather than literal interpretations when the latter might work counter to moral incentives. In opposition to more conservative spirits, Kant held that the Bible had to be expounded according to moral conceptions, not moral conceptions adjusted to the word of the Bible.[10] His insistence upon rational and moral criteria external to the text by which the religious value of individual passages should be judged was adopted by the Jewish Reformers as it was by liberal Christians. Jewish thinkers all across the religious spectrum engaged in forced interpretation of morally problematic passages, but only the Reformers were willing to suggest that their reinterpretations were grounded in a morality that had transcended that of the Bible itself. Ultimately Kant's rational religion was supposed to free itself of all texts and traditions. Kant believed that when humanity entered its adolescence, statutes and traditions, which were once helpful, turned into fetters. Thus all historical religions were destined to give way before the one universal rational and moral faith.[11] Reflecting upon Kant, Reform ideologists felt that what they had to do was to demonstrate that Judaism, once properly reinterpreted and purified of ceremonialism,

9. Ibid., p. 97.
10. Ibid., pp. 100–114.
11. According to Kant this would be especially true of Judaism. "The pure moral religion," he wrote, "is the euthanasia of Judaism." Immanuel Kant, "Der Streit der Facultäten" (1798), in his *Sämmtliche Werke,* ed. Karl Rosenkranz and Friedrich Wilhelm Schubert, vol. 10 (Leipzig, 1838), p. 308.

would be far from the statutory pseudoreligion that Kant had called it; that on the contrary, it could become just that faith which Kant ascribed to the future.

While the Kantian challenge and its influence upon the Reform movement remained strong well into the twentieth century, Enlightenment thought (which in Germany climaxed with Kant) was soon overshadowed by the radically different world view of romanticism. Its outstanding theological representative, Friedrich Schleiermacher (1768–1834), presented a no more positive view of Judaism than did earlier writers. However, his sharply contrasting understanding of religion in general helped to lead modern Jewish thought, too, in a new direction. Like Kant, Schleiermacher believed that Judaism had no future in the modern world. In 1799 he had written that "Judaism is long since dead. Those who yet wear its livery but sit lamenting beside the imperishable mummy, bewailing its departure and its sad legacy."[12] Again like Kant, he deplored Judaism's lack of universalism and tended to minimize the historical connection between Judaism and Christianity; and like Spinoza and Lessing he, too, described it as childlike compared to its successor faith. In his very influential dogmatics, *The Christian Faith*, first published in 1821–22, Schleiermacher placed Judaism, along with Islam and Christianity, on the highest level of monotheistic faith, but Christianity, because both universal and freed of all sensualism, represented its purest and most perfect form. Only a sick soul, he noted, would abandon it for one of its rivals.[13]

Schleiermacher was determined to restore respect for Christianity by insisting that religion was animated by feeling, not rational postulates. Intuition, not logical argument, established its most basic certainties. Since religions did not exist apart from "pious communities," natural religion, which had never served as the faith of any historical entity, was nothing more than the result of abstracting common elements with the tools of reason. In contrast to the Enlightenment, Schleiermacher did not believe that Christianity would be absorbed into a purely rational faith. It was forever bound by its Scripture that placed at its center a Redeemer of humanity, not merely a teacher of moral truths.[14] The effect of Schleier-

12. Friedrich Schleiermacher, *On Religion: Speeches to Its Cultured Despisers,* trans. John Oman (New York, 1958), p. 238. See also Joseph W. Pickle, "Schleiermacher on Judaism," *Journal of Religion* 60 (1980): 115–37.

13. Friedrich Schleiermacher, *Der christliche Glaube,* 2d ed., vol. 1 (Berlin, 1830), pp. 52–53.

14. Ibid., pp. 62–88.

macher's thought for Judaism was to remove it much further from Christianity than had been true during the Enlightenment. Mendelssohn had been able to make his religion appear modern by stressing that it fully embraced natural religion, adding to it only revealed legislation. Schleiermacher cut Christianity loose from Judaism in two respects: not only did Christianity lack historical continuity with Judaism, it was also not joined to it by an underlying bond of natural religion. In fact he declared it a separate species. But thereby—at least implicitly—he also created a rationale for its persistence. For if Judaism was the unique faith of a historical community that possessed its own individuality and was shaped by its own revelation and experience, if it could not be compartmentalized into universal natural religion and particular observance, then neglect of the ceremonial law did not mean the end of Jewish particularity. By reviving respect for positive, historical religion, Schleiermacher's thought became one of the influences that turned the Reformers to examining Judaism in terms of its particular development and not alone its conformity with reason.

If Schleiermacher's reevaluation of individuality among religions unintendedly gave authority to separated, ongoing Jewish existence, Hegel's conception of Judaism within the scheme of historical religions left it once again consigned to the past. For G. W. F. Hegel (1770–1831), as for Lessing, Judaism represented but a single stage of human development. While for Lessing that stage was a level of religious education, in Hegel's thought it became a thrust in the dialectical progress of the World Spirit. Thus in Hegel's mature writings Judaism was presented as the "religion of sublimity," one-sidedly emphasizing a transcendent God toward whom the worshiper assumed an attitude of fear.[15] Christianity corrected this imbalance through the Incarnation, which brought God directly into history. Because Hegel's philosophical thought was predicated upon pantheism, Christianity with its doctrinal immanentism was far more conducive to it than Judaism. Moreover, Hegel's veneration for the state as the highest embodiment of the World Spirit created an atmosphere of political quietism that stifled prophetic morality. For about a generation before midcentury, Hegel's influence in Germany was enormous. Jewish thinkers could not help but be affected by his grand system and its cherished goal of freedom. Yet like Spinoza, Hegel left no room in his thought for significant individual responsibility. And that was es-

15. Rotenstreich, *Recurring Pattern*, p. 67. See also Hans Liebeschütz, *Das Judentum im deutschen Geschichtsbild von Hegel bis Max Weber* (Tübingen, 1967), pp. 24–42.

sential to any conception of Judaism, especially for the Reformers who dwelt upon Judaism's moral imperative. Though thoughtful Jews had to grapple with Hegel's philosophy, ultimately they all rejected its most basic elements.

It is within this intellectual context that the early theological enterprise of the Reform movement in Germany must be understood. It was an environment in which no major thinker believed that Judaism was the equal of Christianity or that it could meet the challenge of modernity. Yet Jewish thinkers could not ignore the Christian philosophers and theologians, for their views represented the very modernity that Judaism had to confront if it was not to retreat into intellectual isolation.

NEW CONCEPTIONS OF JUDAISM

Three important systematic thinkers appeared within German Jewry in the first half of the nineteenth century. One of them, Salomon Ludwig Steinheim (1789–1866), was a physician who remained distant from day-to-day religious controversies and spent the last twenty years of his life mostly in Rome. The other two, Salomon Formstecher (1808–89) and Samuel Hirsch (1815–89), were both rabbis who participated actively in the Reform movement.[16]

It is generally agreed that of the three Steinheim was both the most original and the least influential.[17] He was a man of unusually broad learning and creativity, a writer on medical subjects as well as a poet and

16. The general secondary literature on these three thinkers includes Max Wiener, *Jüdische Religion im Zeitalter der Emanzipation* (Berlin, 1933), pp. 120–65; Albert Lewkowitz, *Das Judentum und die geistigen Strömungen des 19. Jahrhunderts* (Breslau, 1935), pp. 385–418; Hans Joachim Schoeps, *Geschichte der jüdischen Religionsphilosophie in der Neuzeit* (Berlin, 1935), pp. 65–132; Julius Guttmann, *Philosophies of Judaism*, trans. David W. Silverman (New York, 1964), pp. 308–21, 344–49; Nathan Rotenstreich, *Jewish Philosophy in Modern Times: From Mendelssohn to Rosenzweig* (New York, 1968), pp. 106–36, 149–74; Jacob Fleischmann, *Be'ayat hanatzrut ba-mahshavah ha-yehudit mi-Mendelssohn ad Rosenzweig* (Jerusalem, 1964), 68–105; Schweid, *Toldot ha-hagut ha-yehudit*, pp. 219–63, 281–91; and Heinz Moshe Graupe, *The Rise of Modern Judaism*, trans. John Robinson (Huntington, N.Y., 1978), pp. 224–35.

17. There has been a revival of interest in Steinheim, however. See Hans-Joachim Schoeps et al., eds., *Salomon Ludwig Steinheim zum Gedenken* (Leiden, 1966); *Salomon Ludwig Steinheim, 100. Todestag, Gedenkfeier im Christianeum am 23. Mai 1966* (Hamburg, 1966); Joshua O. Haberman, "Salomon Steinheim's Doctrine of Revelation," *Judaism* 17 (1968): 22–41; Aharon Shear-Yashuv, "The Theology of Salomon Ludwig Steinheim" (Ph.D. diss., Hebrew Union College–Jewish Institute of Religion, 1970); Moshe Schwarcz, *Hagut yehudit nokhah ha-tarbut ha-klalit* (Jerusalem, 1976), pp. 37–71; and Gary Lease, "Salomon Ludwig Steinheim's Influence: Hans Joachim Schoeps, A Case Study," *Leo Baeck Institute Year Book* (hereafter *LBIYB*) 29 (1984): 383–402.

theologian. He played an active role in the Jewish community of Altona and wrote in behalf of Jewish emancipation, but his knowledge of Jewish sources seems to have been limited mainly to the Bible. When in his early forties, Steinheim began to interest himself seriously in theology and in 1835 published the first of four volumes on the Jewish doctrine of revelation.[18] Apparently he was agitated by the urging of friends that he convert to Christianity and, like Mendelssohn before him and Franz Rosenzweig much after him, felt challenged to justify his persistence in Judaism. He was also concerned that the centripetal force of assimilation was dissipating Jewish consciousness. While in Christianity, following the Enlightenment, religion had been reunited with culture, the same was not, he believed, true for Judaism. Steinheim therefore set out to defend Judaism philosophically, attempting to shore it up against the erosion that was undermining its foundations. He did so by raising the pillars of Judaism high above history where the waters of time could do them no damage. In a sense he was following in the footsteps of Mendelssohn, who had also believed Judaism eternal, stressing its adherence to the rational truths of natural religion and its legislation revealed to the Jewish people for all historical time. However, Steinheim rejected both of the pillars of Mendelssohn's faith. Natural religion in his eyes was paganism, the biblical legislation national, local, and temporary. What made Judaism eternal was something quite different: a foundation of doctrinal revelation that was as unchanging as the principles of mathematics. This revelation allowed of neither internal development nor growth. Since it was given by God, it was perfect from the first. The history of religion was thus not a history of revelation itself, as Lessing had held, but only a history of its acceptance or rejection. For Steinheim the true revelation that God transmitted to ancient Israel consisted essentially of the doctrines of God's transcendence and uniqueness, divine and human freedom, and God's creation of the world out of nothing. Human reason, Steinheim argued, could not have arrived at these ideas; in fact they contradict the whole tradition of philosophical thought from pagan antiquity to modern times. Yet once revealed, they force rational assent even against preexisting inclination. Revelation does not simply reinforce what is latent in the human spirit; it demands a complete transformation of the inner person, "a spiritual rebirth." Whether or not ancient Israel

18. Salomon Ludwig Steinheim, *Die Offenbarung nach dem Lehrbegriffe der Synagoge,* vol. 1 (Frankfurt a.M., 1835); vol. 2 (Leipzig, 1856); vol. 3 (Leipzig, 1863); vol. 4 (Altona, 1865).

was a primitive people did not really matter for Steinheim since the revelation stood above its bearers.[19]

Of revelation Steinheim tells us that it stands in the sharpest opposition to paganism, with which it engages in perpetual combat. The Jewish people has been and still is the "trustee" of this revelation, while philosophy champions the naturalism of the pagans. Between the two lies Christianity, a mixture of both, which has sought in vain to reconcile what is irreconcilable ever since it carried the biblical revelation to the heathens. Judaism alone preserved the revelation in the "pure, unadulterated, pristine form" in which it was destined eventually to win the struggle with paganism. Steinheim's understanding of revelation clearly placed his own religion above Christianity; Judaism not only preceded Christianity, it was also destined in the course of time to succeed it.[20] He thus provided a personal reason for remaining Jewish and at the same time a reply to all those conceptions of Judaism that made it an anachronism.

Although Steinheim was deeply rooted in the modern European intellectual milieu, his views stand in sharpest contrast to it. Not surprisingly, he utterly rejected Spinozism, which he regarded as a classic example of the pagan tradition, calling Spinoza himself "the great denier of God in the covenanted people." But no less did his views contrast with Hegel's equally deterministic system. While Steinheim shares with Schleiermacher the rejection of natural religion, he specifically objects to the Christian theologian's insistence that the religious consciousness requires no external communication of God's nature, will, or plan for humanity.[21] It is generally thought that, especially in his later writings, Steinheim was closest to Kant.[22] Indeed, among the moderns, it was Kant who first recognized the limitation of human reason, stressed human freedom, sharply separated the "is" from the "ought," and outlined a religion far removed from what Steinheim termed paganism. But Kant was not a believer in supernatural revelation, and Steinheim was.

Among Jewish thinkers, Steinheim likewise stood alone. His theology was a revolt against the Mendelssohnian compartmentalization of Judaism into universal philosophy and particular observance. On one occasion he epitomized this lack of inner unity by calling Mendelssohn "a heathen in his brain and a Jew in his body." Steinheim was no less severe a critic

19. Ibid., 1:vii–xii, 5–12, 360–61; Abraham Geiger, "Salomon Ludwig Steinheim," *Jüdische Zeitschrift für Wissenschaft und Leben* 10 (1872): 285–92.
20. Steinheim, *Die Offenbarung,* 1:358–64, 2:465–66.
21. Ibid., 1:185–87, 4:357.
22. Heinz Moshe Graupe, "Steinheim und Kant," *LBIYB* 5 (1960): 140–75.

of contemporary Jewish orthodoxy, which he accused of rote ceremonialism and gross mystification. He did not believe that revelation extended to the institutions of ancient Israel—explicitly not to animal sacrifices—and he thought that the prayer book had unfortunately incorporated pagan elements. He was thus a proponent of ritual reform and welcomed the Hamburg Temple. He was also a universalist who stressed that the Jewish religion, including its messianic teaching, was free of particularism. Difference with regard to religious forms was justifiable in Judaism only "as long as philosophical paganism is still wandering alive among us." If the forms of Judaism too closely resembled those of Christianity, its fundamental inner distinctiveness would be overlooked and thereby its mission—to propagate the pure revelation—remain unattained. But if Steinheim sympathized with ritual reform, in his later writings he decried the theology of other Reformers. They had been ashamed to speak publicly of revelation to their congregations; some of them, he believed, had in their theoretical writings mistakenly identified the revealed doctrines of Judaism with modern pantheism or idealism.[23]

Steinheim consistently paid little attention to postbiblical Judaism, and in this he differed not only from the orthodox but also from a Reform movement that was becoming increasingly conscious of history. While the Reformers stressed religious development, Steinheim denied it; while the Reformers linked their enterprise to the rationalist tradition of Jewish philosophy, Steinheim was unfamiliar with much of that tradition and rejected what he knew. Those Jews who believed in the supernatural revelation of doctrine believed no less in the divine origins of the *Halakhah,* but Steinheim did not; those Jews who rejected or limited the authority of the ceremonial law were usually also rationalists unwilling to admit a fully supernaturalist conception of revelation. It is not surprising, therefore, that Steinheim remained an isolated, if fascinating, figure.

If there were professors of Jewish theology at German universities, Salomon Formstecher tells us in the preface to his *Religion of the Spirit* (1841), practical men like himself would not have to occupy themselves with writing on the subject in their leisure hours. But at that time and all through the nineteenth century no German university was prepared to

23. Salomon Ludwig Steinheim, *Moses Mendelssohn und seine Schule* (Hamburg, 1840), p. 37: Steinheim, *Die Offenbarung,* 1:xvii, 2:vii–viii, 3:318–22; Steinheim, "Synagoge und Tempel: Ein modernes Schisma," *Allgemeine Zeitung des Judentums* 6, no. 38 (September 17, 1842): 564, 567–68.

establish a chair of Judaica even when funds were offered by the Jews themselves. Thus Formstecher, who throughout his career remained a preacher in the Jewish community of Offenbach, took it upon himself at the age of thirty-three to publish a comprehensive theoretical and historical description of Judaism that would place it into relation with the reigning philosophy of absolute idealism, especially as expounded by Friedrich W. J. Schelling, and also with Christianity and Islam. He remembered from his own university years in Giessen that what was taught in the lecture hall about Judaism was derisive, emotionally biased toward Christianity, and grossly in contradiction with his own conception and firsthand experience of his faith. He had come to the conclusion that only a Jew could write impartially of Judaism. Formstecher therefore attempted at once to raise Judaism to intellectual respectability by applying to it the terminology of academic thought and to set it above the rival faiths, especially Christianity, which claimed to succeed it. He was aware that he could not simply present Judaism within the context of one of the idealist philosophies or theologies, since to do so would necessarily produce a totally unacceptable conception. He could only utilize selectively some of the terms and ideas of the intellectual environment, remaining always conscious of the ramifications for Judaism.[24] The result is that while one can trace the influence on his thought of Schelling, and perhaps also of Johann Gottlieb Fichte and Hegel, Formstecher remained eclectic in his approach, more determined to be a vindicator of Judaism against idealistic philosophy than a Jewish philosophical idealist.

The principal thrust of Formstecher's work was to relate the development of Judaism intimately to the development of humankind. He wanted to show that despite the prevalent tendency to regard it as alien, Judaism had played, and was still playing, an absolutely essential role, that in its further evolution it would become the universal religion of civilized humanity. Like Steinheim, Formstecher raised Judaism above the possibility of historical obsolescence, except that in his case the eternity of Judaism was not determined by a clear, doctrinal revelation communicated to the Jews at the beginning of their history. Rather the historically given revelation had to evolve within the people until the Jews, and indirectly through them the rest of humanity, reached full awareness of the prehistorical, absolute revelation implanted by God in every hu-

24. Salomon Formstecher, *Die Religion des Geistes: Eine wissenschaftliche Darstellung des Judenthums nach seinem Charakter, Entwicklungsgange und Berufe in der Menschheit* (Frankfurt a.M., 1841), pp. v, 4–7.

man spirit. Also unlike his predecessor, Formstecher insisted that every truth of religion must likewise be a truth of reason and that the content of revelation consisted of the absolute good.[25] In this rationalism and ethicism he was much closer to the dominant mood of the Reform movement.

Formstecher distinguished between Judaism as an idea and as a historical phenomenon. While the former was pure, the latter could absorb foreign elements that served it as a protective shell. Jews who despaired of their religion's viability in the modern world had failed to understand either the unchanging idea within or the historical phenomenon's capacity for further development. Formstecher juxtaposes Judaism with paganism, not dialectically but as polar ideal types. Paganism is the religion of nature that represents God as the world soul; Judaism is the religion of spirit that represents God as a purely ethical being who transcends the universe He has created. While pagan religion played an indispensable role in the development of the human spirit, it was destined to oblivion since it could never encompass spirit, while Judaism, the religion of spirit, could eventually encompass nature.[26]

In Formstecher's view, the development of Judaism reflects a "progressive revelation" stretching back to biblical prophets who, far in advance of their *Zeitgeist,* were first enabled by God to bring to awareness the unconscious content of their spirit. Scripture and tradition preserved and refined the prophetic revelation. The further history of Judaism, with all its vicissitudes, could be described as a perpetual striving to realize the spiritual ideal.[27] Its history was therefore coincident with the spiritual history of all humanity. Far from being a mere stage in that history, Formstecher's Judaism became parallel with its entirety. Judaism continues to exercise its influence on the universal spiritual development of humanity through Christianity and Islam, which are here represented as missionary faiths that Judaism has sent into the pagan world. They do not succeed Judaism; they are its agents. And because the success of their task requires the adoption of pagan elements, they—but not Judaism—are "transitory phenomena" that will cease to exist as separate entities once they have purified humanity of its paganism.[28]

Not only does Formstecher thus ascribe to Judaism a very different

25. Ibid., pp. 4, 11, 33.
26. Ibid., pp. 63–72.
27. See Bernard J. Bamberger, "Formstecher's History of Judaism," *Hebrew Union College Annual* 23, pt. 2 (1950–51): 1–35.
28. Formstecher, *Die Religion des Geistes,* pp. 74–82, 196, 393–95.

role in the religious history of Western civilization; he also removes philosophy from its venerated position at the leading edge of human spiritual development, declaring it merely the product of a futureless paganism. Without mentioning their authors by name, Formstecher condemns the philosophies of Fichte, Schelling, and Hegel. He then states unequivocally, "Modern philosophy manifests a subjective paganism that negates itself and therefore, in its incapacity to become the consciousness of humanity, will once again disappear as an ephemeral phenomenon." He singles out Hegel and Schleiermacher as guilty of the gnostic pretension to know God's inner essence and hence unable to appreciate the antignostic, essentially ethical character of Judaism. Formstecher suggests that only a second Kant, who would act positively to supplant metaphysics with ethics, could appreciate the truth of Judaism.[29] But such a philosopher would already have transcended philosophy.

Not surprisingly, Formstecher was no more favorably inclined to Jewish philosophers. He believed there could be no Jewish philosophy, only a Jewish ethics. To his mind, Philo as an Alexandrine mystic and Maimonides as an Aristotelian were both pagan, while Spinoza on account of his pervasive "pagan pantheism" could be neither Jew nor Christian. Mendelssohn, by contrast, had not adopted pagan elements. Aside from medieval Jewish philosophy, Judaism, as a historical phenomenon, had interacted with its environment in other ways as well. The Kabbala, to which Formstecher was not unremittingly hostile, was another product of pagan influence; so, too, were certain Jewish ceremonies. Like his fellow Reformers, Formstecher believed that religious customs had played a positive role in insulating Judaism from detrimental influences. However, despite all his criticism of contemporary philosophy and Christian theology, Formstecher—quite inconsistently—did believe that German Jewry lived in an environment where paganism represented a declining threat. Jewish separation was, therefore, no longer appropriate intellectually, and it would cease to be appropriate politically once German Jewry had achieved full emancipation. In short, Formstecher ultimately looked beyond Judaism to a completely universal faith—just as he looked beyond the state to a supranational spiritual theocracy. Formstecher's messianism thus transcended historical Judaism, though not the universal ideal that he believed had characterized its essence from the first.[30]

29. Ibid., pp. 358–59. See also Lewkowitz, *Das Judentum,* pp. 411–12.
30. Formstecher, *Die Religion des Geistes,* pp. 353–57, 413–52.

Unlike Formstecher, Samuel Hirsch did not make his entire career in a single community. A product of village Jewry in Rhenish Prussia, he attended *yeshivot* in Metz and Mainz before embarking on studies at the universities of Bonn and Berlin. His breadth of knowledge in both Jewish and in general philosophical and historical literature was matched by few Jews in early nineteenth-century Germany. Ordained by Samuel Holdheim, Hirsch served as rabbi first in Dessau, then Luxembourg, and finally in Philadelphia. Over the years his views became progressively more radical, reflecting shifts in the social context as well as the trajectory of his own independent spiritual development.[31] For about half a century, in both Europe and America, he played a guiding and active role in the Reform movement. Already in Dessau, where he preached and taught from 1839 to 1841, he was so mistrusted by some members of the Jewish community that appeal was made to the Prussian order of 1823 prohibiting all religious innovations and—perhaps also on account of a desire to save money—his contract was terminated by a narrow vote. He thereupon wrote to his older friend, Leopold Zunz in Berlin, asking for employment as a teacher at the institute that Zunz headed at the time, and he took the occasion to mention a book on which he had been working for several years. It was to be a "philosophical exposition of the system of Jewish theology," its purpose "to draw sharply the boundaries between Judaism, Christianity, and paganism."[32]

Hirsch's *Religious Philosophy of the Jews,* which appeared in 1842, a year after Formstecher's book, was his largest and most systematic work.[33] And although its author soon went beyond a number of the conclusions, it continued to be influential as theory in the Reform movement.[34] This is the more remarkable as Hirsch, no less than Steinheim

31. On various phases in the development of Hirsch's thought, see Jacob Katz, "Samuel Hirsch: Rabbi, Philosopher and Freemason," *Revue des études juives* 125 (1966): 113–26; Gershon Greenberg, "Samuel Hirsch: Jewish Hegelian," ibid., 129 (1970): 205–15; Greenberg, "The Historical Origins of God and Man: Samuel Hirsch's Luxembourg Writings, *LBIYB* 20 (1975): 129–48 (where reference is made to Greenberg's remaining articles on Hirsch); Michael A. Meyer, "Ob Schrift? Ob Geist? Die Offenbarungsfrage im deutschen Judentum des neunzehnten Jahrhunderts," in *Offenbarung im jüdischen und christlichen Glaubensverständnis,* ed. Jakob J. Petuchowski and Walter Strolz (Freiburg, 1981), pp. 162–79.

32. Samuel Hirsch to Leopold Zunz, April 16, 1841, Leopold Zunz Archives, Hebrew University Library, Jerusalem, 40792–g14.

33. Samuel Hirsch, *Die Religionsphilosophie der Juden oder das Prinzip der jüdischen Religionsanschauung und sein Verhältniss zum Heidenthum, Christenthum und zur absoluten Philosophie* (Leipzig, 1842).

34. Greenberg, "Historical Origins of God and Man," pp. 129–30. The Jewish

and Formstecher, presents a conception of Judaism that yields very little to its intellectual milieu. The propositions put forth in Hirsch's book are grounded in the Bible, as well as in Talmud, Midrash, and traditional commentaries, the latter quoted extensively in Hebrew or Aramaic as well as in German translation.[35] Throughout it seems apparent that Hirsch was not seeking to cut and shape Judaism to fit the dominant philosophy of the day.[36] Quite the contrary, in terms of the reigning Hegelianism, he was determined to show that Judaism as a whole, based on its own sources, could be understood as the hub of a systematic religious philosophy that drew upon Hegel but rejected his most basic assumptions.

At the outset of his book Hirsch places his project into the context of contemporary Jewish history. With Mendelssohn there began a period in which German Jews were determined to acquire the culture (*Bildung*) of their age. Echoing Johann Wolfgang von Goethe, Hirsch calls this time the years of apprenticeship (*Lehrjahre*). In the process Jews had given up their peculiar characteristics. But now the time had come to reverse the thrust. "Today the concern is precisely to understand the peculiarity, the positive world view of the Jewish religion, and to understand in their absolute necessity the forms that it has given itself in order to keep the world view always before it, namely its ceremonies and customs, and to raise them again in the heart to the status of living deeds— to build rather than tear down, preserve rather than abandon."[37] In short, Hirsch felt that the time had come for a reassertion of Jewish particularity. But to be respectable that reassertion had to be made within the context of contemporary philosophical thought.

Hirsch's critique of Hegel has received considerable attention and can be briefly summarized.[38] Against Hegel, Hirsch raises religious knowl-

---

philologist and philosopher, Heymann Steinthal, claimed that Hirsch permanently shaped his conception of Judaism and that he provided him, when he was young, with "armor for battle against the opponent whom I would get to know only at the university— Hegel." Heymann Steinthal, *Über Juden und Judentum* (Berlin, 1910), p. 197.

35. For Hirsch's defense of rabbinic literature, see Hirsch, *Die Religionsphilosophie der Juden*, pp. 460, 593n.

36. See, e.g., Schweid, *Toldot ha-hagut ha-yehudit*, p. 261: Hirsch "succeeded in moving from the measurement of his Judaism by the criterion of his environment to the measurement of his environment by the criterion of his Judaism."

37. Hirsch, *Die Religionsphilosophie der Juden*, pp. v, ix.

38. Aside from the general histories of Jewish thought, see Emil L. Fackenheim, "Samuel Hirsch and Hegel," in *Studies in Nineteenth-Century Jewish Intellectual History*, ed. Alexander Altmann (Cambridge, Mass., 1964), pp. 171–201. For Hirsch's thought in relation to the left-wing Hegelians, especially Ludwig Feuerbach, see Man-

edge to the level of philosophical thought so that philosophy can no longer be seen as absorbing religion's content while superseding it in form. According to Hirsch himself, the major point at which he departs from Hegelian philosophy is in his rejection of the necessity of evil as means to the good. Hegel held that man began in a state of nature but then sinfully set himself into opposition with it. Only when this negation was itself negated could the higher unity of virtue appear. Hirsch refuses to accept the necessity of a dialectical process in which sin, meaning the alienation of man from nature, plays a necessary role. For him sin is not a determined stage in human development and certainly not to be equated with man's separation from nature. Sin is neither necessary nor consigned to the past. It is a permanent option and always the result of individual free choice. Herewith Hirsch rejects not only Hegelian pantheism but also the closely parallel Christian doctrine of original sin overcome by the Incarnation, which Hegel had incorporated into his own philosophical construction. Thus while Hegel's system is congenial to Christianity, it is distinctly inhospitable to Judaism, which is predicated upon free moral choice. There can be a Hegelian Christianity, but not a Hegelian Judaism. Hegelianism, Hirsch tells us, is "the most sublimated paganism." For him, as for Steinheim and Formstecher, a direct line runs from the ancient world to modern philosophy. Hirsch makes a detailed examination of paganism to support his view that it represents a passive religiosity which, in moving from fetishism to the anthropomorphic representations of Greece and Rome, negates itself dialectically. Necessarily it emerges with nothing because it was based on the false proposition that human beings must subordinate themselves to nature. Judaism, by contrast, represents an active religiosity, based on human decisions between the paths of sin and virtue. It is not a further development of paganism; it is essentially different.[39]

For Hirsch, Judaism begins with Abraham, who was the first to recognize that human beings are free and without sin except insofar as they bring it upon themselves. Passing through trial after trial, Abraham emerges as the victor over paganism and becomes the model for true religion. Unlike Steinheim, Hirsch believes that Abraham required no supernatural revelation to achieve his realization of human freedom, but God was active in educating Abraham, as God actively educates (or is the source of religious self-education—Hirsch wavers on this point) for ancient Israel and for all humanity. Here again is Lessing's theme of revelation as divine education, except that Abraham has already achieved its highest level. Here, too, is a rejection of the Hegelian notion that the Jewish God—unlike the Christian—is not directly involved in human history. On the contrary, Hirsch notes, Judaism requires the mediation neither of a church, as in Catholicism, nor of Scripture, as in Protestantism.[40]

On the whole, Hirsch is more favorably inclined to Christianity than either Steinheim or Formstecher. Jesus stands within Judaism and, like Abraham, he represents an ideal for humanity. Although Paulinian Christianity, by promulgating the idea of original sin, left Judaism behind, it was only through this concession to paganism that Christianity was able to perform the "extensive" role vis-à-vis the pagan world that an essentially "intensive," pure Judaism could not enact. For Hirsch, Christianity will not be superseded by Judaism, but together with Judaism it will constitute the absolute religiosity of the future. By contrast, modern philosophy will not endure, for it merely recapitulates on a deeper level the stages of its ancient pagan predecessor. Thus, for example, the skeptical Kant becomes in Hirsch's view the equivalent of Socrates, while Fichte, in building a new system, performs a task equivalent to that of Plato. With Hegel philosophy seeks to encompass all, but Hegel's own disciples, especially those on the Left like David Friedrich Strauss, have already undermined his system. Modern philosophy, as once ancient paganism, lies in shambles.[41]

The way therefore lies open to what Hirsch calls "the philosophy of revelation," which is reflected in the growing awareness of human freedom. For Hirsch the biblical God created miracles and prophecy in order to demonstrate divine sovereignty over nature and to call ancient Israel to its vocation of recognizing the possibility of moral choice. Sinai was the capstone of this revelation since it united miracle with prophecy. But revelation continued providentially until Israel, learning to imitate God as the model of freedom, had become fully aware of its destiny.[42] Although that destiny brought the Jews untold sufferings, their sorrows were to be understood either as divine chastisements on account of those Jews who failed in their vocation to show the world that one need not sin or, in the case of pious men and women, demonstrations that virtuous conduct even under duress was possible without supernatural grace. Hirsch

40. Ibid., pp. xxx, 457–528, 545, 545n.   41. Ibid., pp. 621–839.
42. Ibid., pp. 537–620.

was not an optimist about the future. He believed that hatred of the Jews lay dormant, and he pointed to its recrudescence in the Hep-Hep riots of 1819 and the Damascus blood libel of 1840. At the same time he deplored the fact that Jews had not stood the test of remaining loyal to their vocation despite the temptations of assimilation. Mistakenly they considered themselves a denomination (*Confession*), when in fact they were a "spiritual nationality." Hence the messianic age remained distant. But when it would come, Israel and the other nations would be united in a single religion of human freedom. Sin would remain a possibility, but no one would chocse it. The nations of the world would then bring Israel to Jerusalem, not to establish a state but to found there the "ritual of all rituals, the Jewish national ritual" symbolizing the Jewish national vocation. United with humanity in word and deed, Judaism would remain particular in its mode of religious practice.[43]

CONCLUSION

If we now look back upon all three thinkers we can perhaps better appreciate their independence of the milieu in which they wrote. To be sure, their philosophies of religion were prompted by the reigning systems of thought that they encountered in the lecture halls of the universities they attended and in their own reading. Their writings attest to the shared conviction that the deghettoization of the Jewish community must be accompanied by a deghettoization of Judaism. The old faith could not be expected to survive among cultured Jews unless it could be shown to be still intellectually viable. Such a proof required confrontation with the prevalent philosophical and theological systems of the day.

What seems most striking about the Jewish theological response, however, is that, for all its variety, it evidences so little concession on basic issues. The German milieu presented a series of intellectual and religious challenges to which the reply was characterized less by submission than by reinterpretation and reassertion.[44] Each of the three thinkers recognized clearly the danger to Judaism posed by determinism, whether in Spinozistic or in Hegelian form; necessarily each rejected the milieu's prevailing conceptions of Judaism that, for one reason or another, limited it to the past. In various ways they assigned their own faith—more so than Christianity—to the future. Of course they employed some of the termi-

43. Ibid., pp. viii, 868–82. See also Samuel Hirsch, *Die Messiaslehre der Juden in Kanzelvorträgen* (Leipzig, 1843), pp. 372–93.

44. See Moshe Schwarcz, "Religious Currents and General Culture," *LBIYB* 16 (1971): 9–11.

nology of the leading thinkers, but at every point crucial for Judaism they explicitly or implicitly departed from it. Does it therefore make sense to speak of a Jewish Kantian, Schellingian, and Hegelian respectively? It seems rather we should say that Steinheim, Formstecher, and Hirsch were men concerned with translating Judaism into the new philosophical languages of Europe—that was their modernization and reform. But to a remarkable degree they were unwilling to change the meaning of the words themselves.

German Culture and the Jews

"Jews have not assimilated into 'the German people,' but into a certain layer of it, the newly emerged middle class."[1] This sentence from my doctoral dissertation, written almost half a century ago, has been at times quoted by fellow scholars. Others have arrived at similar conclusions through their own observations. I am quoting the sentence now, however, for the sake of qualification, for my subsequent inquiry into the nature of the historical process designated as assimilation led me to believe that, the experience of certain individuals notwithstanding, the entrance of Jewry as a *collective* into the body of German society did not mean real integration into any part, stratum, or section of it. It meant, rather, the creation of a separate subgroup, which conformed to the German middle class in some of its characteristics.[2]

German Jewry, like the German middle class, belonged neither to the landed aristocracy, nor to the peasants, nor to the proletariat. Its economic function corresponded to that of the middle class but was not identical with it. Jews were not distributed across the whole range of middle-class professions and occupations but remained concentrated in certain pursuits, so that even economically they remained a conspicuous subgroup. Their separateness is demonstrated most tellingly, however, by their endogamy, their habit of marrying only among themselves. Some intermarriage with members of the surrounding society did take place, but

1. Jacob Katz, *Die Entstehung der Judenassimilation in Deutschland und deren Ideologie* (Frankfurt a.M., 1935), p. 32; reprinted in his *Emanzipation and Assimilation: Studies in Modern Jewish History* (Westmead, Farnborough, 1972), p. 236; and in his *Zur Assimilation und Emanzipation der Juden* (Darmstadt, 1982), p. 32.

2. See Katz, "Judenemanzipation und ihre soziale Folgen," in his *Zur Assimilation,* pp. 185–98.

those who intermarried almost always dropped out of the Jewish community; only in exceptional cases did the non-Jewish partner become integrated into Jewish society. As far as actual and active kinship was concerned, Jews remained almost exclusively bound to their own kind—a fact that more conspicuously than any other set them apart from the population at large.

As a separate subgroup within the given frame of state and society, Jews naturally also exhibited some special features deriving from their religious and cultural tradition. The often observed linguistic habit, the residual of their former Yiddish-speaking past, is a case in point.[3] Yet this was a residual only; the basic elements of their culture had been adopted from the surrounding society during a transition period of not more than two or three generations. By the nineteenth century German Jews, largely through their attendance at German or Germanized Jewish schools, had acquired the basic elements of what the Germans call *Bildung*, that is, they were conversant with, and affected by, the same elements of German culture that had shaped the minds of their counterparts in German society. If you like, you may call this assimilation. Benno Jacob, however, distinguishes between "assimilated" in the accusative and "being assimilated" in the dative: you "assimilate" cultural values, that is, in the accusative; if by absorbing the elements of another society you include yourself in that society, you have "been assimilated" in the dative.[4] German Jewry certainly "assimilated" in the accusative. German Jews may have "been assimilated" in the dative. Many of them may have thought they had achieved assimilation in the dative, but in reality they did not. German Jews, with their distinctive economic and familial characteristics, remained a recognizable subgroup. Despite the fact that Jews were exposed to the same stimuli as their counterparts in Gentile society, Jewish cultural behavior continued to reflect distinctive Jewish tradition.

The difference between German and German-Jewish cultural behavior is, first of all, quantitative. Jews were more intensively involved in the cultivation of their *Bildung* than were their Gentile counterparts. They were more avid readers of literature; they frequented theaters and concert

3. See Peter Freimark, "Language Behaviour and Assimilation: The Situation of the Jews in Northern Germany in the First Half of the Nineteenth Century," *Leo Baeck Institute Year Book* 24 (1979): 157–77; Jacob Toury, "Die Sprache als Problem der jüdischen Einordnung im deutschen Kulturraum," in *Gegenseitige Einflüsse deutscher und jüdischer Kultur: Internationales Symposium,* ed. Walter Grab, *Jahrbuch des Instituts für deutsche Geschichte,* Beiheft 4 (Tel Aviv, 1982), pp. 75–96.

4. Benno Jacob, "Prinzipielle Bemerkungen zu einer zionistischen Schrift," *Der Morgen* 3 (1927): 527–31.

halls in numbers far greater than their proportion of the population; and they were similarly overrepresented in all cultural activities. While there are no statistical data to bear out this contention, it has been put forward so often by those involved in these matters as to be beyond dispute. Friedrich Wilhelm Riemer, an intimate friend of Johann Wolfgang von Goethe, for example, remarked on the outstanding attentiveness of the Jewish audience, especially of Jewish women:

> The educated among them [the Jews] were on the whole more obliging and steady in the veneration of his person as well as his writings than many of his own coreligionists. They do reveal in general more pleasing attention and flattering participation than a national German, and their quick power of comprehension, their penetrating intellect, their peculiar wit render them a more sensitive audience than what regrettably can be found among the often somewhat dull and slow-to comprehend genuine Germans. Women possess those talents at times in even more amiable form, and thus it happened that Goethe was willing to present his recent poetical productions to them, either individually or in groups—for instance in Carlsbad (1807, 1808, 1810)—for he could always be assured of a certain response, as I am able to testify from my own observation with regard to Frau von Eibenberg, Frau von Gotthaus, Frau von Eskeles und Fliess, and others.[5]

Here we have not only a testimony to the preponderance of Jews in a literary audience but also an attempt to account for it by identifying some inherent Jewish qualities, a point I shall return to later.

The Jewish participation in the reception of Goethe should not come as a surprise; one of the first and foremost promoters of the Goethe cult was Rahel Varnhagen,[6] who identified with its spiritual tendencies in a penetrating way and was probably more passionate and sophisticated in her response than other early escapees of the ghetto. It must be borne in mind, of course, that the group described by Riemer belonged to the upper layer of German Jewry, and that the women in this group, in the first generation after the exodus from the ghetto, formed a kind of leisure class. Social life in these circles, concentrated in their salons, entailed the cultivation of spiritual intercourse on, *inter alia,* literary subjects. To suggest that the reading habits of other elements of German Jewry were the same as those of its leisure class would be folly. Yet there are ample indications that Jewish families even of modest means read German lit-

---

5. Friedrich Wilhelm Riemer, *Mittheilungen über Goethe aus mündlichen und schriftlichen, gedruckten und ungedruckten Quellen* (Berlin, 1841), pp. 428–29.
6. Solomon Liptzin, *Germany's Stepchildren* (Cleveland and New York, 1969), pp. 12–17.

erature once they had been introduced to it in modern schools. The autobiographies collected by Monika Richarz, especially those from the mid-nineteenth century onward, bear this out abundantly. Preference was given to the German classics—Goethe, Christoph Martin Wieland, Friedrich von Schiller, Heinrich Heine—but there are also many references to now-forgotten authors of historical novels and other works.[7] These were, of course, the books on the shelves of the educated public in general, and there is no way of knowing whether the Jewish boy on his *bar mitzvah* received more of them than did his Christian classmate for his confirmation.

There is, however, reliable information about the preponderance of Jews in theater audiences, and attendance at the theater is frequently mentioned in the autobiographies Richarz collected.[8] Adolph Asch, for example, explains that Jewish families and bachelors in early twentieth-century Posen used to have fixed days of the week for attending the theater. Jewish theatergoers, who, he observed, "occupied the best seats in the house," used the occasion to meet their friends and relatives.[9] Asch's testimony reveals both that Jews constituted an important part of the audience and that they remained a group apart. What was true of Posen was presumably true for many cities with substantial Jewish populations. When the Vienna Ringtheater burned down in 1881, the city's Jewish community mourned the deaths of a high percentage of the victims—a fact the *Allgemeine Zeitung des Judentums* found appropriate to cite as proof for the "disproportionate contingent of Jews in the theater audience, contrary to that in the pubs."[10]

Even more conspicuous was the preponderance of Jews in the audiences of musical performances, paradoxically attested to by the special relationship between Richard Wagner and the Jewish public. In his autobiography Wagner relates how in Breslau in 1863, on entering the stage to conduct a concert, he observed that all the seats in the first rows of the hall were occupied by Jews. At a luncheon in his honor the following day once again the company consisted of Jews.[11] At that time, of course,

---

7. Monika Richarz, *Jüdisches Leben in Deutschland,* vol. 1, *Selbstzeugnisse und Sozialgeschichte, 1780–1871* (Stuttgart, 1976), vol. 2, *Selbstzeugnisse zur Sozialgeschichte im Kaiserreich* (Stuttgart, 1979). See, in both volumes, the discussions listed in the index under "Lektüre."

8. Ibid., the discussions listed in the index under "Theater."

9. Ibid., 2:228–29.

10. *Allegemeine Zeitung des Judentums* 45, no. 52 (December 27, 1881): 862.

11. Richard Wagner, *Mein Leben* (Munich, 1963), p. 747.

Wagner's "Das Judenthum in der Musik" was unknown to the general public, having been published under a pseudonym in 1850 in a musical periodical. When in 1869 he saw fit to republish the essay as a pamphlet under his own name, one of the first reactions was an anonymous letter from Breslau "on behalf of 7,000 Jews," containing, as Cosima Wagner noted in her diary, "abuses and threats."[12] It is not difficult to guess what these threats consisted of—a Jewish boycott of the works of the composer, who had revealed himself to be a reviler of Jewish mentality and character.

Wagner and his entourage feared that Jews—at least in places where there was a heavy Jewish population—might have the power to prevent the success of his performance. Even in Paris, where *Rienzi* was about to open, it was feared that the pamphlet would endanger the opera's reception.[13] Hans von Bülow, a fellow musician who had formerly been married to Cosima and remained loyal to Wagner despite her divorce and remarriage, greeted the *Judenbroschüre* with enthusiasm. Yet, writing from Munich, he warned Wagner that "the rich Jews would not continue to attend the Wagnerian operas so diligently."[14] Those in Wagner's circle were most apprehensive about what might happen in Berlin, however, where the performance of *Lohengrin* was in preparation. The apprehension turned out to be unfounded. The morning after the premiere Wagner received a telegram from Karl Tausig, himself a Jew and an important musician in his own right, yet a devoted Wagnerian all the same: *Lohengrin* "tremendous success; all Jews reconciled."[15] Obviously the Jewish boycott of Wagner and his music was not of long duration. Although the performance of *Lohengrin* in Breslau had to be postponed for fear of strong Jewish protests,[16] the uproar soon subsided. In view of the general situation of German Jewry, this is not difficult to explain. It was an optimistic time, and in 1869, the very year in which Wagner's pamphlet was republished, the formal emancipation of Jews in Germany's northern states, headed by Prussia, was completed. Wagner's pamphlet seemed out of tune with the prevailing trend. Jews could afford—or so they thought—to ignore the inopportune nastiness of an artist whose work was just be-

12. Cosima Wagner, diary, March 15, 1869, *Die Tagebücher,* ed. Martin Gregor-Dellin and Dietrich Mack (Munich and Zurich, 1982), 1:72.

13. Ibid., April 3–11, 1869, pp. 80–81, 83.

14. Ibid., March 10, 28, 1869, pp. 69, 77.

15. Ibid., March 16, April 1, 7, 1869, pp. 76, 80, 82.

16. Ibid., March 28, 1869, p. 77.

ginning to win general recognition. Still, the reactions to Wagner's pamphlet clearly reflect the importance of Jewish participation in the musical life of the country.

The preponderance of Jews in the audiences of musical performances continued, despite the sharp turn in the Jewish destiny a decade later with the emergence of political antisemitism. When the leaders of the new movement asked Wagner to sign their petition to have Jewish emancipation rescinded, the composer declined. He was careful to find some ideological justification for his refusal—Wagner always kept the door open for the de-Judaized Jew—but there is good reason to agree with Bülow, who charged that Wagner declined to sign in order not to antagonize his Jewish audience.[17] Bülow signed the petition, fully aware of the possible consequences once his act became public. "I shall have to face a certain proscription by the press as well as a reduction in my income," he wrote, "at least 50 percent of it. It is a fact confirmed in all my journeys that Shem and Hebron yield the most understanding and generous audience for concerts; more than that: that the participation of the nonsemites is dependent on them."[18]

Can the disproportionate Jewish participation in music and possibly in the theater be taken as an indication for other fields of cultural activity, for instance, the cultivation of literature? Attendance at concerts and plays may have had a very special attraction for the Jewish public. Jews who aspired to social acceptance but had difficulty entering Gentile circles may have found sitting in a mixed audience in the concert hall and theater a convenient way of demonstrating their membership in society at large. Reading at home lacked, of course, this public dimension. The drive for identification with the surrounding society does not necessarily, however, require public confirmation. Initiation into the spiritual life of the nation through acquaintance with its literature was in itself enough to nurture a sense of belonging. Of course a certain measure of literacy was indispensable, and that had been assured back in the first decades of the nineteenth century when attendance at German or German-language schools was made obligatory for Jews. Indeed the replacement of traditional Jewish educational institutions—the *heder* and the *yeshivah*—by secular, modern schools was a turning point for the cultural makeup of

17. Ibid., June 16, July 6, December 20, 1880, 2:546, 564, 643.
18. Hans von Bülow to Hans von Wolzogen, September 10, 1880, *Hans von Bülow: Briefe und Schriften* (Leipzig, 1907), 6:30.

Germany's Jewish community.[19] Once that revolutionary step had been taken—and it met with surprisingly little resistance—Jewish parents were not content with mere elementary-school secular education but made every effort to send their children to secondary schools and later to the university as well. By 1860 the percentage of Jewish children attending secondary schools in the larger cities was three, even four times as high as that of other confessions. In the following decades the percentage became even higher.[20] As more advanced schooling must have resulted in a greater receptivity to German cultural values, a higher percentage of Jews in the reading public may also be assumed.

There are a number of historical and sociological reasons for the disproportionate Jewish participation in cultural activities. Certainly the traditional Jewish aptitude for study, transferred now from religious to secular literature, may have played a role, but this factor, obvious as it seems, cannot have been the decisive one. While it could well explain the peculiar Jewish enthusiasm for intellectual pursuits, it would have no bearing on music, for which there was no antecedent in the life of traditional Jewish society. Similarly the urge for identification with the larger German environment can be only a partial explanation. It may serve to elucidate the peculiar Jewish gift for passive absorption of culture, but it does not explain why Jews also excelled as active contributors to that culture. In other words, Jews were active creators far beyond their numbers in many fields of endeavor, including painting, sculpture, and science, for which they had absolutely no prior training in ghetto times. We can only assume that Jews, in leaving behind their traditional ghetto society, brought with them a special endowment for cultural creativity that, on their joining society at large, found on the one hand a new scope and opportunity and on the other the social stimuli for its realization.

Once out of the ghetto, Jews very quickly moved beyond the passive absorption of German culture to become active creators of that culture as well.[21] The extent of their achievements and the quality of their contribution have been a subject of passionate controversy ever since. It is, of course, easier to count the cultural producers than to assess their relative

19. See Mordechai Eliav, *Jewish Education in Germany in the Period of Enlightenment and Emancipation* [in Hebrew] (Jerusalem, 1960); Jacob Toury, *Soziale und politische Geschichte der Juden in Deutschland, 1847–1871* (Düsseldorf, 1977), pp. 163–78.

20. Toury, *Soziale und politische Geschichte*, pp. 171–75.

21. Ibid., pp. 178–210.

merits, and, in fact, a survey of just this kind was once undertaken. In 1933 a group of leading figures of German Jewry conceived the idea of publishing a collection of essays reciting the contributions of Jews to the various fields of German culture. As the editor, Siegmund Kaznelson, explained in his preface, *Juden im deutschen Kulturbereich* had an exclusive scholarly purpose. It was to state the bare facts to counter "exaggerated notions in one direction or the other, that is, either over- or underestimation" of the Jewish contribution to various fields.[22] The authors of the essays indeed tried their best to execute their task, and the volume remains a useful source of information to this day. Though scholarly in its execution, the purpose of the book was, of course, shaped by the political atmosphere in which it was first published, as Robert Weltsch pointed out in the introduction he wrote to the second edition in 1959.[23] The book was meant to defend Jewish honor in the face of relentless discrimination and the slander of Jewish mentality and character by the Nazis, whose attacks had just become the official policy of the state. This intention was not lost on the authorities. The book shared the lot of many Jewish publications of those years: it was confiscated, its distribution forbidden. It is now available only in the second, enlarged edition prepared by its editor after his emigration to Palestine.

The Nazis banned the book because the reader would, they claimed, receive the impression that "the whole of German culture until the National Socialist revolution was sustained only by Jews" and "an entirely false image of the actual, especially the destructive, activity of the Jews in German culture."[24] The adjective "destructive" (*zersetzend*) was a central smear word in antisemitic propaganda.[25] This clash over the meaning of the Jewish contribution to German culture—for the Jews a vindication for the Jewish presence and for the Nazis the source of all that was destructive—was the culmination of a long-standing conflict whose catastrophic potential was now revealed. The seeds of the catastrophe can be traced back to the time when Jewish integration seemed to be steadily progressing, that is, to the liberal era before the outbreak of political antisemitism of the late 1870s.

Once the new generations of Jews had been initiated into the elements

22. Siegmund Kaznelson, *Juden im deutschen Kulturbereich*, 2d ed., introd. Robert Weltsch (Berlin, 1959), p. xii.

23. Ibid., pp. xiv–xx.

24. Quoted in ibid., p. xvi.

25. Christof Cobet, *Der Wortschatz des Antisemitismus in der Bismarckzeit* (Munich, 1973), pp. 201–3.

of German culture, it was natural that the gifted among them would go beyond mere passive absorption to become active creators and contributors to that culture. Jewish cultural activity could now proceed along two or three different lines. It could use the new elements of German culture to reshape the Jewish cultural tradition, synthesizing Jewish content and the German mode of expression. This was the path taken by those who dedicated themselves to the study of Jewish lore in the broader sense of the term, including not only the scholarly *Wissenschaft des Judentums* but also the reinterpretation of various branches of Jewish tradition—theology or *Halakhah*—whether Orthodox or Reform in approach. This undertaking, though qualitatively as well as quantitatively no mean achievement, remained an internal Jewish development scarcely noticed by German society. On the other extreme there were those who attempted to join the German cultural tradition into which they had been newly initiated and contribute to it, ignoring their Jewish background altogether. This was the path taken by those novelists, poets, composers, and philosophers who considered themselves Germans of Jewish origin, whether baptized or not. Believing they were integrated into the German cultural tradition, they wished their Jewish background to be treated as a more or less regrettable accident.[26]

There was theoretically a third avenue—almost entirely avoided in the first generation of integration. Jewish novelists could have depicted contemporary Jewish society as they experienced it, or the Jewish past as they had learned it, and spun their tales around Jewish characters. Jewish composers could have taken the melodies of the synagogue and the Jewish home and made them the nucleus of their compositions. Jewish poets could have derived their inspiration from the long succession of Jewish poetical tradition, giving it a new lease on life through a new linguistic garb. Why was this potential not realized, or realized only in the most rudimentary form, as, for instance, in Heinrich Heine's unfinished novel *Der Rabbi von Bacharach*? The answer is that such an endeavor ran counter to the idea of integration as conceived by the first generation of Jews initiated into German culture. To them anything Jewish, indeed the very name "Jew," smacked of the disparagement inherited from the millennial defamation and fed by the inferior social position continuously occupied by Jews. The prerequisite for integration into German society was therefore the more or less explicit condition that Jews shed their typical characteristics, both external and internal.

26. Toury, *Soziale und politische Geschichte*, pp. 178–210.

The social history of literature, theater, and the arts in general gives evidence that not all social classes in a society are always regarded as fit subjects for literary or other artistic representation. There was a time when both literature and the stage were the exclusive domain of the aristocracy. Other classes, in the wake of their political enfranchisement, still had to await what may be called their artistic emancipation. Though Jews came to share the political rights of the middle class in Germany, they never achieved artistic emancipation. Jewish spokesmen in nineteenth-century Germany used to complain that though Jews had been emancipated, Judaism was not, meaning that Judaism was never really placed on an equal footing with Christian denominations. We may elaborate on this complaint by saying that though Jews had been emancipated, Jewishness was not. Indeed Jews were not deemed fit to appear on the stage except as objects of ridicule. For this reason writers who wished to present Jewish issues had to disguise them in neutral garb. Michael Beer, for example, the gifted brother of the composer Giacomo Meyerbeer, wrote a most interesting drama about the suffering of a pariah, but critics agreed that he used the figure of an Indian of low caste to depict the lot of the despised and rejected Jew.[27] Why did Beer resort to this disguise? Berthold Auerbach had an explanation: the appearance of a Jew on stage would have undermined the tragic atmosphere necessary for the effect of the drama.[28] When Auerbach himself wished to tell the story of his transformation from a devoted *yeshivah* pupil into a secular university student, he projected his religious crisis onto the life of a Catholic seminarian.[29] The picture of *yeshivah* life, with all its Jewish paraphernalia, would have made the reading public turn away.

The stratagem of the disguise seems at times to have excellent results. It is not true, as often maintained, that the Germans rejected Jewish writers like Heine and Ludwig Börne because of their Jewish origins. Both had a large and admiring public and appreciative critics for most of their active years. So did Auerbach, who was celebrated almost as a national hero for his portrayal of the life of the German peasant.[30] The composers Meyerbeer and Felix Mendelssohn, and many other now-forgotten musi-

27. See Lothar Kahn, "Michael Beer (1800–1833)," *Leo Baeck Institute Year Book,* 12 (1967): 149–60.

28. "Michael Beer," *Galerie der ausgezeichneten Israeliten aller Jahrhunderte; ihre Portraits und Biographien,* ed. Naphthali Frankfurter and Berthold Auerbach, vol. 5 (Stuttgart, 1838), p. 24.

29. Jacob Katz, "Berthold Auerbach's Anticipation of the German-Jewish Tragedy," *Hebrew Union College Annual* 53 (1982): 233.

30. Ibid., pp. 217–18.

cians of Jewish origin, were fully accepted and at times admired practitioners of their art. But whenever these Jewish writers or artists met with opposition, their opponents were quick to use anti-Jewish arguments, attributing all shortcomings to Jewishness. Auerbach, a lifelong democrat but by temperament a lenient critic of political and social conditions who did not antagonize others, was almost never attacked as a Jew despite the fact that his Jewish origins were well known and readily admitted. Börne and Heine, on the other hand, who had strong opinions on political, social, and cultural issues, and even stronger ways of expressing them, were repeatedly the objects of resentment and public condemnation. On such occasions, though both had been baptized, their Jewishness was always remembered. If they deserve to be called "Germany's stepchildren"—in the words of Solomon Liptzin—it is because they were not allowed to be naughty at times, as one's own children always are.[31] It was when they misbehaved—or others thought they had—that the imperfection of Jewish integration into German life came to the fore.

At times the mention of Jewish origins did not need specific occasion but stemmed from the psyche of the critic rather than being prompted by the object itself. Such is Wagner's "Das Judenthum in der Musik," possibly the most elaborate and consequential assault on the Jewish contribution to German culture.[32] Wagner wrote his essay in 1850, following his escape from Dresden, where he had taken part in the ill-fated revolution of 1848–49. In a kind of temporary retirement in Zurich, he reviewed his artistic career and looked ahead toward an altogether unknown future. In the past he had been intimately associated with the two most successful German-Jewish composers, Mendelssohn, who had died three years earlier, and Meyerbeer, who was still living and prospering. To Meyerbeer, Wagner was indebted for repeated financial and other support, but he found himself growing increasingly estranged from Meyerbeer's work, and even contemptuous of it, to the point where he wished to dissociate himself entirely from his former mentor. To make this more than a purely personal act, Wagner evolved the theory that the shortcomings of Meyerbeer's artistic creations, as well as of those of other Jewish composers and writers, were inherent in the peculiar Jewish tradition. Because of its embarrassing overtones, Wagner preferred to publish the article under a pseudonym. Nineteen years later, when he republished it

31. Liptzin, *Germany's Stepchildren*, pp. 27–44, 67–87.
32. The following summary of Wagner's antisemitism is from Jacob Katz, *From Prejudice to Destruction: Anti-Semitism, 1700–1933* (Cambridge, Mass., 1980), chap. 14.

under his own name, he was well on his way to becoming a world-famous celebrity but still frustrated in his insatiable ambitions. He added new names to the original list of those Jews who were unable to appreciate his work and therefore, he thought, conspired to ruin it. Jews who had converted to the Wagnerian creed—and there were many of them—were miraculously exempt from the pernicious effect of their cultural inheritance.

Though strikingly subjective and arbitrary in their exposition, Wagner's arguments were not all of his own invention. Wagner infused his concoction with ingredients from his anti-Jewish predecessors Karl Marx and Bruno Bauer, as well as the stock of traditional anti-Jewish stereotypes. That he could do so is incontestable proof that these elements of early and recent antisemitism were at least present, if dormant, in Germany's liberal era. His essay, both in 1850 and when republished in 1869, was regarded by the general public as untimely, just as the attacks on Börne and Heine had been decried a generation earlier. Still, the recurrence of such anti-Jewish attacks demonstrates that acceptance of Jewish contributions to culture could never be regarded as final, even when and where Jewishness was ignored.

To say this is not necessarily to understand why it should have been so. Given the persistence of stereotypes in general, and of antisemitic stereotypes in particular, the deprecation of the Jewish artistic creations could be attributed to prejudice alone. Historical objectivity compels us to ask if there was anything in the artistic work produced by Jews that actually conformed to the charges repeatedly made against it. Some of these charges may, of course, be dismissed out of hand, as when a disciple of Wagner, following "The Master's" argument, maintained that one could discern, "with frightening clarity," the Jewish ingredient in the work of Meyerbeer and other Jewish composers, in the same way that one could taste the Jewish spices used in Jewish food.[33] But not so easy to dismiss are the comments of Eduard Devrient, one of the great actors of the time and the historian of the German theater. Observing five of his Jewish colleagues, among them Ludwig Dessoir and Bogumil Dawison, he concluded that they acted like brothers—sounding the same notes, gesturing in the same manner. "How," he asked, "can it be that Jews—whose hearts are especially tender and sensitive—cannot find a way to express

---

33. *Richard Wagner und das Judentum: Ein Beitrag zur Culturgeschichte unserer Zeit von einem Unparteiischen* (Elberfeld, 1869), p. 12.

true emotion on the stage, but always allow irony to break through?"[34] This observation, in a letter to his wife, who converted to Christianity for his sake, cannot be attributed to sheer prejudice. Devrient must have been responding to something concrete in the style of the actors he knew. It is well to remember that the use of irony to undercut sentiment was an often-observed feature of Heine's poetry. Students of his work have frequently tried to identify its Jewish motives, elements, and impulses not always to disparage it but, on the contrary, to reclaim its special Jewish genius.[35] Jewish qualities may quite naturally appear—for better or for worse—in the artistic creations of Jews, even of those who have joined non-Jewish cultures. It would therefore be preposterous to dismiss categorically all observations from the mouths of antisemites as prejudicial misconceptions.

The pernicious distortion of the antisemites is not in their observations, which may or may not have been accurate, but in their evaluation of what they observed, pronouncing that whatever derives from Jews must be bad, or at least strange and foreign, unworthy and not to be tolerated in expressions of German culture. The truth is that all during the liberal era in Germany this evaluation of the Jewish contribution to German culture was not just the idiosyncrasy of relatively few vociferous critics of Judaism like Richard Wagner; it was shared also by active supporters of Jewish integration like Gustav Freytag[36] and—it is safe to say—tacitly accepted by the general public as well. Moreover Jews themselves, though sometimes struggling against it, were apt to succumb to the same deadly judgment of their own tradition and mentality.

This state of affairs is best demonstrated by the denunciation of the Jewish accent and intonation in speech and music, one of the main motifs of Wagner's attack. Wagner went so far as to assert that no Jew would ever be capable of speaking German—or, for that matter, any other European language—without betraying his foreign origin by his

34. Eduard Devrient to Therese Devrient, March 1860, *Briefwechsel zwischen Eduard und Therese Devrient,* ed. Hans Devrient (Stuttgart, [1909]), p. 352.

35. For the most recent and thorough treatment of Heine's relation to Judaism, see S. S. Prawer, *Heine's Jewish Comedy: A Study of His Portraits of Jews and Judaism* (Oxford, 1983).

36. On Gustav Freytag's attitude, see Katz, *From Prejudice to Destruction,* pp. 203–5. Freytag was critical of Wagner's pamphlet when it was republished in 1869, arguing that Jews were already on their way toward shedding their unpleasing qualities, some of which he nevertheless recapitulated. "Der Streit über das Judentum in der Musik," *Grenzboten* (Leipzig) I, vol. 2 (1869): 333–36.

way of handling it.[37] Exaggerated though this assertion was, it had some
basis in reality. Given the linguistic peculiarities of their past, the Jews
might very well have retained certain residual expressions, usages, and in-
tonations, just like any other group that once spoke a distinctive dialect.
But while the peculiarity of expression of other groups was taken for
granted and considered no worse than amusing, the Jewish way of speaking was condemned and ridiculed.[38] There is, in fact, a special verb in
German that describes the Jewish manner of speech—*mauscheln* (from
Moshe, or Moses), connoting ridicule and contempt at the same time.
That Jews themselves succumbed to this evaluation of their linguistic peculiarity is evident in the tremendous effort they made both individually
and institutionally to eradicate the traces of their dialect, at least when
speaking outside their own circles.[39]

Yet at times *mauscheln* (in its noun form, *Gemauschel*) had a broader
connotation: it could serve to discredit Jewish artistic creations or performances. Jews themselves used it to dissociate themselves from other Jews,
thus offering antisemites a kind of license for their anti-Jewish denuncia-
tions. Wagner, a master at twisting arguments, contended in the epilogue
to his pamphlet that his Jewish friends, whom he on this occasion exempted from the Jewish taint, were the first to be repulsed by instances
of *Gemauschel* in the works of their coreligionists.[40]

Hans von Bülow resorted more explicitly to this stratagem of justify-
ing antisemitism by citing the anti-Jewish attitudes of Jews themselves.
Though he had signed the anti-Jewish petition of 1881, he later found it
necessary to minimize the significance of that act, suggesting that he had
signed largely to protest the cultural consequences of the mass immigra-
tions into Germany of Russian and Galician Jews, "the mere sight of
whom must be as disgusting to European Jews as to all of us, irrespective
of race or religion." To prove that this indeed was the case, Bülow cited
the reactions of well-known Jews to the *Gemauschel:* how "fatal and
nauseating" the *Gemauschel* in speech was to Ferdinand Lassalle, how
sensitive Karl Tausig and Hermann Levi were to it when it emerged in
music. Bülow recounted Levi's exasperation on leaving the theater in Munich after having conducted an opera that he regarded as an example of
Jewish tastelessness: "If I have to conduct this *Mauscheloper* one more
time, I will join the Anti-Semitic League!" The exclamation became,

37. Richard Wagner, *Das Judenthum in der Musik* (Leipzig, 1869), pp. 14–16.
38. Toury, "Die Sprache als Problem der jüdischen Einordnung."
39. Freimark, "Language Behaviour and Assimilation."
40. Wagner, *Das Judenthum in der Musik,* p. 57; see also his introduction, p. 8.

said Bülow, a kind of household phrase.[41] Given Levi's involvement with the Wagner circle,[42] the exclamation is all too believable, and one more piece of evidence that even during the liberal era the Jewish contribution to German culture was acceptable only if it succeeded in being not Jewish.

In the course of time, the ironies implicit in this state of affairs would become open sores, signaling the precarious situation of German Jewry long before the Nazis' explicit attacks on Jews became the official policy of the state.

41. Bülow to unidentified recipient, February 29, 1884, *Bülow: Briefe und Schriften,* 6:254.

42. See Peter Gay, "Hermann Levi: A Study in Service and Self-Hatred," in his *Freud, Jews and Other Germans: Masters and Victims in Modernist Culture* (New York, 1978), pp. 189–230. The anecdote Bülow relates tallies with other evidence Gay collects to demonstrate Levi's burdened relation to his Jewish origin. Still I do not think the phenomenon falls into the category of self-hatred.

The Invisible Community

Emancipation, Secular Culture, and Jewish Identity in the Writings of Berthold Auerbach

The nature of the secular cultural production of German Jews was an issue that exercised Germans and Jews throughout the modern period. The issue carried weight because the emancipation process had made culture a primary criterion for the achievement of citizenship. Emancipation was conceived as a *quid pro quo* in which the Jews would regenerate themselves morally in return for rights. They were expected to conform to the standards of the German middle class through occupational restructuring, religious reform, and the adoption of German manners and mores including, perhaps above all, German language and culture. For Jews, then, the fact that fellow Jews contributed to the German cultural community was an apologetic fact of the first rank. The existence of Jewish writers, composers, and artists beginning with Moses Mendelssohn attested to the Jews' fitness to attain membership in the cultural nation and, by extension, in the political one. For antisemites emancipation was also the critical factor, since it had succeeded only too well. Emancipation had allowed the Jews not just to enter, but to inundate German culture to the point of domination. This alleged domination threatened the purity of the antisemite's culture, whether conceived as German, Teutonic, or Aryan, because the works of Jews had an ineradicable Jewish essence.

I would like to thank Mary Gluck and Harold Sharlin for helping me to improve this article. The National Foundation for Jewish Culture, the Memorial Foundation for Jewish Culture, and the Newman Fund for Jewish Studies of the University of California, Berkeley, supported the research for it.

While the secular cultural production of Jews retains its intrinsic value as a historical issue, it goes without saying that the viewpoints of neither apology nor prejudice can be utilized to understand it. At present the issue might be reformulated in terms of first, the relationship between secular culture and Jewish identity, and second, the role of a minority group in the majority culture. The first issue turns on how acculturation in general, and cultural production in particular, affected Jewish identity. Did they simply undermine Jewish identity, or did they offer the foundation for new forms of Jewish identity? Were acculturation and cultural production the high road to assimilation, or were they means whereby Jewish identity was recast? If in fact German Jews used German culture to fashion new forms of Jewish identity, would it be profitable to consider the possibility that they created a subculture—that they used the majority culture in a manner peculiar to themselves as a minority group? Moreover, is it possible that the subculture itself served as a form of Jewish identity? This notion of a subculture would in turn provide a category for examining the second issue, the role of the minority group in the majority culture. If the Jews adopted German culture in a peculiar way, did they also produce a correspondingly peculiar sort of German culture? Did a distinct minority group acculturation, in other words, lead to a distinct cultural production that might have had discernible influence on the majority culture? A provisional answer to these questions can be offered by looking at individual cases.

The instance I would like to use is that of Berthold Auerbach. As Jacob Katz has recently written, "If any German Jew could ever have had reason to believe that he had been accepted by German society and integrated into German culture it was Berthold Auerbach."[1] Auerbach achieved an international reputation with his *Black Forest Village Stories,* in which he helped introduce the milieu of rural peasant life into German fiction. He became a representative of German *Kultur* both at home and abroad and enjoyed the friendship of German intellectual and literary

1. Jacob Katz, "Berthold Auerbach's Anticipation of the German-Jewish Tragedy," *Hebrew Union College Annual* 53 (1982): 216. This meticulous analysis of Auerbach's Jewish identity relies entirely on extraliterary sources. I have attempted to show that Auerbach's Jewish identity can be understood through an analysis of his literary work, which is, after all, the reason that we now consider him to be a figure of importance. For an additional analysis of Auerbach's Jewish identity, see Margarita Pazi, "Berthold Auerbach and Moritz Hartmann," *Leo Baeck Institute Year Book* (hereafter *LBIYB*) 18 (1973): 201–18; and for his politics, Pazi, "Revolution und Demokratie im Leben und Werk von Berthold Auerbach," in *Revolution und Demokratie in Geschichte und Literatur: Zum 60. Geburtstag von Walter Grab,* ed. Julius H. Schoeps (Duisburg, 1979), pp. 355–74.

circles as well as of the nobility.[2] Among the noteworthy Jewish writers and artists of the century, he was never rebuked for being Jewish (at least not during his lifetime). From the point of view of Jewish apologetics, Auerbach was the nonpareil *Dichter* of Jewish birth and conviction. In a memorial sermon of 1882 Auerbach was so heralded to the detriment of Heinrich Heine and Ludwig Börne: "Heine and Börne as writers were Jews, but not as men: Auerbach was a Jew as a man but not as a writer."[3] Through a close examination of Auerbach's literary career I will argue that Auerbach was in fact equally a Jew as writer and as man, and that the Jewish identity embodied in his work was in fact emblematic of an entire invisible community of acculturating German Jews who perpetuated distinct cultural forms within the majority culture.

Auerbach was born in 1812 into a financially secure and well-educated family in rural Southwest Germany. He attended a traditional *heder* from ages six to nine, and until his *bar mitzvah* studied at the community school, which featured a dual secular and religious curriculum. Intending to become a rabbi, he moved to Hechingen, where he studied at the *yeshivah* until 1827, when a sudden deterioration of his family's finances forced him on to Karlsruhe, where the support of relatives allowed him to continue his studies, both religious and secular. In 1829 Auerbach moved to Stuttgart to attend a regular *Gymnasium,* since in Württemberg rabbis were now legally required to have formal academic training. After failing the entrance exam Auerbach took private tuition in Latin and entered the *Gymnasium* in 1830. He received his *Abitur* in 1832 and enrolled at the University of Tübingen.

Auerbach's resolve to enter the rabbinate had weakened in the meantime: he thought that with a university education he could aspire to higher things. He vacillated, however, and this was reflected in his choice of faculties: he registered for law in the summer semester of 1832, for theology in 1832–33. At Tübingen, Auerbach became part of a circle of students devoted to secular culture—he himself wrote plays and essays—and political liberalism, *Burschenschaftler* in the movement's second phase when it combined nationalism with liberal politics.[4] In the company of

2. On Auerbach's associations, see the authoritative biography by Anton Bettelheim, *Berthold Auerbach: Der Mann, Sein Werk, Sein Nachlass* (Stuttgart, 1907).

3. Ludwig Stein, *Berthold Auerbach und das Judentum* (Berlin, 1882), p. 5. See also M. I. Zwick, *Berthold Auerbachs sozialpolitischer und ethischer Liberalismus* (Stuttgart, 1933), pp. 13–14.

4. For an insightful summary of the history of the *Burschenschaften,* see Konrad Jarausch, "The Sources of German Student Unrest, 1815–1848," in *The University in Society,* ed. Lawrence Stone (Princeton, 1974), 2:533–69.

some of his friends, Auerbach committed the great sin of his youth: he displayed the German national colors. For this act he was prosecuted and forced to leave the university. Even when he returned, after a three-month incarceration, he had lost his theological stipend and his career options had been conclusively sealed: with a criminal past Auerbach could not hold the civil service post of rabbi.

Auerbach began to look for remunerative literary work and found a commission to write a two-volume biography of Frederick the Great.[5] While working on the biography he became a convert to Thomas Carlyle's religion of literature: if the state would not allow him to preach from the pulpit, he would preach through literature. He soon found a post as theater and literary critic for the influential journal *Europa,* and with that his career as a man of letters was launched.[6]

From the outset of his literary career Auerbach opposed the belated romanticism of the popular *Weltschmerz* literature of the 1820s and 1830s. This literature belonged to the aftermath of a revolutionary age that had failed to achieve revolution. Based on the view that the world, no longer just or balanced, offered neither hope nor consolation to the individual, this literature drew on the literary convention of the isolated and misunderstood individual represented by Johann Wolfgang von Goethe's Werther and Tasso, which had been continued in the works of the German romantics—Friedrich von Schlegel, Novalis, and Ludwig Tieck—and which the cult of Byron that swept Germany in the 1820s and 1830s reinvigorated. *Weltschmerz* poetry—including works by Franz Grillparzer, Karl Leberecht Immermann, Eduard Mörike, Eduard Büchner, Annette Elisabeth Freiin von Droste-Hülshoff, August Graf von Platen, Christian Friedrich Hebbel, Ida Hahn-Hahn, Christian Dietrich Grabbe, and Nikolaus Lenau—was often understood in terms of "Byronismus." To explicate the insoluble situation of their lone character, the *Weltschmerz* poets often invoked the mythical figure of Phaeton, the youth whom Jupiter threw off the sun chariot.[7]

In his reviews in *Europa,* Auerbach characterized this *Weltschmerz* literature as the subjective literature of the self—"Ichpoesie." He meant that this literature was entirely dependent upon the subjectivity of the author. The literature never attained the status of a work of art that could

5. Berthold Auerbach published his *Geschichte Friedrich des Grossen* (1834–36) under the pseudonym Theobald Chauber. He never allowed this biography to be reprinted in his collected works.

6. For Auerbach's life, see Bettelheim, *Berthold Auerbach.*

7. Friedrich Sengle, *Biedermeierzeit* (Stuttgart, 1971), 1:221–38.

stand on its own, because the author injected himself into it in an un-
mediated fashion. He argued that "among the ancients the author and his
personality retreated entirely behind the work; among the moderns the
'I' or the majestic-humble 'we' is to be found in every page." The contents
of such subjective literature were as predictable as they were deplorable:
the "impotent spokesman of the woe of our age," he wrote, could create
only a "blunt juxtaposition of contradictions" and the "refinement of horror and inner strife." In this subjective literature an isolated figure, a mere
extension of the author's personality who did not attain the status of independent literary character, existed apart from any form of collective
life.[8]

In those same reviews Auerbach set out his criteria for the creation of
objective literature. There should be, first of all, a "free and animated
creation of forms." Literature should exist on its own, independent of the
author: he praised Clemens Brentano's *History of Brave Casperl and Beautiful Annerl* (1817) for forming a "fresh whole."[9] Such free forms required two things: characters independent of the author's subjectivity and
a collectivity, a community in which the characters could come to life.
Auerbach found those qualities in the work of Matthias Claudius (1743–
1815), a writer of the preceding age whose collected works he reviewed.
Claudius succeeded, Auerbach thought, because he had turned to the
German people. He was a true "poet of the people," a *Volksschriftsteller.*
In the people Claudius had found not only a community that transcended
mere subjectivity but also true character. Such literature served higher
purposes than the bombast of *Weltschmerz,* for it contributed to "truth
and humanity" as well as to the "highest development [*Bildung*] of
the age."[10]

These literary criteria are significant first, in that Auerbach did in fact
turn to writing an "objective" literature based on character and community and he succeeded in doing so by becoming the *Volksschriftsteller*
par excellence. His early adulation of Claudius was no accident. Yet, as
I will shortly argue, Auerbach did not become the chronicler of the *Volk*
without first writing about his fellow Jews and about the German middle
classes in order to meet the criteria articulated in his reviews. Both of
these attempts were, in fact, major detours of his apprenticeship years.

The criteria are further significant because they are closely connected

8. Berthold Auerbach, review in *Europa: Chronik der gebildeten Welt,* 1838, no. 1,
pp. 37–40.
9. Auerbach, review in ibid., no. 2, p. 86.
10. Auerbach, reviews in ibid., no. 2, p. 421, and no. 1, p. 40.

with Auerbach's Jewish self-understanding. In the two years (1836–38) preceding his appointment to *Europa,* Auerbach wrote a number of portraits of outstanding contemporary Jews, including Gotthold Salomon and Gabriel Riesser. In those pieces he developed a scheme of two distinct generations of German-Jewish intellectuals based on their understanding of the emancipation process.

The previous generation, represented by Gotthold Salomon (b. 1784), the Hamburg preacher, had understood emancipation to be a "question of education and humanity."[11] That generation of preachers, publicists, and teachers following Mendelssohn had accepted the *quid pro quo* of regeneration for rights and articulated a distinct ideology of emancipation. The aim of the ideology was to create a morally regenerated, bourgeois Jewry—a new Jew and a new Jewish community. The ideology proposed a new educational and social ideal based on the major tenets of the pre-Kantian *Aufklärung,* but which it referred to with the regnant ideal of the majority culture, *Bildung.* The individual was to be morally autonomous, freed from the tyranny of the senses through the cultivation of reason and made sensitive and humane through religion and esthetics, the cultivation of the heart. Salomon's generation also envisioned a new sort of Jewish community that would also embody its ideal of *Bildung:* in keeping with the regeneration of the individual, the community would be constituted on the basis of assent rather than authority and would also be humane, decorous, and genuinely pious. Because of the ideology of emancipation and its new ideal, then, Auerbach argued that the previous generation had been "practical-pedagogical."[12]

His own generation, represented by Gabriel Riesser (b. 1806), had transformed emancipation into a "question of law."[13] With the upswing of political life in the 1830s, a new generation of Jews schooled in liberalism (in 1848 Riesser was to be vice-president of the Frankfurt Parliament) had begun to see emancipation in the larger context of German politics. They vehemently rejected the previous generation's understanding based on "education and humanity": instead of the regeneration of the Jews, Riesser proposed their political awakening through the formation of political clubs.[14] In the same spirit Auerbach complained in 1836

11. "Gabriel Riesser," *Galerie der ausgezeichneten Israeliten aller Jahrhunderte: Ihre Portraits und Biographien,* ed. Naphtali Frankfurter and Berthold Auerbach (Stuttgart, 1836–38), 5:3–7.
12. "Gotthold Salomon," ibid., p. 38.
13. "Gabriel Riesser," ibid., pp. 3–7.
14. *Gabriel Riessers Gesammelte Schriften,* ed. Meyer Isler (Frankfurt a.M., 1867), 2:3–89. On Riesser, see Fritz Friedländer, *Das Leben Gabriel Riessers* (Berlin, 1926);

that the *Sulamith* (from 1806), the first German-language journal published by Jews and a major organ for the dissemination of the ideology of emancipation, was an embarrassment that should be eliminated. He further argued that his generation had abandoned the tenets of the *Aufklärung* in favor of the new ideal of *Wissenschaft,* indicating both Hegelian philosophy and historical-critical philology. Auerbach thought his own generation, in contrast to the previous one, was characterized by "science and politics."[15]

Auerbach's generational analysis reveals a close correspondence between the ideology of emancipation, which he obviously disputed, and his own criteria for objective literature. Both turn on character formation and the creation of community. The ideology of emancipation envisioned the formation of a morally autonomous and cultivated individual; Auerbach wanted truly autonomous literary characters. He saw the inescapable need for a genuine community in which individual characters could develop; the ideology of emancipation proposed a new community based on reason, esthetics, and piety. Auerbach's opposition to the belated romanticism of the *Weltschmerz* literature followed, in an uncanny way, from his self-understanding as a Jew *vis-à-vis* the emancipation process. However articulately Auerbach rejected the previous generation's ideology of emancipation, that ideology unwittingly informed his own intellectual composition. He essentially became a second-generation exponent of the ideology, combining political liberalism (emancipation as a question of "law") with regeneration (emancipation as a question of "education and humanity"). His view of emancipation in its general outlines thereby approached that of the German liberal advocates of emancipation from Christian Wilhelm von Dohm onwards, for whom "civic amelioration" meant both an improvement of the Jews as men as well as an improvement of their political status.[16] Auerbach's early literary career (1836–47) was a search for a community that could embody true *Bildung* because, as we have seen, he wanted a literature that would also contribute to the formation, the *Bildung* of his age.

It should be noted that Auerbach's literary and political views are not unique but curious minority variations on majority culture themes. De-

---

and Moshe Rinott, "Gabriel Riesser: Fighter for Jewish Emancipation," *LBIYB* 7 (1962): 11–38.

15. "Gotthold Salomon," *Galerie der ausgezeichneten Israeliten,* 5:40 n. 2, 38.

16. Christian Wilhelm von Dohm, *Über die bürgerliche Verbesserung der Juden* (Berlin, 1781). On Dohm, see Jacob Katz, *Out of the Ghetto: The Social Background of Jewish Emancipation* (Cambridge, Mass., 1973), pp. 57–64, 101–2.

spite his rejection of *Weltschmerz* literature and romanticism, he himself remained within the spectrum of second-generation romanticism through the very categories he used to define his position: subjective *versus* objective and the concern for community were romantic notions. The same holds for his liberalism. Auerbach's liberalism resembled that of his fellow *Burschenschaftler,* and a continuum existed between second-generation romanticism and liberalism.[17] The crucial difference between Auerbach and his Christian fellows was that his minority Jewish experience propelled him toward these issues with additional force. His search for community was even more acute because of the multiplicity of communities in which he lived—German and Jewish, secular and religious, political and cultural. The point is that his minority experience conditioned him to manipulate elements of the majority culture in a way peculiar to the German-Jewish minority. He did not create something totally unknown in German culture, but rather saw the same phenomena through the intensifying prism of his minority experience.

Auerbach attempted to create an objective literature by using the Jewish community in his first two novels, *Spinoza* (1837) and *Poet and Merchant* (1840). These two novels failed, however, precisely because the community could not sustain the characters. Both were intended to be portraits of a Jewish community in a particular age—*Spinoza* the Sephardi community of seventeenth-century Amsterdam, *Poet and Merchant* the Polish-German community during the early days of the *Aufklärung* in Germany—and Auerbach made great efforts to turn them into *Sittengemälde* by limning customs, manners, and practices. But the characters he chose—Baruch Spinoza and the epigrammist Ephraim Kuh—were renegades from Orthodox Judaism (spiritual kindred with whom Auerbach identified) and had lost faith in and broken with the only community available to them. Already on his way toward excommunication, Auerbach's Spinoza attempts to find a place in a community of free spirits, but this circle collapses under the weight of romance and hidden religious tension. Kuh similarly tries to find an alternative community after abandoning his home town—in a university town, among nobles by passing as a Christian, or even beyond the confines of respectable bourgeois society among actors and officers—but he, too, fails. Both these men were doomed, then, in literature as in life, to an existence at

17. For German liberals *Bildung* was also seen as a political act. On this problem in general, see the perspicacious analysis in James J. Sheehan. *German Liberalism in the Nineteenth Century* (Chicago, 1978), pp. 14–18.

best on the margins of society, and however Auerbach strove to overcome this fact of their existence he could not. Spinoza and Kuh are consequently embarrassingly similar to the characters of the *Weltschmerz* literature that Auerbach detested. They are isolated, misunderstood figures, and Auerbach's novels futile searches for community.

While Auerbach's effort to locate genuine characters in a community failed, he did manage in the course of the novels to enunciate the very ideas he was later to embody successfully in the rural society of the German Southwest. Because Auerbach's two novels were clearly intended to be *Bildungsromane,* the characters express the ideas that the novels were designed to embody. Both Spinoza and Kuh, for example, affirm the centrality of character. Spinoza asserts at a critical juncture, "The truly decisive and critical is in the end individual character."[18] In keeping with the *Aufklärung* content of the ideology of emancipation, character is important for Auerbach since it alone engenders morality. Lack of moral sense due to insufficient character turns out to be precisely Kuh's failing. Kuh remarks to Gotthold Ephraim Lessing that "the Socratic demon seemed to have transformed itself in Mendelssohn into an ethical compass." The narrator adds, "How rare that one can correctly recognize and characterize in others what one lacks oneself and does not recognize to be a flaw."[19] The individual achieves the sort of character that is moral through the supremacy of reason, which can subdue the passions and senses. One of the characters in *Spinoza* asserts that "one must learn to be master of one's passions and to act according to the eternal laws of reason."[20] Similarly, Mendelssohn tells Kuh in the conversation that "the finest flowering of reason is self-formation [*Bildung*]." Kuh plaintively voices the need for community in direct opposition to the prototypical hero of the *Weltschmerz* literature, Goethe's Werther. After reading the *Sorrows of Young Werther,* Kuh exclaims: "There must again come a time when, free and without coercion, each man, in harmonious development of all his powers, will feel himself sustained in the harmony of a large whole. . . . How different is the suicide of a Werther from a Cato!"[21]

The problem of community plagued Auerbach the man as well as Auerbach the writer. In one of his portraits of outstanding Jewish per-

---

18. Berthold Auerbach, *Spinoza,* vols. 10 and 11 of *Berthold Auerbachs Gesammelte Schriften* (hereafter *GS*) (Stuttgart, 1858), 11:128–29.
19. Berthold Auerbach, *Dichter und Kaufmann,* vols. 12 and 13 of *GS,* 12:195.
20. Auerbach, *Spinoza, GS,* 11:136.
21. Auerbach, *Dichter und Kaufmann, GS,* 13:159–60.

sonalities (1838) he had capsulized the contemporary situation by saying, "Whereas in previous centuries one developed oneself from the particular to the universal, we must build ourselves back from the universal to the particular."[22] The universal ideals of the *Aufklärung* or of *Wissenschaft* were insufficient, in other words, without a community. Auerbach expressed this same view in a letter he wrote on his thirtieth birthday, just after the appearance of his "ghetto novels," *Spinoza* and *Poet and Merchant,* in which he echoes Kuh's plaint after reading *Werther:* "You know I saw my entire highest calling in life, indeed the fulfillment of my existence for many years, in a rich, full, youthful warm life of love, which was to be the highest point of all existence; I have now acquired the knowledge that I must devote myself to an extended life of duty, a life for the general community without an egotistical foundation."[23] At the moment Auerbach wrote this letter he was embarking on the next two stages of his search for a community.

In the early 1840s Auerbach tried to invest the middle class with the values of character and community. He envisioned the middle class as the repository of both individual and collective character formation (the latter in the form of political liberalism), the two being mutually dependent: individual character formation required political freedom, and the creation of a free community could flow only from formed individuals. "The middle classes," he wrote, "are the core and marrow of all healthy state and national life. The free and developed [*frei und gebildet*] bourgeoisie is the highest flower of the peaceful development of mankind. I say free and developed, not in order to divide the two of these but rather to emphasize that the two are one. Only he who is developed is free."[24] Auerbach saw the accession of the middle class to political power as the "high distinction of our time" and as necessary to the development of humanity: in realizing its program of liberalism, the middle class

22. "Michael Beer," *Galerie der ausgezeichneten Israeliten,* 5:20.

23. Berthold Auerbach to Jacob Auerbach, February 27, 1842, *Berthold Auerbach: Briefe an seinen Freund Jacob Auerbach* (hereafter *Briefe*), ed. Jacob Auerbach (Frankfurt a.M., 1884), 1:46.

24. Auerbach described the sort of middle class he desired in his German version of William Channing's *Self-Culture* (1838), published as *Der gebildete Bürger: Buch für den denkenden Mittelstand* (Karlsruhe, 1843). The American Unitarian preacher had addressed his lecture to the working class of artisans and manual laborers; in reworking the lecture for a German audience, Auerbach had addressed it to the middle classes. Auerbach added new materials to the body of the work as well as a significant introduction and conclusion. I have based my interpretation of Auerbach's views solely on those interpolations and new materials. I have not used direct translation of Channing's work to represent Auerbach's views. For the quoted passage, see p. 2.

would unite the nation and become a contributing member to the comity of nations. Nationalism and cosmopolitanism were complementary consequences of middle-class liberalism. The middle class could accomplish this program only if it were itself united, however. This meant that the tension between the middle class of commerce (*Besitz*) and that of education (*Bildung*) had to cease. A correctly understood notion of *Bildung* as true character formation, rather than miscellaneous knowledge or appearance, could, in Auerbach's opinion, become the basis for a generalized "dignity of the middle classes." Auerbach thought he saw the beginnings of this new middle-class life in the vast network of associations that appeared in the *Vormärz* period, in which a new community emerged that also served as a "preparatory school for political life."[25]

Auerbach's image of the role of the middle class was, of course, entirely visionary. It was essentially a program for the emancipation of the middle class that in its ideas and language drew upon his second-generation ideology of emancipation. The reciprocal dependence of character formation and political freedom had been one of the staples of the emancipation ideology from Dohm's famous 1781 tract onwards. Dohm had framed this relationship in the concepts of the *Aufklärung* as the need for "moral" and "political" development: the Jews had to improve themselves as men and as citizens. The emancipation edict of Baden (1809), for example, cautioned the Jews that the sovereign's gracious act required reciprocity: the Jews would have to match "legal equality" with "political and moral development" (*politischer und sittlicher Bildung*).[26]

Because Auerbach's image of the middle class was visionary, it could not sustain his fiction; that is, the middle class could embody neither his version of genuine *Bildung* nor his liberal politics. In his volume *German Evenings* (1851), for example, Auerbach ended up locating the desired values outside the general community, just as he had in his depiction of the Jewish community. In the short story "Rudolph and Elisabetha" (1842) character formation and liberalism become the basis for a circle of sensibility that, reminiscent of the Berlin salon of romanticism, is hermetically sealed to the outside world.[27] "What Is Happiness?" (1842), in turn, has the bearer of *Bildung* and liberalism suffer scorn, intrigue, and incarceration at the hands of a bigoted and politically con-

25. Ibid., pp. 42-43.
26. Carl Friedrich, Grand Duke of Baden, "Verbesserte Einrichtungen für die Israeliten im Grossherzogthum Baden," *Sulamith* 2, no. 3 (1809): 152.
27. Berthold Auerbach, *Deutsche Abende*, vol. 19 of *GS*, pp. 3-73.

servative middle-class society.[28] Auerbach's visionary image of the middle class clearly could not be realized in his fiction.

In 1840, while he was experimenting with the middle class as the true bearer of *Bildung,* Auerbach had begun writing about the rural life of his Black Forest hometown. He had already started on the stories in February of 1840, and his father's death that August caused him to continue them rather than undertaking other projects. The first two volumes of *Black Forest Village Stories* appeared in the autumn of 1843 and were an immediate literary and commercial success. Auerbach was identified with his creations and became a celebrity feted by the nobility as well as the literary middle class. The overwhelming success of the stories decided the course of his literary career. He was once and for all a *Volksschriftsteller.* Auerbach assumed this identity with characteristic energy and within a few years (1846–47) elaborated a full-blown theory of the relationship between the *Volk* and literature in *Schrift und Volk* (1846) as well as creating the two types of literature his theory entailed—literature "from the people" (*aus dem Volk*) in the continuation of his *Black Forest Village Stories,* and literature "for the people" (*für das Volk*) in his calendar stories entitled *The Godfather's Treasury* (1844–47).

Auerbach envisioned the *Volk* to be the basis of a new German nation, just as he had the middle class a few years before. But this time, in the rural life of Southwest Germany, which he knew from childhood, Auerbach had a flesh-and-blood subject that his literary imagination could reshape. Here he had a real community, the appropriate basis for the "objective literature" he had desired and unsuccessfully sought to create since his reviews of the 1830s.

In this last stage of his quest for community, Auerbach himself points to the relationship between the ideology of emancipation and the regeneration of Germany through the *Volk.* The emancipation of the German nation was to follow the pattern of the Jews' struggle in content as well as in form.

> With one hand they worked, with the other they bore weapons (Nehemiah 4:17). As in the past, according to the biblical passage, the ancient Jews fought and built, as today the Jews striving for inner and outward emancipation attempt to achieve the inner ennoblement of their coreligionists and at the same time their equitable outward position, so similarly does the task of the *Volksschriftsteller* present itself.[29]

28. Ibid., pp. 75–118.
29. Berthold Auerbach, *Schrift und Volk: Grundzüge der volksthümlichen Literatur, angeschlossen an eine Charakteristik J. P. Hebels* (Leipzig, 1846), p. 359.

Auerbach's program rests on the twin pillars of *Bildung* and liberalism. As in the ideology of emancipation, *Bildung* and freedom are inseparable, the two progressing necessarily in tandem. "Human development and the free civic life [*Menschenbildung und freies Bürgerleben*] must go hand in hand."[30] His vision of Germany's regeneration through the *Volk* is clearly a transposition of the ideology of emancipation.

For Auerbach *Volksliteratur* is to be midwife to a new age. He sees the *Volk* as the basis of all national life. "The people is the internal life condition of all circles of a national body." The *Volk* holds this crucial position because it is the prototypical community bound together by primary ties. The rural *Volk* represents the "sanctity of a human community united within itself."[31] While that community must become paradigmatic—the foundation for the regeneration of society as a whole—in order to fill that role it must itself be restored to its pristine state for it is no longer intact. The *Volk* has been subjected to the combined pressures of foreign culture and the bureaucratic state.[32] The *Volk* must assimilate these influences and reshape itself into an organic whole at the same time that it is made the paradigm for the rest of society. Auerbach assigns *Volksliteratur* a crucial role in accomplishing that dual task.

Volksliteratur is to bring forth the new age by maintaining the "form of *Volk* life" while concomitantly laying the basis for new forms of national life.[33] Auerbach entrusted this task to literature because he thought it to be the one remaining institution that could overcome the two great ills of the age: a political state and a high culture divorced from the life of the *Volk*. Because it focused on the actual life of the *Volk,* this literature could create a new national *Bildung* rooted in the organic life of the people. In the case of the state, the bureaucracy, which could act only to "order, prohibit or supervise" precisely because it lacked genuine relationship to the *Volk,* would in the long run lead only to despotism. Were a liberal state to emerge based on legal equality and legal guarantees, with *Bildung* replacing authority, then literature would play the critical role of integrating the populace into it through "inward clarification" rather than the mere imposition of law. Auerbach's visionary "Bildungsstaat" would be the perfect embodiment of freedom since it would derive "organically from life and spirit."[34] In the case of culture, *Volksliteratur* would reintegrate the realm of spirit into the life of the *Volk* by joining religious and national culture. But this was not to be the old religion. Just

30. Ibid., p. 361.   31. Ibid., p. 136.   32. Ibid., p. 197.
33. Ibid., pp. 140–41.   34. Ibid., pp. 88, 387, 358–59.

as authority was to give place to *Bildung* in the state, so revelation was to give way to *Bildung* in religion. Religion was to be reintegrated into life by becoming totally ethicized, devoted to the concrete realization of ethical life through character formation: "The cult must be culture, religion must become *Bildung,* inward liberation and redemption of mankind, his true rebirth; not in words and practices, but in deeds, in character, in the totality of life, in the purification and sanctification of all human action."[35] The old confessional distinctions were to fall away as religion became the basis of community. Religion, because it leads man beyond himself and his family, was to help him become active on behalf of the commonweal: "Every unselfish act for others must claim recognition as the essential content of religious activity."[36]

Yet Auerbach was fully aware that he was not the first to discover the *Volk.* The romantics had discovered it long before him. He was therefore quick to point out how his relationship to the *Volk* was fundamentally different from theirs. The romantics' relationship to the *Volk,* he argued, was entirely in keeping with their subjective view of literature in general. Literature did not serve the community but remained the esthetic pursuit of isolated individuals. The romantics thus had no relationship to the flesh-and-blood *Volk* but came to the *Volk* out of a literary construct, as a subject to be exploited for their pursuit of the exotic and fantastic. They consequently always chose figures on the margins of the *Volk,* such as musicians, and these figures never became autonomous characters; they remained dependent upon the author's subjectivity.[37]

Auerbach wanted *Volksliteratur,* in contrast, to be quintessentially objective. He saw a need for two types. The first, literature "from the *Volk,*" was to be the more descriptive. It was to show the "quiet development of life in homely situations," proceeding from the actuality of *Volk* life to reveal the "holy" and "eternal" spirit that inheres in the mundane. As a poetry of daily life it was not, however, to slip into moralizing; rather, the "ethical foundation" and "humanitarian" direction were to be immanent in the work. The work was to stand on its own without the author's superimposed interpretation, to be fully autonomous or objective in that the author's personality was to have "entirely retreated" from it. Moreover, the "destructive forces" of *Volk* life had to be allowed to play themselves out, even if the results were tragic. Auerbach's main concern in this literature "from the *Volk*" was that it "show the free individual in

35. Ibid., p. 300.   36. Ibid., pp. 297–98. See also pp. 302, 303, 315, 322–23.
37. Ibid., pp. 78–95.

his connection with the world and human life," in other words, the formation of individual character in a community.[38]

The *Black Forest Village Stories* met this bill of particulars. The stories were concerned with the mundane events of daily life that are made dramatic by the conflicts of character they exemplify, the community in which they are set, and a romance that helps to quicken the plot. "The War Pipe," for example, demonstrates a peasant couple's strength of character in their ability to compromise, as well as the basic humanity of peasant life: when troops pass through the town during the Napoleonic Wars, the couple rush to help the wounded regardless of whether they are allies or enemies. "The Palace Peasant's Vesele" is a tragedy that stems from the inability of a wealthy peasant family to recognize that the peasant community embodies true *Bildung* and humanity in its own hoary, if unsophisticated form. The narrator points out:

> One makes a great mistake to believe that one can live in the country-
> side undisturbed and alone by oneself. . . . In the country, in a village,
> where the small number of residents know each other, one must to some
> extent give everyone an account of one's goings-on, one cannot self-
> satisfiedly shut oneself off. . . . In this pronounced participation in the
> affairs of others lies a certain sensible community of life [*Gemeinschaft
> des Lebens*] that extends itself over everything.[39]

Another story, "The Command," shows the peasant community to be the fount of liberalism. When the peasants resist the order of an imperious bureaucrat to give up a venerable tradition, their spokesman says: "In the major issues of life every individual must provide for himself and every community for itself, that is not for the masters to do. . . . You are our servants and we are the masters. You are servants of the state and we the citizens are the state."[40]

Literature "for the *Volk*," in contrast, was to be prescriptive since it was intended to instruct the *Volk*, restoring it to its true essence. Here again Auerbach's stories, this time in *The Godfather's Treasury*, successfully met the criteria he established. The primary task of literature "for the *Volk*" was to recount contributions to the commonweal: it was "to emphasize and teach us to appreciate that diligent act for the benefit of the common good that attracts no particular attention but contains in itself the health and abundance of life."[41] This idea is embodied in the

38. Ibid., pp. 270, 49–51, 77, 85, 173.
39. Berthold Auerbach, *Schwarzwälder Dorfgeschichten*, vol. 1 of *GS*, pp. 89–90.
40. Ibid., pp. 179–80.
41. Auerbach, *Schrift und Volk*, p. 270.

image of the venerable grandfather, in "The Grandfather's Blessing," who would pause on his walk to kick rocks out of the path to ease the way for those who would follow.

Literature for the *Volk,* because it was expressly didactic, was to differ from its counterpart literature "from the *Volk*" in two important ways. First, in order for the work to be pedagogically effective, an instrumental use of the author's subjectivity was necessary. This use of subjectivity did not bear any relationship to that of the *Ichpoesie* or belated romanticism which Auerbach opposed, for here the author's spirit pervaded the work as a sign of his "total surrender to it."[42] The fictional world had an objective status that the author's presence was simply to make accessible, for otherwise the *Volk* would not be able to learn. The author's subjectivity made the work a credible example, seemingly drawn from life, that would appear fully in accord with the character of the *Volk.*

In the second place tragedy is impermissible in literature for the *Volk.* Conflicts were to be resolved through the reconciliatory power of religion so that morality could be shown to remain preeminent. Here morality was to be explicit and predominant, whereas in literature "from the *Volk*" it was immanent and subordinate. In "The Savings Book," for example, a locksmith's apprentice is saved from tragedy at two turns. Unjustly accused of stealing a diamond brooch, the apprentice is kept from hatred and rash vengeful acts by a trip to the church that restores his inner peace. In the second instance the treasury official who had charged him with theft apologizes and asks his forgiveness just as the young apprentice is about to embezzle money. Through the affirmation of pure humanity, crime is avoided, morality upheld, and class conflict reconciled. All of the stories feature this sort of moralizing. The apprentice saw his conflict in terms of the moral struggle between a high and lower man ("there are two kinds of men in everyone, and everything depends on which one we invoke"), and that theme recurs frequently in *The Godfather's Treasury.*[43]

Auerbach's fiction succeeded in carrying out the program elaborated in his *Schrift und Volk.* His fictional theory and practice coincided not merely because he wrote his theory after having written stories in both categories, but rather because the vision of his theory also informed the stories, giving them life and shape. While his works cannot lay claim to

42. Ibid., p. 236.
43. Berthold Auerbach, *Schatzkästein des Gevattermanns,* vol. 17 of *GS,* pp. 4, 26, 160.

much enduring artistic value, they are a notable instance of an ideology creating a (commercially) successful fiction rather than impairing it. In other words, Auerbach created his fiction from the ideology of emancipation rather than in spite of it.

With the appearance of his *Black Forest Village Stories,* Auerbach had achieved literary fame and brought to a successful close his quest for community and an "objective" literature. In the *Volk* Auerbach had discovered the community that could embody the values of the ideology of emancipation he had futilely tried to invest first in the Jews and then in the middle classes. And in creating that fictional world out of the ideology of emancipation Auerbach became the unacknowledged and unwitting emblem for the acculturating secularist segment of the Jewish community.

What was this secularist community, and who were its members? The nature of that community can be defined only within the context of the transformation of German Jewry in the age of emancipation, for in that ninety-year period (1781–1871) German Jewry made the transition from a subgroup on the margins of the corporate order to a subsociety within bourgeois society. The most representative development of that transition was the improvement of German Jewry's economic situation: the mid-eighteenth-century pattern of mass destitution at one extreme and inordinate wealth at the other gave way to a new commercial middle class that by 1850 encompassed the majority of the Jewish community.[44] That new commercial middle class, which benefited from the enormous growth of the German commercial sector, also urbanized at a far higher rate than the German populace.[45] This new middle class, affluent and urban, attempted to alter its social existence to fit its economic standing in two directions. On the one side Jews pressed to enter German associational life, the *Vereine,* which were the core of bourgeois German life. While Jews did succeed in gaining acceptance to some of these organizations, especially during the liberal eras of the 1830s and 1840s and again during the 1860s and 1870s, they were never admitted in numbers commensurate with their economic standing.[46] At the same time, these mid-

44. Jacob Toury, "Der Eintritt der Juden ins deutsche Bürgertum," in *Das Judentum in der Deutschen Umwelt, 1800–1850,* ed. Hans Liebeschutz and Arnold Paucker (Tübingen, 1977), pp. 195–98, 210, 232.

45. Monika Richarz, ed., *Jüdisches Leben in Deutschland,* vol. 1, *Selbstzeugnisse zur Sozialgeschichte, 1780–1871* (Stuttgart, 1976), pp. 27–31.

46. Henry Wasserman, "Jews, *Bürgertum* and *Bürgerliche Gesellschaft* in a Liberal Era in Germany, 1840–1880" [in Hebrew] (Ph.D. diss., Hebrew University, Jerusalem,

dle-class Jews transformed the associational life of the Jewish community, gradually giving previously religious associations secular content and establishing new associations on unequivocally secular foundations.[47]

This new Jewish subsociety created a corresponding subculture. Although acculturation had preceded emancipation in Germany,[48] the Jews' adoption of German language and culture was subsequently conditioned by the emancipation process, as I mentioned earlier; German Jewry's subculture consequently emerged out of the ideology of emancipation, whose two generations Auerbach delineated. While the subculture ranged along a spectrum from Neo-Orthodox to secularist, its center position, created by the ideologues who understood emancipation to be a "question of education and humanity," in Auerbach's words, rested on an attempted synthesis of Judaism and secular culture. In this synthesis secular culture was accorded primacy, as illustrated by a passage from the first volumes of printed sermons in German: "Religion is an essential requirement of the educated man."[49] Neo-Orthodoxy attempted to reverse this relationship while preserving the synthesis. For Samson Raphael Hirsch and his followers, Judaism becomes the highest form of humanity, and thus secular culture serves to illuminate its inherent ideals.

The secularist segment of the Jewish community attempted to revise this synthesis in the opposite direction of the Neo-Orthodox. Indifferent to, or rejecting Judaism but without converting, this group went beyond a synthesis to treat secular culture as a substitute for Judaism. But in serving as a substitute for Judaism, this secular culture became an unwitting Jewish identity. The secularists' German culture was not a random German culture but one adopted and reshaped through the ideology of emancipation. It was, then, a belated *Aufklärung,* the ideals of which pervade Auerbach's thought. The secular Jews held fast to this culture as the basis of their political emancipation and their potential social integration. Through the emancipation process, then, a very different form of Jewish identity had begun to emerge.

Yet the assimilation (i.e., social integration) of these acculturated Jews occurred infrequently if at all. They had few contacts with non-Jews beyond the business world, a fact to which the memoir literature of the

n.d.), pp. 43–46; Jacob Katz, *Jews and Freemasons in Europe, 1723–1939* (Cambridge, Mass., 1970), pp. 113, 145–47.

47. Wassermann, "Jews, *Bürgertum* and *Bürgerliche Gesellschaft,*" pp. 83–88.

48. Azriel Shochat, *Im Hilufei Tkufot Reshit ha-Haskalah be-Yahadut Germanyah* (Jerusalem, 1960); Yehezkel Kaufmann, *Golah ve-Nekhar* (Tel Aviv, 1929–32), 2:5–8.

49. Joseph Wolf, *Sechs Deutsche Reden* (Dessau, 1813), 2:56–57.

period clearly attests.[50] A fictional reconstruction of the period, Georg Hermann's *Jettchen Gebert* (1906), also demonstrates this: the highly secularized family of the *Vormärz* era, for whom Judaism is a mere memory, associates within the extended family or with a handful of other secularized Jews, and this suffocating insularity is the underlying cause of the heroine's suicide.[51] As a group, then, these Jews lacked a formal institutional identity. Their institutional ties beyond the family could not provide them with an adequate form of social cohesion. As a community they were invisible. Only their German culture could serve to identify them as a group. For this reason an ideal figure with whom to identify that culture and, through it, themselves as a group, was crucial.

Auerbach functioned as such an ideal figure for this group. Here was a Jew who was recognized as fully German and associated with Germans without disavowing his Judaism. The fiction that gained him his reputation, moreover, was based on the version of German culture they shared with him. For these secular Jews, Auerbach was a latter-day Mendelssohn: just as Mendelssohn had served as an ideal for the ideologues of emancipation trying to create a synthesis of Judaism and secular culture, so Auerbach served these Jews trying to use German culture as a substitute for Judaism. Auerbach served as the epitome of both *Bildung* and social integration.

The subculture of these Jews, for whom Auerbach was emblematic, had a particular place in German culture at the same time that it served as a peculiar Jewish identity. The subculture helped to keep alive the *Aufklärung* tradition in a romantic and romanticizing culture.[52] It helped to preserve a cosmopolitan tradition based on notions of the supremacy

50. Richarz, *Jüdisches Leben in Deutschland*, vol. 1, passim. Richarz points this out in her introduction, p. 57.

51. Georg Hermann [Borchardt], *Jettchen Gebert*, vols. 1 and 2 of his *Gesammelte Werke* (Berlin, 1922).

52. In an admirable essay, "Theologischer Rationalismus und Vormärzlicher Vulgärliberalismus," Hans Rosenberg has shown the afterlife of the *Aufklärung* among the German Protestant middle classes in the form of theological liberalism. Theological liberalism was a direct continuation of the *Aufklärung* tradition of rational theology and therefore shared many of its assumptions with the ideology of emancipation; indeed the ideology of emancipation was modeled after theological liberalism. For understanding the role of the minority subculture in the majority culture, it is important to note that theological liberalism was reaching its peak as a movement and heading into decline at the very moment that Auerbach was writing his novels. Doctrinally, theological liberalism had matured by the first decade of the century; as a movement it peaked in the late 1830s and early 1840s. Thus the role that theological liberalism had played was subsequently assumed by the minority subculture. Rosenberg's essay has been reprinted in *Politische Denkströmungen im deutschen Vormärz*, ed. Hans Rosenberg (Göttingen, 1972), pp. 18–50.

of reason and a community based on *Bildung.* In Auerbach in particular the subculture helped introduce a liberal version of *völkisch* thought into a German culture that was soon to take a mystical and racial turn.[53]

The case of Berthold Auerbach and the secular minority subculture cannot be taken as conclusive evidence for the relationship of cultural production to Jewish identity or of the minority subculture to the majority culture. But in leading us beyond the viewpoints of apology and prejudice, the one instance does demonstrate that the issue of cultural production is historically significant. In fact, if seriously pursued the issue might well lead us to rethink some of our categories for understanding German-Jewish history. Auerbach and the subculture for whom he was emblematic point out the possibility of acculturation without assimilation in German-Jewish history as a direct result of the emancipation process, and beyond that the possibility that virtually total acculturation might itself create valid forms of Jewish identity for the individual and the group.

53. For the change in middle-class culture, and especially its institutionalization from the 1870s onward, see George L. Mosse, *The Crisis of German Ideology* (New York, 1964).

Heine's Jewish Writer Friends

Dilemmas of a Generation, 1817–33

About 1817 young Jewish writers and intellectuals in Germany began to reassess their situation. They now doubted that either the spread of new ideas and secular education or the participation of Jews in the Napoleonic Wars would strengthen the prospects for civic equality. The political alliances that had been forged in the wake of Napoleon's downfall and the slowly evolving conception of a Christian-German state—which excluded Jews from significant involvement in public affairs—staggered their optimism. With the Enlightenment slowly yielding to romanticism and the ideals of the French Revolution to Metternich's reaction and exclusivism, young Jewish intellectuals were beginning to wonder whether perhaps they had not fought the wrong enemy and battled against their own interests.[1]

The young Jewish writers and intellectuals with whom I shall be concerned were all friends of Heinrich Heine. They are Michael Beer (1800–33), Ludwig Robert (1778–1832), Daniel Lessmann (1798–1831), and Moritz Gottlieb Saphir (1795–1858). Though all were roughly Heine's age, only Robert was a fully established writer. Robert, Beer, and Lessmann died between 1831 and 1833, and, from a literary standpoint, Saphir did as well. Though he lived on for more than two decades, what there was of interest in his life and work—his ability to arouse admiration and fear—lay clearly in the past.

---

1. For an effective account of the disillusionment of young Jewish intellectuals, see especially Hans G. Reissner, "Rebellious Dilemma," *Leo Baeck Institute Year Book* (hereafter *LBIYB*) 2 (1957): 179–93.

These were not, of course, the only Jewish literary figures whose lives and works touched on Heine's. There were the old men, David Friedländer and Saul Ascher, whom Heine both praised and mocked. His lasting respect for Rahel Varnhagen, differences notwithstanding, is well known. His relations to members of the Culturverein, whose names recur in his correspondence, have been noted in learned articles in the *Leo Baeck Institute Year Books*. Other Jewish writers, such as Alexandre Weill, entered his life after his move to Paris. Nor can I deal here with Heine's complex relationship to Ludwig Börne.[2]

In previous portraits I have painted of this quartet of writers, I made no attempt to abstract common features or draw conclusions beyond each writer separately.[3] I shall aim here for such conclusions, asking key questions in the process. To what extent were these writers outsiders, involuntary outsiders, men wishing to get inside, mix, and blend with the landscape? To what extent did they judge accurately their acceptance or lack of it in the increasingly German-Christian state? Did the defensive, reactive psychology, to which they seemed condemned at times, leave scars on their psyche? To what extent did the Enlightenment's ideal of humanity offer them sustenance, or, to state it another way, to what degree was their past experience as Jews reflected in their *oeuvre?*

Responses to these questions will entail other issues: their relationship to Heine as a source of embarrassment or pride; their attitude toward Napoleon and the hated French; their acceptance of post-Napoleonic Germany; their attitude toward the Jewry that all but one had left and their surviving sensitivity to anti-Jewish slurs; a possible sense of solidarity with those who had shared common origins, faced common problems, fought similar battles.

I

Michael Beer was the only one of the quartet to remain a Jew. Of his various tragedies only one, *Der Paria* (1826, 1829), carries a semblance of interest today. An Indian of low cast pleads for recognition of his humanity, a chance to prove his mettle—to die for his country if necessary, and live for its glory if possible. Though issuing from the mouth of an

---

2. I have touched on this relationship in my "Ludwig Börne: First Jewish Champion of Democracy," *Judaism* 25 (Fall 1976): 420–34.

3. See Lothar Kahn, "Michael Beer (1800–1833)," *LBIYB* 12 (1967): 149–60; Kahn, "Ludwig Robert: Rahel's Brother," ibid., 18 (1973): 185–99; Kahn, "Moritz Gottlieb Saphir," ibid., 20 (1975): 247–57; and Kahn, "Daniel Lessmann," ibid., 23 (1978): 201–12.

Indian, the story is also that of the Jewish outcast of his time, a man still struggling for recognition of his existence, his dignity, his right to define himself and not be judged on the basis of birth and label.[4] Like so many children of the Enlightenment, Michael Beer—in spite of strongly romantic features in his tragedies—believed in the supremacy of reason and education. This play, which Giacomo Meyerbeer, his brother, should have set to music instead of *Strünsee* (1829), another of Michael Beer's plays, was intent on demonstrating the nobility of the pariah Jew, his willingness to live and die for a noble cause, but demanding that he be judged on the basis of merit and merit alone.

Heine subverted Michael Beer's hopes for the recognition of Jewish humanity, as he did later the hopes of Berthold Auerbach and Gabriel Riesser. Heine, outside of the Rothschilds the best known Jew of the time, was hardly the man through whom one could comfortably demonstrate the virtue of the Jew.[5] While *Das Buch der Lieder* (1827) had netted him far more praise than blame—the latter directed primarily at the poet's sentimentalism and eroticism—the third volume of the *Reisebilder* (1831) had transformed a naughty poet into an evil character. The Platen affairs, which had its origins in August Graf von Platen's nasty antisemitic remarks and ended with Heine's merciless mockery of the count's sexual aberration, did nothing to enhance the reputation of either poet, but did the more serious damage to Heine. Writing from Paris to Karl Leberecht Immermann in 1830, Beer spoke of the indigestion and nausea he felt upon reading Heine's satire.[6] Beer never questioned Heine's poetic talent, whereas Heine frequently expressed mocking contempt for Beer's plays.[7]

4. The following lines from *Der Paria* leave little doubt as to the applicability of the Jewish situation of the time. Gadhi, the Indian, begs, "Stellt mich Euch gleich und seht, ob ich euch gleiche"; "Ich hab' ein Vaterland, ich will's beschützen, / Gebt mir ein Leben und ich zahl's mit Wucher"; "Wagt's und erprobt des Unterdrückten Kraft." Michael Beer, *Der Paria,* in *Sämtliche Werke von Michael Beer,* ed. Eduard von Schenk (Leipzig, 1835), p. 240.

5. Jeffrey L. Sammons has been frank and honest as biographer throughout his "modern biography" of Heine, *Heinrich Heine: A Modern Biography* (Princeton, 1980). He states that Heine "did not strike his contemporaries as a person of integrity, and it must be said in frankness that he cannot always appear so to his biographer today" (p. 15).

6. Michael Beer to Karl Leberecht Immermann, April 11, 1830, *Michael Beers Briefwechsel,* ed. Eduard von Schenk (Leipzig, 1837), p. 182.

7. In various letters, especially to Moses Moser (e.g., December 1, 1823, *Heinrich Heines Briefwechsel,* ed. Friedrich Hirth [Munich, 1914], 1:128–29), Heine deprecated the literary value of Beer's dramas, including *Der Paria,* of which he approved only in human terms. He wrote an anonymous review of Beer's *Strünsee,* then promptly informed his friends that he did not mean the praise at all and merely wanted to be in

Though they knew each other well in Berlin and vacationed together at Boulogne, there was no love lost between them. The difficulty extended beyond Beer's low esteem for Heine's character and Heine's equally low regard for Beer's poetry. Heine was almost surely envious of Beer's inherited wealth and carefree existence, as his own struggle to stay financially afloat was so difficult.

The two men were, moreover, fundamentally different. Heine was outspoken when he was so inclined, polemical if it suited him, deceptive and flattering when the need arose. Beer was gentle throughout, so that Heine accused him of handling everything with kid gloves (*Glacéhandschuhe*). The suggestion of weakness that Heine's remark implied hurt Beer, who reacted more sharply than was his custom.[8]

Their respective attitudes toward political conditions in Germany and the evolving condition of Jews were also dictated in part by their personalities and temperaments. Beer was far more consistent on the issues, leaving a clearer line of thought, though hardly a well-defined one. He was a moderate, an early liberal,[9] in favor of a constitutional monarchy that would respect human freedoms as they were understood at the time and maintain peace and security. Beer evinced little enthusiasm for political developments at home, where his relations with the Bavarian king and his minister Eduard von Schenk called for public silence. Occasionally he did express mild views in his letters to Immermann, ironically edited by the same Schenk. At least part of the timidity that Beer showed on domestic matters resulted from favor which the Bavarian king and also the Prussian king accorded the Beer family, especially to Amalie Beer, the matriarch of the family, whom even Heine somehow treated with reverence.

But for the events in France, before and during the July Revolution, Beer demonstrated a lively interest and considerable support. He restrained his enthusiasm on only one or two occasions, when he voiced fear that the new French government of Louis Philippe might be adventurous in its relations with the German states, thus provoking another

Beer's good graces, given Beer's influence with Eduard von Schenk and Schenk's power at the Bavarian court. S. S. Prawer, in *Heine's Jewish Comedy: A Study of His Portraits of Jews and Judaism* (Oxford, 1983), seriously underestimates Beer's literary talent and the esteem in which he was held.

8. Beer's sensitivity on the subject is clear in his letter to Immerman, April 11, 1830, *Beers Briefwechsel*, p. 182.

9. In letters from France, Beer asked Immermann not to think of him as a "Liberaler Schwärmer." See, e.g., Beer to Immermann, August 4, 1830, ibid., p. 206.

war.[10] Though Beer spent a sizable portion of his adult life in France—as did his brother Meyerbeer—his political and cultural allegiance belonged entirely to Germany. He detested Emperor Napoleon I, condemning him as a bloodthirsty tyrant. The French people as such lacked the virtues of *Innigkeit,* so dear to him as a German. French literature, he felt, was greatly overrated, and not even Victor Hugo escaped his sallies against its lightheartedness and artificiality. Why, then, was Beer in France so often and so long? Why does he refer to French culture heroes as true human beings? Why does his excitement over French politics far exceed his response to developments in Germany? Why earlier, had he advised his brother Wilhelm not to remain any longer in the Prussian army, considering the reaction that followed the victory over the hated tyrant?

Like the other writers to be discussed shortly, Beer wondered whether his anger had been directed at the right party. Certainly the antisemitism of the Hep-Hep riots had something to do with his estrangement from Germany. In 1830 he commented bitterly on the canes of the people of Hamburg descending once more on the backs of hapless Jews.[11] He never lost his sensitivity to Jew-hate in any form, though there are also signs of a stoic resignation. The hope unleashed by the Enlightenment that Jews would eventually be accepted as equal citizens died slowly in him, but events finally convinced him that the end had not come for the violence or prejudices of centuries.

Beer's prolonged stays in France may have had something to do with the freer and more equal atmosphere of the French capital, the lower incidence of antisemitic outbursts, the chance of being viewed more readily as a human being. Beer makes no reference to these facts[12] that, especially in Börne, find frequent expression. Nevertheless it would be a mistake to assume that Beer, any more than the other authors under consideration here, was guided in his values and manner of living mainly by Jewish considerations. He was not. He aspired first to be recognized as a human being, second to be integrated into German society, third to be allowed to be a Jew if he chose to be a Jew. Like others of his time, he may have thought of baptism from time to time, but Schenk's wishful

10. Beer to Immermann, September 16, 1830, ibid., p. 213. Beer believed the French were *kriegslustig,* and any false move by Prussia would unite the French while accentuating differences at home.

11. Beer to Immermann, September 13, 1830, ibid., p. 211.

12. Beer's silences are significant, suggesting inner conflicts more clearly than some direct statements.

thinking on the subject was no more than just that.[13] Michael Beer offered no written promise, as did Meyerbeer, of remaining a Jew, but his exceptional devotion to his mother sufficed to preclude any act that would hurt her, and conversion would have.

Michael Beer was hardly a religious Jew. He had little use for organized, traditional, and prescriptive religion. His belief in God came close to the deist position. As for Jewish teachings, they were sorely in need of reform even for those who believed. His father opened up his home for Reform worship when the government forbade more public Reform services. Beer's poem "Der fromme Rabbi" (1830?) is a fierce attack on a type of orthodoxy that, carried to literal extremes, might result in foolish if not criminal acts.

Michael Beer was a restless, rootless young man, who moved from city to city, from Germany to France and back again. He was occasionally vain and always ambitious, not averse to currying favor with the powerful or to using such power as his inherited wealth conferred on him. But he was also quiet and moderate at home, eager to fit in, living up to Gotthold Ephraim Lessing's image of the Jew of *Bildung* and *Besitz*. Though politically attracted to French liberal institutions, Beer was culturally immersed in things German. In his mother's salon and those of other Jewish hostesses he attached himself only to Schenk and Immermann. The concerns over money that mark the correspondence of his composer brother, equally wealthy, were not in evidence. Beer was proud of his brother and devoted to him, urging Immermann and others to induce Meyerbeer to become once more a German composer. Finally, Beer was sensitive to personal slights and, if we are to believe Adolf Friedrich Graf von Schack, a slight aimed at his Jewish physiognomy caused him to fall ill and die shortly thereafter.[14]

Except for his authorship of *Der Paria*, Beer was not very actively involved in the battle for emancipation. He established a foundation for Jewish artists. On the whole, however, he held back, sensing that the love he felt for Germany was only partly returned. He recognized the dichotomy between the desire and the reality, the ought-to-be and the is.

13. Beer to Immermann, September 13, 1830, *Beers Briefwechsel*, p. 211.
14. This questionable story, absurd from a medical standpoint, was told by August Friedrich Graf von Schack in *Ein halbes Jahrhundert* (Stuttgart, 1888), pp. 341–42. Although Beer allegedly had a special costume made for an important ball, none of the ladies would dance with him because of his Jewish looks. Beer's hurt was supposedly so great that he became ill and died shortly thereafter.

II

Ludwig Robert (b. Liep Levin), Rahel Varnhagen's brother, converted to Christianity early in life. While Beer's ties with his parents were close, and with his mother pathologically so, Robert's relations to his autocratic businessman-father were strained. The tension between *Kaufmann* and *Dichter,* which Berthold Auerbach already discerned in his fictionalized biography of Ephraim Kuh, constituted a disruptive presence in the Levin house. Yet we cannot be certain that this tension was a factor in Robert's baptism. Robert seemed serious about his Christianity, as, indeed, he appeared serious about all religion. In spite of a generally good though not untroubled relationship with Heine, Robert disliked Heine's jibes at Christianity, as he also disapproved of Heine's conduct in the Platen affair. It was rumored at the time of Robert's death that his friendship with Heine had recently been broken by Robert's outspoken revulsion over Heine's role.[15]

Curiously, Robert himself was at times castigated for alleged bad taste in his epigrams; he was chided for a Heinean lack of measure, excessively severe critical judgments, and quarrelsomeness. Men like F. H. K. Fouqué or Wilhelm Dorow, not friendly to Jews, remembered at crucial moments that Robert was, after all, one of the children of Israel, and what else could one expect? He belonged to those who had introduced humor into German culture, initially an admired attribute. But then, Hermann Marggraff asked, why did Jews turn their wit against values and institutions dear to the Germans and not against their own antiquated beliefs?[16] Perhaps it was to appear pure in the eyes of some Judeophobe friends that Robert led the literary charge against Moritz Gottlieb Saphir, who could much more surely be accused of irresponsibility and dubious taste.

What Robert was mainly guilty of was a dearth of talent and even more a lack of success. The latter gnawed at him deeply, and, along with some friends, he felt that nonliterary matters accounted for his neglect and lack of recognition. A remnant of prejudice against his Jewish birth was surely present, but, even more, a sense of failure turned him from a charming and witty conversationalist into an embittered, often querulous

15. Friedrich Hirth, ed., *Heinrich Heines Briefwechsel,* 5:79. Hirth's claim is largely refuted by a letter in the *Nachlass* of Erich Löwenthal, June 1, 1832. Though critical of Heine's politics and his role in the Platen affair, Robert called Heine "our only living poet." Erich Löwenthal, *Nachlass,* Archives of the Leo Baeck Institute, New York.

16. Hermann Marggraff, *Deutschlands jüngste Literatur- und Culturepoche* (Leipzig, 1839). While directed at all Jewish-born writers with some talent at humor, Marggraff's anger is aimed especially at Moritz Gottlieb Saphir.

man. Wilhelm Haape claimed that intrigues against him were at the root
of his failures, while Gustav Schwab saw him as the victim of mediocre
critics.[17]

Of all of Robert's plays, only two are of modest interest. *Die Über-
bildeten* (1803) is a satire on Jean Baptiste Molière's *Les Précieuses
ridicules* (1659), ridiculing the overrefined ladies of the French salons.
This play could easily have served Robert as an outlet for his resentment
at being overshadowed first by his sister Rahel, whom he yet loved deeply,
and later his wife, Friederike, whom he loved even more.

Die Macht der Verhältnisse is thematically a replay of Beer's *Paria*.
It, too, is a drama of protest against the humiliations that may stem from
the accident of birth that forever stamps some people as superior and
others as inferior, casts some into a dominant position and others just as
surely into the role of the dominated. Published only in 1819, *Die Macht
der Verhältnisse* may actually have been written as early as 1811. It tells
the story of the writer Weiss, son of a pastor, who feels that his honor has
been violated by an officer. Weiss challenges the officer to a duel, but is
refused on the grounds that duels are the prerogative of the aristocracy.
Thereupon Weiss shoots the officer in cold blood. So much for its social
theme—the remainder is standard romantic plot.

Robert publicly claimed neutrality in the dispute he brought to the
stage. Yet his sympathies are clearly with the man of lower birth whose
pride and humanity have been violated. In a sense, the drama is the cry,
if not conscious, of the erstwhile Jew who still senses his second-class
status and the occasional thrusts of his enemies. This Jewish link becomes
all the more credible when we remember that the play's plot was based
on an actual incident involving the Jew Moritz Itzig, whom Achim von
Arnim refused to meet on the field of honor. Itzig did not shoot Arnim,
but the affair became public knowledge.[18]

It is possible that, as the cautious Robert claimed, *Die Macht der
Verhältnisse* was not antiaristocratic. In fact, critiques of *Die Nichtigen*
(1825, also known as *Es Wird zur Hochzeit Gebeten*) chided Robert for
pronobility sentiments. Robert occasionally displayed some rebelliousness
in his plays and journalistic essays for J. G. Cotta, but even in his journal-

17. Wilhelm Haape, *Ludwig and Friederike Robert: Eine Baden-Badener Erinnerung*
(Karlsruhe, 1896), p. 22. Gustav Schwab's comment is quoted by Ignaz Hub, *Deutschlands Balladen- und Romanzendichter* (Würzburg, 1864), 1:342–46.

18. Certain similarities between the Itzig-Arnim affair and *Die Macht der Verhältnisse* remain incontestable, despite the fact that Robert continued to deny that it was
the basis of the play. See Robert to Rahel Varnhagen, Löwenthal Nachlass, January 27,
1816 (?). The letter was originally made available to me by Percy Matenko.

ism he was cautious and centrist. Once Cotta reprimanded him for his gentleness; newspapers demanded something more exciting and extreme. But in his poetry, much of it published in his *Die Kämpfe der Zeit* (1817), Robert appears the staid Prussian who denounces Napoleon, deprecates the *Franzmann* for whom he has other pejorative terms, is intolerant of the "blöde Pöbel," and doubts the ability of the masses to govern themselves.[19] He extols all things German—both Germanic virtues and his benevolent government's mildness and justice. Again and again, even in his correspondence, Robert speaks of "our mild and just government."

Perhaps earlier, under Johann Gottlieb Fichte's influence, Robert's patriotic sentiments were entirely sincere. At times, as the reaction spread, one cannot escape the suspicion that here was a man eager to protect and even to ingratiate himself. Later, in the 1820s, he moved toward a more liberal stance, ultimately landing more or less in the middle. Though in a letter to Ludwig Tieck he pictured himself as a man of the Left,[20] since he favored the future over the past and present, he made more modest claims in a letter to Cotta.[21] While reaffirming his opposition to hereditary privileges, he also described himself as equally removed from the more liberal Eduard Gans who preceded him as Cotta's correspondent. Not too much should be made of Robert's occasional liberalism. When the old and deaf Börne visited a nearby spa, Robert disavowed any desire to see him, due to Börne's *sans-culottism*.[22] Shortly before his death Robert denied a report in the *Schwäbische Merkur* that the police were after him for political reasons, and the report appears highly dubious.[23]

Dorow maintained that Robert's Jewish origins made proof of his loyalty absolutely imperative, and that assessment is worth repeating,

19. In a poem "Der König," *Die Kämpfe der Zeit* (Stuttgart, 1817), p. 126, Robert doubted the ability of the masses ever to determine their own destiny and laws. What the masses needed was the guidance of a wise and paternal king. Robert's monarchism in 1813 was naive enough to be suspect. Whenever he uses the term *Freiheit* (freedom), it is clearly not freedom within the nation he has in mind, but freedom from a foreign oppressor. "Ein Preusse kann nicht ehrlos leben / Ein Deutscher keine Ketten sehen." Ibid., p. 19.

20. Robert to Ludwig Tieck, n.d. [ca. 1820], *Briefe an Ludwig Tieck,* ed. Karl von Holtei (Breslau, 1864), p. 147.

21. Robert to Cotta, September 5, 1829, *Briefe an Cotta,* ed. Herbert Schiller (Stuttgart, 1927), p. 325.

22. Robert to Cotta, September 1, 1831, ibid., p. 333. There are similar remarks in other letters.

23. *Schwäbischer Merkur,* August 11, 1832. The story was denied in the same paper a few days later.

regardless of Dorow's anti-Jewish reputation. Like Beer, Robert was willing to supply this proof, though internally resentful—it must be presumed—at having to do so over and over again.

If Robert had any Jewish interests, they ceased with his baptism[24]—not always the case. He did not actively participate in any of the internal Jewish debates then raging. But Rahel and he occasionally exchanged notes in Hebrew script, a thin reminder of their "unhappy birth."

III

Whereas personal injury due to second-class citizenship marked the better works of Beer and Robert, the key to Lessmann's work was *Schwermuth* (melancholy).[25] The term has a high frequency in his literary vocabulary, and *der Schwermüthige*, a figure suffering from *Weltschmerz*, is a recurring character. Daniel Lessmann (b. Daniel Lewin Philipp), concluded his life by hanging himself from a tree. None of the reasons offered by his friends and foes are entirely acceptable explanations for his suicide. Heinrich Stieglitz believed Lessmann suffered severely because of neglect. Moritz Veit speaks of Lessmann's "unstetes Treiben" and his "wirre Phantasie." Friedrich Wilhelm Gubitz sensed deep emotional conflict behind an outwardly even temper. Maximilian Heine, a close friend, thought Lessmann witty, lovable, a bit eccentric, his suicide probably an impulse of the moment.[26]

A peculiarity worth noting is Lessmann's negative treatment of women and his total silence on his mother, while his "enlightened father" re-

24. Yet Robert was distrustful of *Frömmelei* and argued the Christian church was in need of cleansing. "As soon as Christians will be Christians, the better Jews will cease to be Jews. As long as this doesn't happen, however, these cross-bearing Jews are the true Christians and these sinful Christians the real Jews." In this letter to his sister Rahel (cited in n. 18, above), Robert added, "If suffering is the mark of the Jew, he is a Jew, and if to be a Christian means to bear one's earthy cross in humility . . . he is a Christian."

25. See also, Hans G. Reissner, "Daniel Lessmann in Vienna and Verona," *LBIYB* 14 (1969): 203–14. I am deeply indebted to the late Professor Reissner for his guidance in the preparation of this section on Lessmann.

26. For these assessments of Lessmann's character and suppositions concerning his suicide, see Heinrich Stieglitz, *Gruss aus Berlin* (Leipzig, 1838); Ludwig Geiger, "Moritz Veit und das deutsche Geistesleben," in his *Die Juden in der deutschen Literatur* (Berlin, 1910), p. 186; Friedrich Wilhelm Gubitz, *Bilder aus Romantik und Biedermeier,* ed. Paul Friedrich (Berlin, 1922), p. 383; Maximilian Heine, *Erinnerungen an Heinrich Heine und seine Familie* (Berlin, 1868), p. 23, who reports that many at first suspected murder, given that his body was found in a forest. This notion was repeated in "Lessmann," *Jüdisches Athenäum: Gallerie berühmter Männer jüdischer Abstammung und jüdischen Glaubens* (Leipzig, 1851), p. 123.

ceives frequent mention in his work.[27] A prolonged engagement to a girl
in the village in which he was recuperating from a war wound failed to
lead to marriage and adversely affected his career plans. The same restlessness already observed in Beer and Robert is also discernible here.
Lessmann, too, seemed in aimless pursuit of something ill defined, moving from one city to another and spending a long period of time in France.
He ultimately settled in Berlin, a city he did not like.

While the bulk of Lessmann's associations in the capital tended to be
with Jews, first in the Wissenschaftszirkel and later in the Veit circle,[28]
he had no abiding interest in Jewish questions. He depicts Jews positively,
as energetic and hard working. But he also jokes about them, suggesting
that the modern Jew is more apt to wait for the arrival of a general he
can tap for financial gain than for the advent of the Messiah. Lessmann is
also uncharitable to the "uncultured Jews" from the East. But his Jewish
characters in the novellas are depicted warmly. Where they are the victims of prejudice, Lessmann introduces an enlightened Christian to instruct the culprits as to the error of their thinking or deeds. It is a reflection of the times that Lessmann needed old Jews to depict real Jews. In
Die Heidenmühle (1833), the old Jew Manasse is at first proud of his
son, but then pride turns to despair when the rootless youngster, attracted
by the worst of modernity, lands in jail. Throughout, Manasse retains the
reader's sympathy.

During his years in Vienna and Verona,[29] Lessmann had been intrigued with the sacral-emotional aspects of Catholicism. After his conversion to Protestantism in 1824, he became increasingly anti-Catholic,
antimissionary, and anticlerical. As with Heine, there was one last flicker
of concern with Jewish matters, as though there might be a need to
atone.[30] Then it died out. Occasionally Lessmann was to refer to himself
as a Protestant, but the claim does not always carry the ring of conviction.

27. A character with only a slightly different name, Gottlieb (instead of Lessmann's
father's name, Gotthold) Lessmann keeps reappearing in Daniel Lessmann's Die
Heidenmühle (Berlin, 1833). In Das Wanderbuch eines Schwermüthigen (Berlin,
1831), 1:94, Lessmann pays specific tribute to his father, then a very old man, "who
would have won my very high esteem, even if he had not been my father."
28. In the Veit circle, consisting of Jews and Jewish converts, Lessmann associated
with Moser, Maximilian Heine, Leopold and Adelheid Zunz, Eduard Gans, and the
now aged Lazarus Bendavid.
29. See Reissner, "Lessmann."
30. Like so many other converts, Lessmann did not have himself baptized until after
his father's death. He informed the authorities that he had been contemplating this step
for some time. Hertha Schumann, "Daniel Lessmann" (Ph.D. diss., University of Leipzig, 1920), p. 86.

Lessmann came from a family in which the ideals of the Enlightenment were highly regarded. His father's very choice of a name—Lessmann— suggests Lessing. After his Austrian-Italian interlude, which produced medieval Christian romances and histories that bear the imprint of romanticism, Lessmann returned in his final years to a renewed appreciation for the eighteenth century. With Beer and Robert he held French letters in low regard.

Unlike the other Jewish authors, Lessmann fought Napoleon on the battlefield. For a while it appeared that his fiction was beginning to romanticize the life of the soldier—the night watches and heroism in the face of danger. But his work displayed little of the passionate patriotism of Robert's *Die Kämpfe der Zeit*. In fact, Lessmann left no doubt as to his disenchantment with the post-Liberation reaction. He did not, however, involve himself in controversy *à la* Heine and Börne. Lessmann thought a limited monarchy on the British model desirable for Prussia. Where Heine detested British life and Börne was more attracted to France and the new country across the Atlantic, Lessmann found value in the balance of British institutions.

IV

Moritz Gottlieb Saphir was a much-debated, highly controversial figure, enjoyed by many, dreaded by some, despised by more. His fame skyrocketed in the 1820s and shrank rapidly in the mid-1830s. Today his puns, verbal tricks, exercises in tortuous reasoning, and clever but uninspired poems strike the reader as hopelessly antiquated. It seems hard to believe that Saphir once delighted kings, their courts, and the literate bourgeoisie, and frightened actors and dramatists alike with his sharp, pitiless theater criticism. According to rumors of the time, he was repeatedly beaten up by those scorned and forced to flee in the dark of night. Always under a cloud that he was for hire, he did indeed serve Metternich after he finally resettled in Vienna. But if his theater criticism was not always fair, it did display both taste and judgment. Like his political views, his theater reviews showed a strong conservative bent, but when he had no axe to grind, they were on the side of reason, decency, and balance.

Heine offered this correct estimate in an 1825 letter to Moses Moser. "Saphir . . . is still unpolished," he wrote; "Wit isolated is worth nothing. Wit becomes sufferable only when built on a solid foundation of seriousness." Saphir's seldom was. Heine subsequently modified his judgment, claiming that Saphir could occasionally rise to true humor. In the same letter to Joseph Lehmann, he also expressed displeasure that Saphir had lent his journal to an insult of Heine.[31]

Though Saphir admired Heine's talent, he sided with Börne in their dispute. Saphir possessed neither the talent of the former nor the character, sincerity, and dedication of the latter. Yet an anti-Jewish, ultraconservative pamphlet lumped the three together under the title *The Eternal Jew in the Guise of Börne, Heine, and Saphir.* The pamphlet openly decried the incursions of Jewish wit, denouncing it as a detriment to German letters and culture.

The *Kaufmann-Dichter* polarity manifested itself in tensions between Saphir and his father, centering on Saphir's decision to abandon exceptionally promising rabbinic studies in favor of a career as a free-lance journalist. In his testament, the older Saphir asked the younger son, not Moritz, to say the Kaddish for him. Moritz was not cut out of his father's will in other respects, and he waited for his father's death before embracing Christianity. Saphir's mother died before he was ten, and among the few tender pages in his work is the memory of her death.[32] With the exception of Daniel Lessmann, mother-son relationships were generally happier for Jewish writers than relationships with their fathers.

What happened to remove this Orthodox young Jew from a thoroughly observant family, deeply steeped in Judaism, from the path of Talmud studies? Saphir tells us that a priest he befriended in Prague introduced him to secular studies. Until age seventeen, the *yeshiva bochur* knew only *Judendeutsch* and could not speak German at all. Aided by a prodigious memory, he learned in quick succession German, French, English, and Italian, reading copiously in all these literatures. At first they merely distracted him from Jewish studies, then he abandoned Jewish studies altogether as the call of the wider world took him from the ghetto.

Saphir's first stories of exclusively Jewish interest—especially "Der falsche Kaschtan"—were immensely popular,[33] living for decades after

31. Heine to Moser, July 1, 1825, *Heines Briefwechsel,* 1:367; Heine to Joseph Lehmann, May 26, 1826, ibid., p. 419.

32. Saphir himself provides considerable biographical information, all within the customary humorous frame. See his *Meine Memoiren und anderes,* Reclam Ausgabe (Leipzig, 1877?). See also Saphir, *Ausgewählte Schriften* (Brünn, n.d.), I, vol. 7, p. 52, and I, vol. 8, pp. 32–39.

33. For the success of this story about a *chazan* and a tale in a similar vein "Variation der falschen Katalani," see Yomtov Ludwig Bato, "Mortiz Gottlieb Saphir, 1795–1858," *Bulletin des Leo Baeck Instituts* 2, no. 5 (1958): 28–29. Leopold Löw described Saphir's *Schnoke* as epoch making. Ibid.

their initial appearance in Yiddish. They brought him to the attention of editors in Vienna, who gave him a variety of assignments. Brief periods in various South German cities were followed by a nearly five-year stay (1825–29) in Berlin. Here he published his *Berliner Schnellpost,* known mainly for its predilection for scandal but also for giving budding writers a chance to display their wares, and later his *Berliner Courier.* The pet peeves of Saphir's journals were Fouqué, Gubitz, Willibald Alexis (Wilhelm Häring), and Robert. In the ensuing battle of the pamphlets, Saphir emerged the victor in intellectual feats, but the loser in the war. His skill in circumventing the censors became legendary; his mastery of evasion and mock legality—perhaps residues of his talmudic training— amused His Majesty at the breakfast table.[34] When Saphir, now overconfident, pleaded for freedom of the press, His Majesty's humor declined markedly. Suddenly his ministers remembered Saphir's transgressions along with the fact he had only foreign citizenship. He was expelled from Berlin. Eventually he settled in Munich, where the same experience was more or less repeated. Then he was off to Paris, where he met with Heine and Börne. In 1834 he returned to Vienna, edited various journals, and gave witty lectures.

Saphir suffered more virulent abuse than the other three writers. His often-vicious attacks invited counterinvective.[35] Wit sometimes became the weapon of his victims. He had no illusions about himself, calling himself a humorous Satan on one occasion and a "gemütlicher Bösewicht" on another. Saphir reenforced the impression, widely current, that wit was a Jewish trait. He was conscious of the relative newness of wit in Germany. He contrasted the police-authoritarian mentality of the Prussia of his time and the Jewish need for laughter—"the defense and weapon of the oppressed." Germans did not see the Jewish recourse to laughter as a reaction to suffering but instead—and wrongly—as motivated by revenge and reprisal.[36] On the subject of antisemitism, however, Saphir remained deadly serious, long after his conversion. Not only did he react to antisemitism fiercely, but he explained and fought it courageously.[37]

34. Hubert Houben, *Der gefesselte Biedermeier* (Leipzig, 1924), pp. 187ff.

35. Some called Saphir a snake, others a reptile. Karoline Bauer, in her *Memoirs,* vol. 1 (London, 1895), p. 182, described him as a malicious, venal critic. F. W. Gubitz dismissed him altogether as a critic because he was "bestechlich." *Bilder aus Romantik und Biedermeier,* ed. Paul Friedrich (Berlin, 1922), p. 523.

36. For Saphir on wit and Germans, see his *Ausgewählte Schriften,* II, vol. 1, p. 17, also III, vol. 10, p. 20; on wit and Jews, ibid., p. 22.

37. Ibid., III, vol. 2, pp. 177–210. Saphir anticipated modern theorists by depicting antisemites as sick individuals for whom Jew-hate filled a psychological need.

Saphir's conservativism was the result less of positive conviction than of a rampant skepticism that permeated all his work. To him, the more things were different, the more they were the same. Belief in change and perfectability was chimera; it took God six days to create the world and now liberals were trying to remake it in three. To all intents and purposes Saphir had no politics at all because he did not and could not believe. (Curiously he accused Heine of just this deficiency which supposedly accounted for his lack of "godliness."[38]) Was it Saphir's lack of commitment to any belief that deepened the impression he was a writer for hire? His skepticism extended to such questions as German unification, the hope of a better world in America, the achievements of the French Revolution, and Napoleon, whose meteoric rise had intrigued him as a young man, but whom he later scorned.[39]

In literature, there were some beliefs. Culturally Saphir, too, was a Germanophile, believing the French received more from German literature and philosophy, German idealism, than they gave in return. In addition, Saphir, who liked his women in the drama (and the theater) to be chaste, found French drama and theater intensely immoral. This man whose personal sincerity and seriousness were open to doubt, insisted on love of virtue and fear of vice in the genre he loved most of all.[40]

After his baptism, Saphir's Jewish interests waned except for his continuing concern with Jew-hate and, as with Heine, his preoccupation with Jewish cuisine—*schalet* and *kugel* being "perfect mixtures of the romantic and the classical." But he was just as prone as Heine and Börne to be critical of Jews, to call the Jews of Munich *Judenfische,* and take aim at other Jewish targets. Even emancipation—the new Jewish God—came in for some hard-hitting criticism.[41] First, Saphir doubted that emancipation would come, and, if it came, he felt it might not be worth coming. New-fangled Jews did not have his respect, they bent, adjusted, conformed. Old-fashioned Jews might be stiff and stubborn, but they were also firm and dependable.

As I survey this small field of early writers of Jewish birth that grew to maturity in the German language and was given some latitude in its choices of identity and belief, I am struck by a number of things. First, with the exception of Michael Beer, they were sufficiently detached from

---

38. Ibid., II, vol. 3, p. 220.   39. Ibid., p. 238.
40. Ibid., I, vol. 6, p. 166.   41. Ibid., II, vol. 1, p. 182.

their heritage to leave Judaism in favor of Christianity, a step they thought would help them overcome the last hurdle to full equality. Second, they were overly optimistic about achieving this integration, recognizing too late that, as Michael Beer put it, it was not the *Parisian Letters* that were attacked, but the Jew in Börne;[42] similarly, without exception, they were to encounter hostile reminders of their Jewish origins, suggesting an early racial component in Jew-hate. Third, they died young, and only Heine and Robert married. Is there significance in the fact that not one of the six—Heine and Börne included—had a child? Fourth, there is no indication that Maimonides, Rashi, or even Moses and Moses Mendelssohn, consciously or otherwise influenced their thinking; they were caught up all the more in the conflict between the Enlightenment and romanticism, as partisans of Johann Wolfgang von Goethe, Immanuel Kant, Fichte, and G. W. F. Hegel. Fifth, with the partial exception of Lessmann, they were considered representatives of a vibrant new quality in German letters—humor—but soon this quality was regarded as a serious Jewish threat to basic German traditions. Sixth, the preponderant presence of Heine and Börne gave early Jewish writers the reputation of Jacobins and radicals, when actually several among them were conservative by any standard. Seventh, they were drawn to—and defended—German cultural products, and often unfairly deprecated the literature of especially the French. Eighth, while regarding themselves as intensely German, they spent suspiciously large amounts of time in France, suggesting some mild discomfort in the Fatherland whose praises they chanted in all sincerity. Ninth, the antisemites of the time—and they proliferated rapidly—remarked on the restlessness, nervousness, and haste of these writers and complained about their lack of internal consistency—all justified observations—but the Jew-haters did not recognize their own causative role in this.

Finally, the star figure among the Jewish writers, Heinrich Heine, made all of them a bit nervous with his quarrels, polemics, and satiric images of Jews and Gentiles alike. His own public image made him less than the ideal virtuous Jew, whom, after Moses Mendelssohn, the Gentile world demanded. Heine was not the ideal figure whom a Berthold Auerbach or a Gabriel Riesser needed in the 1840s to further the cause of emancipation. The great poet may have deepened the defensive-reactive psychology to which all were already subject without him. To complete this picture of the social and psychological side of the dilemma, let me

42. Beer to Immermann, December 27, 1831, *Beers Briefswechsel*, pp. 268–71.

observe that the writers possessed in extraordinary measure a *Geltungs-gefühl,* an unwholesome craving for recognition, and they suffered deeply when it was denied. Like Beer's pariah, they seemed to be saying, "Give us half a chance, and you will see the stuff we are made of."

Fin-de-Siècle Vienna

The Jewish Contribution

Old Vienna, Gay Vienna: is the operetta city of wine, women, and song little more than a myth? The vitriolic Viennese satirist Karl Kraus once observed, "I have shattering news for the aesthetes: Old Vienna was new once."[1] Distance, hindsight, and nostalgia tend to transfigure things, to paper over conflicts and clashes, to bathe the misery, the strife, the poverty of a city or a period in the glow of rosy romanticism. After all, in 1889, 200,000 of Vienna's almost two million inhabitants lived at the starvation level, and shortly after the end of World War I Bruno Frei painted a similarly bleak picture in *Jüdisches Elend in Wien* (1920). To a present-day Viennese, Old Vienna, or Altwien, usually means the Biedermeier period, between the Congress of Vienna (1815) and the abortive revolution of March 1848, also known as the *Vormärz,* the *Backhendlzeit,* when everything was still *gemütlich* in the city, when a chicken was roasting on every spit and Schubert's melodies filled the air. (How the Viennese, with their proverbial hearts of gold, treated Franz Schubert and his kind is another story). To a non-Viennese, Old Vienna is apt to mean the age of Johann Strauss, which was the second half of the nineteenth century, and particularly the so-called *fin de siècle,* which is perceived as a period of intellectual brilliance, the kind of cultural florescence that only a politically decaying and socially changing age can produce, the poignant twilight years of a six-hundred-year-old empire

---

1. Karl Kraus, *Half-Truths and One-and-a-Half Truths: Selected Aphorisms,* ed. Harry Zohn (Montreal, 1976), p. 60.

that the German poet Stefan George has described as "der farbenvolle Untergang"—the colorful sunset or decline.[2]

Vienna at the turn of the century (which we may define as the dying decades of the Habsburg Empire, from the late 1880s to the end of World War I in 1918) has been very much in the consciousness of to-day's American intellectuals. Near the turn of another century, they are searching for the roots of modernism and parallels to our troubled times, for the guidance and wisdom of a period of tremendous political and cultural change through a better understanding of the problems and solutions (or nonsolutions), the insights and ideas that have shaped the modern world—in music, psychoanalysis, art, architecture, and, of course, literature. Names like Arnold Schönberg, Gustav Mahler, Anton Webern, Alban Berg, Sigmund Freud, Alfred Adler, Adolf Loos, Ludwig Wittgenstein, Otto Wagner, Josef Hofmann, Gustav Klimt, Oskar Kokoschka, and Egon Schiele come to mind right away. The literary contributions of Viennese Jewry have long been one of my own fields of special interest. A little bio-bibliographical handbook I published in 1969 has 238 entries of Jewish men of letters who were born in Vienna or lived there for at least two decades; it lists only those who published one or more books, so it excludes most of the numerous Jewish journalists.[3] A revised edition, on which I have been working, will probably include as many as 400 names. To highlight the disproportionate outpouring of talent that this represents, let me review a little history and some statistics.

Jews were first documented as living in Vienna around the year 1200; periods of relative toleration and prosperity were punctuated by expulsions in 1421, 1670, and—most horrendously—1938. The eighteenth century brought some easement under the "enlightened despot" Joseph II, who issued his celebrated *Toleranzpatent* (Edict of Toleration) in 1781–82, even though his mother, Queen Maria Theresia, displayed little fondness for the Jews. Around that time there lived the first Jew, albeit a converted one, who was able to become a force in Austrian intellectual life: Joseph von Sonnenfels, a man of tremendous versatility—a courtier and statesman, a prolific writer on many subjects, and one of the sponsors of Austria's national theater. Thanks to such men as Joseph II and

2. Stefan George, "Den Brüdern," dedicated to Leopold von Andrian-Werburg and included in his *Der Teppich des Lebens* (Berlin, 1900). See Harry Zohn, ed., *Der farbenvolle Untergang: Österreichisches Lesebuch* (Englewood Cliffs, N.J., 1971), p. 8.
3. Harry Zohn, *Österreichische Juden in der Literatur* (Tel Aviv, 1969).

Sonnenfels, Austrian Jews were at last able to take the giant step from the ghetto into the world, and it is hardly surprising that all through the nineteenth century talented and ambitious Jews flocked to Vienna from all parts of the Habsburg Empire. At the turn of the century there was a veritable outpouring of Jewish genius in Vienna, and, as usual, it was far out of proportion to the numbers involved.

Vienna in the reign of Emperor Franz Joseph (1848–1916) was the imperial-royal capital city of a multinational empire comprising about fifty million souls, of whom twelve million were German-speaking. The Jewish population of Vienna grew rapidly in the declining decades of Austria-Hungary, the Dual Monarchy created after the *Ausgleich* (compromise) with Hungary in 1867. Between 1880 and 1938 the Jews amounted to no more than 8–11 percent of the population of Vienna. In 1880, there were 72,000 Jews in the city; in 1890, 118,000; in 1900, 147,000; and in 1910, 175,000, which means that before the outbreak of World War I, Vienna was second only to Warsaw as far as the Jewish population in Europe was concerned. At any given time, about 90 percent of Jews in the German-speaking part of Austria lived in the capital city. The steady increase in the Jewish population was due to the fact that Vienna promised greater opportunities, more culture, and less virulent antisemitism—at any rate, not the pogrom variety, though it must be noted that *fin-de-siècle* Vienna had an avowedly antisemitic mayor, Dr. Karl Lueger. This man's Jew-baiting, to be sure, was selective and largely an opportunistic political device (Lueger reserved the right to decide who was a Jew in his eyes) and did not compare with the menace posed by men like Georg Ritter von Schönerer, whose antisemitism was based on German nationalistic and racial principles and thus foreshadowed the Nazis. Fortunately the time was not ripe for an extremist like Schönerer, who despised other groups and institutions as well: "Ohne Juda, Habsburg, Rom / Bauen wir den deutschen Dom" (Without Judah, Habsburg, Rome / We will build the German dome) was his rallying cry.

Vienna was always the *Wasserkopf,* the hydrocephaloid city, the German-speaking tail that wagged the multinational, predominantly Slavic dog. Though Emperor Franz Joseph was an intellectual and cultural cipher, the personality of this basically decent and unprejudiced man held the often reluctant and restive nationalities together for a few more decades. At the end of World War I, however, the various nationalities that had served in the army went right from the front to their now independent countries of origin—with one exception: the Jews, who really had

no place to go but Vienna; *they* were the true patriots—professional Austrians, almost. In Franz Theodor Csokor's play *3. November 1918* (written between 1929 and 1937, for which a good English title would be
"The Army That Never Returned"), Colonel Radosin, a true Austrian
patriot, commits suicide when he realizes that multinational cooperation
and aspirations will now be replaced by an atavistic, crude nationalism
and particularism; another such patriot in the play is Grün, the Jewish
army doctor. Such Jews were virtually traumatized by the breakup of the
empire. One eastern Jew from Brody, Joseph Roth, a gifted novelist,
identified with the various features of Old Austria to such an extent that
he intoned dirges for a bygone world, affected the stance of an Austrian
army officer, called himself "a Catholic with a Jewish brain," and once
signed a letter as "Mojsche Christus."[4] After 1918 Roth was rent by con-
flicting loyalties and sought spiritual refuge in monarchist ideology. But
his Catholic leanings coincided with a fresh creative interest in his Jewish heritage. He strove to create a special symbiosis between *imperium*
and *shtetl,* and in *Juden auf Wanderschaft* (1927), a series of vignettes
of the life and character of European Jewry, he viewed the Zionist movement as the direct result of internal conflicts within the Habsburg realm.
Roth, alas, could not achieve a synthesis between his Jewish origins, his
allegiance to, and indeed fixation on, the lost empire, and his desire to
embrace the predominant religion of that empire, namely Catholicism,
and so he drank himself to death in Paris in 1939, at the age of forty-five.

It is hardly surprising that the majority of Viennese Jews opposed the
Zionist movement, though political Zionism was the creation of one of
their own, Budapest-born Theodor Herzl, who abandoned his literary
career after writing thirty plays and numerous prose works and went to
an early grave because of overwork, tension, and frustration. Herzl's
greatest support came not from Viennese Jewry but from the Jewish
masses of Eastern Europe and the East End of London. He found himself
in an untenable position as a "wage slave" of the *Neue Freie Presse,*
Vienna's foremost newspaper and probably the greatest liberal journal
of Europe at the time. Its proprietors were Jews but, like the great majority of their coreligionists, professional Austrians, as it were. Looking
forward to ever more complete assimilation, Moriz Benedikt and Eduard
Bacher saw to it that not one word about Zionism and the wide-ranging
political activities of their cultural editor, Theodor Herzl, ever appeared

4. Joseph Roth to Benno Reifenberg, February 16, 1926, *Joseph Roth, Briefe, 1911–
1939,* ed. Hermann Kesten (Cologne and Berlin, 1970), p. 81.

in the pages of the *Neue Freie Presse*. While Herzl found little encouragement or understanding among his literary contemporaries, his activities did cause a certain self-awareness and Jewish culture to blossom, inspiring Jewish study associations, athletic organizations, and the like. But how many Jews in *fin-de-siècle* Vienna considered emigrating to a prospective Jewish homeland? These mostly assimilated and sometimes even converted Jews felt they were living in "dos gebenshte Estreich," as the Yiddish writer Avraham Goldfaden once called it. Hebrew writers like Perez Smolenskin, Abraham Broides, Reuben Brainin, and Hayyim Nahman Bialik lived and flourished in Vienna, and so did noted rabbis like Adolf Jellinek, Moritz Güdemann, Zevi Perez Chajes, Max Grunwald, and Israel Taglicht. The old story of assimilation and Jewish attenuation *l'dor vador* is exemplified by the cloth and silk merchant Isak Löw Hofmann, born in 1759, who became Edler von Hofmannsthal in 1835, and thus ennobled cofounded the *Kultusgemeinde* (Jewish community council) of Vienna. His son was already baptized, and his great-grandson, Hugo von Hofmannsthal, one of the giants of modern Austrian literature, born in 1874, was a Catholic (though hardly parochial) writer. One has to look hard for vestiges of a Jewish sensibility in this poet's writings. In "Terzinen über Vergänglichkeit," Hofmannsthal writes, "I existed a hundred years ago, and my ancestors in their shrouds are as related to me as my own hair." In another poem, "Manche freilich . . . ," he repeats, "I cannot shed from my eyelids the weariness of completely forgotten peoples." Presumably, these are references to his Jewish ancestry, but why should the Jewish people have been "completely forgotten," except perhaps in the poet's own consciousness? At any rate, in 1905 Hofmannsthal expressed the *Lebensgefühl,* the sense of life, of *fin-de-siècle* Vienna when he wrote: "We must take leave of a world before it collapses. Many know it already, and an indefinable feeling makes poets out of many."[5]

It was a rich literary scene. At one end of the spectrum, there are self-hating Jews like Arthur Trebitsch and Otto Weininger; the latter shot himself in 1903, in the house in which Ludwig van Beethoven had died, a newly minted doctor of philosophy at age twenty-three and the author of a very original and sensational book called *Sex and Character* (1903), in which he managed to attack both Jews and women. At the other end of the spectrum, there is the only *homo judaicus* of the circle often referred to as Jung-Wien (Young Vienna), the markedly Jewish patri-

5. Cited in Jakob Laubach, "Hugo von Hofmannsthals Turmdichtungen" (Ph.D. diss., University of Fribourg, 1959), p. 88.

archal figure of Richard Beer-Hofmann. His orientation may be regarded as a protest against the assimilated, feckless Jewry of his time, and to this end he invoked the heroic biblical period of the Jewish people in a grandly conceived, fragmentary cycle of poetic plays about King David. Beer-Hofmann achieved early fame in 1897 with his "Schlaflied für Mirjam," a philosophical lullaby for his firstborn. While this beautiful poem does express the *fin-de-siècle* feeling that life is impenetrable, disconnected, and evanescent, that we cannot communicate our deepest experiences even to those nearest and dearest to us, and that each generation is doomed to recapitulate the past with its errors and sorrows, it also reminds us that we may derive solace from our community and a definite continuity of existence, with ancestral values and voices shaping us and guiding us to a more meaningful, purposeful life. Even though Mirjam herself and Beer-Hofmann's latest biographer, Esther Elstun, stress the universality rather than the Jewish significance of this poem,[6] I feel that the "Schlaflied," which betokened Jewish dignity even to a man like Rainer Maria Rilke, who was no particular friend of the Jews, is one of the most beautiful *Jewish* poems in the German language. There are several translations of the "Schlaflied" into English. What follows is the one by the poet's younger daughter, Naëmah Beer-Hofmann:

Lullaby for Mirjam

Sleep, my child, it's late, go to rest.
Look how the sun sets in the west,
Over the mountains its last dying breath.
You—you know nothing of sun and of death,
Turning your eyes to light and to shine.
Sleep, so many more suns are thine.
Sleep, my child, my child, go to sleep.

Sleep, my child, the evening wind blows.
Nobody knows whence it comes, where it goes.
Dark and hidden the ways are here
For you, and for me—and for all of us, dear!
Blindly we wander and wander alone,
No companion for you—or for me here below.
Sleep, my child, my child, go to sleep.

Sleep, my child, and don't listen to me,
Meaning for me is but sounds for thee,
Sounds like the wind, like the falling of rain

---

6. See Esther Elstun, *Richard Beer-Hofmann: His Life and Work* (University Park, Pa., 1983), p. 13.

Words—but maybe a lifetime's gain.
All that I've reaped will be buried with me.
None can to none an heir here be.
Sleep, my child, my child, go to sleep.

Mirjam—my child, are you asleep?
We are but shores, and blood in us deep
Flows from those past to those yet to be,
Blood of our Fathers, restless and proud.
All are within us, who feels alone?
You are their life—their life is your own.
Mirjam, my life, my child, go to sleep.[7]

Clearly, Beer-Hofmann's vibrant Judaism helped him overcome his own dandyism and decadence, his passivity and pessimism. In his novel *Der Tod Georgs* (1901), the protagonist's reveries and stream-of-consciousness reflections on his esthetic existence lead him to an affirmation of life and of his Jewish heritage.

In *fin-de-siècle* Vienna, artistic personalities like Beer-Hofmann and Hofmannsthal, and particularly the great Burgtheater, were a formative influence on Martin Buber when he returned from Poland to his native city in 1896 as an eighteen-year-old student. As Maurice Friedman has pointed out, Buber discovered in Vienna "the spokenness of speech . . . the life of dialogue. . . . This reality of speech-as-event was particularly connected for Buber with Vienna."[8]

Most of the members of the Young Vienna circle were Jews, or at least of Jewish birth or descent. These included, in addition to Beer-Hofmann, Herzl, and Hofmannsthal, Stefan Zweig, Felix Salten (born in Budapest as Sigmund Salzmann), Arthur Schnitzler, Leopold von Andrian-Werburg, Felix Dörmann (b. Biedermann), Siegfried Trebitsch, Raoul Auernheimer, and Peter Altenberg. The characteristic constellation of many of these men of letters was a patriarchally run Jewish family from which the gifted son broke away at the earliest opportunity, spurning the business opportunities provided by the self-made father in favor of a literary career. Cases in point are Stefan Zweig, Siegfried Trebitsch, Felix Salten, and Karl Kraus in Vienna and Franz Kafka and Franz Werfel in Prague. We have Kafka's poignant letter to his father, one of many evi-

---

7. Naëmah Beer-Hofmann's translation of Richard Beer-Hofmann's "Schlaflied für Mirjam" is printed in Klaus W. Jonas, "Richard Beer-Hofmann and Rainer Maria Rilke," *Modern Austrian Literature* 8, nos. 3/4 (1975): 63. See also Rainer Maria Rilke to Ilse Blumenthal-Weiss, April 25, 1922, in Rilke, *Briefe aus Muzot: 1921 bis 1926*, ed. Ruth Sieber-Rilke and Carl Sieber (Leipzig, 1937), p. 145.

8. Maurice Friedman, *Martin Buber and the Theater* (New York, 1969), p. 4.

dences that he strove to recapture his Jewish heritage and Jewish values. But what Jewish values shall we distill from the life and work of Peter Altenberg, born in 1859 as Richard Engländer, a gentle, lovable ancestor of beatniks and flower children, a man who tramped around Vienna's streets in sandals and spent his days and nights in cafés, the confidante of cabbies and prostitutes as well as the friend of literary figures, a man who wrote enchanting vignettes of Vienna's little people as well as more exotic visitors from Africa, especially of lovers of all kinds, a bohemian whose nervous breakdowns symbolized the dichotomy between his preachments as a health fanatic and his use of alcohol and drugs, a figure who poignantly reminds us of the transitoriness of a bygone age with its forced gaiety, its surface smiles, its amorous dalliance, and its unheroic passivity? What Jewish values, indeed, except perhaps the fact that Peter Altenberg was both a notable receiver and a dispenser of *tzedakah?* And what about the Jewishness of Karl Kraus, the foremost German-language satirist of the past century, a man whose savage satire and mordant wit for decades filled his own periodical *Die Fackel* (The Torch), whose uncompromising blasts aimed at crushing iniquity, deflating pomposity, exposing lies and shams in life, language, and literature, the man who wrote *The Last Days of Mankind* (1919), a mammoth drama widely regarded as the most telling indictment of war ever written, a ringing denunciation of the martial spirit and the corrupt and moribund empire and society that precipitated the carnage? Kraus, like Weininger, is often labeled a self-hating Jew, and in some of his intemperate attacks he was indeed unsparing of his fellow Jews. But Kraus also had a Jew's burning sense of justice, a Jew's reverence for language and its uses, a Jew's quest for truth in human relationships as well as literature.

From an altogether different social class was the Moravian-born writer Jakob Julius David, all but forgotten today, who spent most of his short life in Vienna. Hard hit by poverty and infirmity, David wrote melancholy stories and novels that are marked by a pronounced social consciousness. They include *Das Blut* (1891), about the problems of Jews living in rural areas; *Die am Wege sterben* (1900), about the misery of students in Vienna; and *Der Übergang* (1903), about the decline of a respected Viennese family.

What the Jews meant in the culture of *fin-de-siècle* Vienna has been expressed most effectively by Stefan Zweig in his remarkable autobiography *The World of Yesterday*. After making the point that the Jews replaced the somewhat jaded Austrian aristocracy as the carriers of culture and the patrons of the arts, Zweig writes, "Nine-tenths of what the world celebrated as Viennese culture in the nineteenth century was promoted, nourished, or even created by Viennese Jewry." Zweig's rosy picture of the nostalgically remembered Vienna of his youth must, of course, be viewed in the context of his despair at the time he wrote his book near the tragic end of his life, though he was insightful enough to admit that "the world of security was naught but a castle of dreams."[9] A contemporary of his viewed the same scene and sounded an alarm. Jakob Wassermann, a native of Franconia, came to Austria in 1898 and spent the rest of his life there. He found the banks, the press, the theater, the literature, and the social organizations of Vienna in Jewish hands. In his autobiography, *My Life as German and Jew,* first published as *Mein Weg als Deutscher und Jude* in 1921, Wassermann severely criticized the Jews of *fin-de-siècle* Vienna for their servility, lack of dignity and restraint, and their self-seeking opportunism—qualities that Theodor Herzl had also identified as being part of a ghetto mentality. Wassermann's animadversions foreshadow what a German Jew named Moritz Goldstein wrote in 1912, pointing out that the Jews were acting as the self-appointed literary and cultural guardians of a heritage to which their right was highly dubious.[10] It was an alarm that for the non-Jews, particularly the antisemites, only confirmed what they had long felt and what the Jews disregarded at their peril. Among the Jews of Vienna there does not seem to have been a Gershom Scholem to point out forcefully that the German-Jewish symbiosis there had no future. Theodor Herzl tried to respond to the perceived danger, but he merely looked forward to transplanting his own, German-language culture to the Jewish homeland, whereas Scholem saw salvation only in a Hebrew-based Jewish culture.

At that time, however, salvation was sought in greater assimilation and adaptation, even conversion. The two greatest Jewish-born musicians of *fin-de-siècle* Vienna, Gustav Mahler and Arnold Schönberg, both converted to Catholicism. Mahler's act (1897) may be regarded as largely opportunistic, leading to his appointment as musical director of the Imperial Opera House, though it is also true that he found Catholicism intellectually satisfying and more in line with his philosophical and mystical leanings. Schönberg returned to the Jewish fold during the Hitler period. Vienna's chief musicologists and music critics—Eduard Hanslick,

9. Stefan Zweig, *The World of Yesterday* (New York, 1943), pp. 22, 5.

10. Moritz Goldstein, "Deutsch-jüdischer Parnassus," *Der Kunstwart* 25, no. 11 (March 1912), pp. 281–94. See also Goldstein, "German Jewry's Dilemma: The Story of a Provocative Essay," *Leo Baeck Institute Year Book* 2 (1957): 236–54.

Julius Korngold, Max Graf, Egon Wellesz, Richard Specht, Paul Stefan (b. Grünfeld), and Guido Adler—were also of Jewish birth, and so were the foremost contributors to the Silver Age of the Viennese operetta: Charles Weinberger, Emmerich Kálmán, Leo Fall, Oscar Straus, Bruno Granichstädten, Edmund Eysler, and Leo Ascher. Jews even made an imperishable contribution to the quintessentially Viennese genre of the *Wienerlied,* the wine garden songs in which the Viennese, with more than their share of *amour propre,* have long celebrated themselves, their way of life, and their beautiful city; suffice it to mention Gustav Pick (the author of the *Fiakerlied*), Adolf Hirsch (known as Adolfi), and Alexander Krakauer, who in his short life equated his beloved Vienna with paradise.

Jews made no great contribution to the art and architecture of the time; there was no Jewish Gustav Klimt, Egon Schiele, Oskar Kokoschka, or Adolf Loos. The architect Oskar Marmorek deserves to be remembered—if only because he supported Herzl's Zionism and was active in the Vienna Jewish community. Richard Gerstl, born in Vienna in 1883, was a promising early expressionist artist whose haunting, manic, bitter paintings were in the mainstream, but his contact was with musicians rather than other artists, and his suicide at age twenty-five was caused by his unrequited love for Mathilde Schönberg. The painter Victor Tischler, born in Vienna in 1890, also deserves mention in this context. Another painter of partly Jewish descent was Max Kurzweil, who took his own life in 1916; he is remembered for his portrait of the young Herzl. Among Jewish artists from other parts of the empire who lived and worked in Vienna for a time may be mentioned Emil Orlik, Mauricy Gottlieb, Isidor Kaufmann, Jehuda Epstein, Eugen Jettel, and Leopold Horowitz. The builder of Austria's Social Democratic party, Victor Adler, was of Jewish parentage, but he embraced Protestantism and in his political pursuits was not above making antisemitic remarks. In the field of education, philanthropy, and social welfare, Eugenie Schwarzwald, a native of Czernowitz and the founder of a legendary girls' school that boasted faculty members like Loos and Kokoschka, deserves to be mentioned.

The story of Moravian-born Sigmund Freud, who spent almost his entire life in Vienna, a city with which he had a love-hate relationship, is too well known to bear repeating here. Suffice it to say that Freud remained conscious of his Jewishness, which by turns was a burden and an inspiration to him, and was a longtime member of B'nai B'rith. In this context a Freudian psychoanalytic apostle turned apostate should not be forgotten. Unlike Freud, Alfred Adler, the originator of Individual Psychology, was a native of Vienna who related with pleasure that he had had a real Viennese street-urchin childhood and zestfully spoke the city's dialect and sang its songs.

A writer whom Freud both admired and shunned as his "double" and who in his writings anticipated many of Freud's clinical findings and insights was the dramatist and storyteller Arthur Schnitzler, who was himself trained as a physician. Today Schnitzler is regarded as the perfect literary representative of a declining age, a great diagnostician of earthly evanescence, the psychologically penetrating chronicler and critic of interpersonal relationships and social and cultural decay, in particular the moral relativism of an aristocracy aware that it was fighting a rearguard action against the encroachments of dimly understood economic, social, and political forces. Arthur Schnitzler repeatedly wrote on Jewish themes. Between 1899 and 1912 he worked on his play *Professor Bernhardi* in which he highlighted the burning social issue of antisemitism as well as the problem of euthanasia and its religious considerations. A simple act of mercy on the part of a Jewish doctor is trumped up by prejudice-ridden clerical Vienna and inflated into a *cause célèbre.* In this thesis play the dramatist gives a cheerless picture of Viennese society and weaves into it the many social, religious, political, and ideological crosscurrents that were leading to its disintegration. The *Diskussionsroman* (novel of discussion) *Der Weg ins Freie* (translated as *The Road to the Open* in 1923), which Schnitzler wrote between 1902 and 1907, betrays the influence of Herzl and his largely unsuccessful attempts to win Schnitzler's support for the Zionist cause. It presents a whole typology of Austrian Jewry floundering between the Scylla of antisemitism and what to Schnitzler appeared to be the Charybdis of Zionist endeavors. The author did not believe that roads to freedom—from prejudice, erotic entanglements, artistic frustration, and other aspects of an unfulfilled life in a constricting atmosphere—could be traveled jointly. Dr. Schnitzler's only prescription seems to have been that everyone search his soul and find that inner road for himself. He considered it proper that Jews should be a kind of ferment in the brewing of humanity (a position close to that of Stefan Zweig, that great believer in the Diaspora) and that what Herzl called *Judennot* (Jewish distress) should be borne by them proudly, with dignity, and without yielding to the blandishments of any party or movement that promised a panacea.

In an undated letter found in 1942, more than ten years after his death, Schnitzler had written:

> Neither Jewish-Zionist resentment nor the stupidity and impudence of German nationalists will make me doubt in the least that I am a German writer. . . . I would not want Zionism eliminated from the world's political scene of today or from the soul-economy of contemporary Jewry. As a spiritual element to elevate one's self-reliance, as a possibility for reacting against all sorts of dark hatreds, and especially as a philanthropic action of the highest rank, Zionism will always retain its importance even if it should some day prove to have been merely a historic episode. I find it proper that authors whose language is Hebrew should call themselves Hebrew writers or Jewish writers. Neither could I object if poets of Jewish background who have hitherto written in another language became outraged at the stupidity and vulgarity of anti-semitism, which would deny them membership in a nation on whose territory they were born, in whose speech they were reared and which they even helped to shape; and if, as a result, these poets abjured the beloved language hitherto employed by them and turned to Hebrew as the medium for their creative works. Such poets would thereby have obtained the right to designate themselves as Jewish poets. But as long as they continue to write in German, they must call themselves German poets. . . . They are German poets as surely as Heine, Börne, Gundolf, and a hundred others of Jewish origin are German; as surely as Brandes is a Danish writer and Proust a French writer. Just ask any genuine living German poet, ask Heinrich Mann, Thomas Mann, Gerhart Hauptmann, Hesse, Unruh, whom they feel to be more German: Wolzogen, Dinter, and that crowd, or Wassermann, Werfel, Beer-Hofmann, and a dozen others of Jewish origin that I could name.[11]

By way of summing up, it may be stated that the quantitatively and qualitatively outstanding Jewish community of *fin-de-siècle* Vienna participated wholeheartedly in what one of its descendants, Frederick Morton (b. Mandelbaum), has described as the "nervous splendor" of the time,[12] which betokens a certain isolation, dislocation, political paralysis, cultural pessimism, and other evidences of a spiritual malaise. Most of these Jews were unaware, or tried to deny, that the demise of the liberal tradition which they were experiencing also sounded the death knell of as-similationism. It is undeniable that the Jews of Vienna made many contributions to the culture of the time that are part of the enduring legacy

---

11. Quoted in Harry Zohn, "The Jewish World of Arthur Schnitzler," *Jewish Quarterly* 10 (1963): 29.

12. Frederick Morton, *A Nervous Splendor: Vienna 1888/1889* (Boston, 1979).

of what has come to be known as modernism. To what extent these contributions may be regarded as Jewish—that is, springing from Jewish
self-awareness and embodying Jewish values—is, however, open to argument.

GUY STERN

German-Jewish and German-Christian Writers

Cooperation in Exile

As early as 1933 Leo Baeck prophesied that the thousand-year-old history of German Jewry had ended.[1] Unlike Baeck, few German-Jewish writers and intellectuals foresaw that Adolf Hitler's seizure of power meant, in effect, the inexorable extinction of an established, mutually beneficial relationship between German Jews and Christians. Gradually and, of course, in retrospect, German-Jewish writers arrived at the same conclusion. For example, in *Süsskind von Trimberg* (1972), Friedrich Torberg's novel about a Jewish troubador of the Middle Ages, the novelist enters the story and assigns himself the symbolic role of the last representative of the countless generations of German-Jewish writers who preceded him.[2] In a similar vein Hans Sahl entitles one of his poems "Wir sind die Letzten" (We Are the Last).[3] Even the few fledgling Jewish writers, living today in the Federal Republic of Germany, question whether a once-sustaining matrix is still viable. Leon Brandt, for example, who returned to his native Berlin after years of residence in Israel

1. Leo Baeck's prophetic (verbal) statement was reported by Robert Weltsch, "Das Leo Baeck Institut" in his collection of essays *An der Wende des modernen Judentums* (Tübingen, 1972), p. 67: "[Baeck] hat im Jahre 1933 die Worte gesprochen: 'Die tausendjährige Geschichte des deutschen Judentums ist zu Ende.' "
2. Friedrich Torberg, *Süsskind von Trimberg*, vol. 7 of *Gesammelte Werke in Einzelausgaben* (Frankfurt a.M., 1971), p. 299.
3. Hans Sahl, *Wir sind die Letzten,* Veröffentlichungen der deutschen Akademie für Sprache und Dichtung, Darmstadt, no. 50 (Heidelberg, 1976), p. 13.

and the Uni⟨...⟩ ⟨...⟩ an autobiographical essay despairingly,
"An Anoma⟨...⟩ ⟨...⟩tion without a Future."[4]

In the f⟨...⟩ ⟨...⟩tive assessments, it appears all but
quixotic t⟨...⟩ ⟨...⟩'s tradition, a few decades at best
as compa⟨...⟩ ⟨...⟩lent history, beyond its savage
suppress⟨...⟩ ⟨...⟩ng so, by portraying its mani-
festatio⟨...⟩ ⟨...⟩resent, not only can its final
evolut⟨...⟩ ⟨...⟩n backward, also elements
of its ⟨...⟩ ⟨...⟩no means offering a coun-
tert⟨...⟩ ⟨...⟩ers, will try to modify it.
Or, ⟨...⟩ ⟨...⟩stroyed continuity," coined
by ⟨...⟩ ⟨...⟩ngeborg Drewitz,[5] I should
li⟨...⟩ ⟨...⟩ulness of the Hebrew term
⟨...⟩ ⟨...⟩ short, isolated vestiges of the
⟨...⟩ ⟨...⟩hristians remained even after
⟨...⟩ ⟨...⟩s of the earth, in fact, except in
⟨...⟩ ⟨...⟩ Alfred Kantorowicz put it, the
⟨...⟩ ⟨...⟩ore slowly than is assumed, and

⟨...⟩cteristics defined the interaction be-
⟨...⟩s during the exile years. For one, col-
⟨...⟩s continued as before, but now with an
⟨...⟩ctful, awareness of each other's different
⟨...⟩. German writers, from poets to essayists,
⟨...⟩rnalists, left Germany, it became clear that
⟨...⟩er how much the refugees wished it to be
⟨...⟩d unaltered in only the rarest of cases. The
⟨...⟩hip that had often marked the interaction be-

⟨...⟩ales Miteinander, ein Zustand ohne Zukunft," in *Fremd*
im eig⟨...⟩ ⟨...⟩*r Bundesrepublik* ed. Henryk M. Broder and Michel R.
Lang (Frankfur⟨...⟩ ⟨...⟩pp. 69–75.

5. *Die zerstörte K⟨...⟩ität: Exilliteratur und Literatur des Widerstandes* is the
title of Ingeborg Drewitz's latest collection of essays (Vienna, Munich, and Zurich,
1981).

6. Alfred Kantorowicz, *Politik und Literatur im Exil: Deutschsprachige Schriftsteller
im Kampf gegen den Nationalsozialismus* (Hamburg, 1978), especially his subchapter
"Das Ende deutschjüdischer Symbiose," pp. 124–38: "Dem [i.e., der Symbiose] hat die
Gegenaufklärung, die mit Hitler siegte und sehr weitgehend auch die Nachkriegsent-
wicklung im kontinentalen Westeuropa beeinflusste, ein Ende gesetzt" (p. 138).

tween German Christians and German Jews in their professional encounters subtly shifted.[7] Where Jews and Christians had previously collaborated or worked together, minimally cognizant of their differences, this
naturalness and acceptance became often impossible in the face of the
strident propagandizing of Nazi racism. In refuting the Nazis' pseudo-
science—in mere reaction to it—the subject of similarities and differences
between Christians and Jews was raised despite the disinclination to do
so on the part of the well intentioned. In consequence, respect and appreciation of each other's background, frequently implicit and spontaneous
in the past, now often became explicit and conscious.

One aspect of interaction in the field of literature may be taken as symptomatic. Ever since the eighteenth century, when Gotthold Ephraim Lessing and Moses Mendelssohn collaborated in the editing of the *Briefe, die
neueste Literatur betreffend,* up to Karl von Ossietzki's and Kurt Tucholsky's joint editorship of the *Weltbühne,* there had existed a mutually
beneficial, complementary working relationship between German Jews
and Christians in the editorship of journals and magazines.[8] But in these
relationships, the religious or ethnic background of each collaborator,
qua collaborator, was ignored or considered fortuitous. In the entire editorial correspondence of the *Neue Merkur,* for example, which for several years united the Jew Efraim Frisch and the Protestant Wilhelm
Hausenstein, there is at most an incidental and insignificant mention of
their different backgrounds. My subsequent interviews confirmed that this
was simply not a topic of their conversations.[9] This ingenuousness continued to characterize Ferdinand Lion's and Klaus Mann's joint venture
of editing the exile journal *Mass und Wert.* While Klaus Mann's correspondence, recently made accessible to scholars, does contain occasional
antisemitic, if jocular, remarks, Mann does not jibe at Lion or his Jewish
collaborators and, in fact, ignores such externalia.[10]

But, in interviewing the German-Jewish author Robert Jungk in the

7. A study of German-Jewish writers by Klara Pomeranz Carmely, *Das Identitäts-
problem jüdischer Autoren im deutschen Sprachraum: Von der Jahrhundertwende bis
zu Hitler* (Kronberg Ts., 1981), comes to excellent conclusions on the contradictions
and dilemmas of both assimilated socialist and Zionist authors but does not give sufficient weight to successful "symbioses" in the intellectual world.

8. For a brief survey of such collaborations, see Guy Stern, *War, Weimar, and
Literature: The Story of the "Neue Merkur," 1914–1925* (University Park and London,
1971), p. xix.

9. Ibid.

10. The correspondence between Ferdinand Lion and Klaus Mann is available at the
Handschriftenabteilung der Stadtbibliothek, Munich.

summer of 1983, I gained the impression that a heightened awareness of each other's background characterized the behavior of the editorial staff of another exile magazine, *Die Flaschenpost,* published in Switzerland. It involved, at various times, the Protestant Arnold Künzli, a Swiss writer (now also a professor of political science at Basel) and several Jewish writers, including Jungk. Each knew (and respectfully commented upon) the other's affiliation, down to the fact that Alfons Rosenberg, one of the editors, had converted from Judaism to Catholicism. Here and elsewhere the former spontaneity had been replaced by a more conscious behavior.[11]

The same attitude of respectful awareness can be sensed where Jewish and Christian writers collaborated on a book, even as late as 1947. In the foreword to the anthology *Verboten und Verbrannt,* Alfred Kantorowicz stresses his feelings of respect for the "inner immigration"; later in the book his Christian collaborator, Richard Drews, is identified as one of its representatives. The anthology itself is marked by a careful balance of excerpts by Jewish and non-Jewish writers.[12] Similarly, when Wilhelm Sternfeld corresponded with the Deutsche Bibliothek in search of a collaborator for the *Exil-Lexikon,* one of the earliest bio-bibliographical tools for the study of exile literature, he asked for a "German" library scientist.[13] That undoubtedly meant, in the context of the time, a German Christian.

II

My second point is closely related to the first. Even a random enumeration of literary circles in exile reveals the same type of mix, crossing religious lines, as had existed in the German or Austrian homelands. With a greater sensitivity than they had often shown at home, the exiles provided mutual support for one another—ranging from criticism of each other's works to financial help—while all the while more conscious of each other's religion. In New York, a group loosely conjoined around the husband-and-wife writers and collaborators Hertha Pauli and E. B. Ash-

11. The interview with Robert Jungk took place in July 1983, at the Akademie der Künste, West Berlin.

12. See Richard Drews and Alfred Kantorowicz, *Verboten und Verbrannt: Deutsche Literatur 12 Jahre unterdrückt* (Berlin and Munich: Ullstein and Kindler, 1947), p. 215. Because of the erratic publishing history of books that appeared in exile, publisher's names will be given in these cases.

13. The correspondence of Wilhelm Sternfeld is part of the archival holdings of the Deutsche Bibliothek, Frankfurt a.M.

ton (Ernst Basch), themselves an example of a mixed marriage, included the Jews Walter Mehring and, on a transient basis, Paul Frischauer, and the Christians George Grosz and Lucy Sabsay, a film editor.[14] As a member of the group, more spectator than participant, I noticed the tact and restraint that characterized the conversations when the ethnic or religious background of a fellow exile was under discussion. George Grosz, whose correspondence is not without highly ambivalent remarks toward Jews, was far more restrained during these gatherings.

Whatever we know of the Yorkville round table of Oskar Maria Graf, which included the Jewish writer-editor Manfred Georg, or the circle around Thomas Mann, to which such Jewish writers as Alfred Neumann, Bruno Frank, and Lion Feuchtwanger belonged,[15] the same conscious goodwill seems to have prevailed. In Mexico City, Anna Seghers, Egon Erwin Kisch, Bruno Frei, and other socialists, Jews and non-Jews, collaborated on journals and newspapers and met frequently for literary and political discussions. But we can infer that here, too, ingenuousness had given way to awareness. Bruno Frei, in a recent essay, significantly called for a creation or restoration of naturalness as an antitoxin to antisemitism: "An incessant education and self-education toward unself-consciousness [zum Selbstverständnis] will become necessary. . . . The relationship of Jews and non-Jews must become as natural, as unencumbered by the past, as that of Allemanians to Friesians."[16]

III

Third, literary works increasingly accentuated interreligious relationships. The problem of intermarriages or liaisons, though not a new subject in German literature, became far more frequent. This accentuation was to be expected, of course, in works set in Germany or German-occupied countries—such as Ferdinand Bruckner's Die Rassen.[17] More significant, the subject also occurs quite often in works about exiles or exile situations. It is as if the assimilation of the Jews and the related problem of intermarriages, once they were halted in Nazi Germany, forced a reex-

14. See Guy Stern, "Hertha Pauli," in Deutsche Exilliteratur seit 1933, ed. John M. Spalek and Joseph Strelka, vol. 2, New York (Bern, 1985).
15. For an account of Oskar Maria Graf in New York, see Helmut F. Pfanner, Exile in New York: German and Austrian Writers after 1933 (Detroit, 1983). For a description of gatherings in the house of Thomas Mann, see Mann's Die Entstehung des "Doktor Faustus": Roman eines Romans (Frankfurt a.M., 1949), passim.
16. Bruno Frei, "Das Feindbild," in Fremd im eigenen Land, p. 155.
17. Ferdinand Bruckner (Theodor Tagger), Die Rassen (Paris: Thalia, 1933) and (Zürich: Oprecht und Helbling, 1934).

amination of attitudes even upon those who had escaped the enforcement of the Nuremberg Laws.

Yet these works vary in their resolutions. In Solomon Dembitzer's unpublished novel, "Das Mädchen aus Flandern," the strain of living in an inhospitable New York breaks apart the Jewish protagonist's relationship with his Christian fiancée.[18] Hans Habe, on the other hand, in his first novel, *Drei über die Grenze,* depicts how a relationship between a young Jewish refugee woman and a Christian political exile is sustained and strengthened by the shared experience of flight and exile.[19] Similarly, a self-sacrificing Christian gives a young Jewish couple a chance to establish a new life in Mexico in Erich Maria Remarque's *Liebe deinen Nächsten.*[20] Also in a remarkable novel by Horst Schade, *Ein Engel war mit mir: Ein Tatsachenroman,* a Christian girl from the Silesian town of Gleiwitz helps the Jewish hero escape across the border. In the autobiographical sequel, *Denn Dämmerung herrscht auf der Welt,* the Christian protagonist leaves Germany with his Jewish fiancée, later his wife, to emigrate to Palestine. His experience as bohemian, boxer, and free-lance writer enables him to survive the struggle for daily existence, and his robust health helps him overcome injuries from the rifle shot of an Arab terrorist. With the understanding of his wife, he masters the challenges and confrontations of being a Christian among Jews in an emerging State of Israel.[21] It appears equally symptomatic that a Jewish writer, Carl Seelig, wrote an epilogue to *Ein Engel war mit mir* and aided in its publication.[22]

Conversely, exiled Jewish writers in their belletristic works singled out Christians *as Christians* for particular acts of nobility. Alfred Kerr's poem "Helmuth von Gerlach," for example, begins with an implicit recognition of that exile's background: "Verächter seiner Väter Sitten / Zog er in eine fremde Welt" (Despiser of his fathers' customs / He wandered to a foreign world).[23]

18. The manuscript of "Das Mädchen aus Flandern" is in the Solomon Dembitzer Collection, Archives of the Leo Baeck Institute, New York.

19. Hans Habe, *Drei über die Grenze* (Geneva: Editions Union, 1937).

20. Erich Maria Remarque, *Liebe deinen Nächsten* (Stockholm: Bermann-Fischer, 1941).

21. Horst Schade, *Ein Engel war mit mir: Ein Tatsachenroman* (Zurich: Steinberg Verlag, 1947), and Schade, *Denn Dämmerung herrscht auf der Welt* (Zurich: Steinberg Verlag, 1949).

22. Carl Seelig, "Bericht über Horst Schade" in Schade, *Ein Engel war mit mir,* pp. 297–304.

23. Alfred Kerr, "Helmuth von Gerlach," in his *Melodien: Gedichte* (Paris: Editions Nouvelles Internationales; Internationale Verlags-Anstalt, 1938), p. 55.

IV

My fourth observation is that where Christians and Jews joined in efforts at help and rescue of the persecuted or of exiles, they stressed their
impartiality and, if they showed preferences, they would lean over back-
wards, Christians often championing Jewish writers and Jewish writers
their Christian colleagues. Clearly the collaborations of German-Jewish
and German-Christian writers in those apocalyptic times were not confined to literary concerns or creations, and writers of all persuasions
joined in this humanitarian mission. It is to the credit of many that they
programmatically eschewed appeals or actions preferential to helping one
or the other group. Most surprising in tracing these efforts is the fact that
they disprove the assumption often put forth in exile studies, but particularly in East Germany, that writers persecuted as Jews did not join forces
with those persecuted as political opponents of the Nazis, be they Jews
or Christians. While clashes did abound, as Alfred Kantorowicz details in
his autobiographies,[24] there were also remarkable acts of mutual support.
Wherever possible, victims of religious and political persecution joined
together for sheer survival, even when outright antipathies had previously existed among them.

In certain groups, the composition of the leadership alone, perhaps by
design, reflected mutual support among Jews and Christians. In the
United States the American Guild for German Cultural Freedom subsi-
dized writers, secured sponsors for affidavits, and occasionally acted as
contact to publishers. It relied heavily, of course, on American dignitaries
and intellectuals for its board members and officers, but its European
Council, with Thomas Mann as chairman, consisted of an illustrious
cadre of German Christians and Jews: R. A. Berman-Hoellriegel, Lion
Feuchtwanger, Bruno Frank, Leonard Frank, Sigmund Freud, Bronislav
Hubermann, Otto Klemperer, Emil Lederer, Heinrich Mann, Father
Georg Moenius, Robert Musil, Alfred Neumann, Rudolph Olden, Max
Reinhardt, René Schickele, Erwin Schroedinger, Paul J. Tillich, Ernst
Toch, Ernst Toller, Fritz von Unruh, Veit Valentin, and Franz Werfel.

This council was led, from the beginning, by Prince Hubertus zu Loewenstein as general-secretary. Its statement of purpose (1937), probably
drafted by Peter de Mendelssohn, explicitly states that the humanitarian
problem it seeks to address is not "circumscribed to any area or class [of

24. See, e.g., Kantorowicz, *Politik und Literatur im Exil*, pp. 82–87.

persecuted]."[25] And Prince zu Loewenstein, in an interview in 1983, added, "We political immigrants never gave recognition to the differences either among religions or among emigrants for political or ethnic reasons—neither before, nor at that time, nor now."[26]

A similar though far more Marxist-oriented organization in England, the Free German League of Culture in Great Britain, espoused identical principles: "The path of all refugees from Germany, whether they be Jews or non-Jews, is a common one in our fight against Hitler-Fascism."[27] The organization's executive council included both German Jews and Christians, such as John Heartfield and Johanna Klopstock, and solicited and—surprisingly—gained support from communist writers like Bodo Uhse, after the war a party functionary and feature writer for the German Democratic Republic. In 1942 the Free German League devoted a special issue of its magazine, *Unser ist der Morgen,* to the eradication of antisemitism. Uhse concluded his article by asking for a common effort to defeat Hitler, because his defeat alone could end the suffering of Jews in Europe.[28] Jan Petersen, likewise a non-Jewish communist, wrote the foreword: "A free Germany is unimaginable without the complete removal of the injustices that victimize the Jews. . . . The fight for the restoration of equal rights of all mankind, regardless of religious or racial affiliation, must form an essential part of the German people's struggle for freedom."[29] Even more surprising, another contributor to this special issue was Alexander Abusch. Although he later became an instrument of Stalinist suppression, he contributed an extremely sensitive article on the spiritual and intellectual richness of German Jewry.[30] It is idle to ask whether it was sincere; it served the purpose of presenting a united front in behalf of the oppressed German Jews, especially the intelligentsia. Given the appeal by Abusch, it is only to be expected that the far less dogmatic, if leftist, Jew Arnold Zweig, then living in Palestine, should

25. American Guild for German Cultural Freedom, *Statement of Purpose* (New York, [1937]), inside panel, Archives of the Deutsche Bibliothek, Frankfurt a.M. Much of the American Guild's correspondence is located here.

26. The interview with Prince Hubertus zu Loewenstein took place at his home in Bad Godesberg, in August 1983.

27. *Eine Frage der Wiedergutmachung des Unrechts an den Juden: Eine Erklärung deutscher Antifaschisten* (London: Almorris Press, for the Free German League of Culture in Great Britain, [1943]), p. 8.

28. Bodo Uhse, "Der Pogrom geht weiter," *Unser ist der Morgen,* August 1942, p. 27.

29. Jan Petersen, foreword, ibid., p. 4.

30. Alexander Abusch, "Der gelbe Stern und das jüdische Volk," ibid., pp. 5–9.

declare his solidarity with Jews of all political persuasions. Zweig described himself as "equally oppressed . . . by the cruelties inflicted upon the Left. But in the main this book [of mine] is a declaration in behalf of the Jews."[31] In the lengthy epilogue to the postwar reissue of the book authorized by Zweig, Achim von Borries emphasized Zweig's loyalty to Judaism: "As he remained a Jew as a German, he also remained a Jew as a Marxian Socialist."[32]

There were also, much to their credit, Jewish organizations that tried to help non-Jewish exiles. The German-Jewish Club of New York, later the New York World Club, while primarily a form and forum of Jewish self-help in such matters as job procurement, also served some Christian exiles, among them Kurt Kersten.[33] And, according to Hans Steinitz, its publication the *New York Aufbau* drew upon "non-Jewish journalists and members of the editorial staff in large numbers."[34] To find validation for Steinitz's assertion, one need only to recall that the *Aufbau* offered a first American foothold to Fritz von Unruh, published Oskar Maria Graf immediately after his arrival in America, and gave editorial positions to Siegfried Anhäuser, a German-Christian editor and former member of the German parliament, and to the postwar political writer Gert Niers.[35] In England, Jewish communities no doubt repeatedly heeded the plea of Dr. Ignaz Maybaum of Berlin, a prominent immigrant rabbi, who enjoined his fellow Jews to aid intellectuals of both religions, because "the world of tomorrow has need of the Christian intellectual who is a Christian and of the Jewish intellectual who is a Jew."[36] In turn, the archbishop of Canterbury wrote the foreword to one of Maybaum's books, *Man and Catastrophe*.[37]

There are also many instances in which individual writers bent over

31. Arnold Zweig, *Bilanz der deutschen Judenheit: Ein Versuch* (Amsterdam: Querido Verlag, 1933), 2d ed. (Cologne, 1961), p. 5.

32. Achim von Borries, epilogue to 2d ed. of ibid., p. 318.

33. For a biographical account of Kurt Kersten's first years in New York, based largely on material at the Leo Baeck Institute, see Guy Stern, "Ob und wie sie sich anpassten," in *Leben im Exil: Historische Perspektiven,* ed. Wolfgang Frühwald and Wolfgang Schieder, no. 18 (Hamburg, 1981), p. 70.

34. Hans Steinitz, "Aufbau, Neubau, Brückenbau: Ein Geleitwort," in *Aufbau, Reconstruction: Dokumente einer Kultur im Exil,* ed. Will Schaber (New York and Cologne, 1972), p. 15.

35. Fritz von Unruh, "Fürtwangler und das Hitler-Regime," in ibid., p. 225; Oskar Maria Graf, "Die Juden stehen nicht allein!" ibid., p. 203; interview with Hans Steinitz, September 1983, at Leo Baeck Institute, New York, N.Y.

36. Ignaz Maybaum, *Synagogue and Society: Jewish-Christian Collaboration in Defense of Western Civilization,* trans. Joseph Leftwich (London: James Clarke, 1944), p. 111.

37. Ignaz Maybaum, *Man and Catastrophe* (London: Allenson & Co., 1941).

backward to rescue others of different religious persuasions. Most notable among them was, of course, Thomas Mann.[38] In the past Mann—as is now well known—had flirted with antisemitism—and not only in his *Betrachtungen eines Unpolitischen* (1918). But in his lecture "The Decline of European Jewry," delivered in San Francisco in July 1943, he singled out Jewish writers for defense and approbation. He pointed to the contributions of Jewish artists, musicians, and scientists, and he closed with a moving appeal in behalf of the persecuted Jews: "May this hall, this meeting radiate waves of compassion, of indignation and of our determination to help, which will reach perhaps and frighten the murderers of right and humanity, but above all may they move those who have the power and the means to alleviate the suffering of our time!"[39] Mann also wrote recommendations and forewords for Jewish writers, even when he might have had reservations about the work, in order to help them succeed. A long-forgotten novel by Frederick Hollander (b. Friedrich Hollaender), for example, received an almost lyrical tribute in Mann's preface:

> I have read this book with genuine delight and I am happy for the opportunity to congratulate both the author and the publisher before its release for this extraordinary and beautiful work. It is a splendid novel, new, tense with life, courageous, and artistically entertaining, written in a visible, vigilant, and colorful English, in the rhythmical charms of which one can sense the musicianship of the author.[40]

Heinrich Mann was no less eloquent than his brother in his intercession on behalf of German-Jewish writers and intellectuals. In an appeal written in France and intended to encourage revolution against the Nazis, he also invoked the injustice done to German-Jewish writers: "[Hitler] drove creative, talented people out of Germany. . . . The Jews had contributed very heavily to German intellectual life. They had done their duty beyond their numerical representatives. That alone was reason enough to be persecuted by a despot who has set naked tyranny as his only goal and purpose."[41]

38. Herbert Lehnert, "Die Dialektik der Kultur: Mythos, Katastrophe und die Kontinuität der deutschen Literatur in Thomas Manns *Doktor Faustus*," in *Zur Ästhetik der Exilliteratur seit 1933*, ed. Alexander Stephan and Hans Wagener (Bonn: Bouvier, 1985).

39. Thomas Mann, "The Decline of European Jewry," in *Thomas Mann: Sieben Manifeste zur jüdischen Frage, 1936–1948*, ed. Walter A. Berendsohn (Darmstadt, 1966), p. 46.

40. Thomas Mann, preface to Frederick Hollander, *Those Torn from Earth* (New York: Liveright, 1941), p. [i].

41. Heinrich Mann, foreword to *Der Pogrom* (Zurich and Paris: Verlag für soziale Literatur, 1939), p. iii.

Paul Tillich, from his religious and ethical convictions, reminded his Christian listeners, even when making an appeal for help for non-Jews via the American Christian Committee for Refugees from Germany, of the historic plight of the Jews: "God separates men, if He elects them. He separates Israel from the nations and makes her an exile in Egypt, in Babylon, in the Hellenic, in the Roman Empire, and now in the occidental world and its nations."[42]

German-Jewish writers showed a similar spirit of generosity and altruism. One example among many will suffice. It could happen that two former rivals or enemies, whether or not such antagonisms were nurtured in part by a Jewish-Christian conflict, forgot such antipathies once they were in exile. The Jewish director Max Reinhardt, unfavorably disposed toward his rival Erwin Piscator when both were in pre-1933 Germany, became supportive to the point of self-denial when both were exiles. In May 1939, when Piscator had just arrived in America, Reinhardt, already somewhat more established, supplied him with a letter of recommendation in which he unselfishly declared, "One is even fully justified in saying that the last phase of development of the German theatre, before the beginning of the socalled [sic] Third Reich, bears your name."[43]

Similarly Alfred Kerr, in his capacity as president of the PEN Club in Exile, stressed time and again that the common exile fate united them all. As his notes for his agendas and short addresses show, he frequently used his forum to solicit aid for German-Christian writers. "Perhaps," he recorded, "we together can do something for Kurt Kersten who is still a prisoner in the South of France."[44] The full extent, however, to which Christian exiles were helped by Jews—of course not by German Jews alone and certainly not only by German-Jewish writers—can be gauged by an editorial that accompanied the printing of Paul Tillich's speech in the *Presbyterian Tribune* of October 29, 1936:

> There are [among the refugees from Germany] 14,000 Christian exiles, and these 14,000 have received woefully inadequate help. In most instances such help as has been given was contributed by Jews. . . . [At the meeting addressed by Dr. Tillich] profound gratitude was expressed

42. Paul Tillich's speech, "Christianity and Emigration," was originally delivered on October 6, 1936 at Riverside Church, New York, then printed in the *Presbyterian Tribune*, October 29, 1936, p. 1, and finally reprinted separately. A copy is in the Abteilung Exilliteratur, Deutsche Bibliothek, Frankfurt a.M.

43. Max Reinhardt to Erwin Piscator, May 3, 1939, Literaturarchiv, ibid.

44. Alfred Kerr's notes for his agendas and short addresses to the London PEN Club in Exile are in the Alfred Kerr Archive of the Deutsche Akademie der Künste, West Berlin.

that relief had in many instances been extended to Christian refugees by Jewish organizations, despite their crushing responsiblities for refugees of their own faith.[45]

V

Finally, a new cooperation between German-Jewish writers and German-Christian writers of the postwar generation has developed in the more recent past. It has often been claimed, and correctly so, that Jewish exile writers were not particularly welcomed back by the German book trade, by the German reading public, or by their colleagues after 1945. But it is fair to add that exceptions abound. The sociologist Friedrich Oppler has repeatedly reminded the German government of its obligations to Germany's postwar Jews: "Every state, unless it is one with a Hitlerian ideology, must be interested in bringing about the true integration [of those Jews] who wish it and are capable of it."[46] Erich Lüth, drama critic and an admirer of the exiled Erwin Piscator, expressed similar sentiments, but also made a special plea for German-Jewish writers and intellectuals: "We want to renew the remembrance of great Jews in the world and in Germany and do everything to be able to profit from the insights of Jewish men and women, scholars, and poets."[47]

Among the newly established fiction writers of postwar Germany, several raised their championship of works by Jewish exiles to the level of a personal crusade. Three examples will illustrate the point. Ingeborg Drewitz, well-known lyricist and novelist, has reviewed, in a long succession, every book from the pen of a German-Jewish author, both newly published, and republished, and she has used her position as a publisher's reader to advance the careers of others, among them Jean Améry, H. G. Adler, Ulrich Becher, Alfred Döblin, Irmgard Keun, Nelly Sachs, who became a personal friend, and Hans Sahl. Drewitz explains her missionary zeal as follows: "And then, after 1945, came the avid eagerness—more than curiosity—to get to these unknown works." She also details her friendships with several of these authors and explains how those friendships prompted her to use her presidency of the PEN Club in their behalf: "To prepare exhibitions, to get [the exiled writers] invited, to investigate possibilities for their return was for me one of the most noble

45. Editorial, *Presbyterian Tribune,* October 29, 1936, p. 11.

46. Friedrich Oppler, *Das falsche Tabu: Betrachtungen über das deutschjüdische Problem* (Stuttgart, 1966), p. 299.

47. Erich Lüth, *Deutschland und die Juden nach 1945,* Vortrag . . . gehalten vor der Evangelischen Akademie in Loccum am 19. Sept. 1957 (Hamburg, n.d.), p. 15.

tasks among my work and my responsibilities to the Writers Club and it accompanied my work as a reviewer."[48]

Similarly Horst Bienek has championed the rediscovery of German-Jewish writers. In his so-called Silesian Trilogy he has deliberately included Jewish writers who once lived in Silesia, even unearthing some completely forgotten, such as Alphons Silbergleit, a poet and short story writer who died in a concentration camp.[49] In addition, Bienek became, for a while, a kind of unpaid literary agent for Hermann Kesten, whose descriptions of the literary world he particularly admired. At last Bienek was able to convince the Ullstein-Verlag to publish Kesten's works in their entirety.[50]

Heinrich Böll, for his part, has appointed himself—to use his word—the "minesweeper" for Germany, which, in his opinion, is still mined with antisemitism. Therefore he reviews books and encourages radio and television series that are likely to dispel prejudices. He most clearly defines his intent in a foreword to a reprint edition of Heinz Liepman's *Das Vaterland* (1933, 1981): "May this book remind younger readers how much of Germany was driven out of Germany."[51] It is important to add that Drewitz, Bienek, and Böll do not stand alone.[52]

Perhaps this paper calls for an epilogue. There are, at most, sixty thousand declared and undeclared Jews today in Germany and Austria, some of them born there, some born in Eastern Europe. Among this tiny number there are established and neophyte German-Jewish writers. Of the generation over sixty there is Wolfgang Hildesheimer, living in Switzerland, but a frequent visitor of West Germany and Austria. He has stated that his Jewishness is, salutarily, never a topic of conversation with his non-Jewish fellow writers.[53] There is Hilde Domin, who sees in Judaism

48. Drewitz, *Die zerstörte Kontinuität,* pp. 13–14, 18.

49. See Horst Bienek's description of the genesis of the Silesian Trilogy entitled *Beschreibung einer Provinz* (Munich, 1983). References to Alphons Silbergleit are on pp. 56, 62, 91, 99, 115, 130–32, 142, 149, 164. Exiled writers mentioned include Max Tau (pp. 84, 91, 121), Hermann Kesten (p. 185), Manés Sperber (p. 218), Nelly Sachs (p. 225), and Elias Canetti (p. 226). See also the discussion of exile in general, p. 217.

50. Interview with Horst Bienek at his home in Ottobrunn, August 1983.

51. Heinrich Böll, foreword to *Das Vaterland,* by Heinz Liepman, in Böll, *Vermintes Gelände: Essayistische Schriften, 1977–1981* (Cologne, 1982), pp. 83, 28.

52. Rudolf Krämer-Badoni was among the first to discover Arno Reinfrank; Hermann Kasack and Fritz Usinger encouraged the publications of essays by exile writers under the aegis of the Deutsche Akademie für Sprache und Literatur, Darmstadt—to give, randomly, a few further examples.

53. See Wolfgang Hildesheimer's untitled essay in *Mein Judentum,* ed. Hans Jürgen Schulz (Stuttgart, 1978), p. 271.

a *Schicksalsgemeinschaft,* a joint fate.[54] And there are Günter Anders and Robert Jungk. In East Germany there is Stefan Heym, who has just written an Ahasverus novel.[55] But among the middle generation there are other luminaries such as Jurek Becker, Günter Kunert, and Wolf Biermann. And strange as it may seem, given the uncertainties of their stay, there are some very young Jewish authors in West Germany, born there after World War II or the born-abroad children of refugees, who have begun to write. Names such as Peter Finkelgrün, born 1943 in Shanghai, or Jeannette Lander, born 1931 in New York, who writes promising poems and novellas, will scarcely evoke recognition as yet.[56] Are they and others like them harbingers of tomorrow, and will their lives call for a continued study of the cooperation between German-Jewish and German-Christian writers? This relationship would be, in the opinion of Hilde Domin, the repatriated poet, something bordering on the miraculous. But she adds lines from one of her poems that command us not to rule out the occurrence of miracles:

> Nicht müde werden
> sondern dem Wunder leise
> wie einem Vogel
> die Hand hinhalten.

> Do not tire
> but towards the miracle
> softly,
> as if to a bird,
> hold out your hand.[57]

In the ongoing dialectic between despair and faith, that seems a small enough thing to ask, especially by a Jewish exile writer continuing to live and work in Germany. And in the light of the findings detailed above, this tentative hope of a hope may not be entirely unjustified.

54. See Hilde Domin's untitled essay in ibid., p. 107.

55. Stefan Heym, *Ahasverus* (Munich, 1981).

56. See Peter Finkelgrün, "Freunde von gestern—und Feinde von heute," in *Fremd im eigenen Land,* pp. 116–31; Jeannette Lander "Unsicherheit ist Freiheit," in ibid., pp. 28–64.

57. The poem concludes Hilde Domin's untitled essay in *Mein Judentum,* p. 117.

WERNER E. MOSSE

Wilhelm II and the *Kaiserjuden*

A Problematical Encounter

THE TWO CULTURES

Imperial Germany was a nation not of one national culture but of at least two cultures, which one might label, respectively, the official "Knackfuss culture" and the "Fontane-Liebermann counterculture."[1] Theodor Fontane was well aware both of the dichtomy between the two cultures and of the relationship between each and ethnicity. These are delineated in perhaps his best-known poem, written in 1894, "On My Seventy-Fifth Birthday":

> At the head of battles and my enthusiasm
> Marched the Pfuels and the Itzenplitzes,
> The Ribbecks, the Kattes, the Bülows and Arnims,
> The Treskows and Schliefens and Schliebens
> Marched from the Uckermark, Havelland, and Barnim—
> And I wrote about all of them.

> But those who came on this day of rejoicing
> Bore very different names.
> They also were "sans peur et reproche," without fear
>   and reproach,
> Yet of almost prehistoric nobility:
> We cannot name all of those ending in "berg" and "heim,"
> They came in crowds,
> The Meyers came in battalions,

---

1. What could be considered a third subculture—that of modernism/expressionism—lies outside the purview of the present study.

Also Polacks and those who live further east,
Abram, Isack, Israel,
All the patriarchs were on the spot
And put me kindly in the lead.
Why should I still want the Itzenplitzes!
I have been somebody for everybody,
They all read me.
They all knew me long ago.
And that is what counts . . . "Come on, Cohn."[2]

The association between culture and ethnicity is clearly implied.

Two years later, the antisemitic Baroness Hildegard von Spitzemberg described in her diary two cultural events of the Berlin season. The first was the premiere, in December 1896, of Gerhart Hauptmann's *Die versunkene Glocke:* "The house was filled to the last place with Jews and Jew-companions and with the representatives of press and literature, Harden, Sudermann, Erich Schmidt, Fontane, Pietsch, the last of whom, however, shook their heads disapprovingly and did not join in the frenetic applause of the poet's supporters."[3]

A few months later, to celebrate the hundredth anniversary of the birth of Wilhelm I, the court poet, Ernst von Wildenbruch, concocted an allegorical play. The baroness, who denied herself the pleasure of witnessing the premiere performance in person, recorded the impression of her acquaintances: "The play *Willehalm* must be terrible, a pedestrian allegory, stale, wearisome, in parts with a positively comical effect. It is said that, besides Wildenbruch, the Kaiser and Kuno Moltke also had a hand in it, which would explain the flop."[4] Again, the two events recorded in the diary of Hildegard von Spitzemberg indicate both the existence of "two cultures" and their ethnic overtones.

Finally, Heinrich Mann, some years later, included in one of his less admirable productions the following characteristic dialogue:

"This Klempner is an insufferable person!"
"What do you want? These people from Silesia and Posen stand everywhere in one's way. They manage everything these days."
He shrugged his shoulders.

2. Theodor Fontane, "Am meinem Fünfundsiebzigsten," in his *Gesammelte Werke*, ed. Ernst Heilborn (Berlin, 1915), 1:191–92.
3. Hildegard von Spitzemberg, diary, December 2, 1896, *Das Tagebuch der Baronin Spitzemberg*, ed. Rudolf Vierhaus, 3d ed. (Göttingen, 1963), pp. 348–49.
4. Ibid., April 7, 1897, p. 355: "Marschall von Bieberstein," the baroness added, "war entsetzt wie alle, die das Stück gelesen und noch mehr die, die es gesehen haben." The sentiments were echoed by Ernst Bassermann. See Karola Bassermann, *Ernst Bassermann* (Mannheim, 1919), p. 86.

"There's something of an eastern flavor about the new German Culture."[5]

The adepts of the "Fontane"—or, perhaps more appropriately, the "Fontane-Liebermann culture"—were largely, though by no means exclusively, Jews, and it is, perhaps, not accidental that while its representative artistic figure was the Jewish painter Max Liebermann[6] and the leading literary exponent Theodor Fontane from the French colony, Fontane's counterpart in the "Knackfuss culture" was Ernst von Wildenbruch, an illegitimate offspring of the house of Hohenzollern.[7] Wildenbruch's poetry was not of a quality designed to ensure immortality—as the following samples show:

Christmas on Strange Seas

Christmas wanders faithfully, quickly
Up to the far and strange bay;
White ships rock in the wind,
German ships which it had been looking for.
Christmas swings on board,
A light goes on above the ships,
The crew is sleeping and takes no notice,
Its sweet word rises in a song. . . .

Germany and the World

The large and rich world
Became bare, poor and empty.
The world no longer has a soul,
It no longer has a Germany![8]

5. Heinrich Mann, *Im Schlaraffenland* (1900; reprint, Hamburg, 1966), p. 189.

6. Max Liebermann, descendant of an old Jewish industrial family in Berlin and related to the Rathenaus, may be regarded as the representative painter of the alternative culture. Not only did he paint an often-reproduced portrait of Emil Rathenau for the AEG, but, through the intermediary of his friend Eduard Arnhold, he obtained commissions to paint, among others, director Henry Nathan for the Dresdner Bank and Geheimrat Franz Oppenheim for the Agfa. For Liebermann's relations with Eduard Arnhold, see *Eduard Arnhold, Ein Gedenkbuch* (Berlin, 1928), pp. 221–22. James Simon humorously described the celebrated painter's self-esteem: "Es gibt doch nur zwei Maler, Sie, Herr Professor Liebermann und Velasquez." "Wieso Velasquez?" *Heute sprach ich mit . . .* , ed. Cecile Lowenthal-Hensel and Arnold Paucker (Stuttgart, 1971), p. 153. For Liebermann's place in German and Jewish culture, see Peter Gay, "Encounter with Modernism: German Jews in German Culture, 1888–1914," *Midstream* 21, no. 2 (February 1975): 28–30.

7. The dramas of Ernst von Wildenbruch, an offspring of Prince Louis Ferdinand of Prussia, were accepted for the stage by the Duke of Meiningen. See Ernest K. Bramstedt, *Aristocracy and the Middle-Classes in Germany* (Chicago and London, 1964), p. 292; and Alfred Biese, *Deutsche Literaturgeschichte* (Munich, 1917), 3:459.

8. Ernst von Wildenbruch, "Christmas on Strange Seas" and "Germany and the World," in Theodor Echtermeyer, comp., *Auswahl Deutscher Gedichte* (Halle, 1931), pp. 381, 715.

Perhaps the most prominent product and exponent of the "Knackfuss culture," however, was no less a personage than Kaiser Wilhelm II himself.

THE PROTAGONISTS

The major components of Wilhelm II's cultural world have been perceptively analyzed by Lamar Cecil. The foundations of the young prince's personal culture were well and truly laid at the aristocratic university of Bonn in the aristocratic student corps Borussia and among the aristocratic officers of a regiment of Grenadier Guards then stationed in the city.[9] It is, however, characteristic that the future Kaiser also took pleasure in the lectures of the eminent art historian Karl von Justi. The professor's assessment of his pupil was perceptive and not uncritical: "He is lively and quick in perception, but of by no means outstanding ability. . . . For the rest, he appears as decided in his opinions as he is quick in forming them and then to close his mind to any countervailing considerations."[10] A further facet of the prince's cultural background is represented by his marriage (early in 1881) to princess Auguste Viktoria of Schleswig-Holstein. What linked him to a wife devoid of beauty, social graces, and wealth, was the fervent Protestantism (verging, at least in her case, on Puritan bigotry) that the pair had shared since early youth. Characteristically, they had figured among the early admirers of court preacher Adolf Stöcker.[11] A further component of the prince's general culture had been the experience of military service among aristocratic guards officers. "So geht es mir nun mit meinem Sohn," his father lamented in 1883, "er ist der richtige Gardeleutenant."[12] Even after his marriage the prince continued to divert himself in the officers' messes, particularly those of aristocratic regiments stationed in Potsdam, and to enjoy the society he found there.[13]

It was in this general cultural matrix that the more specific elements of the "Knackfuss culture" germinated and took root. Besides the sickly sweet patriotic imperialism of a Wildenbruch, three further manifestations might be mentioned. If Wildenbruch could be considered the bard of the "Knackfuss culture," its artistic exponent was, beyond a doubt, court painter Professor Hermann Knackfuss. Among the professor's representative paintings, one, in the genesis of which the Kaiser himself had

9. Lamar Cecil, "Wilhelm II und die Juden," in *Juden im Wilhelminischen Deutschland, 1890–1914,* ed. Werner E. Mosse (Tübingen, 1976), pp. 313–18.

10. Quoted in ibid., p. 317.   11. Ibid., pp. 319, 325–27.
12. Quoted in ibid., p. 319.   13. Ibid.

taken a hand, concerned itself with one of Wilhelm II's lifelong obsessions, the so-called Yellow Peril. As Lamar Cecil has explained:

> With the intention of opening the eyes of Europe to the peril . . .
> Wilhelm designed, in the summer of 1895, a sketch of an imaginative
> picture, which he entitled "Peoples of Europe, Safeguard Your Most
> Sacred Possessions!" He then commissioned Professor Hermann Knack-
> fuss, an artist renowned for his vast religious canvases, to create a paint-
> ing based on this sketch. The result was a monumental oil painting
> showing the Archangel Michael, patron saint of the Germans, urging on
> the peoples of Europe—Germania in the van, Britannia skulking sub-
> missively in the background—to take up together the struggle against the
> Asiatic menace represented by a Buddha spawning hordes of yellow
> gnomes.[14]

Wilhelm II was delighted with the result. Not only did he dispatch copies
of the picture to European dignitaries—including the president of the
French Republic and the cardinal archbishop of Naples—but he also advertised it through high officials in Berlin and through German overseas
shipping lines.[15]

Of the court sculptor Reinhold Begas, a further representative of the
"Knackfuss culture," Carl Fürstenberg, a personal friend whose own
artistic taste (like his general culture) was not above suspicion, wrote
diplomatically in his memoirs: "Wahrscheinlich hätte sich seine Kunst in
noch reineren Bahnen entwickelt, wenn nicht der Geschmack seiner
Auftraggeber . . . ihn zu einem allzu grossen Reichtum der Formenge-
bung gedrängt hätte. Als er dann gar, unter der Regierung Wilhelms II,
zum offiziellen Bildhauer des Kaiserreichs gemacht wurde, erlitt seine
Kunst eine Belastungsprobe, der sie in vielen Fällen nicht gewachsen
war."[16]

Wilhelm's musical interests, in his youth, had been Wagnerian (one of
the few areas where the "Knackfuss culture" overlapped, if to a limited
extent, with the tastes of the counterculture). Through his intimate friend
Philipp zu Eulenburg-Hertefeld, himself an amateur composer, he was
introduced to the Wagner family. When, in 1889, the young Kaiser paid
his first visit to Bayreuth, Cosima Wagner recorded her impressions:
"The emperor is personally very sympathetic, but to explain to him even
the rudiments of art, I would have to spend with him three years on a

14. Ibid., pp. 333–34.   15. Ibid., p. 334 and n. 72.
16. Carl Fürstenberg, *Die Lebensgeschichte eines deutschen Bankiers Niedergeschrie-
ben von Hans Fürstenberg* (Berlin, 1931), p. 227.

desert island alone."[17] It is interesting to speculate whose sufferings would have been the more intense. In fact, as Cosima may well have felt, the Kaiser's enthusiasm for the works of "The Master" was probably little more than skin deep. His musical preference, it seems, lay in a different direction: "Although the horn of his car sounded the thunder-motif from *Rheingold,* Wilhelm preferred the operas of Lortzing, Auber or Meyerbeer to Wagner's vast spectacles."[18] It was, at any rate, not yet the time of Franz Lehár's *Merry Widow.*

A more lasting enrichment of the Kaiser's "Knackfuss culture" arising from the Wagner connection resulted, however, from his meeting with Houston Stewart Chamberlain, Wagner's son-in-law. Chamberlain's recently published *Die Grundlagen des neunzehnten Jahrhunderts* (1899) became, for a time at least, the Kaiser's bible and the basis of his philosophic-historical world view. The impact of the work is described by Lamar Cecil:

> Chamberlain's popular work . . . soon attracted the emperor's attention. Wilhelm, never able to concentrate for long, had difficulty in reading anything to the end, let alone a swollen work of over a thousand pages. He therefore obliged wholly unsuited persons, as for example General Anton von Mackensen, to read the book aloud. The contents of the work he digested so thoroughly that he could quote whole pages by heart. Wilhelm II found many of Chamberlain's arguments irresistible, and before long he inflicted on Auguste Viktoria and her suite nightly readings from the masterpiece. To be subjected to such a long and meandering treatise induced in many listeners . . . a yawning boredom, but, given the Kaiser's enthusiasm, there was no escaping.[19]

In a letter after their first meeting, the Kaiser had gushed to Chamberlain: "Ihr Buch dem deutschen Volk und Sie persönlich mir, sandte Gott, das ist bei mir ein unumstösslich fester Glaube."[20] More serious, Wilhelm II tried to spread the gospel by making the book compulsory reading in all Prussian colleges for the training of secondary school teachers.[21] Such, in brief, was the cultural profile of the most prominent exponent of the "Knackfuss culture."

The representatives of the counterculture, whose company the Kaiser sought, were drawn from a very different cultural background. They tended to represent *Besitz-* rather than *Bildungsbürgertum,* though at any

---

17. Quoted in Cecil, "Wilhelm II und die Juden," p. 330.
18. Quoted in ibid.   19. Ibid.   20. Quoted in ibid., p. 331.
21. Ibid., pp. 330–31.

rate in the case of the Jews among them, the boundaries between the two were fluid. The men of Jewish extraction honored by the Kaiser's attention have gone down in history as the *Kaiserjuden*. This was a derogatory term coined almost certainly by the Zionist leader Chaim Weizmann and originally employed in a sense different from subsequent usage. In his autobiography *Trial and Error,* published in London in 1949, Weizmann, commenting on a conversation with two prominent spokesmen of the Hilfsverein der deutschen Juden, observed, "They were the usual type of *Kaiserjuden,* like Albert Ballin and Max Warburg, more German than the Germans, obsequious, super-patriotic, eagerly anticipating the wishes and plans of the masters of Germany."[22] While Weizmann, carried away by his double prejudice against German Jews and against Germany in general (clearly British patriotism was, in his eyes, a less venial sin) meant to stigmatize a particular *type* of German Jew, the term *Kaiserjuden* came later to be applied to the small group of men of Jewish origin whom Wilhelm II would meet on occasion and with whom he liked to converse. It is with this group that the present paper is concerned.

To translate the term *Kaiserjuden* as "court Jews"—though tempting—is inappropriate. These were men of wealth, standing, and independent position, by no means dependent financially or in any other respect on the ruler—not even to the extent that the belated "court Jew" Gerson Bleichröder had been on Otto von Bismarck. *Kaiserjude,* in fact, was not a clearly defined status and carried no recognizable badge of office. Who qualified for the appellation lay largely in the eye of the beholder, or to adapt the famous words attributed to Karl Lueger, the antisemitic burgomaster of Vienna, "Wer Kaiserjude ist, bestimme ich." Withal, there exists a consensus that points to Albert Ballin of the Hapag as the quintessential *Kaiserjude,* perhaps also the first. It was through Ballin that the Kaiser met, in turn, the Jewish bankers Max Warburg and Carl Fürstenberg. Independent of this trio, Wilhelm II also developed friendly relations with the Jewish "Cotton-King" James Simon, the coal magnate Eduard Arnhold, and the former banker Ludwig Max Goldberger. He also met, if less frequently, a number of others, among them Emil and Walther Rathenau, the veteran industrialist Wilhelm Herz, and the coal magnate Fritz Friedländer (after his baptism Fritz von Friedländer-Fuld). Usually included among the *Kaiserjuden* were the banker brothers Franz and Robert von Mendelssohn, as well as their

22. Chaim Weizmann, *Trial and Error* (London, 1949), pp. 183–84.

cousin Ernst von Mendelssohn-Bartholdy.[23] Associated with the *Kaiserjuden*, though still further removed from Jewishness, was the banker-politician Bernhard Dernburg. The dozen or so *Kaiserjuden* accordingly represented an important segment of the Jewish *haute bourgeoisie* of Wilhelmine Germany.[24]

In cultural terms, these *Kaiserjuden* formed a somewhat heterogeneous group. The common denominator, perhaps, was that they represented, in the widest sense, a "commercial culture" or, perhaps, subculture, distinct from the military-feudal-landowning, nationalist, Lutheran "Knackfuss culture." It was a distinction, moreover, that overlapped, even if it did not fully coincide, with another. In contradistinction to the proponents of the official culture, prominent members of the counterculture tended to be maritime, outward looking, liberal, and, broadly, Anglophile. Friedrich Naumann perceptively distinguished the two cultures in an essay published in 1909 in the *Neue Rundschau* under the title "Potsdam und Hamburg."[25]

In a more narrowly cultural sense, the *Kaiserjuden* were a mixed batch. On the one hand, they included among their number highly cultured men like the great art collectors and connoisseurs Eduard Arnhold and James Simon. Thus Arnhold, described as "one of the most knowledgeable collectors of modern French and German paintings," owned, besides the works of many German painters, paintings by Goya and Manet, Pissaro, Sisley, Renoir, and Degas.[26] His wider cultural interests

23. For the relations of the Mendelssohns and the Kaiser, see Felix Gilbert, *Bankiers, Künstler und Gelehrte* (Tübingen, 1975), pp. xliv–xlv; and Wilhelm Treue, "Das Bankhaus Mendelssohn," in *Mendelssohn-Studien*, vol. 1 (Berlin, 1972), p. 49.

24. This was in part a loosely structured group, in part a collection of individuals. Carl Fürstenberg, in his memoirs, speaks of a circle "der, in mehr oder weniger direkter Fühlungnahme, aus Albert Ballin, Walther Rathenau, Bernhard Dernburg, Max Warburg, einigen anderen [Fürstenberg might at least have named his erstwhile friend Fritz Friedländer, but they had quarreled and broken off relations] und mir selbst bestand." Fürstenberg, *Lebensgeschichte,* p. 426. Of the rest, while Arnhold and Isidor Loewe were fast friends, the others, although all knew each other, had no particular ties. In the most comprehensive list of *Kaiserjuden,* Jacob Toury names in the first place Albert Ballin, Eduard Arnhold, James Simon, Carl Fürstenberg, Ludwig Max Goldberger, and Emil and Walther Rathenau. As *Kaiserjuden* of the second order (*In zweiter Linie*), he includes Georg Solmssen (b. Salomonsohn), Wilhelm Herz, Franz von Mendelssohn, Max Steinthal, Maximilian Kempner, Max M. Warburg, Heinrich Grünfeld, Benjamin Liebermann, and Fritz von Friedländer-Fuld. Jacob Toury, *Die politischen Orientierungen der Juden in Deutschland* (Tübingen, 1966), p. 239. For the purposes of the present paper, it is unnecessary to discuss the economic activities and personalities of these men.

25. See Eduard Rosenbaum, "Albert Ballin," *Leo Baeck Institute Year Book* 3 (1958): 270.

26. Karl Schwarz, "Kunstsammler," in *Juden im deutschen Kulturbereich,* ed. Siegmund Kaznelson, 3d. ed. (Berlin, 1962), p. 121.

were far ranging, as witnessed by his correspondence with a galaxy of artistic and scientific luminaries of the age.[27] The interests of the great patron and collector James Simon, on the other hand, lay in a different direction. Cofounder of the German Orient Society, he offered munificent support to its excavations in Babylon, Assur, Jericho, Galilee, and Egypt. For the opening of the Kaiser-Friedrich Museum in Berlin, he donated a whole room of Italian paintings, bronze statuettes, medallions, coins, and miniatures. In 1920 he presented to the Deutsches Museum a collection of early Christian art, wooden sculptures, and Gobelins. His gifts represented the greatest ever made to a German museum.[28]

Moreover, the collecting activities and patronage of an Arnhold or Simon were harmoniously blended into a patrician life-style. Thus Arnhold's art collections, which included mainly works of the Renaissance and impressionism, "created a precious and harmonious setting for the distinguished sociability cultivated here."[29] In a similar manner, the home of Robert von Mendelssohn and his Italian-born wife Giullietta provided a tasteful background for the delicate musical culture practiced there. It is described by Leila von Meister, an American-born friend of the Mendelssohn family:

> The Mendelssohns' music room in itself is a frame that promotes inspiration. Finely proportioned and sparingly furnished in perfect taste the room is dominated by three magnificent Corots. The characteristic silvery-grey tones of the landscapes, so full of mysterious charm, seem to invite the recueillement necessary for the true appreciation of the art to which the room is dedicated.

The star of the musical counterculture, its Liebermann or Fontane, may well have been Richard Strauss. "We had a thrilling evening a little while ago," Leila von Meister wrote in April 1904,

> when Richard Strauss, who is at this moment undoubtedly Germany's greatest composer, conducted one of his recent works at the Philharmonic—"Ein Heldenleben: Sinfonische Dichtung für Orchester." . . . We found our seats were almost directly behind the Mendelssohns and old Joachim the violinist who, with the score of the work that was to be performed on his knees, was deeply engrossed in it.[30]

27. Wilhelm Treue, "Caesar Wollheim und Eduard Arnhold," *Tradition* 6 (June 1961): 104–5. Arnhold's cultural contacts were wide ranging, even if their quality may, of necessity, have been somewhat uneven.

28. Schwarz, "Kunstsammler," p. 121.

29. Paul Landau, "Gesellschafts-Kultur," in *Juden im deutschen Kulturbereich*, p. 912.

30. Leila von Meister also observed: "Robert Mendelssohn upholds the family tra-

Culture of a different—if more dillettantish—kind was represented by Walther Rathenau, scientist, philosopher, and publicist, as well as amateur painter with a lively interest in the visual arts.[31] On the other hand, self-made men like Albert Ballin, from a lower-middle-class background, or Carl Fürstenberg, offspring of a provincial merchant family, lacked conspicuous cultural interests or attainments. Formal education, in many cases, did not go beyond a modest secondary schooling, topped off, however, by extensive travel and by practical and commercial experience gained through high-level business contacts both in Germany and, significantly, abroad. The *Kaiserjuden,* typically, were men of experience who, through their numerous contacts, had learned also to be "men of the world." As a rule they distinguished themselves from the bulk of their non-Jewish peers by the extent of their intelligence, intellectual agility, range of cultural interests, and knowledge of the world and its ways. The common denominator for most was, perhaps, a form of worldly wisdom coupled with diplomatic skills and psychological insight. (In this as in other respects, the unfortunate Walther Rathenau, who strove so hard to be a true imperial *Kaiserjude,* was atypical.) The cultural contrast, thus, between the disciple of Houston Stewart Chamberlain and the Jewish subjects whose company he sometimes sought could hardly be greater.

ENCOUNTERS

There are a few accounts of early encounters between Wilhelm II and members of the Jewish economic elite. In January 1891, with the liner *Auguste Victoria* about to set sail from Cuxhaven for the Hapag's first pleasure cruise in the Mediterranean, the Kaiser, who happened to be in town, gave in to a spontaneous desire to visit the ship. It was the occasion of his first meeting with Albert Ballin.[32] On leaving the *Auguste Victoria* after the inspection, Wilhelm II was heard to tell Ballin: "Brin-

---

ditions by always having wonderful music in his house. He is himself a good cellist and his wife Guillietta [*sic*]—an Italian by birth—is an absolutely first-class pianist. That this rare combination of talents attracts the best artistic elements to the Mendelssohns' house is not surprising. Eleonora Duse always stays there when she is playing in Berlin, and Joachim is an old intimate and a regular guest at the little 'Sunday supper' gatherings. . . . On these occasions Joachim and the two Mendelssohns combine a programme of heavenly chamber music—trios, quartets, quintets, according to what artists happen to be present—to fill the different parts." All quotations from Leila Meister, *Gathered Yesterdays* (New York, 1964), quoted in Treue, "Das Bankhaus Mendelssohn" pp. 54–55.

31. Hans Fürstenberg, *Erinnerungen* (Düsseldorf and Vienna, 1968), pp. 101–2.
32. Rosenbaum, "Albert Ballin," p. 267.

gen Sie unsere Landsleute nur auf die See, das wird der Nation und Ihrer Gesellschaft reiche Früchte tragen."³³ Ballin, however, dates the beginning of his closer acquaintance with the Kaiser from the preparations for the opening of the Kiel Canal in 1895. As member of a committee to plan the opening ceremony, which met under the Kaiser's chairmanship at the palace in Berlin, Ballin spoke up boldly for the interest of the Hapag against the officially favored Lloyd.³⁴ The opening disagreement was characteristic of the Kaiser's first meeting with more than one of the *Kaiserjuden*. It proved, however, no obstacle to cordial relations between the two men. While Ballin came to enjoy free access to the Kaiser in Berlin, the latter's visits to the Ballin villa became so frequent—at least for a time—that the press, with gross exaggeration, chose to dub it "Klein-Potsdam."³⁵

Through Ballin, Wilhelm II met his friend and banker Max Warburg. Warburg himself recorded their first meeting: "It was in the year 1903 that I came face to face with him [Wilhelm II] for the first time. Prince Bülow had told Ballin that it was desirable, perhaps even necessary, to deliver a lecture about financial reform to the Kaiser. He proposed me for the task, and Ballin took it upon himself to talk with me." Warburg was to meet the Kaiser after a dinner to be held in Cuxhaven in connection with the annual Elbe regatta. But only ten minutes were allocated for the interview, so Warburg declined. A few weeks later the authorities conceded thirty-two minutes. Warburg, not unreasonably, asked for more. "Nun aber wurde Ballin heftig, und mir blieb nichts anderes übrig, als mich zu fügen." The conversation with the Kaiser took an unexpected turn. Wilhelm, it appears, chose to open it with the statement: "Die Russen gehen nächstens pleite," with which Warburg courageously disagreed. "Nein Majestät, die Russen gehen nicht pleite." The Kaiser insisted: "Die Russen gehen doch pleite." After three minutes of this argument Wilhelm turned his back and left Max Warburg standing.

An inauspicious beginning. But the following year, after the Elbe

33. Quoted in Bernhard Huldermann, *Albert Ballin* (Oldenburg and Berlin, 1921), p. 282; also quoted in Rosenbaum, "Albert Ballin," p. 270.

34. "Ballin objected in his usual low voice, that the Lloyd of Bremen should precede the Hapag ship at the festivities starting from Hamburg on June 20th. The Kaiser said that he had already given his promise to the Lloyd. Ballin withdrew, but emphasized that he nevertheless felt justified in making his objection." Huldermann, *Albert Ballin*, p. 194; also quoted in Rosenbaum, "Albert Ballin," p. 270. For a fuller and more picturesque account, see Carl Fürstenberg, *Lebengeschichte*, pp. 434–36.

35. Cecil, "Wilhelm II und die Juden," p. 341. For a more detailed account, see Lamar Cecil, *Albert Ballin: Business and Politics in Imperial Germany, 1888–1918* (Princeton, 1967), pp. 98–142.

regatta, the Kaiser himself called Warburg and invited him to explain *Finanzreform.* Warburg did so for more than one hour. It was the beginning of regular, if infrequent, meetings. "Von da an traf ich den Kaiser alljährlich in ungezwungener Weise nach den Regatten beim Diner in Cuxhaven und wurde auch einmal ins Schloss in Berlin gebeten."[36]

This encounter as described (in, perhaps, a slightly embellished form) by Warburg, is interesting in several respects. In the first place, it shows the Kaiser in his typical position regarding his dealings with the *Kaiserjuden*—that of learner. Second, there are his characteristic slightly vulgar (*burschikos*) language, the opening disagreement, oddly reminiscent of Ballin's first encounter with the Kaiser, the notable fact that the Kaiser, as in the case of Ballin, bore Warburg no lasting resentment. Finally, there is no sign whatever of the servility alleged by Weizmann against the *Kaiserjuden.*

Another whom the Kaiser met through Ballin was Carl Fürstenberg, who recalled:

> To my friendship with Ballin I owe the beginnings of my acquaintance with Kaiser Wilhelm II. One day, Ballin had been received by the Kaiser and found him in a very depressed state. He complained about the difficulties created for him on all sides and the lack of understanding for his inexhaustible efforts for the well-being of the Fatherland. Finally he expressed a wish to talk at long last to someone amusing and intelligent placed completely outside the usual cliques of the court and political parties. Ballin had then considered it appropriate to mention my name. The result was an invitation calling me to the imperial castle for a small supper party.

Hitherto, Fürstenberg had met the Kaiser only on stiff official occasions that he had not enjoyed. "Das Zusammensein im kleinsten Kreise dagegen erwies sich nicht nur als eine grosse Auszeichnung, sondern auch als ein wirkliches Vergnügen."[37]

What is significant here is not only the mode of the Kaiser's approach to Ballin—both the fact in itself and the nature of the request—but also the reasons given. It is also important to note the operation of an informal "network" through which both Max Warburg (though the original initiative in his case came from Bernhard von Bülow) and Fürstenberg were introduced to the Kaiser through the agency of Ballin. The three men were closely acquainted not only professionally but also personally and socially.

36. Max M. Warburg, *Aus meinen Aufzeichnungen* (New York, 1950), pp. 30–31.
37. Carl Fürstenberg, *Lebensgeschichte*, p. 439.

James Simon, who did not belong to this particular circle, met the Kaiser in a manner no less characteristic. Simon had secured the election of his friend Admiral Fritz von Hollmann, who enjoyed Wilhelm II's favors, to the vice-presidency of the reorganized German Orient Society. It was through Hollmann that Simon was introduced to Wilhelm II. Simon's friend and biographer, the journalist Ernst Feder, recorded:

> Presented to the monarch in Kiel on the yacht *Hohenzollern* in pouring rain, he [Simon] knew how to interest him in the society. When the emperor asked whether they had any special wishes for their excavations, Simon remarked that the Director-General of the Turkish museums in Constantinople created difficulties for them everywhere. Whereupon Wilhelm II observed in his temperamental way: "I will wring the creature's neck." He helped wherever he could, and his personal intervention removed many obstacles.[38]

Simon's housekeeper of many years, Therese Marner, emphasized that it was not Simon but the Kaiser who at all points took the initiative[39]— and the same is true in the Kaiser's relationships with most of the other *Kaiserjuden.*

Walther Rathenau became acquainted with the Kaiser in a different but no less characteristic manner when, in February 1900, he gave a talk in the Postmuseum in Berlin on "Elektrische Alchymie"—the use of hydroelectric power in electrochemical works. After the talk Rathenau demonstrated some electrochemical experiments, an acetylene burner (for signaling and the use of lighthouses), an explosion of natrium on water, Becquerel rays, and the Nernst electrical bulb long promoted by the AEG. A conversation between the Kaiser and Rathenau ensued, with the former opening the exchanges in characteristic style: "Danke Ihnen für den Vortrag. Ausserordentlich interessant. Famos, mit solchen Kräften rumzuwirtschaften, als ob es gar nichts wäre." "Schönes Licht, die Azetylenflamme," was a further comment. And, a little later in the con-

---

38. Ernst Feder, "James Simon," MS in the Archives of the Leo Baeck Institute, New York. The bulk of this document (hereafter "James Simon" MS) has been incorporated in Feder's "James Simon: Industrialist, Art Collector, Philanthropist," *Leo Baeck Institute Year Book* 10 (1965): 3–23 (hereafter "James Simon," *LBIYB*). A section in the printed essay entitled "The 'Kaiserjude'" (p. 8), casts some doubt—perhaps rightly—on Chaim Weizmann's originating the term; it may be that he only gave it currency.

39. "J.S. hat sich nicht um Hofgunst gemüht [*sic*], aber als der Kaiser den Wunsch äusserte, ihn kennen zu lernen hat er sich nicht dagegen gesträubt. Admiral von Hollmann führte ihn dem Monarchen zu u. es war keine Audienz im üblichen Sinne keine nach Minuten bemessene. 1 1/2 Stunden sprachen Kaiser u. Untertan miteinander u. weder der eine noch der andere hatten bemerkt wie die Zeit verflog." Therese Marner to Ernst Feder, n.d., Archives of the Leo Baeck Institute, New York.

versation: "But above all, don't talk to me about petroleum! A foreign product—always price increases. And these petroleum lamps ruin the air in small apartments. We have to expand the hydroelectric facilities! In Silesia. Think of the waterfalls!"[40] What is characteristic, besides Wilhelm II's well-known idiosyncratic mode of expression and his perfectly legitimate dilettantism, is the fact that once again the Kaiser was in the position of learner in his relations with a *Kaiserjude*. The Kaiser's Jewish acquaintances were, in fact, almost invariably people capable of imparting information unobtainable from the assorted *Knackfüsse* of the imperial entourage.

There is no evidence to suggest, however, that Wilhelm II took to Rathenau as he did to several of the others. Rathenau, unlike other *Kaiserjuden,* was very much a member of the second generation, not only younger than the rest (except for Max Warburg) but, more significant, even younger than the Kaiser himself. In addition Rathenau possessed, and to a high degree, a quality uncongenial to Wilhelm II. Whereas the other *Kaiserjuden* carefully kept their distance both metaphorically and physically, the pompous Rathenau, to his own detriment, did not.[41] James Simon would later recall an unfortunate occasion when Wilhelm II had organized a talk on *Luftschiffahrt:* "In widerlicher Weise machte sich Walther Rathenau an den Kaiser heran, ihm dabei nahe auf den Leib rückend, was der Kaiser nicht liebte."[42] It is not surprising that the meetings between Wilhelm II and Rathenau—barely a dozen before 1914—remained infrequent compared to those with some other *Kaiserjuden.*

Most of Wilhelm II's encounters with representatives of the counterculture took place, significantly, in Hamburg, with the annual Elbe

40. The conversation is recorded in *Walther Rathenau: Hauptwerke und Gespräche,* ed. Ernst Schulin, vol. 2 of *Gesamtausgabe* (Munich, 1977), p. 621.

41. Hans Fürstenberg, who admired Rathenau, writes: "Schon in der Jugend hatte Walther Rathenaus aufrechte Gestalt etwas feierlich Würdiges. Er war stets gewählt gekleidet, mit einer Vorliebe für dunkelgestreifte Hosen, farbige Westen und hohe Kragen. . . . Das geradezu Erhabene an ihm beruhte in der Hauptsache auf seinem tiefen, sinnenden Blick, auf der Überlegenheit seiner Rede, auch auf seiner Grösse." *Erinnerungen,* p. 99. Rathenau was didactic and humorless, hardly company for Wilhelm II, with whom, however, he shared at least one vice: "Ähnlich wie Kaiser Wilhelm II, machte er manchmal Notizen mit einem Bleistift auf der blendend weissen Manschette, die damals gestärkt getragen wurde." Ibid., p. 106.

42. Quoted in Feder, "James Simon" MS, p. 267. The same unfortunate characteristic of Rathenau, again in something like a "teaching situation," is described by Hans Fürstenberg, who knew Rathenau from childhood: ". . . auf seiner Grösse, die ihm gestattete, den etwas Kleineren, wie mir, einen Arm lässig über die Schulter zu legen und dann, auf- und abschreitend, eine Ansprache zu halten, die man zunächst als unwiderleglich empfand." *Erinnerungen,* p. 99.

regatta at Cuxhaven, the German Derby, and the extension of the Hamburg season to the Kiel regattas the focal points. Symbolically Albert Ballin, the first *Kaiserjude* and the one closest to the Kaiser, was the presiding genius, next to Wilhelm himself, at these festivities. It was in Cuxhaven that Wilhelm had first met Max Warburg, and the city would remain the major venue of their contacts, and it was at Kiel on the imperial yacht that James Simon had been presented to the Kaiser. Eduard Arnhold's meeting with the Kaiser also had a nautical flavor. Arnhold accompanied Wilhelm II on two voyages that afforded opportunities for much informal conversation. Ernst Graf zu Rantzau recalled:

> The Kaiser appreciated him extraordinarily. Arnhold went on two boat trips with the Kaiser, and afterward he liked to talk about the goings-on on board, but without committing any indiscretions. It was noticeable that the Kaiser had talked with him frequently, and probably not always about unimportant topics. On several occasions Arnhold was called to Potsdam or the palace in Berlin for an audience.[43]

In July 1913, Ballin invited Arnhold, a close friend, who had recently been elevated to the Prussian Herrenhaus, to join him on the maiden voyage of the new Hapag liner *Imperator*. Those on board included, besides the Kaiser and Ballin as host, a plethora of high officials as well as a few "others." As Arnhold, in a telegraph letter, reported to his wife: "86 Gäste, darunter etwa 60 Exzellenzen; von der plebs nur Fürstenberg, Salomonsohn, Warburg, James Simon und meine Wenigkeit, M.d.H. sonst Delbrück, Breitenbach, Trott, Dallwitz, Kraetke, Sydow, Krupp und tausend andere Bekannte. Eben habe ich mit Ballin, dem 'Imperator' gefrühstückt."[44] It was also at the Kiel regatta that Wilhelm II showed much-appreciated kindness to the young daughter of Carl Fürstenberg[45] and that Marie-Anne von Friedländer-Fuld, Fritz Friedländer's only daughter, met her first (and short-lived) husband, the Hon. John Mitford.[46] Carl Fürstenberg described the general setting for the Kiel regattas against the background of German naval policy and thought that by

43. Ernst Graf zu Rantzau, "Der Mann des öffentlichen Lebens," in *Eduard Arnhold*, pp. 45–46.

44. Quoted in ibid., p. 174.

45. Described in Carl Fürstenberg, *Lebensgeschichte*, pp. 444–45. Carl Fürstenberg was exceptional among the *Kaiserjuden* in being distinctly susceptible to imperial condescension.

46. Fritz Friedländer, the delighted father of the bride, wrote to an acquaintance, "Die Bekanntschaft meiner Tochter stammt von der Kieler Woche her und ist, um es kurz zu sagen, gegenseitig eine absolute Liebesheirat." Fritz Friedländer to Graf Bogdan von Hutten-Czapski, October 29, 1913, Reichsarchiv in Potsdam VI 1 Hu. No. 1 5.

founding the Imperial Yachting Club in Kiel the Kaiser sought to provide that policy with a social setting:

> Competition with the imperial yacht *Meteor* drew a number of wealthy foreigners and Germans, who acquired great yachts. . . .[47] At the Kiel Week, the German society of the day met in a selection approved by the Kaiser. Ballin owed it to his, one might well say, friendly relations with the Kaiser that in this select society he played a prominent part. The Hapag, for these occasions, always provided one of its finest vessels, on which Ballin then gathered a good part of the guests assembled in Kiel. Kiel Week was generally preceded by regattas in Hamburg. The Kaiser then sailed either round the Skagerrak to Kiel—a voyage on which I was once privileged to accompany him on board the *Hohenzollern*—or through the Kaiser Wilhelm Canal, built for strategic reasons at great expense.[48]

It would appear that the Kaiser's contacts with subjects of the counterculture, however limited in number, were not without their psychological effect on this volatile monarch. In Hamburg and Kiel, in Friedrich Naumann's view at any rate, the Kaiser was a different person from the man he was in his court circle. At the Elbe regatta or at the Kiel Week, he mixed freely with men from different walks of life, unhampered by the strict etiquette of the court. Here the web of servility and intrigue that usually surrounded him was absent.[49] In short, in the freer atmosphere of the "maritime-commercial" culture, Wilhelm II was able, at least to some extent, to shed the old "Knackfuss."

The "Hamburg culture," at the same time, extended its tentacles—if weakly—in the direction of Berlin. It was, perhaps, not wholly accidental that contacts between Wilhelm II and the *Kaiserjuden* reached their apogee during the chancellorship of Bernhard von Bülow, himself an alien in the "Knackfuss culture," who was married to a foreign wife and had associations with Hamburg. Not only was Bülow on terms of respectful friendship with Ballin and his near-neighbor in Blankenese, Max Warburg (and to some extent with Walther Rathenau),[50] but he was

---

47. These included, besides a member of the Krupp family, such men of Jewish origin as the retired Silesian industrialist Oskar Huldschinsky and the Berlin banker Carl Hagen, broker of the better-known banker Louis Hagen of Cologne. For some details, see Carl Fürstenberg, *Lebensgeschichte,* p. 443. The history of the yachting exploits of "commodores" from the German-Jewish economic elite remains to be written.

48. Carl Fürstenberg, *Lebensgeschichte,* p. 443.

49. Friedrich Naumann is quoted in Rosenbaum, "Albert Ballin," pp. 270–71.

50. In the face of some opposition, Bernhard von Bülow in 1908 defended the conferment of some decoration on the overeager Walther Rathenau "weil er ein sehr fähiger, brauchbarer Mensch ist, und um zu zeigen, dass bei uns auch ungetaufte Juden

instrumental in the appointment of Bernhard Dernburg as state secretary
for the colonies and was at least prepared to consider further ministerial
appointments for men of the Jewish economic elite. More significant
than the role of Bülow, however, was that of Admiral Fritz von Hollmann, state secretary for the navy until 1897. Hollmann, who coinci-
dentally had been chosen by Emil Rathenau as chairman of the board
(*Aufsichtsratsvorsitzender*) of the AEG, became the major link in Berlin between the Kaiser and such of his prominent Jewish subjects as he
desired to meet. As Hildegard von Spitzemberg, in gross misrepresenta-
tion of the true state of affairs, confided to her diary in the autumn of
1908, "His Majesty, as everybody knows, is very fond of Hollmann, and
therefore people like Ballin, Rathenau, Fürstenberg, Friedländer, and
similar new men flatter him in all directions."[51] In fact, the initiative for
the bachelor luncheons occasionally organized by Hollmann, at which
Wilhelm II from time to time met some of the *Kaiserjuden,* came solely
from the Kaiser himself. At the same time, it is no doubt true that Emil
Rathenau had made the admiral chairman of his board (unquestionably
a lucrative appointment), while James Simon, as has been seen, had secured his election (no doubt less profitable) to the vice-presidency of the
German Orient Society. Whatever the relationships, was it pure accident
that a major link-man between Wilhelm II and his subjects of the alternative culture was a retired admiral?[52]

Why, it may be asked, did Wilhelm II, notwithstanding his strongly
articulated antisemitic prejudices, seek from time to time the company of
members of the Jewish economic elite?[53] For this there were several
reasons. One—perhaps not the most important—was that throughout his
life the Kaiser enjoyed the company of the wealthy[54]—if they were aris-

nicht immer als Parias behandelt werden." Bülow to Friedrich Wilhelm von Loebell,
December 27, 1908, quoted in *Walther Rathenau Tagebuch, 1907–1922,* ed. Hartmut
Pogge von Strandmann (Düsseldorf, 1967), p. 101.

51. Spitzemberg, diary, September 12, 1908, *Spitzemberg Tagebuch,* p. 488.

52. The German imperial navy, in general, yielded in nothing to the army in its
antisemitism. The naval officer who married Ballin's adopted daughter, a Christian, had
to quit the service immediately.

53. Wilhelm II's later argument that he had never known Ballin was a Jew (see
the sources given in Cecil, "Wilhelm II und die Juden," p. 343, n. 112) is, of course,
disingenuous. A good deal more interesting is the Kaiser's claim, recorded by his chief
of naval cabinet, Admiral Georg Alexander von Müller, and paraphrased by Lamar
Cecil, "dass sie in Wirklichkeit überhaupt keine *echten* Juden waren." Ibid., p. 342.
See also Cecil, *Albert Ballin,* pp. 98–99. "Real" Jews for Wilhelm II were people he
detested, like the journalists Maximilian Harden and Theodor Wolff of the *Berliner
Tageblatt.*

54. And a number of the wealthy were Jews: "So bewunderte er eine Reihe be-

tocratic to boot, that was just a bonus. A more important attraction—and a significant one—was that these men were disinterested (it was by this test that Walther Rathenau failed so miserably, as did the greater number of *Adelsjuden* to be considered later). Thus the former lord chamberlain, Robert Graf von Zedlitz und Trützschler, later recorded that of all the private individuals he invited, the Kaiser had held James Simon and Franz von Mendelssohn in the highest esteem, as he knew that neither would ever proffer a personal request.[55] "Kennen Sie James Simon?" Hollmann once overheard Wilhelm II ask Bülow. "Der will keine Orden und Auszeichnungen, der tut, was er tut, nur der Sache wegen."[56] Carl Fürstenberg, in turn, records a characteristic incident, once again on the authority of the ubiquitous Hollmann. When, on one occasion, a large sum of money was needed for a "good cause," the Kaiser's civil cabinet drew up a list of wealthy men to be approached (with offers of appropriate rewards). After preliminary contacts, Hollmann submitted the list to the Kaiser. "Als dann mein Name herankam," Fürstenberg reported, "bestimmte der Kaiser, dass man ihn von der Liste streichen möge. Ich bin sicher, dass er nichts von mir will, und er soll nicht glauben, dass ich etwas von ihm will, war seine Begründung."[57] Albert Ballin, in his turn, actually declined the proffered patent of nobility (an offer facilitated, in his case, by the absence of male descendants).[58]

The Kaiser's own attitude, however, notwithstanding his disclaimer in the case of Fürstenberg, was less disinterested. In the first place, men like Arnhold, the Mendelssohns, Ballin, and Fürstenberg were a valuable source of economic information not available elsewhere. Their wealth and goodwill, moreover, could be tapped for a great variety of public and patriotic objects. They would munificently support what they saw as good causes—among them relief in Silesia,[59] officers' homes in Bad Hom-

---

güterter Juden wie die Baroness Mathilde Rothschild und den Industriellen James Simon, die beide als Kunstmäzene galten und für ihre Wohltätigkeit bekannt waren." Cecil, "Wilhelm II und die Juden," p. 342.

55. Feder, "James Simon," *LBIYB*, p. 7.
56. Quoted in Feder, "James Simon" MS, p. 9.
57. Carl Fürstenberg, *Lebensgeschichte,* p. 442. "Ich verdanke die Kenntnis dieses Zwischenfalls einer Indiskretion des Freundes Hollmann." "Der Kaiser wusste," writes Fürstenberg (but was he wholly truthful?), "wie vollkommen gleichgültig ich nicht nur nach aussen, sondern auch innerlich den Auszeichnungen gegenüberstand, die zu verteilen er in der Lage war." Ibid., p. 441.
58. Feder, "James Simon" MS, p. 123.
59. Hildegard von Spitzemberg recorded in her diary: "Am 24. und 25. [March 1897] fand der Bazaar statt für die Überschwemmten Schlesiens. . . . Es war ein Komitee gebildet, meist aus Damen, die aus Schlesien stammen oder dorthin gravitieren,

burg,[60] the development of Zeppelins,[61] and the equipping of sanatoriums (usable as military hospitals in the event of war).[62] Wilhelm II's appeals to the generosity of his Jewish acquaintances generally succeeded, though on occasion they met with refusal—without, however, provoking imperial resentment. An instance of this kind was later recalled by James Simon:

> Once the Kaiser told him [Simon] that he would like to plant a rose garden in the Tiergarten and had talked with his gardener about it, who estimated the cost at 20,000 marks. "I don't find that at all expensive; what do you think, Mr. Simon?" "I don't find it expensive either," answered the one to whom the question was directed, and with that the affair was settled for him.[63]

On a more private level, Wilhelm II sometimes obtained, for court favorites or himself personally, useful and potentially profitable financial tips. Eduard Arnhold, for instance, promoted the sale of tiles produced in

---

neben der Herzogin von Ratibor und andern gros bonnets viele Frauen von Industriellen, Bankiers und 'Schlesingern' aller Kategorien. Diesen kumulierten sich andere." Spitzemberg, diary, November 27, 1897, *Spitzemberg Tagebuch*, pp. 360–61.

60. Carl Fürstenberg, *Lebensgeschichte*, pp. 441–42.

61. James Simon recalled: "Dann, wie der Kaiser sie einmal einlud, ihnen sagte, heute verlange er nichts von ihnen, er lasse ihnen nur einen Vortrag über Luftschiffahrt halten, als sie dann aber gingen meinte Hollmann, sie müssten eine Luftschiffahrt-Gesellschaft gründen, was dann auch mit einem Kapital von einer Million Mark geschah. [Daher stammt die Anekdote: "Meine Herren, heute gibt es Freibier!"]. Quoted in Feder, "James Simon" MS, pp. 266–67.

62. The equipment of sanatoriums concerns Oskar Tietz, who, with his oppositional liberal attitudes and his South German connections, was very different from the other *Kaiserjuden*. The story is so engagingly told by his son Georg that it deserves inclusion here: "Da liess der Innenminister meinen Vater ins Ministerium bitten und eröffnete ihm, er glaube er könne die Angelegenheit des Lessinghauses [a building owned by the Prussian state needed for an extension of the Tietz department store] zu einem guten Ende bringen. Es hätte sich die seltene Gelegenheit ergeben, dass Seine Majestät der Kaiser den Wunsch geäussert habe, ein Lungensanatorium als private Stiftung des Roten Kreuzes erbaut zu sehen, dass man in einem Kriegsfalle auch als Lazarett benutzen könnte. Es seien schon erhebliche Fonds für den Bau aufgebracht worden, doch es fehlten noch Gelder für Betten, Wäsche und Röntgeneinrichtungen. Ob unsere Firma dieses nicht im Interesse der Volksgesundheit stiften wolle. Wenn Vater dabei einen Wunsch nach Orden oder Titel äussern würde, so könne dieser erfüllt werden. Vater lehnte dankend jede Ehrung ab, aber er stiftete neben den Betten und der Wäsche noch einen Flügel für Kinderheilung, den man allerdings nicht als Lazarett gebrauchen konnte. Genehmigung und Kaufverbriefung des Lessinghauses erfolgten umgehend." Georg Tietz, *Hermann Tietz Geschichte einer Familie und ihrer Warenhäuser* (Stuttgart, 1965), p. 104. Such were the characteristic dealings between Wilhelm II and wealthy Jews who were not—and did not wish to be—*Kaiserjuden*. For further instances, see ibid., pp. 104–5.

63. Feder, "James Simon" MS, p. 10. Feder writes, "Alle Stiftungen, die James Simon machte, gingen aus seiner eigenen Initiative hervor, und er liess sich auch durch den Kaiser nicht zu öffentlichen Zuwendungen bestimmen." Ibid., p. 9.

the imperial estate of Kadinen.[64] On another occasion one of the Kaiser's closest friends, Prince Max Egon Fürstenberg, in company with Christian Kraft Fürst zu Hohenlohe-Oehringen, found himself in serious financial difficulties on account of misguided industrial speculations. The Kaiser, in alarm, called in Carl Fürstenberg to advise on ways of clearing up the mess. Fürstenberg duly provided detailed reports on the financial affairs of the two aristocrats, for which he was thanked profusely. But Fürstenberg declined the Kaiser's request that he take charge of the rescue operation, instead convincing Wilhelm II that the job must be done by others. Following the interview, while accompanying his guest across the anterooms, Wilhelm II took his leave with the comment that Fürstenberg was the cleverest of his *Bankdirektoren*. Did he, indeed, realize just how clever Fürstenberg had been? At any rate, Wilhelm II showed his appreciation by presenting Fürstenberg with his picture with a handwritten dedication thanking him for his good advice.[65]

Notwithstanding incidents of this kind, it seems likely that purely material considerations, however relevant, played a secondary role in the Kaiser's relationship with the *Kaiserjuden*. Not only did Wilhelm II enjoy the company of these experienced and sometimes witty men of the world,[66] but he found it, above all, instructive. "Mit James Simon," he once observed admiringly, "kann man nicht zusammen sein, ohne von ihm zu lernen."[67] In his relationship with Simon in particular, who felt the Kaiser treated him like an older brother,[68] Wilhelm II was happy to relax. A small incident—presumably described to Ernst Feder by Simon himself—is revealing. When Simon brought the Kaiser an invitation to visit the wedding chamber of the new synagogue in the Fasanenstrasse, which was decorated with tiles from the imperial brickworks, the following dialogue ensued:

"Tell me Mr. Simon, what will the people say about my strong interest in Jewish things?"

64. *Eduard Arnhold,* p. 46.

65. Carl Fürstenberg, *Lebensgeschichte,* pp. 498–500.

66. Ballin had first recommended Carl Fürstenberg to Wilhelm II among others for his well-known "entertainment-value." The Kaiser had expressed the wish "doch endlich einmal einen amüsanten und gescheiten Menschen zu sprechen." Ibid., p. 439. Of the Kaiser's liking for the company of Eduard Arnhold, it was said, "Er liebte den vorzüglichen Gesellschafter, den witzigen, immer schlagfertigen Debatter." *Eduard Arnhold,* p. 46.

67. Quoted in Feder, "James Simon" MS, p. 9.

68. "James Simon hat . . . oft betont dass der Kaiser mit ihm verkehrt habe wie mit einem älteren Bruder." Marner to Feder, cited in n. 39 above.

"Your Majesty, perhaps the rabbis will assume that your Majesty wants to convert to Judaism."

"Why, I did not know that the gentlemen raised their expectations so high."[69]

In general the *Kaiserjuden,* without overlooking the Kaiser's defects, commented appreciatively on his genial manner, quick intellect, and retentive memory. Typical in this respect is the appreciation of Carl Fürstenberg:

> The person I met here was not the Kaiser but a human being. Endowed with exceptional intellectual power, he could display unusual charm when he wished to do so. . . . What perhaps stands out among his mental dispositions was an outstanding memory. . . .
>
> Besides his innumerable official duties, he took an interest, not merely as a layman but in depth, in excavations, in biblical studies, in the history of the house of Hohenzollern, and especially in Frederick the Great. . . . Joined with a thorough factual knowledge was a remarkable linguistic talent. All this enabled the Kaiser to be one of the most brilliant conversationalists of his age. That not many people have had the opportunity to draw unmixed enjoyment from these talents has to be admitted. More particularly, in relations with his immediate entourage, Wilhelm II was inclined to play the monarch.[70]

As part of this cautious assessment of his erstwhile conversational partner—Wilhelm II was at the time still living, in exile in the Netherlands—Fürstenberg noted the Kaiser's disturbing propensity, when he did relax the bands of discipline, to play more or less infantile practical jokes on members of his entourage. Nor was the Kaiser's taste or artistic expertise wholly beyond reproach:

> The Emperor in no way resented it, when James Simon corrected his naïve views of artistic matters, thus, when he once compared the painter of a quite insignificant picture to Rembrandt or when he recommended for display at the Berlin Art Exhibition a sculpture he considered a Renaissance piece, but which turned out to be an insignificant decoration from the World Exhibition in Paris.[71]

Perhaps expressive of the Kaiser's artistic predilections is his remark to Eduard Arnhold about an equestrian statue representing his much-admired grandfather Wilhelm I as "Imperator." "I find it wonderful,"

69. Feder, "James Simon" MS, p. 10.
70. Carl Fürstenberg, *Lebensgeschichte,* pp. 439–40. "James Simon in his turn, 'ohne seine Schwächen zu verkennen,' appreciated 'das Wissen und das grosse Gedächtnis des Kaisers.' " Feder, "James Simon" MS, p. 9.
71. Feder, "James Simon" MS, p. 12.

said the Kaiser. "My father can be dressed up as Siegfried, Lohengrin, Barbarossa, Emperor Sigismund, whereas Emperor Wilhelm tolerates only one presentation; as Emperor he belongs on a battle-horse."[72] But while neither the Kaiser's taste nor his information might be above reproach, there is agreement that he accepted polite corrections and even harmless jokes with general good humor.[73]

Against this background it is possible to consider some of the topics touched on in conversations between Wilhelm II and his Jewish subjects. Some surviving reports will illustrate their range. On the Kaiser's part, "Knackfuss-style" indiscretions on international affairs were common, as when he confided to James Simon in 1912 in—of all places—the synagogue in the Fasanenstrasse "Wenn ich die Österreicher nicht zurückgehalten hätte, hätten die Kerls uns in einen Krieg verwickelt."[74] In general, however, topics from the economic and cultural spheres predominated. From Eduard Arnhold, for instance, the Kaiser occasionally wished to learn about economic conditions in Upper Silesia, or the prospects of drilling for oil in Palestine. More often, however, he chose to discuss questions related to art or to the affairs of the German Academy in Rome.[75] The Kaiser's infrequent conversations with Walther Rathenau, on the other hand, touched on topics as diverse as the affairs of the Mannesmann brothers, Rathenau's castle in Freienwalde, the princess of Orange whose remains were buried there, England, the death of Edward VII, jewelry, cotton, architectural styles (with Rathenau, as ever, ready to offer a decided opinion on any subject under the sun), and a mysterious

72. *Eduard Arnhold*, p. 46.

73. That the imperial favor could, however, be lost, is shown by the case of Ernst von Mendelssohn. As the former lord chamberlain, Robert Graf von Zedlitz und Trützschler recalled: "Unter allen, die er am Hofe kennenlernte, waren die Vornehmsten und Würdigsten wohl James Simon und Ernst von Mendelssohn, die nichts für sich wollten, alles ablehnten, von den Hofschranzen viel umworben waren, mit manchmal nur fingierten Wünschen des Kaisers. James Simon sei keine Kampfnatur, Mendelssohn widersprach bei zwei Gelegenheiten dem Kaiser, der ein Vorgehen gegen die russischen Papiere wünschte, und wurde dann nicht mehr eingeladen." Quoted in Feder, "James Simon" MS, p. 160. For Mendelssohn, economic interests were the more important.

74. Feder, "James Simon" MS, p. 194. Simon reports another incident, characteristic of the Kaiser's silliness and irresponsibility: "Bei einer Einladung zur kaiserlichen Tafel nahm er, ehe man zum Essen ging, James Simon beiseite und machte ihm eine vertrauliche Mitteilung über die politische Lage. 'Nun darf ich wohl erwarten,' fügte er lachend hinzu, 'dass das *Berliner Tageblatt* diese Dinge morgen veröffentlicht.'" James Simon assured the Kaiser of his complete discretion and was not a little surprised when at dinner, Wilhelm II repeated his "revelation" in front of twenty guests. Feder, "James Simon" MS, p. 10.

75. *Eduard Arnhold*, pp. 46–47. A conversation in January 1911, mainly about artistic matters, is described in ibid., p. 46.

item summarized by Rathenau as "reluctance to fight."[76] On another occasion the conversation ranged from the illness of Emil Rathenau, or Walther Rathenau's part in a recent merger of two private banks, to France and Paul Cambon, the French ambassador in London, Adolf Freiherr Marschall von Bieberstein, a recent article by Rathenau in the *Neue Freie Presse* in Vienna, a brochure entitled *Rheinischer Bismarck,* and architectural matters relating to the new opera building.[77] On yet another occasion, at a luncheon at Hollmann's, the Kaiser seems to have delivered himself in the presence of Rathenau and Simon, "ohne weitere Zeugen," of a lengthy and fairly revealing soliloquy on the state of international affairs.[78]

If conversations with Rathenau tended to turn to political themes, those with Carl Fürstenberg were mostly of a more general nature.[79] Exchanges with James Simon, on the other hand, tended to cover mainly artistic matters or affairs of the German Orient Society.[80] Wilhelm II also characteristically advised the brothers Franz and Robert von Mendelssohn on the interior decoration of their new villas in Grunewald.[81] Overall, it is difficult to escape the conclusion that there was in the Kaiser's dealings with Jewish economic leaders—as indeed in everything he did—a good deal of talented dilettantism. No doubt in the eyes of his conversational

76. Rathenau, diary, March 16, 1911, *Rathenau Tagebuch,* p. 133.

77. "Ich riet, die Kirchhofsmauer des Moltkedenkmals zu beseitigen." Ibid., June 6, 1912, p. 167.

78. Ibid., February 13, 1912, pp. 156–58.

79. "Mein Gedankenaustausch mit dem Kaiser sollte sich nicht auf allgemeine Unterhaltungen beschränken." Carl Fürstenberg, *Lebensgeschichte,* p. 445.

80. Feder, "James Simon," *LBIYB;* Feder, "James Simon" MS, passim; Marner to Feder, cited in n. 39, above.

81. Treue, "Das Bankhaus Mendelssohn," p. 57. The history of cultural exchanges between the Hohenzollern and Mendelssohn families is curious. It began when Frederick the Great had forced Moses Mendelssohn to buy a so-called *Juden-Affe* from the Royal Porcelain Manufacture. "Die Affen gehörten zu den sonst schwer absetzbaren Stücken, die von Juden gekauft werden mussten. Einer dieser Affen hatte seinen Platz im Bankhaus Jägerstrasse und ist wohl mit diesem vernichtet worden." Ibid., p. 58. Later, Moses Mendelssohn's descendants reciprocated in an unusual manner, at least according to the family tradition: "Obwohl in Geschichtsbüchern berichtet wird, dass wenn die Königliche Familie baden wollte, eine Badewanne von Unter den Linden aus dem Hotel de Russie nach dem Berliner Schloss transportiert wurde, so meldet die Familientradition, dass die Badewanne aus dem Mendelssohnschen Hause in der Jägerstrasse kam, das damals das einzige—oder eines der wenigen—Berliner Privathäuser war, in dem sich eine Badewanne befand." Gilbert, *Bankiers, Künstler und Gelehrte,* pp. xli-xlii. Now Wilhelm II reciprocated by acting as unpaid adviser on interior decoration. His relations with the Mendelssohns were friendly. As Feder records in his diary from the recollections of James Simon: "Hübsch, wie er der 8-jährigen Lilli von Mendelssohn auf ihre briefliche Einladung sofort seinen Besuch in eigenhändigem Schreiben ankündigte." Feder, "James Simon" MS, p. 124.

partners, this was more than compensated for by the imperial condescension, goodwill, and eagerness to learn. Nor was there lack of human sympathy on either side.

Wilhelm II's abdication probably contributed to Ballin's presumed suicide.[82] Eduard Arnhold, whose sympathies remained with the monarchy, offered his entire fortune, should it be needed, to help the imperial family.[83] James Simon, who had not met with the Kaiser since 1914, bitterly resented his abdication.[84] Carl Fürstenberg, in his memoirs, included a sympathetic appreciation of the former monarch.[85] And when, in 1931, James Simon, bereft of his splendid collections and now a relatively poor man, celebrated his eightieth birthday, he received from Wilhelm II in Doorn, accompanied by a greeting and a picture with a personal dedication, a drawing from the ex-imperial hand depicting the construction of the Tower of Babel (which, Wilhelm asserted, was—contrary to conventional wisdom—a symbol not of human hubris but of pious veneration).[86] It was a last pathetic greeting from the leading exponent of the "Knackfuss culture" to a last representative of the doomed and withering culture of Fontane and Liebermann.[87]

REFLECTIONS

What can be concluded about the encounter between the devotee of Knackfuss and the protagonists of Liebermann? There can be little doubt that the contacts between Wilhelm II and the *Kaiserjuden* can be seen as the meeting of the two distinct cultures, existing side by side. The culture of Wilhelm II was, in essence, that of the official establishment which had as its pillars, besides Protestantism, a cult of Prussia and the Prussian

82. Rosenbaum, "Albert Ballin," p. 299.
83. "Es ist der 10. November 1918. . . . Der Kaiser nach Holland übergetreten. . . . Um 9 Uhr früh ruft mich Arnhold an: 'Lieber Graf, das Furchtbare ist geschehen, ich glaube, es ist unabänderlich. Vielleicht bedeutet es die Morgenröte einer neuen Zeit. Ich möchte Ihnen nur eines sagen: ich halte es für möglich und wahrscheinlich, dass eine Familie, die uns beiden sehr nahesteht . . . materieller Hilfe bedürfen wird. Ich wollte Sie bitten zu melden, dass ich in dem Falle mit meinem Vermögen und meinen Besitzungen jederzeit zur Verfügung stehe.' Fürwahr ein stolzes Wort! *Wer* hat, ich frage es, *so* am 10. November 1918 gesprochen und gehandelt?" Ernst Graf zu Rantzau, "Der Mann des öffentlichen Lebens," in *Eduard Arnhold*, p. 48.
84. Feder, "James Simon" MS, p. 264. Simon did not, however, object to repeated visits to Doorn by his son Heinrich. Ibid., p. 13.
85. "Mir gegenüber hat Wilhelm II stets so viel Güte an den Tag gelegt, dass ich mich gewiss nicht befugt fühle, einer so oberflächlichen Aburteilung beizutreten." Carl Fürstenberg, *Lebensgeschichte*, p. 243.
86. Feder, "James Simon" MS, p. 13.
87. For Liebermann, 1933 *Ausstellungs- und Malverbot.*

monarchy, elements of German imperialism and pan-Germanism, a goodly dose of antisemitism, and an even larger one of questionable artistic taste. How far it may be considered the specific culture of the nobility, landowning *Junkers,* high officialdom, and the Prussian officer class may be a matter for discussion. The counterculture represented by the *Kaiserjuden* can be seen as, essentially, that of the Jewish *Besitz-* and, to a lesser extent, *Bildungsbürgertum* (the two, though overlapping, are, of course, not identical). How far this culture was specific to the Jewish *Besitzbürgertum* will be considered later. What should be noted here, however, is that this was not the *avant-garde* culture of modernism and the radical intelligentsia with which, of course, Jews also had close connections.

Peter Gay has described the essentially conservative nature of Max Liebermann, who may be considered as perhaps the leading exponent of the counterculture of the German-Jewish bourgeoisie.[88] As Liebermann observed about himself, discreetly omitting the Bohemian aspects of his life: "In my daily habits I am the perfect bourgeois; I eat, drink, sleep, take walks, and work with the regularity of a tower clock. I live in my parents' house where I spent my childhood, and it would be difficult for me if I had to live anywhere else."[89] In his art, after the early rebellion of the *Sezession,* Liebermann turned conservative. For *avant-garde* art and modernism, he showed neither sympathy nor understanding.[90] Could not the evolution of Fontane, another representative figure, be seen in similar terms from the early scandal of *Irrungen, Wirrungen* (1888) to the respectful acceptance of *Der Stechlin* (1899) and the old man's head-shaking, noted by Hildegard von Spitzemberg, at the premiere of Hauptmann's *Die versunkene Glocke?* And did not the same apply—*mutatis mutandis*—of two other representative figures of the same culture, Richard Strauss and Thomas Mann?

It was thus a conservative, or perhaps liberal-conservative, bourgeois culture that Wilhelm II with his Borussian "Knackfuss culture" encountered in the *Kaiserjuden.* On a purely cultural plane, this was, of course, a meaningless encounter: Knackfuss could no more influence Liebermann than Liebermann Knackfuss. On a narrowly cultural level, there were no points of contact (except possibly a doubtful and peripheral overlap through a partial apostasy from the "Liebermann culture" expressed in

88. Peter Gay, "German Jews in German Culture"; and Gay, "Begegnung mit der Moderne" in *Juden im Wilhelminischen Deutschland,* pp. 248–49, 251–52.
89. Quoted in Gay, "Begegnung mit der Moderne," p. 252.
90. Ibid., pp. 252, 254.

occasional enthusiasm for Bayreuth and Richard Wagner). The half-hearted attempts of Wilhelm II to bridge the cultural divide, though creditable to his personal aspirations and witnessing to a certain openness of mind, could only be described as pathetic. As for his Jewish partners, he could hardly hope to convert them to the philosophical gospel of Houston Stewart Chamberlain.

On a different plane, Wilhelm II's contacts with the *Kaiserjuden* could be seen, following Friedrich Naumann, as an encounter between the spirit of Potsdam and that of Hamburg, between a residual feudal culture and an *arrivée* commercial one. At this level, also, Wilhelm II as a modern monarch showed a creditable desire to bridge the gap between *Borussentum* and *Ballinismus*.[91] While the Kaiser's interest in economic development and particularly in the overseas activities sponsored by men like Ballin and his friend Max Warburg was genuine enough, it could never overcome his prior commitment to the combined interests of the Bund der Landwirte and *Schlotbarone* represented by the favored family of Krupp. Bülow's attempt to establish a balance came to naught when the chancellor was forced to resign to make room for the second-rate establishment bureaucrat Theobald von Bethmann-Hollweg. Alfred von Tirpitz, supported by the Kaiser, by "heavy industry," and popular naval agitation would inevitably defeat Ballin, who after early support for naval expansion (1898–99),[92] became progressively more alarmed at the growing dangers of Anglo-German naval rivalry. There was not the slightest chance, at any time, of the "Hamburg system" prevailing over that of Potsdam, or the Hansabund over Bund der Landwirte and heavy industry. In fact at anything remotely approaching a political level, the encounters between Wilhelm II and the *Kaiserjuden* were doomed to sterility.[93] Wilhelm II was and remained, first and foremost, a *Borusse*. The hopelessness of the situation in this respect was evidently apparent to James Simon as well as to Albert Ballin from an early moment.[94] In

91. Antisemites, perceptively selecting Ballin as the representative figure of the counterculture, actually coined the term "verballinisiert." "Es ist dahin gekommen, dass unsere höchsten Stellen verballinisiert sind, dass bis an die höchsten Stufen des Thrones die Fremdlinge aus Palästina und Amerika Zutritt haben." Otto Böckler, Reichstag deputy of the Deutsche Reformpartei, Reichstag XI. Legislaturperiode, I Session, erster Sessionsabschnitt (1903/4) Bd. 1, 11. Sitzung (Donnerstag den 14. Januar 1904), p. 277.

92. Volker R. Berghahn, *Der Tirpitz-Plan* (Düsseldorf, 1971), p. 141.

93. As Feder reports from the reminiscences of James Simon: "Politisch war mit dem Kaiser nicht zu reden, das konnte auch Ballin nicht." "James Simon" MS, p. 123.

94. "Er [James Simon] erzählte noch, dass er dem Kaiser einmal ein Memorandum über die Aufgaben des modernen Monarchen überreichen wollte, wollte es mit P.[aul] N.[athan] ausarbeiten, unterliess es aber weil zwecklos." Ibid., p. 124.

any case, the "system of Potsdam" could hardly be reformed or even modified by some casual encounters between its titular head and a few representatives of the rival "system of Hamburg."[95]

At the same time this was, of course, an encounter between the official head of the bureaucratic German state and representatives of a Jewish elite group, a German-Jewish encounter at the highest level. But in this respect, also, it was an encounter with little meaning, even if James Simon could on occasion act as intermediary between the Berlin Jewish community and the monarch[96] or persuade the Kaiser to pay a visit to a synagogue as a return for the purchase of imperial tiles.[97] Once Simon's standing with the Kaiser may even have enabled him to mitigate marginally the effects of a piece of antisemitic legislation in Romania. However, when it came to anti-Jewish discrimination nearer home, nothing could be achieved, as James Simon would soon discover. In fact, it proved impossible to so much as raise the so-called Jewish Question in Germany with Wilhelm II.[98] Moreover, the Kaiser, himself an antisemite in his basic attitudes, was, in this regard at least, hardly a free agent. It was scarcely necessary for him to demonstrate his unwillingness to recognize the existence of any Jewish problem by the disingenuous pretenses that he had never known of Ballin's Jewishness or that other Jews with whom he maintained occasional contacts were not *real* Jews at all. The furthest he was prepared to go was to break the rules for the benefit of two Jewish friends of his youth, Walter Mossner and Siegfried Sommer. Beyond this, he remained a true embodiment of the *Borussisch* spirit in all its essentials—hardly affected by some casual contacts with *Kaiserjuden* (and a few others) from beyond the pale.

It is interesting and perhaps significant, however, that Wilhelm II chose his Jewish companions from among the unbaptized, unennobled,

---

95. The history of the deliberately named Hansabund of 1909, the economic pressure group representing economic interests including those of the *Kaiserjuden,* lies outside the scope of this paper.

96. Feder, "James Simon" MS, pp. 10, 175.

97. "Jüdische Gemeinde liess durch Simon den Kaiser bitten, für den Trausaal der Synagoge Fasanenstrasse Kadiner Kacheln zu liefern. Simon bat den Kaiser, die Synagoge zu besuchen, Rabbiner würden sich riesig freuen." Ibid., p. 123. The Jewish Notables, were, however, not used to the honor of receiving the Kaiser, as proved by a picture James Simon showed his friend Ernst Feder. "Dann, die sehr originelle Fotographie des Moments, in dem der Vorsteher der jüdischen Gemeinde Jacoby, den Kaiser vor der Synagoge Fasanenstrasse empfängt, aber in seiner Verlegenheit weder seinen Zylinderhut abnimmt noch die ihm vom Kaiser entgegengestreckte Hand ergreift." Ibid., p. 75.

98. Ibid., pp. 287, 291.

and, essentially, unfeudalized. Only one of the erstwhile *Kaiserjuden,* and a marginal one, Fritz Friedländer apostatized to become a Roman Catholic, as Fritz von Friedländer-Fuld. Like Georg von Caro, Paul von Schwabach, and Otto von Mendelssohn Bartholdy, he thus joined the small group of *Adelsjuden* who had bought their titles by means of conversion and/or cash.[99] There is a world of difference between Fritz Friedländer, who paid a million marks for ennoblement, and Albert Ballin, who refused it when offered *gratis.* Somewhat different was the position of the Mendelssohns, whose first ennoblement, like their Christianity, reached back to an earlier date.

Significantly, members of the Mendelssohn family themselves distinguished between Franz (I) Mendelssohn, ennobled *ex gratia* by Kaiser Friedrich III in 1888, and Ernst Mendelssohn-Bartholdy and Otto Mendelssohn Bartholdy, ennobled respectively in 1902 and 1907 in consideration of contributions to favorite projects of Wilhelm II.[100] The ennobled members of the family also were Christians from birth. Nor were the Mendelssohns inclined to build themselves palaces (their *grossbürgerliche* villas in Grunewald were, however, luxurious and entirely "appropriate to their station"), nor did they yet acquire *Rittergüter* (their relatively modest vacation home, characteristically, was located for generations at Horchheim near Koblenz). The other exception among the *Kaiserjuden,* in both social and ethnic background, was Bernhard Dernburg, who shared with the rest not their religion but their attitudes. Bernhard Dernburg was not ennobled, did not acquire an estate, and, politically, stood somewhat to the left of the others.

Indeed the majority of the *Kaiserjuden* steadfastly resisted the blandishments of conversion, a fact that Weizmann was too purblind or prejudiced to acknowledge. In their Judaism there were indeed nuances with the spectrum ranging from active involvement in Jewish affairs (as with James Simon, Max Warburg, their friend Paul Nathan, the offspring of Jewish bankers, or Ludwig Max Goldberger), through the Judaism from

99. Baroness von Spitzemberg, for instance, noted in her diary in March 1906: "Sehr bestürzt und betrübt war ich durch das, was mir die alte Frau von Wedel über die Nobilitierungen anlässlich der Silberhochzeit [of Wilhelm II in 1906] erzählte, und zwar als ihr vom Minister Wedel [Prussian minister of the Royal House] selbst mitgeteilt. Danach haben Friedländer und Caro jeder dem Kaiser eine Million zur freien Verfügung gestellt als Kaufpreis für das 'von,' und zwar wollte ersterer Anfangs nur 1/2 Million geben, liess sich aber dann steigern! Paul Schwabach verweigerte diesen Kuhhandel! und blieb deshalb ungeadelt!" [He was ennobled the following year, 1907]. Spitzemberg, diary, March 22, 1906, *Spitzemberg Tagebuch,* pp. 456–57.

100. Gilbert, *Bankiers, Künstler und Gelehrte,* p. xlv.

pride and filial piety of an Albert Ballin[101] or Eduard Arnhold[102] to the lukewarm and residual Jewishness of Carl Fürstenberg (who baptized his children) or Walther Rathenau (who, however, very deliberately and not without much agonizing, resolved to remain a Jew). And with the various levels of Jewish engagement went a consistent allegiance to the standards and life-style of the *haute bourgeoisie,* with a patrician tinge perhaps, as in the cases of Arnhold, or James Simon, and to some extent Max Warburg and the Mendelssohns. In fact, the life-style cultivated by these men was not that of the feudal landowner but rather the belated patrician, merchant prince, or royal merchant. In other times and in another place they might have become, if not Medicis, at any rate Fuggers or Welsers. Their heirs, and this also is significant, contracted modest marriages well within the ambit of the social group into which they had risen. Their social ambitions, on the whole (except for Aniela Fürstenberg and Walther Rathenau), appear to have been measured, though James Simon at least did not disdain aristocratic companionship. In their political views, contrary to Weizmann's stereotype, none were, or indeed could be, conservatives.

It was, in fact, precisely their relative lack of social ostentation or demands that made the companionship of the *Kaiserjuden* agreeable to Wilhelm II. Hobnobbing in Hamburg and Kiel, if not precisely in private between consenting adults, did take place at a safe distance from the watchful eyes of the court, the bigoted empress and her devout and narrow-minded clique. From such socializing as did occur wives were rigorously excluded, though Wilhelm II could show endearing condescension to children like the younger Aniela Fürstenberg or Lilli von Mendelssohn (in fact, both Mendelssohn spouses were probably *hoffähig*). Again, the Hollmann contacts and the relatively more frequent meetings with Ballin were discreet, though they could not, of course, escape the Argus eyes of Baroness Spitzemberg and others of her ilk. The *Kaiserjuden,* however, to the great gratification of Wilhelm II, put forward no official social pretensions (Walther Rathenau, who might have, was precluded from doing so by being unmarried). James Simon, Eduard Arnhold, and the rest, and perhaps more particularly their wives, either had renounced higher social ambitions or, more probably, had never entertained them. It was on this basis alone that relatively sustained friendly contacts with Wilhelm II were possible.

101. Kurt Zielenziger, *Juden in der deutschen Wirtschaft* (Berlin, 1903), p. 187.
102. Geheimer Bergrat Ewald Hilger, in *Eduard Arnhold,* p. 124.

What the *Kaiserjuden* on their part gained from relations thus circumscribed must remain a matter of conjecture. Did they genuinely value—and the evidence suggests that this may have been the case—personal relationships with a *Knackfuss* ready to invest some personal charm and imbued with a genuine desire to learn and a good deal of curiosity about the alien world of Hamburg and Liebermann? Did those, like James Simon, treated by the Kaiser like "older brothers," derive some satisfaction from their presumed (to a slight degree real) educative opportunities? Did some secretly flatter themselves with the illusion that they might, one day, at some critical juncture, exercise some actual influence over policy decisions affecting areas of special interest—Jewish, commercial, or patriotic? Or were they susceptible, perhaps even involuntarily, to the personal flattery involved in imperial condescension? Or were they, finally, simply passive participants in a show not scripted by themselves? No doubt all these factors played a part, in different proportions and measures in different individuals. The common denominator, however, was probably a degree of personal sympathy and even affection for their imperial acquaintance.[103]

Finally, Kaiser and *Kaiserjuden* may be considered to have met at a high level as representatives of two great forces in German society, a feudal class eroded by capitalism and a capitalist class partially corroded by feudalism. The *Kaiserjuden,* however, for reasons already indicated, represented, on the whole, a "pure" form of capitalist bourgeoisie. How typical, then, were they of the German *haute bourgeoisie* as a whole? Were they its vanguard or a peculiar and slightly exotic variant? The answer, probably, lies in the latter direction. The Kaiser, indeed, hobnobbed also with a number of non-Jewish industrialists. His relations with these non-Jewish *Kaiserjuden* await elucidation, but the evidence would seem to suggest that these may have been neither Borsigs nor Thyssens, neither Dierigs (perhaps a Gentile equivalent of the Simons) nor Wiegands (Ballin's opposite number at the Norddeutscher Lloyd). Perhaps the nearest Gentile counterpart to the *Kaiserjuden* were the Delbrücks. Dearer to the Kaiser's heart, however, were Karl von Stumm-Halberg or Guido Henckell von Donnersmarck, respectively *Freiherrn* and *Grafen,* not to speak of the industrialist Christian Kraft Fürst zu Hohenlohe-Oehringen. So far as contacts with members of the commercial elite

---

103. The applicability of the term "friend," used in connection with Ballin and, occasionally, James Simon, would seem to depend largely on the meaning attached to "friendship." If these were indeed "friends," they were so in the Anglo-Saxon rather than the Germanic sense.

were concerned, the *Kaiserjuden* as commoners and "pure capitalists" were, probably, distinctive.

What perhaps distinguished them in the eyes of the Kaiser from their non-Jewish peers may have been less that they asked little or nothing of him—indeed this was a characteristic they may have shared with the industrial magnates—as the fact that they represented a distinctive culture, which the bulk of the magnates (not to speak of "pure" non-Jewish industrialists and capitalists) did not. It is at least suggestive and indicative of Wilhelm II's genuine interest. in cultural pursuits that one of the things that between 1890 and 1900 linked him to his closest friend and confidant in the aristocracy, Philipp Fürst zu Eulenburg-Hertefeld, was shared cultural interests.[104] Indeed it may have been the antisemitic prince who unconsciously helped to promote Wilhelm II's rapprochement with the *Kaiserjuden.* Wilhelm II's interest in the "other" culture, however and whenever acquired, was genuine; and the only way of satisfying it effectively was by contact with the *Kaiserjuden.* The same, to a large extent, is true of the Kaiser's genuine interest in the "Hamburg culture" represented by Ballin and Warburg. Contact with the *Kaiserjuden* alone could satisfy both cravings—as well as some of Wilhelm's more materialistic requirements. For benefits such as these it was worth reining in a deeply ingrained prejudice.

The encounter between Wilhelm II and the *Kaiserjuden,* however interesting in terms of cultural and social history, had no political and little practical significance. On the pages of German history as a whole, it remains little more than a gloss. In all matters of importance, while the Kaiser went his way (and that of Tirpitz, Bethmann, and Ludendorff), his Jewish companions went theirs. While he helped, fatefully, to guide the destinies of the German Empire, they helped to guide the fortunes of their commercial enterprises. Both came to grief—the Kaiser in the lost war, his partners in conversation in inflation and depression—before Adolf Hitler put an end to their economic activities and their culture alike. The encounter between Kaiser and *Kaiserjuden* thus remained an episode: *Das Wasser war viel zu tief.*

104. "Zum ersten Mal begegnete er [Eulenburg] Wilhelm 1885, und der Prinz, der bereits mit Eulenburgs Musik vertraut war, entwickelte eine grosse Zuneigung zu diesem Mann. [His counterpart, for the *Kaiserjuden,* was in some respects the former actor and publicist Maximilian Harden]. Beide teilten die Begeisterung für die Schönen Künste und waren sich einig in ihrem Abscheu gegen üppige Jüdinnen." Cecil, "Wilhelm II und die Juden," p. 328.

SHULAMIT VOLKOV

The Dynamics of Dissimilation

Ostjuden and German Jews

The historiography of modern German Jewry has usually followed one of two lines: it has either presented the story of Jews in Germany as a gradual, consistent, and successful process of assimilation, or it has concentrated on the obstacles to legal, social, or cultural integration, considering the hopes of true emancipation, not to mention full assimilation, illusionary and deceptive. The first line of interpretation was prevalent first in Germany itself, and then in the main ports of German-Jewish emigration in England and in the United States. The second dominated the so-called Zionist school, primarily in Israel. In effect, the old controversies of the early twentieth century, the arguments of the Centralverein deutscher Staatsbürger jüdischen Glaubens (CV) versus the Zionistische Vereinigung für Deutschland (ZVfD), were repeatedly rehashed in this historiography, and some historians apparently still find them relevant. While the Holocaust and its aftermath have altered the relative strength of the two camps, the essential debate seems to have remained intact and is being revived time and again.

During the last few years, however, chances for a different kind of historiography have greatly improved. Written mainly, though by no means exclusively, by historians of a new generation, this historiography is, of course, not entirely free of old ideologies, but it is at least ready to experiment with new methods and tools and apply other viewpoints. It is not only that one is simply bored with arguing an anachronistic case, but that both life in the Diaspora and life in the Zionist homeland have developed otherwise than expected. As is so often the case, we are called upon to revise our view of the past by new information and new research strategies, but above all by the changing circumstances of our own life.[1]

In an effort to rethink the story of German Jewry and apply a somewhat different perspective to it, I would like to emphasize in what follows neither the assimilatory forces in the development of the Jewish community in Germany, making Jews increasingly more like other Germans, nor the repelling forces of an antisemitic host society, reaching inconceivable dimensions under National Socialism. Instead I wish to focus upon the forces from within, which were drawing German Jews back together again even despite themselves. I do not wish to argue that these forces were more powerful or more important than the assimilatory trends, in the short or in the long run. I simply wish to try and focus upon them, treating them this time as the main, rather than a marginal, theme. By examining dissimilation one may after all gain some insight concerning assimilation, too. In fact, one may discover that the two were inseparably and, I would argue, dialectically interwoven.[2]

I

It is more or less accepted by historians of Wilhelmine Germany that certain new trends, counteracting the primary assimilatory drive of Jews living within German society, became noticeable sometime during the last decade of the nineteenth century. These were actually at work throughout the century. They may account for the widespread and persistent conception of emancipation among German Jews as a call for integration *and* some upholding of tradition. They may account for the continuing efforts of Jews everywhere in the country to preserve at least something of what was special and unique to them. Indeed they may prove indispensable for explaining a major characteristic of German-Jewish social, cultural, and intellectual history: the insistence upon integration *and* identity, *Verschmelzung* and *Eigenart*.[3] For the specific purpose of this essay,

1. A clear reflection of this changing historiography can be gained by reviewing the volumes of the *Leo Baeck Institute Year Book*. For the new areas of interest, new methods, and, last but not least, for the work of a growing group of younger historians working on these topics, see now especially the volumes since 1981.

2. The term "dissimilation" and some of its potential analytical advantages has been brought to my attention by Professor Saul Friedländer of Tel Aviv University, whom I wish to thank for sharing with me some of his insights.

3. For the intellectual aspects of these efforts, see Uriel Tal, "German-Jewish Social Thought in the Mid-Nineteenth Century," in *Revolution and Evolution: 1848 in German Jewish History,* ed. Werner E. Mosse, Arnold Paucker, and Reinhard Rürup (Tübingen, 1981), pp. 299–328. For the social and cultural side, see Shulamit Volkov, "Jüdische Assimilation und jüdische Eigenart im deutschen Kaiserreich: Ein Versuch," *Geschichte und Gesellschaft* 9 (1983): 331–48.

however, one may leave aside this general, panoramic perspective and assume only the operation of some dissimilatory forces among Jews in Germany from the 1890s onward. By then these reveal a distinct trend, and must be dealt with in any study of the intellectual controversies or the organizational history of German Jewry at that time.[4] A particularly pressing task is to explain this dissimilatory tendency among the consciously, conscientiously, and willingly assimilating Jews. What made *them* revitalize and reassert their Jewish uniqueness? What made for the reupholding of Jewish identity by these men and women—a minority to be sure, but not an insignificant one—when they seemed to have completely abandoned it?

Dissimilation was nurtured, I would argue, by two main forces: the hostility and exclusiveness of the host society, and the inner dynamics of assimilation itself. I shall here first attempt to indicate the manner in which these forces, each in its turn, brought forth dissimilatory reactions within the Jewish community and among individual Jews in Germany, and then more fully sketch the ways in which one single factor in the modern history of German Jewry affected this process, gave it a special momentum, and helped bring hidden trends onto the surface. I shall thus be dealing briefly with the objective and then with some aspects of the subjective side of dissimilation; first with the phenomenon itself and then with the process of its perception.

Any attempt at explaining dissimilation must clearly begin with the outside barrier, with the forces of antisemitism. Under the circumstances in Imperial Germany, it must have been the one single most important factor in the revival of Jewish self-consciousness. Individual biographies, telling the story of a return to some form of Jewishness in response to the push from the outside world—bigoted, prejudiced, and hostile—are many and are familiar enough. More interesting, perhaps, are the collective dissimilatory responses of German Jewry on the organizational and communal level. From midcentury onward, restrictions on Jewish membership in a variety of social clubs and local associations caused the es-

4. See Arnold Paucker, "Zur Problematik einer jüdischen Abwehrstrategie in der deutschen Gesellschaft," in *Juden im Wilhelminischen Deutschland, 1890–1914,* ed. Werner E. Mosse and Arnold Paucker (Tübingen, 1976), pp. 514–18; Eva Reichmann, "Der Bewusstseinswandel der deutschen Juden," in *Deutsches Judentum in Krieg und Revolution, 1916–1923,* ed. Werner E. Mosse and Arnold Paucker (Tübingen, 1971), pp. 511–612; Jehuda Reinharz, "Deutschtum and Judentum in the Ideology of the Centralverein deutscher Staatsbürger jüdischen Glaubens, 1893–1914, *Jewish Social Studies* 36 (1974): 19–34; Marjorie Lamberti, *Jewish Activism in Imperial Germany* (New Haven, 1978); and Ismar Schorsch, *Jewish Reactions to German Antisemitism, 1870–1914* (New York, 1972).

tablishment of parallel Jewish bodies.[5] Characteristic is the story of B'nai
B'rith, which was created as a Jewish counterpart to the presumably free-
thinking Masonic lodges and intended to form a response to the antisemitism prevalent among their members.[6] In the long run, however, more
influential were the emerging Jewish student associations, and above all
the CV. Here was an organization built explicitly in response to the antisemitic challenge, but although it was established to provide a forum for
the common work of *Abwehr,* it, too, gradually became yet another center and one more starting point for *Rückkehr.* Moreover, the network of
parallel Jewish social groups enhanced the process of "negative integration" and created institutions that in fact worked for the further absorption of the social and cultural values of the dominant society. The CV
was instead a unique Jewish body, having no parallel in the general German environment, intended not to compensate for rejection but to fight
against it.[7]

It was the timing and the specific content of the modern antisemitic
movement in Germany that eventually determined the elements within
Jewry to be worst hit by it. It was they who were driven to seek a fitting
response. It was not the traditional, Orthodox elements that were forced
to react, but the liberals, the Reform Jews; not the still half-segregated
communities in villages and small towns, but the integrated, the assimilated, the "successful," in the large urban centers. *They* were brought to
reassess their position; *they* felt the pressure and *they* were plunged into
a new soul searching. It was not only professional qualifications that made
highly successful or promising lawyers take up the leadership of the CV,
but the fact that it was *they* or their kind for whom public prejudices
posed significant and often insurmountable obstacles.[8]

The new antisemitism was not as threatening for the striving, up-

5. See Henry Wassermann, "Jews, *Bürgertum* and *Bürgerliche Gesellschaft* in a
Liberal Era in Germany, 1840–1880" [in Hebrew] (Ph.D. diss., Hebrew University,
Jerusalem, n.d.); Jacob Toury, *Soziale und Politische Geschichte der Juden in Deutsch-
land, 1847–1871* (Düsseldorf, 1977), chap. 3.

6. For the story of Freemasonry in this context, see Jacob Katz, *Jews and Freemasons in Europe, 1723–1939* (Cambridge, Mass., 1970); and for Germany especially,
Louis Maretzki, *Geschichte des Ordens Bnei-Briss in Deutschland, 1882–1907* (Berlin,
n.d.).

7. For the history of the CV, see the works cited in n. 4 above and Jehuda Reinharz, *Fatherland or Promised Land: The Dilemma of the German Jew, 1893–1914* (Ann
Arbor, 1975).

8. The best source for assessing the mood of these men is the CV monthly *Im
deutschen Reich,* which began publication in July 1895. Outstanding among the CV
leadership were several lawyers, among them the first and the second chairmen of the
organization, Maximilian Horwitz and Eugen Fuchs.

climbing Jews, characteristic of the first and the second generation of emancipation, as it was for those who had apparently made it, who had arrived. Fully equipped through the efforts and sacrifices of their parents, and fully qualified by their talents and their confident handling of all the elements of German *Bildung,* they were now prevented from reaching the very top, from becoming *Ordinarii* at the universities or occupying prestigious posts at the higher echelons of the bureaucracy. They were now finally rebuffed by fellow members of their own rank, regardless of their achievements. Half a century earlier, men—and women—had often been brought to conversion in their efforts to overcome the last hurdle on their road to success. But by the end of the nineteenth century, this was clearly marked as a false route and regarded openly with contempt.[9] Conversion, or the inofficial but parallel secular move away from Judaism, was indeed still chosen by some. But many, who sincerely felt that Judaism was merely thrust upon them by the vagaries of fate, nevertheless chose now to take another look at it. Instead of turning further away, they were beginning to seek for new ways of turning back.

But antisemitism, clearly a powerful force in the direction of dissimilation, was by no means the only one. I have elsewhere tried to explain at some length that while the particular process of Jewish social integration and cultural assimilation in Germany promoted the disintegration of the old, traditional Jewish community, it simultaneously created a new bond among Jews, based on a shared, distinctly modern "intimate culture."[10] Furthermore, the unique capacity of German Jews to respond to the challenge of modernity gave them a relative advantage over the competing German bourgeoisie and eventually made them a distinct substratum within it. Considering the prejudices of the surrounding environment and the restrictions placed upon their upward social mobility, the members of this substratum proved admiringly successful. But precisely those elements that made for their spectacular social climbing and their far-

9. For attitudes to conversion, see especially the programmatic article by Maximilian Horwitz, "Ehrenpflicht," *Im deutschen Reich* 4, no. 4 (1898) as well as Emil Lehmann's analysis, ibid., 3, no. 12 (1897); Rabbiner Maybaum's article, ibid., 6, no. 11 (1900); and, with special vehemence, Ismar Elbogen, ibid., 10, nos. 7/8 (1904); and Alphons Levi, ibid., no. 10. Compare also the useful summary of the controversy during the so-called Mugdan affair in Lamberti, *Jewish Activism,* pp. 95–105, and the comments by Gershom Scholem in "On the Social Psychology of the Jews in Germany, 1900–1933," in *Jews and Germans 1860–1933: The Problematic Symbiosis,* ed. David Bronson (Heidelberg, 1979), pp. 20–22. This issue, however, being symptomatic for the position of Jews within German society, needs to be researched further.

10. For a fuller argument and more data, see Volkov, "Jüdische Assimilation und jüdische Eigenart."

reaching assimilation turned out eventually to be the catalysts of dissimilation.

Jews concentrating in the large towns, and in a limited number of
occupations, were everywhere reaching equal levels of education and de-
veloping and upholding similar attitudes to family life, to the upbringing
of children, to the life-style they ought to establish and the careers they
should choose. They shared a common enthusiasm for the German theater, for literature and the arts, often a knack for Wagner and an outspoken taste for modernism. They were only naturally moving within
the same social circles and brought into new kinds of contacts with each
other. Surely they were protecting themselves against insults and rebuffs
coming from the outside world, but they were also positively attracted to
their own unique milieu by a multitude of common experiences, life
strategies, hopes, and aspirations. Despite themselves, they were made
into a partly segregated social element, though theirs was not a community of social exclusiveness but of the social attraction among the
likes.

All this indicates a complex dynamics that surely requires further in-
vestigation. Clearly, however, the community of the successful, the talented, the educated, and the influential, became an object of identification
even for the poor, the ordinary Jews. They were drawn together, indeed,
as a result of social segregation and a shared domestic culture, but also
by the common pride in their collective achievement and the common
belief in its promise. They were pushed back together by the negative image of themselves prevalent in an antisemitic society, but also by the positive counterimage that a successful assimilation allowed them to form
and uphold. Thus both antisemitism and the process of assimilation helped
set in motion a dialectical process of dissimilation.

II

But for this to become more than a marginal phenomenon, the entire
process had to be recognized and appreciated for what it was. It is in the
nature of dissimilation, just as it is in the nature of its counterpart—
assimilation—that it cannot but be weakened if its existence is disregarded
or denied. At this point, several elements in the history of German Jewry
combined to enhance not only the dissimilatory trends themselves but also
the need to perceive, recognize, and accept them. Among these elements
the so-called *Ostjudenfrage* became particularly important. Here was perhaps the issue that, more than anything else, continually forced a process

of reevaluation and reassessment upon German Jews and made dissimilation into a conscious process, its denial almost impossible, and its acceptance increasingly inevitable.

The *Ostjuden* issue is particularly clouded by "folklore" and mythology, even among other topics in modern German-Jewish history habitually laden with preconceptions and conventional wisdom. Recently, however, two outstanding works, supporting and complementing each other, have cleared much of the confusion and provided us with a wealth of new facts and figures, calling for a renewed discussion and further interpretative efforts. These are Steven E. Aschheim's *Brothers and Strangers,* and Jack L. Wertheimer's doctoral dissertation, as yet unpublished, "German Policy and Jewish Politics."[11] I am heavily relying upon their work in the following examination of the effects of the *Ostjudenfrage* upon the issue of dissimilation. I shall deal with this particular matter, as in the previous, more general section, first from the perspective of antisemitism and then through the analysis of assimilation.

That the influx of *Ostjuden* into Germany was an element in the rekindling of German antisemitism during the late nineteenth century was considered axiomatic at the time. From the beginning of the 1880s' immigration wave, Jewish organizations, such as the Deutsch-Israelitischer Gemeindebund (DIGB), and Jewish newspapers, such as the *Allgemeine Zeitung des Judentums,* were seriously alarmed. In fact, the overall unity that the DIGB strove to achieve was believed to be particularly necessary in face of the new social and cultural danger from the East. The organization even tried to appeal to the authorities in order to control and limit the scope of this immigration, and the problem then aired was later endlessly rehashed. All Jews were implicated in the deeds and misdeeds of the *Schnorrer* from the East, ran the argument, and the hard-won respectability and solid citizenship of the local German Jews was thus in serious danger of discredit.[12]

Heinrich von Treitschke's comments on the filth and degradation brought into Germany by the Eastern Jews, coming as they did at the outset of the new antisemitic wave in the late 1870s, and venemous even for that notorious defamator, received the expected ambivalent response. Typ-

11. The full titles are Steven E. Aschheim, *Brothers and Strangers: The East European Jew in German and German Jewish Consciousness, 1800–1923* (Madison, 1982); and Jack L. Wertheimer. "German Policy and Jewish Politics: The Absorption of East European Jews in Germany, 1868–1914" (Ph.D. diss., Columbia University, 1978). Among the older books, most useful, though exceedingly short on the earlier period, is Shalom Adler-Rudel, *Ostjuden in Deutschland, 1880–1940* (Tübingen, 1959).

12. See Aschheim, *Brothers and Strangers,* pp. 21–22.

ical was Harry Breslau, who reiterated the distinction between local Jews and the backward newcomers, only to plead eventually for more time and patience for the full integration process of *all* Jews into the superior culture of Germany.[13] Even twenty years later, the newly established Hilfsverein, impressive as its charity work among the *Ostjuden* had really been, clearly operated on the assumption of a deep cultural gap between *Ost-* and *Westjuden,* and the absolute superiority of the latter. As an umbrella organization for extensive social work among the needy immigrants, it nevertheless preferred to see them as transient elements and to speed as many of them as possible further on to America.[14] In a CV meeting in Hanover in 1904, James Simon openly argued the need for vocational training of Russian and Galician Jews, so as to make them eventually "exportfähig."[15] Here was an expression of active and engaged solidarity combined with fear of the reaction of non-Jews and a deep-seated, authentic antipathy toward the Eastern intruder.

The constant flow of Jews from the East kept alive the old stereotype of the religiously orthodox Jew, a small speculator and a *Schnorrer.* It strengthened the need of the assimilated to dissociate themselves from it. By rekindling traditional anti-Jewish prejudices, *Ostjuden* may have marginally strengthened the antisemitic movement in Germany. More important, however, was their role in keeping alive the negative Jewish image for the assimilated, in defining all they were trying not to be, in deepening and hastening their alienation from Judaism.

But like antisemitism in general, its anti-*Ostjuden* version, too, had a dissimilatory effect. Aschheim has convincingly shown the intermingling of old and new Jewish images, the "Caftan" and "Cravat," as he has fittingly called them.[16] From Treitschke to *Der Stürmer,* he explains, the link between the two was always constitutive for both the theory and the practice of German antisemitism, while the distinction between them remained marginal. Gradually, German Jews, too, were made to perceive this

13. Heinrich von Treitschke's articles are now easily available in Walter Boehlich, ed., *Der Berliner Antisemitismusstreit* (Frankfurt a.M., 1965). See especially "Unsere Aussichten," pp. 9–10. Harry Breslau's and other replies are also reprinted in Boelich; see especially pp. 65–67.

14. For the history of the Hilfsverein, see Moshe Rinott, *Hevrat haezrah liyehudei Germanyah biyezirah uve-maavak* (Jerusalem, 1963). For some revealing and interesting comments from the perspective of an Eastern Jew, see Shmaryah Levin, *Youth in Revolt* (New York, 1930), pp. 252–57.

15. James Simon, "Die Erziehung zur Bodenkultur und zum Handwerke, eine soziale Frage," *Im deutschen Reich* 10, no. 3 (1904): 213.

16. I owe much of this discussion to Aschheim's presentation in *Brothers and Strangers,* chap. 3.

fact. As time passed, and with the continuing stream of Jews from the East coming into Germany, it became increasingly clear that antisemitism was not only, or even primarily, directed against the old-type, unassimilated, ghetto Jews, personified by the *Ostjuden*. It was even impossible to deflect some of the hostility toward them, be it only temporarily. The actual existence of the Caftan Jew in the streets of urban Germany was immaterial for the antisemites. They could conjure up his image in his absence, too, and there was more than sufficient popular cultural material for doing so. The main burden of the attack was in any case to be borne by the local Jews, the Cravat-type, the assimilated. As the antisemitic campaign continued, its real nature was made increasingly clear, and German Jews gradually comprehended it.

III

Central to this process of recognition was the main fact about the *Ostjudenfrage*, namely that it really did not exist—or rather that it never existed in isolation and was intrinsically inseparable from the greater issue of assimilation. From this perspective it becomes essential to look at a few relevant figures with greater care and precision.[17]

By 1910 between 11 and 12 percent of all Jews in Germany—that is about seventy thousand men, women, and children—mostly from the so-called East, did not possess German citizenship and were legally aliens. The majority of these immigrants settled in a few of the larger German cities and constituted one of the most urbanized groups in Germany of that time. Some came from cities in the East, but the majority combined a movement from country to country with a transition from rural or semirural living to an urban, or even metropolitan environment. On the eve of the First World War, 57 percent of all foreign Jews came from Galicia, and between 8 and 10 percent from Hungary. Thus for about two-thirds of these immigrants, the German language was a mother tongue, and they had grown up, prior to immigration, into a Germanized or Germanizing society. These men and women often had more than a touch of Yiddish in their German speech, and normally carried with them a discernible foreign intonation, the remnants of talmudic colloquialism,

---

17. For data on *Ostjuden* after 1880 used throughout this section, I have relied largely on Wertheimer, "German Policy and Jewish Politics," app. B. See also the *Zeitschrift für Demographie und Statistik der Juden* (hereafter *ZDSJ*) 1 (June 1905): 10, and (December 1905): 4–8; as well as Bruno Blau, "Die Entwicklung der jüdischen Bevölkerung in Deutschland von 1800–1945" (New York, 1950, photocopy), pp. 58–59 and passim; Adler-Rudel, *Ostjuden im Deutschland,* esp. chap. 3.

and a dose of Galician wit. They were, however, often surprisingly well versed in Schiller, or at least well trained in the literary subculture of the *Gartenlaube*.[18] They may have been, indeed, "children of two cultures," but only rarely complete strangers in Germany.[19] The better educated— and these were not only the better situated—usually received some German *Gymnasium* instruction before they left for Germany. Others had at least the fluency in the language and a large measure of spiritual openness to absorb new cultural contents. Among the *Galizianer* many were energetic, adaptable, and open minded, though of course some very poor and very ignorant were invariably there too.[20]

The legal compulsion that brought these immigrants right into the established German-Jewish communities perfectly corresponded to their own wishes and ambitions. Significantly, many of the newly arrived joined the central liberal synagogue communities in the large cities, clearly indicating their wish to become part of the respectable, upward-moving, outwardly oriented Jewish social milieu.[21] Their eventual absorption into the existing local communities was virtually inevitable. From a local perspective the continuous immigration made the communities ever more heterogeneous. The local establishment was continually confronted with the need to absorb new elements. Willingly or reluctantly this had to be done, and it was rarely accomplished without some pain.[22]

There was, however, nothing new in this situation. Looking back some sixty to eighty years we cannot but observe a very similar picture. The large-scale immigration from across the Prussian borders had not yet begun, but the *Ostjudenfrage* was certainly there. Between 1824 and 1871 about fifty thousand Jews from the newly acquired Polish province of Posen migrated into the older Prussian regions.[23] Another fifty thousand

18. An example for this kind of background is to be found in Marcus Ehrenpreis's autobiography, *Between East and West* [in Hebrew] (Tel Aviv, 1953).

19. This is how Ernst Simon saw Martin Buber (born in Vienna but educated in Brody). See his "Martin Buber and German Jewry," *Leo Baeck Institute Year Book* (hereafter *LBIYB*) 3 (1958): 3–39.

20. On the quick acculturation of the *Ostjuden,* see Wertheimer, "German Policy and Jewish Politics," pp. 503–17. For their burning desire to adapt, it is instructive to compare Joseph Roth, *Juden auf Wanderschaft* (Berlin, 1927), pp. 9–25.

21. On the integration of immigrants into the life of the local communities, see the discussion in Wertheimer, "German Policy and Jewish Politics," chap. 8, esp. pp. 409–13, 422–31.

22. For the struggle between local and incoming Jews within the communities, and its internal political implications, see ibid., chap. 9.

23. Data for the following discussion on migration from Posen is from the *ZDSJ* 6 (May 1910): 65–76; Jacob Segall, *Die beruflichen und sozialen Verhältnisse der Juden in Deutschland* (Berlin, 1912), pp. 7–8; Joseph Letschinsky, *Das wirtschaftliche Schick-*

traveled the same route between 1877 and 1905. They, too, were mainly moving into the large urban centers, especially in and around Breslau and Berlin. They, too, were often already German speaking, ready and eager for acculturation. They, too, sought rapid entry into the established local Jewish community.

The Polish *Hosenverkäufer,* who threw Treitschke into a rage, were Jews coming from Posen. The model *Ostjude,* described by Georg Hermann for posterity, the presuming nephew Julius Jacobi, who sent the cultivated Jettchen Gebert into fits of sheer physical nausea, came from Posen.[24] Those of Gershom Scholem's *Urgrosseltern* who did not come from the previously Polish province of Silesia, came from Posen.[25] Salman Schoken, Rudolf Mosse, Heinrich Graetz, Eduard Lasker, and Arthur Ruppin were all born in the province of Posen.[26] While in the early nineteenth century more than 40 percent of all Prussian Jews lived in that province, they constituted by 1910 just over 7 percent of the total Jewish inhabitants in Prussia. Their migration westward continued almost uninterruptedly from 1833 onward. When the first study of the Jewish mass immigration from the East was published in 1881, one could speak of a large-scale Jewish migration only with reference to Posen.[27] Even during the 1880s, the decade of the Russian pogroms, migration from Posen was still numerically larger than that of Jews from further east. Posen Jews were still widely considered *Ostjuden,* though by that time they were occasionally seen as *Mischlinge.*[28] *Vis-à-vis* the new Galician masses, they were finally beginning to be accepted as *bona fide* German Jews.

The story of German Jewry during the century of emancipation is in-

---

sal des deutschen Judentums (Berlin, 1932), chap. 2; Eugen von Bergmann, *Zur Geschichte der Entwicklung deutscher, polnischer und jüdischer Bevölkerung in der Provinz Posen seit 1824* (Tübingen, 1883), chap. 4; and Bernhard Breslauer, *Die Abwanderung der Juden aus der Provinz Posen* (Berlin, 1909).

24. Georg Hermann, *Jettchen Gebert* (Berlin, 1906).

25. See Gerschom Scholem, *Von Berlin nach Jerusalem,* rev. ed. [in Hebrew] (Tel Aviv, 1982), p. 11.

26. See Siegfried Moses, "Salman Schoken: His Economic and Zionist Activities," *LBIYB* 5 (1960): 73–104; Werner E. Mosse "Rudolf Mosse and the House of Mosse, 1867–1920, ibid., 4 (1959): 237–59; Georg Herlitz, "Three Jewish Historians: Jost—Graetz—Täubler," ibid., 9 (1964): 69–90; James F. Harris, "Eduard Lasker: The Jew as National German Politician," ibid., 20 (1975): 151–78; Alex Bein, "Arthur Ruppin: The Man and His Work," ibid., 17 (1972): 117–42.

27. Salomon Neumann, *Die Fabel von der jüdischen Massenwanderung* (Berlin, 1881).

28. See the comments to this effect in Hermann Zondek's memoirs, *Auf festem Fusse: Erinnerungen eines jüdischen Klinikers* (Stuttgart, 1973), pp. 33–34.

deed above all a story of migration, from one culture to another, from village to town, from the small town to the metropolis, from the East to the West.[29] These elements of mobility were overlapping for most Jews in Germany, but immigrants from the East combined them most clearly. They personified the essence of the assimilation process, best presented its difficulties, and reflected its absurdities. Watching them struggle through turned out to be an educational experience for many local Jews, and watching them was increasingly unavoidable.

Jews from the East immediately joined the main effort of German Jews at the time—namely, the effort of social climbing. German Jews were by then turned into a segment of the German bourgeoisie, leaning upon their private and communal achievements in acquiring its two indispensable marks, *Besitz* and *Bildung*. The *Ostjuden* were from the very beginning part and parcel of this development. In fact, they made it appear all the more spectacular. After all, their geographic and cultural starting point was particularly distant. The Posen Jews, settled far east in the former Polish lands, were deeply steeped in an Orthodox, Yiddish culture until well into the 1830s. But both inside the province and everywhere they went as they moved westward, these Jews managed a feat of acculturation and upward social movement—often within one generation.[30] They energetically took part in the economic development of the province and repeatedly overtaxed its educational facilities. The percentage of Jewish boys and girls who received better than elementary education in Posen was the highest in Prussia.[31] Jewish families seemed to be sending at least one outstanding physician each generation into the wealthy, and sometimes into the poorer, suburbs of Berlin. Those who moved out on the strength of their business connections and entrepre-

---

29. On the scope and significance of migration for German Jewry throughout the nineteenth century and into the twentieth, see Usiel O. Schmelz, "Die demographische Entwicklung der Juden in Deutschland von der Mitte des 19. Jahrhunderts bis 1933," in *Zeitschrift für Bevölkerungswissenschaft* 8, no. 1 (1981): esp. pp. 46–52.

30. See Jacob Jacobson, "Zur Geschichte der Juden in Posen," in *Geschichte der Stadt Posen,* ed. Gotthold Rhode (Neuendettelsau, 1953), pp. 243–56. On the linguistic aspects of acculturation and its peculiar success, also with regard to the Posen Jews, see Jacob Toury, "Die Sprache als Problem der jüdischen Einordnung in dem deutschen Kulturraum," in *Gegenseitige Einflüsse deutscher und jüdischer Kultur: Internationales Symposium,* ed. Walter Grab, *Jahrbuch des Instituts für deutsche Geschichte,* Beiheft 4 (Tel Aviv, 1982), pp. 75–95.

31. Data in Jacobson, "Zur Geschichte der Juden in Posen," pp. 252–55; Breslauer, *Die Abwanderung der Juden,* pp. 9–10; Jakob Thon, *Der Anteil der Juden am Unterrichtswesen in Preussen* (Berlin, 1905), pp. 26–28; ZDSJ 4 (January 1908): 13–14. See also the interesting comments of Adolph Asch in *Jüdisches Leben in Deutschland,* vol. 2, *Selbstzeugnisse zur Sozialgeschichte im Kaiserreich,* ed. Monika Richarz (Stuttgart, 1979), pp. 221–30.

neurship were sure to contribute their share of doctors, lawyers, and scholars at some later date. Within the context of a large community in which social success was a primary goal, these striving, industrious, ambitious men were bound to become an integral part. They may have not been entirely welcome while they were still the incoming parvenus, but they could no longer be left out once they had made it.

The list of Jewish contributors to German cultural and scientific life is full of men from Posen. A rapid review of those who made the pages of the first twenty years of the *Leo Baeck Institute Year Book* reveals a third *born* in Posen and Galicia, not counting those whose parents had made the move just before their birth. Some of the most distinguished German Jews were, after all, nothing but *Pollacken*. Among the Easterners, Moravian and Bohemian Jews were first to be accepted as Germans. Posen-born immigrants were then slowly drawn in as a respectable part of the community. The Galicians, coming in at the turn of the century, simply continued a process that had started earlier, and on the eve of the First World War were well on their way in, or perhaps indeed on their way up.

The best description of the position of the Galician Jew in prewar Germany is to be found in Shmuel Yosef Agnon's prose. Among his contemporaries, Agnon was outstandingly free of group prejudices and the tyranny of archetypes. He perceived and exposed the dichotomy of *Ost-* and *Westjuden* in all its complexities and absurdities, with its occasional tragedy and hilarity.[32] Herr Lublin, in whose warehouse Agnon was somehow forced to spend an idle Saturday night, came to Leipzig from his Galician *shtetl* as an eleven-year-old runaway.[33] He was first employed—if such a respectable term might describe the situation—by a female relative, as a peddler-help. He then quickly made his way up by displaying a unique tenacity and an outstanding business acumen. On the eve of the First World War, Agnon explains, Lublin considered himself, like other German Jews in town, a loyal, patriotic German citizen of the Jewish faith. Of his faith, Agnon dryly comments, little was left by then; German he was in body and soul. Lublin had married his former boss's daughter and established with her a model German home, bringing up his children, Heinz, Thomas, and Gerde to be as fully bourgeois and as fully German

---

32. See Baruch B. Kurzweil, "The Image of the Western Jew in Modern Hebrew Literature," *LBIYB* 6 (1961): 170–89; but more especially Dan Miron, "German Jews in Agnon's Work," ibid., 22 (1978): 265–80.

33. This and the following discussion is based on Shmuel Yosef Agnon, *Behanuto shel mar Lublin* (Jerusalem, 1974).

as he himself had become. To the astonishment of his local relatives, Lublin was apparently respected even by the non-Jewish city elite, who found him always ready with clever, original, and useful advice. With unfailing insight Agnon describes the paradoxes of this man's social existence, alluding to the hidden details that disclosed his Galician origins—his unease at the theater, his special family sensibilities, and above all his peculiar wit and humor. In a parallel way, remnants of a Jewish origin repeatedly surfaced at the home of his assimilating parents-in-law, making for particularly sarcastic passages.

After all, Lublin was only one, perhaps two generations later to acquire the benefits of the German culture of his *Schwiegereltern.* His neighbors, for instance, among the famous Leipzig fur merchants, had come into town—from Russia, Lithuania, or Posen—only slightly earlier.[34] Now it was the turn of the Galicians. By the end of the nineteenth century they were everywhere on the move. Sigmund Freud was a son of an immigrant *Galizianer.* Fritz Kortner's father, a small street-corner watchmaker, was one such Hebrew-reading, Yiddish-speaking Galician-born Jew. Victor Adler was born in a small Moravian town on the Galician border.[35] This list, too, can easily be expanded.

IV

In contradistinction with the Posen immigrants, however, the absorption of the Galician Jews was complicated by a number of factors. First, the wave of East European immigrants that began in the 1880s included a fairly large segment of Russian Jews. Following the pogroms, many were trying to flee the tsarist lands, and in 1890 about ten thousand of them were more or less permanent immigrants in Germany.[36] Unlike the *Posener* and the *Galizianer,* and even unlike the Hungarian immigrants, these men and women were easily distinguishable as foreigners. Their language, their habits, their discourse, their spheres of interests, all disclosed their origin, and *they* were in any case rarely trying to hide it. Their share in the wave of immigration, however, was quickly diminishing, and in

34. See Wilhelm Harmelin, "Jews in the Leipzig Fur Industry," *LBIYB* 9 (1964): 239–66.

35. For Sigmund Freud's father in this context, see Ernst Simon, "Sigmund Freud, the Jew," ibid., 2 (1957): 270–305. For Fritz Kortner, see his autobiography, *Aller Tage Abend* (Munich, 1959). On Victor Adler, see "The Jewish Background of Victor and Friedrich Adler: Selected Biographical Notes" (by R. W.), *LBIYB* 10 (1965): 266–76.

36. For the breakdown of Jewish immigrants according to countries of origin, see Wertheimer, "German Policy and Jewish Politics," app. B, esp. p. 588.

comparison with the Galician and the Posen contingencies, the Russian element was gradually becoming negligible.

Second, the Eastern Jewish immigrants in the late nineteenth century were presumably characterized by a lower social profile than their Posen predecessors in midcentury, though precise data are not available. While the German-Jewish population was becoming increasingly prosperous, *Ostjuden* were crowding the Jewish houses of charity and were significantly "expanding the occupational spectrum" of the Jewish community.[37] Finally, and perhaps most significant, the new immigrants, primarily the Galicians, coming into Germany at the late nineteenth and early twentieth centuries, were confronted with a local Jewish community that had left behind the early stages of emancipation and assimilation and was entering a new phase. While time was cut short by the approaching war, entrance into the established Jewish milieu was becoming ever more difficult. The barriers were growing higher.

By the time Agnon's Lublin was making his way up within the German-Jewish and the general German society, a relatively large number of previously Germanized Jews were already at the top of their social climb—either because there was simply nowhere further to go or because the obstacles piled up by a bigoted society were found to be insurmountable. These second, third, and occasionally even fourth generation social climbers were now gradually losing interest in the route up. The struggle for *recognition* was quickly replacing the efforts of social upward mobility. Men were busy protecting what had so far been achieved, seeking to add status to class, prestige to prosperity. They were struggling not merely to become properly acculturated, but also to be known as such. Under the circumstances they were forced to make special efforts in order to do slightly better than the non-Jewish German bourgeoisie on all counts. Above all, they were striving to excel in performing the rituals of middle-class life-style and civility. The still existing old generation of parvenus were, at this stage, posing an acute problem; but the newcomers were truly insufferable.[38]

Norbert Elias, laboring to describe the transformation of the old war-aristocracy into a civilized court-nobility, has inadvertently commented

37. See Jacob Toury, "Ostjüdische Handarbeiter in Deutschland vor 1914," *Bulletin des Leo Baeck Instituts* 6, no. 21 (1963): 81–91.

38. See the somewhat erratic, but nevertheless interesting, discussion in John M. Cuddihy, *The Ordeal of Civility: Freud, Marx, Levi-Strauss, and the Jewish Struggle with Modernity* (New York, 1974). See also Shulamit Volkov, "Selbstgefälligkeit und Selbsthass: Die deutschen Juden zu Beginn des 20. Jahrhunderts," *Geschichte in Wissenschaft und Unterricht,* forthcoming.

upon the history of German Jewry.[39] His distinction between an early
stage of social mobility and assimilation on the one hand, and a period of
consolidation and a new self-awareness on the other, is central for this
discussion. Thus at the early stages of emancipation, *Ostjuden* aroused
some unease and irritation, mingled with a measure of familiarity and
sympathy, and were eventually absorbed into the community on the
strength of their economic, social, and cultural achievements. Later, however, when status became the central issue, *Ostjuden* began to be conceived as a major source of embarrassment, haunting the better-situated,
better-acculturated, better-assimilated Jews. According to Elias's analysis,
shame and embarrassment (*Scham und Peinlichkeit*) were indeed the
two main emotional poles of this generation. Shame was experienced
when one forgot or neglected, even for a moment, the strict rules of the
civilization game. Embarrassment was aroused by the inappropriate behavior of others. Because of the strict rules of behavior that German Jews
imposed upon themselves, shame was something they would always experience. Their peculiar sense of responsibility and solidarity kept them
almost continuously in a state of embarrassment, too. Jewish solidarity,
indeed, was often aroused and appealed to in the service of the *Ostjuden*,
mostly the poor and the needy. But these remained, by the strict rules of
a class society, largely outside the good Jewish homes. The rich, the
prosperous, and energetic *Galizianer* "entered," despite their defective
manners and culture, even as other Jews had "entered" bourgeois society
despite their Jewishness.

At this stage of assimilation the antisemitic idiom helped some Jews
break their final ties with their Jewishness. Others, however, were beginning to face and appreciate the depth of the necessary break. They now
began to see that it must too often amount to a complete break with their
closest relatives; in a sense to a break within themselves. In addition, in
confronting the ever-continuing flow of *Ostjuden*, they were forced to
reflect upon their own lives and seek new definitions of their existence as
Jews. They were beginning to reach out beyond the limits of their own
complacent, solid, bourgeois German identity.

In a letter to his parents in June 1916, Franz Rosenzweig wrote:

> One does not write more illogically about the *Ostjuden* than about the
> *Westjuden;* it is only that in the case of the *Ostjuden* it all seems to

39. For the following discussion, see Norbert Elias, *Über den Prozess der Zivilisa-
tion: Soziogenetische und psychogenetische Untersuchungen* (Basel, 1939), esp. 2:
424–34, 397–409.

come at once, but if one could conceive of the whole literature about the *Westjuden* written—let's say—in the last twenty years, as condensed into one single year, so that literature too would turn out to be, as our Eastern-Jewish grand- and great-grandfathers would have called it, a nice *Bilbul. There is no Ostjudenfrage, there is only a Judenfrage*—and even that doesn't really exist. By the way, imagine only that all that German fear of the *Ostjuden* were to be directed not at the *Ostjuden as such,* but at these same people as future *Westjuden* (well, your kind).[40]

A generation of Jews who were relatively free from the anxiety of social climbing was beginning to look inward. These were the years of Freud and the great Jewish cultural critics, the time of the inflow of Jews into the membership and leadership of the Social Democratic party, and of the emergence of Zionism. The constant handling of the *Ostjudenfrage*—the confrontation with the parvenus—served well the purposes of this reassessment. Recognizing the foreigners as a reflection of oneself was essential for the entire process. It is not by chance that the Viennese Jews took such an important part in it. After all, Vienna was the real capital of Galicia, constantly refilled with new Eastern immigrants.

As an aspect of this process of reconsideration, *Ostjuden* were beginning to be looked upon with a different eye—not by everyone, not everywhere, but surely by a significant, articulate, and outspoken minority. "It is a fact that not only I," wrote Gershom Scholem in his memoirs, "but many, many of my contemporaries felt this pull toward the *Ostjuden.*"[41] This was to a large measure, no doubt, a matter of a generational conflict, as Scholem indeed hastened to add, but it may have also been something else: an expression of a new sense of self. Jews were beginning to accept the heterogeneity of their communality and to acknowledge the positive potential of this pluralism. It was for many of them a matter of reaching the limits of assimilation and promptly halting at the brink. From that point one could only turn backward and inward, seeking a new definition for one's identity, and often also a new self-respect.

40. Franz Rosenzweig to his parents, [June 7, 1916], *Briefe,* ed. Edith Rosenzweig in cooperation with Ernst Simon (Berlin, 1935), p. 95. Italics mine.
41. Scholem, *Von Berlin nach Jerusalem,* p. 47.

STEVEN E. ASCHHEIM

"The Jew Within"

The Myth of "Judaization" in Germany

The history of the strange doctrine of "Judaization" has gone relatively unremarked. Yet this idea in its various permutations was an integral part of the discourse surrounding the modern *Judenfrage*. In Germany, where the debate on the Jewish Question was particularly protracted, programmatic, and philosophically oriented, the notion took on special salience. The idea became a sort of reference point, and most parties were impelled to employ it and bend it to their own purposes (whether in advocatory, oppositional, or deflective ways).

At its most elementary level, the term "Judaization" simply reflected the belief that Jews wielded disproportionate influence and occupied (or were about to occupy) pivotal positions of inordinate economic, political, and cultural power. This was its most obvious and familiar meaning. But it often went beyond this to refer to a more subtle, deeper danger: *Verjudung* connoted a condition in which the "Jewish spirit" had somehow permeated society and its key institutions, one in which Jewish *Geist* had seeped through the spiritual pores of the nation to penetrate and undermine the German psyche itself. Toward the end of the nineteenth century this theme had become an ideological reflex of the political anti-semites, but in terms of its genesis and development, the sensibility it conveyed and the functions it fulfilled, the idea was not limited to such circles. For here was a powerful, polyvalent myth with a life of its own, one that was able to provide comforting explanations for a variety of crises and unfamiliar situations. Elastic in application, easily adapted to different interest groups and ideological orientations, its strength lay precisely in its indeterminate symbolic allusiveness.

The question of Jewish emancipation in Germany was often accompanied by fears of the debilitating effects Jewish integration would have on the larger body politic. Critics of emancipation regarded Jewish assimilation as a potentially corrupting agent, dissolutive of society itself.[1] Already at the beginning of the nineteenth century, however, Jakob Fries argued that it was not Jews as such but Judaism and the "Jewish spirit" which constituted the problem: "We declare war not against the Jews, our brothers, but against Judaism. Should one we love be stricken by the plague, is it not proper that we wish him deliverance from it? Should we abuse those who, stricken by the plague, lament its horrors and conjecture how to free themselves from it? . . . In fact, improving the condition of the Jews in society means rooting out Judaism."[2]

This claim, that the attack upon Judaism was based upon a humanist, even redemptive concern for the Jew, later became, as we shall see, a *leitmotif* of many antisemites. But from the beginning there was agreement that some form of "de-Judaization" (vague as the demand may have been) was the precondition for emancipation. Defenders and opponents of the Jews alike shared this view. In this way the difficulties of *Entjudung* became part of the problematic of the modernizing, intellectual German Jew. Judaism was increasingly "psychologized," experienced, in the words of Hannah Arendt, as a kind of character trait, a personal defect. In his deeply ironic yet compassionate way, Heinrich Heine depicted it as an "Incurable deep ill! defying treatment. . . . Will Time, the eternal goddess, in compassion / Root out this dark calamity transmitted from sire to son?"[3]

The frustrations of de-Judaization were not only felt by Jewish *literati,* for the apparent failure of the *Entjudung* project also became an obsessive ingredient of nineteenth-century anti-Jewish mythology. But here it

1. There are innumerable examples of this. Among the better known are Jakob Fries, *Über die Gefährdung des Wohlstandes und Charakters der Deutschen durch die Juden* (Heidelberg, 1816); Christian Friedrich Rühs, *Über die Ansprüche der Juden an das deutsche Bürgerrecht* (Berlin, 1815).

2. Fries, *Gefährdung des Wohlstandes,* pp. 9–11. The translation here is by Mark Gelber, in *The Jew in the Modern World: A Documentary History,* ed. Paul R. Mendes-Flohr and Jehuda Reinharz (New York, 1980), pp. 258–59.

3. Hannah Arendt's still fresh comments on the nature of modern Jewish identity are in her *Rahel Varnhagen: The Life of a Jewish Woman* (New York, 1974), p. 218. Heine's poem "The New Israelite Hospital in Hamburg" (1841), translated by Margaret Armour, can be found in *The Poetry and Prose of Heinrich Heine,* ed. Frederic Ewen (New York, 1948), p. 285.

was not so much the intractability of Jewishness that was held to be alarming. It was, rather, the claim that the assimilation process had been reversed: instead of Jews being absorbed into German life, Germany itself was being "Judaized." That the notion of *Verjudung* achieved its greatest popularity and plausibility in the postemancipation period is not surprising. The full myth of a "Judaized" society was dependent upon the perception that Jews had access to the levers of power, a state of affairs that had been facilitated by the abolition of previous disabilities. It reflected anxieties that accompanied the introduction of legal equality and the dismantling of traditional protective barriers separating Christians from Jews. It provided a theory to explain the process and fact of newly acquired Jewish "dominance" over national institutions.[4] This myth was essentially one of social and ideological contagion. Not Jewish purification but German pollution and powerlessness, it held, was the outcome of emancipation.

I am concerned in this essay with some of the *modern* manifestations of the theme of "Judaization." This does not imply, of course, that such a notion was limited to the modern period. Indeed, people have been labeled as "Judaizers" almost from the inception of Christian theology itself. The original Judaizers, for example, were St. Peter's followers who urged conformity to Jewish ritual law against St. Paul. Since then the accusation of "Judaization" was pinned onto all manner of challenge against Christian Orthodoxy.[5] Heresy and "Judaization" became virtually synonymous activities. Given the historic Jewish-Christian tension, it was easy for the Christian to regard Jews in terms of the theological abomination of dissent. But the myth of "Judaization" went further than this: the Jew not only embodied dissent, he also became a metaphor for heresy itself, symbol of subversion whether or not its agents were themselves Jewish. All signs of heresy, any kind of dissent, could be labeled as "Judaizing" activities.[6]

A similar generalizing, symbolizing function attended the traditional

4. On the difference between pre- and postemancipation conditions, see Reinhard Rürup, "Emancipation and Crisis: The 'Jewish Question' in Germany, 1850–1890," *Leo Baeck Institute Year Book* (hereafter *LBIYB*) 20 (1975): 13–25.

5. On the history of the term "Judaizer," as well as a case history in which the notion is employed somewhat differently from here, see Paul Lawrence Rose, *Bodin and the Great God of Nature: The Moral and Religious Universe of a Judaiser* (Geneva, 1980), esp. pp. 5–9.

6. See the still important work by Joshua Trachtenberg, *The Devil and the Jews: The Mediaeval Conception of the Jew and Its Relation to Modern Antisemitism* (Cleveland, 1961), p. 181. See, too, Lewis Feuer, *Spinoza and the Rise of Liberalism* (Boston, 1966), p. 48. I thank Stephen Whitfield for this last reference.

association between Jews and moneylending. Indeed, these medieval roots lent resonance to the myth in its later modern garb. Words like *judeln* (1522)[7] and *mauscheln* (1680)[8] entered into general German usage as pejorative terms indicating distasteful (Jewish) ways of thinking, talking, and economic dealing. Christians, too, could be said to indulge in *judeln*. Indeed, those who engaged in usury were often themselves labeled as *Kristenjuden*. In fifteenth-century Germany, Christian usury was termed the *Judenspiess,* or "Jews' spear." (Such symbolic equations were, of course not limited to Germany. Even though Jews had been officially absent from England for many years, in his 1612 essay *Of Usury* Sir Francis Bacon recommended that all usurers "should have tawny orange bonnets, because they do Judaize." And in words strikingly close to later nineteenth-century rhetoric, we find Bernard of Clairvaux, who preached the Second Crusade, commenting, "I keep silence on the point that we regret to see Christian usurers judaizing worse than Jews."[9])

There are striking continuities between the medieval and modern versions of the myth: the attribution of great Jewish power and subversive intention; the combined use of the Jew as concrete embodiment *and* symbol; the detachable nature of the "Jewish spirit" and its ability to penetrate non-Jews in thought and behavior; the obvious secularization of religious heresy into the appropriate political ideology of which Jews were presumed to be both the carriers and symbols (liberalism, Marxism, etc.).

The subject of usury and moneylending, however, was not so much secularized as extended and elaborated to fit the new socioeconomic circumstances of the nineteenth century. The association with money, the equation of Judaism with egoism and materialism, persisted and was reinforced. Regardless of its other variations, no version of the "Judaization" myth was without this dimension. Thus Jakob Fries, whom we have already mentioned and whose arguments were not untypical, identified Judaism with "the whole lot of deceitful, second-hand pedlars and hawkers." Unless their social structure and mental constitution were revolutionized, they would not be able to give up old economic habits. They would "acquire power through money wherever despotism or distress

7. Friedrich Kluge and Alfred Götze, *Etymologisches Wörterbuch* (Berlin, 1951), p. 347.
8. See Jacob Grimm and Wilhelm Grimm, *Deutsches Woerterbuch,* vol. 6 (Leipzig, 1855), pp. 1819–20.
9. This treatment of the relation between usury and "Judaization" is taken mainly from Trachtenberg, *Devil and the Jews.* For the quotation from Sir Francis Bacon, see p. 192; for Bernhard of Clairvaux, p. 191.

engenders oppressive taxation . . . wherever the well-being of the citizen is so endangered that indebtedness on a small scale grows ever worse." Like later commentators, Fries linked the rise of Jewish power to faults within the host society. "Judaization" was the consequence of local wastefulness and sloth: "The idle, stagnant capital of these countries is devoured by the Jews like worms gnawing on rotting matter."[10]

In the late eighteenth and early nineteenth centuries, however, there was still no developed theory as to the overall *Verjudung* of German society and its collective soul. For contemporaries in this preemancipation phase, the problem was not so much the "Judaization" of Germans as skepticism concerning either the Germanization or Christianization of the Jew. As Friedrich Buchholz wrote in 1803, even if the Jewish youth was raised and educated in a Christian home he "would return to huckstering [*Schacher*] and again become a Jew." Baptism, too, would be ineffective, for instead of renouncing *Schacher*, the Jew was "bound to transform the sacrament itself into the object of huckstering." The only effective path to Jewish reform, Buchholz concluded, was participation in military life.[11] Only as Jewish incorporation into German society and culture increased did a more inclusive notion emerge. The theory of *Verjudung* was the negative mirror image of assimilation.

It is perhaps no accident that the first clearly secular and more systematic idea of "Judaization" was formulated and circulated, in the main, by estranged Jewish intellectuals of the radical neo-Hegelian school. It was these men who were groping toward the articulation of an incipient socialist theory. In psychological terms the struggle involved in this "breakthrough," in the early critique of bourgeois society, entailed not only Jewish self-criticism but the compulsion to self-immolation as they increasingly identified bourgeois society with Judaic principles.[12] Regardless of the psychological wellsprings of socialist ideology in Germany, in the present context what counts is the fact that these intellectuals invented a kind of "theory" that was applied to society as a whole and employed socioeconomic rather than theologically informed categories; ironically, the medieval tradition of depicting certain Christian economic practices

10. Fries, *Gefährdung des Wohlstandes*, in *The Jew in the Modern World*, p. 259.
11. Friedrich Buchholz, *Moses und Jesus: Über das intellektuelle und moralische Verhältnis der Juden und Christen—Eine historisch-politische Abhandlung* (Berlin, 1803), pp. 215–16, 208–9. On military life as the solution, see pp. 217ff.
12. These suggestive connections appear in the interesting article by Orlando Figes, "Ludwig Börne and the Formation of a Radical Critique of Judaism," *LBIYB* 29 (1984): 351–82. Although the present essay does not deal specifically with Börne, he very much fits the pattern under discussion.

as "Jewish" was revived. The young Heinrich Heine, for instance, did not merely associate Jews with philistine wealth; he categorized the obsession with moneymaking as such as a Jewish activity. In an early letter (1816) he wrote, "I call all Hamburgers Jews, and those I call baptized Jews in order to distinguish them from the circumcised are called *vulgo:* Christians."[13] The radical attack on wealth, its identification with Jewry, and the gradual "Judaization" of Christian society as it transformed itself into a capitalist one were captured in vignette rather than systematic form by Heine. Baron James de Rothschild he termed "Herr von Shylock in Paris, the mightiest Baron of Christendom."[14] In an unpublished passage from the *Baths of Lucca* (1829) he wrote that finance capital had become the new religion, and, as a result, Rome was dying from the "Jewish poison."[15]

But these were the rather inchoate sentiments of a Jew always profoundly ambivalent toward his own Jewishness. They were never articulated into a general theory. Indeed the more mature Heine did an about-turn and proposed a positive and quite different understanding of "Judaization":

> In Northern Europe and in America, especially in the Scandinavian and Anglo-Saxon countries, among the Germanic peoples, and partly among the Celtic ones, the Palestinian way of life has prevailed to such a marked degree that we seem to be living among Jews. . . . The genuine, the ageless, the true—the morality of ancient Judaism—will bloom in these countries just as acceptably to God as once in the lands by the Jordan and the heights of Lebanon. One needs neither palm-trees nor camels to be good; and goodness is better than beauty.
>
> The readiness with which these nations adopted Jewish life, customs and modes of thought may not be altogether due to their susceptibility to culture. The cause of this phenomenon should always be sought in the character of the Jewish people, who have had a great affinity with the Germans. . . . Judea has always seemed to me a fragment of the West which has somehow gotten lost in the East.[16]

It should be noted that the priority of ethics over esthetics reflected the change in Heine's previous preference of Hellenism over Nazarenism. The broader relevance here lies, however, in the fact that Heine, like

13. Heinrich Heine to Christian Sethe, November 20, 1816, quoted in Jeffrey L. Sammons, *Heinrich Heine: A Modern Biography* (Princeton, 1980), pp. 38–39.

14. Quoted in Helmut Hirsch, "Karl Marx zur 'Judenfrage' und zu Juden: Eine weiterführende Metakritik?" in *Juden im Vormärz und in der Revolution von 1848,* ed. Walter Grab and Julius Schoeps (Stuttgart and Bonn, 1983), p. 207.

15. Quoted in Sammons, *Heine,* pp. 249–50.

16. Heinrich Heine, "Moses" (1854), trans. Frederic Ewen, in *Poetry and Prose of Heine,* pp. 665–66.

many German Jews before and after him, sought in the Bible, in ethics, in Jewish rationalism, and in other elements of Jewish life areas where it could be argued that Judaism had had a beneficial, shaping, even osmotic, effect on the course of Western civilization. There is a long and interesting history of countermodels of "Judaization" worth exploring. Suffice it to say that the attempts to give the matter a more positive valence did not usually prevail; from its earliest beginnings the notion was overdetermined, saturated with negative connotations.

It is with Moses Hess and especially Karl Marx that "Judaization" was placed within a clearly theoretical framework.[17] In Hess's moralistic essay "On Money" (1845), the Feuerbachian critique of religion was located squarely within the socioeconomic sphere and the language of theologico-anthropological projection applied to the relationship between capital, Judaism, and Christianity. "Money," wrote the impassioned Hess, "was alienated spilt blood," and the modern commercial state, which was based upon the worship of money, was based upon the deepest denial of the species-essence of man as a social being. Hess argued that Christianity represented the logic of egoism, the belief that isolated individual existence was a desirable state. As the egoistic man externalized himself theoretically in God, in the real world man externalized himself through money. The world had been transformed into a vast stock exchange that Hess identified as the "Jewish-Christian peddler world":

> The Jews, who in the natural history of the social animal world had the world-historical mission to elicit the predator in humanity, have now at last completed their task. The mystery of Judaism and Christianity has been revealed in the modern Jewish-Christian peddler world. The mystery of the blood of Christ, like the mystery of the ancient Jewish blood worship, finally appears undisguised as the mystery of the predator. In ancient Judaism the blood cult was only prototypical, in medieval Christendom it was theoretically, ideally, logically realized . . . but only in the imagination. In the modern Jewish-Christian peddler world it is no longer symbolic or mystical but a daily, prosaic matter.[18]

Hess's later conversion to Jewish nationalism obviously entailed a repudiation of such views. But even in this essay the theme of "Judaization"

17. I am not concerned here with the question of priority and influence. For a detailed discussion of the ideational links between Moses Hess and Karl Marx, see Julius Carlebach, *Karl Marx and the Radical Critique of Judaism* (London, 1978), pp. 110–24.
18. Moses Hess, "Über das Geldwesen" (1845), in *Moses Hess: Sozialistische Aufsätze, 1841–1847*, ed. Theodor Zlocisti (Berlin, 1921), p. 182. There is a good discussion of Hess in Robert S. Wistrich's excellent *Socialism and the Jews: The Dilemmas of Assimilation in Germany and Austria-Hungary* (London and Toronto, 1982), pp. 36–44.

was mentioned merely in passing. It is only with Marx's essay *On the Jewish Question* (1844) that it becomes the central informing category, that the analysis is invested with apparently more theoretical and socio-historical sophistication. Few essays have been more thoroughly analyzed than this one: here only its relation to the theme of "Judaization" will be discussed.

A polemic against his fellow Young Hegelian Bruno Bauer's opposition to Jewish emancipation,[19] Marx's advocacy of Jewish civil rights in bourgeois society was ambiguous in the extreme. That one could not deny political emancipation to the Jew, Marx argued, was somehow beside the point, for it was political emancipation itself that was the object of criticism. For Marx, *political* emancipation, which Bauer had identified with emancipation of the state from religion, had to be radically distinguished from its final and absolute form, *human* emancipation. Precisely because Jews could be emancipated politically without renouncing Judaism completely, it was necessary to keep in mind the goal of human emancipation and locate the problem "in the *nature* and *category* of political emancipation."[20]

All these reflections were prompted by Marx's exceedingly negative conception of Judaism. Historical progress required its complete renunciation: "What is the profane basis of Judaism? *Practical* need, *self-interest*. What is the worldly cult of the Jew? *Huckstering*. What is his god? *Money*. . . . What was, in itself, the basis of the Jewish religion? Practical need, egoism. . . . Money is the jealous god of Israel, beside which no other god may exist. . . . The bill of exchange is the real god of the Jew. His god is only an illusory bill of exchange."

It is, however, Marx's rendering of the "Judaizing" process as a definitive force in modern society that, in the present context, is crucial: "The Jew has emancipated himself in a Jewish manner, not only by acquiring the power of money, but also because *money* had become through him and also apart from him, a world power, while the practical Jewish spirit has become the practical spirit of the Christian nations. The Jews have emancipated themselves in so far as the Christians have become Jews."[21]

It is noteworthy that Christianity was regarded here as a kind of vehi-

19. Bruno Bauer, *Die Judenfrage* (Braunschweig, 1843). For a translation, see Bruno Bauer, "The Jewish Problem," in *The Young Hegelians: An Anthology*, ed. Lawrence L. Stepelevich (Cambridge, 1983), pp. 187–97.

20. All quotations from Karl Marx's *On the Jewish Question* are from *Karl Marx: Early Writings*, ed. and trans. Tom Bottomore (New York, 1964). See pp. 10–11, 31, 21.

21. Ibid., pp. 34, 36, 37, 35.

cle through which Judaism could realize itself. This perception—that
Christianity had been infected by Judaism and was never really able to
overcome it—was later to obsess many racist antisemites:

> From the beginning, the Christian was the theorizing Jew; consequently
> the Jew is the practical Christian. And the practical Christian has be-
> come a Jew again. It was only in appearance that Christianity overcame
> real Judaism. . . . Christianity is the sublime thought of Judaism;
> Judaism is the vulgar practical application of Christianity. But this prac-
> tical application could only become universal when Christianity as
> perfected religion had accomplished, in a *theoretical* fashion, the aliena-
> tion of man from himself and nature. It was only then that Judaism
> could attain universal domination and could turn alienated man and
> alienated nature into *alienable,* saleable objects, in thrall to egoistic need
> and huckstering.[22]

The world had internalized and "become" the Jew. In the age of "species-
being," human emancipation was therefore conditional upon emancipation from Judaism.

Despite its familiarity, Marx's *On the Jewish Question* remains an
extraordinary document. While the conceptual garb is secular, apparently
sociological, its content is decidedly mythological in nature.[23] The transformation of the Jew into a collective symbol (in this case, into a metaphor for the evils of bourgeois society) was present in all versions of the
Verjudung myth. The "Jewish spirit," moreover, could encompass a wide,
and often contradictory, range of human qualities. How were such attributes discovered? In the myth the specific characteristics of Jewish *Geist*
were always deduced from the nature of the object under criticism—liberalism, capitalism, secularism, or whatever—and then identified as such.
With Marx, as with others, these qualities were then posited as virtually
immutable, incorrigible. The "Jewish spirit" was inevitably dehistoricized,
hypostatized into static, eternal qualities.

Beyond this, however, Marx's analysis contained a thrust that other,
later doctrines of "Judaization" would also emphasize: the contention that
unchanging Jewish *Geist* possessed immense power and was capable of
penetrating all of society, permeating even those who seemed as far away
from Judaism as possible. The notion of *Verjudung* could work in this

---

22. Ibid., p. 39.

23. See the analysis by Nathan Rotenstreich, "For and against Emancipation: The
Bruno Bauer Controversy," *LBIYB* 4 (1959): esp. pp. 23–27. See also, Wistrich,
Socialism and the Jews, pp. 25–31; Carlebach, *Marx and Judaism,* pp. 148–84.

way because it posited a "spirit" that was a part of, and yet at the same time disengaged from, its original carriers. The medieval identification of non-Jewish usurers as *Kristenjuden* was one indication of such an infection. What was new with Marx was the generalization of this principle into one of total social change. If in the medieval version Christian usurers were an indication of such a "Jewish" infection, they were stigmatized as such and held in contempt. In all modern versions of the myth such containment was impossible. This reflected obvious social changes: Jewish penetrability was facilitated because the dividing walls of the ghetto had crumbled, traditional boundaries had eroded, and the secularization of general and Jewish life had proceeded apace. Consequently, society as a whole could be infected and the Jewish principle more plausibly represented as universally operative.

Marx's apologists usually contend that Marx did not attack Jews as such but only the "spirit of Judaism," which, in turn, was symbolic shorthand for the "spirit of capitalism."[24] But this kind of distinction, one that as we shall see was constantly invoked during the nineteenth and early part of the twentieth centuries, was always exceedingly problematic. Marx's crude equation of the Jew and his religion with money, huckstering, and materialist egoism could not but reinforce anti-Jewish stereotypes at the most basic level.

Jewish participation and visibility in the cultural, economic, and political life of nineteenth-century Germany provided the myth with the necessary generating fuel. Such myths assume plausibility only if they contain some relation, however tenuous, to social reality. And *Verjudung*, in its many variations, was never an entirely arbitrary myth: the "Jewish spirit" always transmitted a corrupting *materialist* message. The traditional stereotype, perpetuated in much of nineteenth-century German philosophy and popular literature, hypostatized the Jew as exclusivist, egoistic, and materialistic. This was a convenient foil on which to displace the distaste and anxieties that accompanied the transformation of Germany into a modern, capitalist society. The myth of "Judaization" helped to simplify considerably the analysis of essentially complex abstract processes: the sociological was transformed into the metaphysical, the institutional into the religioethic or racial, cause and effect inverted. Moreover, the myth melded with a new, peculiarly modern consciousness of the role

24. See, for instance, I. Meszaros, *Marx's Theory of Alienation* (London, 1970), esp. pp. 30–31; Hirsch, "Marx zur 'Judenfrage.' "

of "material" forces in molding culture, with a heightened awareness of the "economic" as an autonomous factor in social and political affairs.[25]

Marx, it should be noted, never resorted to biological or racist conceptions. Moreover, this essay was written when he was twenty-six years old, and he never again wrote on the Jewish Question. Whether or not he privately clung to these early convictions, the more mature Marx employed only impeccably "impersonal" categories such as class, means and relations of production, and so forth. Materialist method replaced the original idealism, and the sociological prevailed over the religioethic. What, however, was the fate of the *Verjudung* thesis in the socialist movement?

By and large, socialists retained their support for Jewish emancipation and their disdain for traditional Judaism. As late as 1921 Karl Kautsky could not have put it more bluntly: "The Jews have become an eminently revolutionary factor, while Judaism has become a reactionary factor."[26] But the theme of "Judaization" as such appeared only sporadically and then usually in somewhat defensive form. Given the orthodox materialist emphasis, it is not surprising that Marx's "idealist" essay on the Jewish Question was virtually forgotten until it was reprinted in the *Neuer Sozial-Demokrat* in 1872.[27] When Eduard Bernstein reprinted extracts from these essays in *Der Sozialdemokrat* in 1881, however, a certain ambiguity remained apparent. Bernstein accepted the notion of the "Jewish spirit" but, especially in the light of the climate created by Adolf Stöcker's anti-semitic Berlin movement, tried to "contextualize" the problem. Somewhat disingenuously he warned of the danger of "assuming precisely the opposite of what Marx excellently expounds, namely that the so-called Jewish spirit is a result of bourgeois society based on the capitalist mode of production, which when there are no Eastern Jews produces Christian Jews, like the Christian-Germanic Jews in America."[28] This attack upon antisemitism *in terms* of the "Judaization" thesis, the attribution of "Jew-

25. On this general point, see Louis Dumont, *From Mandeville to Marx: The Genesis and Triumph of Economic Ideology* (Chicago and London, 1977); Joyce Oldham Appleby, *Economic Thought and Ideology in Seventeenth-Century England* (Princeton, 1978).

26. Karl Kautsky, *Are the Jews a Race?* reprint ed. (Westport, 1972), p. 246. See also the important essay by George L. Mosse, "German Socialists and the Jewish Question in the Weimar Republic," in his *Masses and Man: Nationalist and Fascist Perceptions of Reality* (New York, 1980), pp. 284–315.

27. For this entire section on the socialist movement and the theme of *Verjudung*, I base myself upon material drawn from Wistrich's important study, *Socialism and the Jews.* See pp. 47, 362 n. 161.

28. Eduard Bernstein, quoted in ibid., p. 48.

ish" characteristics to non-Jews as a form of Jewish defense, was a somewhat dubious tactic, a double-edged sword at best. In an article entitled "The Judaization of the German Reich" (1881), Bernstein maintained this ambiguity: "Jewry" still symbolized huckstering. He deplored the fact that popular revulsion was directed only "at the circumcised Jews, while uncircumcised Jewry at the helm (of State) was paid homage to and glorified." What had happened was that "Huckstering had become the fundamental principle of the German Reich . . . thanks to the Judaized outlook of the Imperial Chancellor, the monarchical principle and the German monarchy itself is completely judaized."[29] In Austria there were moments when socialists lost all the ironic, ambiguous connotations. Thus Otto Bauer, the Austro-Marxist theoretician, could approvingly quote the antisemite Baron Karl von Vogelsang's remark: "If by some miracle all our 1,400,000 Jews were to be taken from us, it would help us very little, for we ourselves have been infected with the Jewish spirit."[30]

Thus Marxist socialists, while at times inclined to equate the vulgar commercialism of the *Gründerjahre* with things Jewish, did not use the *Verjudung* myth regularly, and, when they did, it was usually in a deflective, albeit ambivalent, way. Their materialist class analysis and internationalist commitment prevented them from going much further than this. Such inhibitions did not pertain to those who were gradually building an ideology of socialism that was neither materialist nor cosmopolitan but rather idealist and nationalist. The rise of a national socialist ideology was, as is well known, a *völkisch, fin-de-siècle* reaction to both bourgeois liberalism and Marxist socialism. These were propitious circumstances in which the *Verjudung* thesis could flourish. The role of the famous economist Werner Sombart in this development was both central and exemplary.

Sombart, significantly, began as a radical sympathetic to Marxism but ended up by including it in his pantheon of "Jewish products."[31] He was

29. Bernstein, "Die Verjudung des Deutschen Reiches," *Der Sozialdemokrat*, January 9, 1881, pp. 1–2, quoted in Wistrich, *Socialism and the Jews*, p. 97. For a similar attack on antisemitism that also contains certain ambiguous comments, see August Bebel, "Vorschlag einer Resolution zum Thema Antisemitismus und Sozialdemokratie," in *Marxisten gegen Antisemitismus*, ed. Irving Fetscher (Hamburg, 1974), pp. 58–76.

30. Otto Bauer, "Das Ende des Christlichen Sozialismus," *Der Kampf* 4, no. 9 (June 1, 1911): 393–98, quoted in Wistrich, *Socialism and the Jews*, p. 191.

31. For good biographical accounts of Werner Sombart and his career, see Herman Lebovics, *Social Conservatism and the Middle Classes in Germany, 1914–1933* (Princeton, 1969); and Arthur Mitzman, *Sociology and Estrangement: Three Sociologists of Imperial Germany* (New York, 1973). Marxism, according to Sombart, had its roots in the Greek philosophy of decadence and the "Jewish spirit." Marx himself was "the

also, of course, instrumental in lending academic legitimacy to the identification of the "Jewish spirit" with that of modern capitalism. His famous *Die Juden und das Wirtschaftsleben* (1911), while written in the idiom of social science, in reality simply systematized older, popular perceptions of the Jews and their facility for moneymaking and materialist gain.[32] The *Verjudung* of Germany could be counteracted only by the creation of a *German* socialism opposed to both the Jewish merchant and Marxist spirit.[33] In the best traditions of the "Judaization" myth, Sombart, who had done so much to diffuse the image of the materialist Jew, argued that the "Jewish spirit" was both an integral part of the Jewish group and was yet detachable and transmittable to non-Jews. Writing in 1934 in a Germany that had indeed attained National Socialism, Sombart stated: "Here it is a question of overcoming and removing, in a feasible way, what is called the 'Jewish spirit.' . . . This spirit first struck root in the Jewish people, and we must assume that it extended itself among them, because it corresponded with a frequently recurring racial trait in the Jewish people." This was a kind of "spiritual" rather than biological racism, for Sombart argued that not all Jews were necessarily afflicted by the "Jewish spirit": some could even be animated by its German antithesis. More to the point, however, was Sombart's insistence that the "Jewish spirit" had radically spread: this did not attenuate the antisemitic animus; it meant simply that the range of attack had to be correspondingly widened, for Germany itself was "Jewish":

> Under the influence of the Jewish spirit the entire external structure of our existence has been formed and, as a matter of fact, *exists*, whether Jews are present or not. In other words, the Jewish spirit has become a part of us, it "objectivates" in a thousand regulations and practices: in our law, our constitution, our style of life, our economics, etc. Our economy, above all. . . . In order to free ourselves from the Jewish spirit—said to be the chief task of the German people and, above all, of Socialism—it is not enough to exclude all Jews, not even enough to cultivate an anti-Jewish temper. It will be far better to so transform the institu-

---

most rootless and contradictory of all socialists." See Lebovics, *Social Conservatism*, pp. 62–66.

32. See Paul R. Mendes-Flohr, "Werner Sombart's *The Jews and Modern Capitalism*: An Analysis of Its Ideological Premises," *LBIYB* 25 (1976): 87–107.

33. For examples of the *völkisch* way in which Sombart employed the term *Verjudung*, see his "Artvernichtung oder Artverhaltung, in *Der Jud ist Schuld: Diskussionsbuch über die Judenfrage*, ed. Hermann Bahr et al. (Basel, 1932), esp. p. 252. See also his *Die Zukunft der Juden* (Leipzig, 1912) and *Judentaufen* (Munich, 1912).

tional culture that it will no longer serve as a bulwark for the Jewish spirit.[34]

We should keep in mind that in Wilhelmine Germany the perception of "Judaization" was not limited to outright antisemites, conservative critics, or such circles as I have discussed above. The deep ambivalence attached to the transformation of Germany into a modern capitalist culture did not apply only to traditional classes or the new proletariat.[35] The very liberals and bourgeoisie who were bringing this metamorphosis about were plagued by similar doubts and anxieties, as older values came into conflict with newer economic practices. Given the obvious fact of Jewish participation in this process, liberal bourgeois non-Jews also voiced the sentiment—sometimes publicly, sometimes privately—that Germany was becoming *verjudet* without, for one moment, reneging on liberal support for Jewish emancipation. *Verjudung* was so useful precisely because it could function as a sublimative "symbolic" tool.

As one liberal put it in an address to the Freies deutsches Hochstift in Frankfurt in 1880, the new antisemitism, though attacking "the Jews," was not really aimed at the Israelite population: "Far from it, that movement represents an inarticulate manifestation of the feeling which has seized hold of our whole people. They feel that the insensate dance round the golden calf, the purblind pursuit of the pleasures of the flesh threaten to lead us, too, astray and onto paths of evil from which the lofty instinct of our people shrinks in horror." Jews, the speaker went on, had of course contributed considerably to these materialistic developments, but "Jewish" activities were not necessarily Israelite ones.

> Indeed it is no secret that this circumstance led a long time ago to the adoption of a common useage [*sic*] of a new terminology which—let it be said, quite unjustly—designates all ruthless money-grabbers as "Jews," even though they may be of German stock, no matter whether they are high or low born. It is these so-called Jews and their society, and not the Israelites, who are the targets of the movement of outraged indignation that is spreading wider in Germany every day. The German

---

34. Werner Sombart, *A New Social Philosophy* (New York, 1969), pp. 177, 178–79. See also pp. 175ff. This is a translation by Karl F. Geiser of Sombart's *Deutscher Sozialismus* (1934).

35. This has been superbly captured by Fritz Stern in his *Gold and Iron: Bismarck, Bleichröder and the Building of the German Empire* (New York, 1977). See also Stern, "Money, Morals, and the Pillars of Society," in his *The Failure of Illiberalism: Essays on the Political Culture of Modern Germany* (Chicago and London, 1975), pp. 26–57.

people are beginning to realize that they are in danger of losing their holiest and most cherished treasure, the heritage of our fathers, that noble contempt for worldly things, that humble reverence for the holy, that sublime striving for inner worth and the transfiguration of the soul, all those traits which have so far been shared by all Germans irrespective of differences of religous denomination.[36]

Liberals did not consistently distinguish between "Jews" and "Israelites." The attack on Jewish civil rights was one thing, condemning the Jew as the embodiment of the "Jewish spirit" quite another. Thus even self-consciously liberal periodicals, journals that advocated Jewish emancipation and opposed political antisemitism, reinforced this link. As Henry Wassermann has decisively shown, popular liberal publications such as the *Fliegende Blätter* consistently connected Jews to the mammonization of German society:[37] Jews were granted a virtual monopoly in caricatures concerned with moneymaking and commerce in its dishonest and vulgar forms. This stereotype was reinforced by the popular middle-class German novels of Gustav Freytag and Wilhelm Raabe, in which the distinction between honorable Christian and dishonest Jewish dealings was of central importance.[38] Liberal German *Bürgertum,* embracing capitalism but locked into an older, competing system of values, found it easy to project the distasteful activity of making money and the commercialization of society onto the Jew.

There were, then, differing intentions behind, and divergent versions of, the "Judaization" myth. But it was, nevertheless, fairly generally disseminated. Because they chose (or were constrained) to use its terminology, to speak its language, all circles described above provided the idea with a certain legitimacy. Their role in the diffusion of this kind of thinking should not be underestimated. Still, here *Verjudung* was used mainly as a form of collective metaphor and in a deflective manner. This was not true for *völkisch* ideologues, certain conservatives, and political antisemites. They constantly hammered the theme home: their attack was

36. Reported in *General-Anzeiger* (Frankfurt a.M.), December 22, 1900, no. 300, quoted in Rürup, "Emancipation and Crisis" p. 23.

37. Henry Wassermann, "The *Fliegende Blätter* as a Source for the Social History of German Jewry," *LBIYB* 28 (1983): 124–28.

38. Particularly noteworthy are Gustav Freytag's *Soll und Haben* (1855) and Wilhelm Raabe's *Hungerpastor* (1864). For historical context, see Ernest K. Bramsted, *Aristocracy and the Middle Classes in Germany: Social Types in German Literature, 1830–1900* (Chicago and London, 1964); George L. Mosse, "The Image of the Jew in German Popular Literature: Felix Dahn and Gustav Freytag," in his *Germans and Jews: The Right, The Left, and the Search for a "Third Force" in Pre-Nazi Germany* (London, 1971).

frontal, and the distinction between "Jew" as symbol and as concrete embodiment was academic at best. While these distinctions must be kept in mind, certain links and continuities need to be noted. The explicitly antisemitic versions of "Judaization," at least in terms of their theoretical outlines, were also enunciated by radicals such as Richard Wagner and Wilhelm Marr. They, too, combined the traditional German "noble contempt for worldly things" with the "Judaization" myth; they also used the idealist tradition for their critique of Jewish materialism.

The translation of these ideas into a self-proclaimed, revolutionary, redemptive antisemitism was effected by Richard Wagner. Although the idea and major themes of "Judaization" had been circulating for a long time, it was a concept that awaited its name. No specific term had been coined. It was in Wagner's essay "Judaism in Music" (1850) that the German neologism *Verjudung* first appeared.[39] There the term connoted the transposition of the material onto the ideal, the corruption of the cultural by the philistine, the demeaning of the spiritual by the commercial. This concern—that the insides of German culture were being polluted and its basic values leveled by the "Jewish spirit"—did not arise in a vacuum; it reflected the anxieties generated by the remarkable and rapid emergence of a new kind of Jew, the secular intellectual and artist destined to play a major role in the shaping of nineteenth-century German culture (Wagner focused his attack on Heinrich Heine, Felix Mendelssohn, and, of course, Giacomo Meyerbeer). Despite the conversion to Christianity of most of these intellectuals, many critics dismissed their work as "arid" and "soulless." Juxtaposed to the noble, organic qualities of German culture, the "Jewish spirit" was stigmatized as an agent of decomposition. Jews, it was held, thrived in "mechanical" rather than "organic" situations. They thus flocked to Berlin—the very embodiment of "Judaized" society—for there, as Heinrich Laube put it, even spiritual exercise was the product of mechanical forces.[40]

Wagner systematized these sentiments in sophisticated and radical terms, combining anti-Jewish rhetoric with sharp social observation. In what, he asked, did the "Verjudung der modernen Kunst" (Judaization of modern art) consist?

39. This is the first mention of the term that I have found. Jacob Katz, in *From Prejudice to Destruction: Anti-Semitism, 1700–1933* (Cambridge, Mass., 1980), pp. 186–87, suggests the same.

40. For an interesting treatment of Heinrich Laube, see ibid., pp. 182–84. For an analysis of the relation between the rise of "new" assimilated Jewry and modern antisemitism, see Steven E. Aschheim, *Brothers and Strangers: The East European Jew in German and German Jewish Consciousness, 1800–1923* (Madison, 1982), chap. 3.

According to the present constitution of the world, the Jew in truth is already more than emancipated: he rules, and will rule, so long as Money remains the power before which all our doings and dealings lose their force. . . . That the impossibility of carrying farther any natural, any beauteous thing, upon the basis of that stage whereat the evolution of our arts has now arrived, and without a total alteration of that basis— that this has also brought the public Art-taste of our time between the busy fingers of the Jew, however, is the matter whose grounds we here have to consider somewhat closer. . . . What the heroes of the arts, with untold strain consuming lief and life, have wrested from the art-fiend of two millennia of misery, today the Jew converts into an art bazaar [*Kunstwaarenwechsel*]: who sees it in the mannered bricabrac, that is glued together by the hallowed brow-sweat of the Genius of two thousand years?[41]

For Wagner the "Judaization" process was partly the product of Jewish power over money; but it was also the beneficiary of a wider trend toward the "commoditization" of culture. German culture was in a state of degeneration, and the decline of standards was clearly in the interest of the modern Jew who, given his "rootlessness" and inalienable status as an outsider, was devoid of all authentic creative capacities. Cut off from its own tradition and the host society, the destructive "Jewish spirit" merely reflected the Jewish condition. Genuine artistic creativity was a function of deep, unconscious, historical belonging.[42]

Wagner illustrates particularly well the fact that all theories of *Verjudung* functioned—in a more or less sophisticated way—as a means of self-appraisal, as foils for cultural criticism. Both the preconditions for, and ultimate success of, "Judaization" were located in flaws and weaknesses in the German self and society.[43] The specter of *Verjudung* was thus

41. For this translation, see *Richard Wagner's Prose Works*, trans. William Ashton Ellis, vol. 3, *The Theatre* (London, 1907), pp. 81–82.
42. Ibid., p. 84.
43. This perception of weakness and the attribution of almost uncanny powers to the "Jewish spirit" were not, of course, limited to Germany. France was also a center of this kind of thinking. Gougenot des Mousseaux's *Le Juif, le judaisme et la judaisation des peuples chrétiens* (1869) not only influenced Edouard Drumont and other leading French antisemites but was translated by Alfred Rosenberg into German in 1921. The notion of "Judaization" also became a key slogan in Austrian antisemitism. See Karl Türk, *Die Verjudung Österreichs: Eine Warnung für das deutsche Reich* (Berlin, 1889). In certain cases, as with political Zionist activity, Jews sometimes even encouraged notions of their great power and influence. For all that, it is still surprising to read empirical British statesmen dealing with the problem of the Balfour Declaration and the later British mandate. Sir Mark Sykes wrote in 1916 that it may seem "odd and fantastic," but "when we bump into a thing like Zionism which is atmospheric, international, cosmopolitan, subconscious and unwritten—very often unspoken—it is not possible to work and think in ordinary lines." Of the draft mandate Lord Curzon

clearly linked to the insecure sense of German national identity: the "Judaized" society provided a countermodel against which the desired national state of affairs could be posited. In his essay "Was ist Deutsch?" (1878) Wagner drew a picture of Jewish power and German failure where cultural pessimism and utopian vision functioned as necessary correlates. He stressed a theme that later antisemites were constantly to reiterate. *Jüdischer Geist,* he argued, had penetrated so deeply, had so undermined the people, that, under the spell of liberal Jewish organs, they would no longer be able to utter a sensible word. *Verjudung* was a kind of opiate. In terms of its purported capacity for spiritual contagion, as an agent of ideological contamination, Wagner could seriously foresee a situation, close at hand, in which although the German *Volk* would persist in external form, its *Geist* would completely disappear.[44]

Wagner was even able to take the *Verjudung* critique beyond the hope for German national regeneration. Here the Jew and his negative "spirit" became the negative symbol, the antitype, not only of the German nation but the counterconception to Wagner's idea of humanity itself. A redeemed, revolutionized world was a de-Judaized humanity.[45]

Like Marx's apologists, defenders of Wagner contend that Wagner did not attack "ethnic" Jews but Judaism as a moral symbol.[46] Was not Wagner friendly with Jews like Hermann Levi, Karl Tausig, and Jacob Rubinstein?[47] The symbolic, plastic nature of the *Verjudung* argument made this distinction a popular one; many antisemites claimed that they had nothing against individual, particular Jews.[48] Judaism was here presented as a state of mind, a psycho-spiritual condition. Houston Stewart Chamberlain, an enthusiastic initiate of the Wagner entourage, put it thus:

---

commented that it "reeks of Judaism" and had "been drawn up by someone reeling under the fumes of Zionism." These quotations appear in the fascinating review by Conor Cruise O'Brien, "Israel in Embryo," *New York Review of Books,* March 15, 1984, pp. 36, 37.

44. Richard Wagner, "Was ist Deutsch?" in *Richard Wagners Gesammelte Schriften,* vol. 13 (Leipzig, n.d.), pp. 166, 171.

45. See the insightful remarks by Paul Lawrence Rose in "The Noble Anti-Semitism of Richard Wagner," *Historical Journal* 25 (1982): 751–63.

46. For a recent example, see L. J. Rather, *The Dream of Self-Destruction: Wagner's Ring and the Modern World* (Baton Rouge, 1979).

47. The way in which Wagner really treated his Jewish "friends" is a matter of dispute. See Rose, "Anti-Semitism of Wagner," pp. 754–59. See, too, Peter Gay, "Hermann Levi: A Study in Service and Self-Hatred," in his *Freud, Jews and Other Germans: Masters and Victims in Modernist Culture* (New York, 1978), pp. 189–230.

48. For just one example, see Wilhelm Marr, *Der Judenspiegel* (Hamburg, 1862), pp. 3, 11.

One does not need to have the authentic Hittite nose to be a Jew; the word indicates rather a special kind of feeling and thinking; a person may very rapidly become a Jew without being an Israelite; some need only to associate actively with Jews, read Jewish newspapers and become accustomed to the Jewish conception of life, literature and art. . . . We must agree with Paul, the apostle, when he says: "For he is not a Jew who is one outwardly in the flesh, but he is a Jew who is one inwardly."

This kind of "spiritual anti-Judaism" allowed for the "humanization of the Jew." As Chamberlain archly put it, "A wholly humanized Jew is no longer a Jew." Of course, he stressed, it was easier to "become a Jew" than the almost impossible task of "becoming a German."[49] But, at least in theory, the exceptional Jew could overcome the "Jewish spirit" within him.

The overwhelming majority of German Jews, while accepting the need for Jewish "modernization," tried to balance their "Germanism" and Judaism within some kind of honorable synthesis. A few extreme cases, however, not only accepted the antisemitic onslaught on Judaism in its entirety but made its purported "spiritual" basis the means for "overcoming" their own Jewishness. The Jewish writer Conrad Alberti (b. Konrad Sittenfeld), for example, totally accepted the anti-Judaic critique. He opposed active antisemitism on the grounds that it merely strengthened Jewishness! "Judaism," he wrote, "can be successfully combated only by Jews—the experience of Christ and Paul should have taught us that. . . . Only inner, spiritual self-disintegration [*Selbstzersetzung*] can liquidate and destroy Judaism."[50] The self-proclaimed Wagnerian Otto Weininger made this spiritual anti-Judaism the cornerstone of a systematic and ultimately tragic attempt to transcend his Jewishness. Judaism was, for him, not a historical tradition or an ethnic or racial category. It was rather a Platonic idea, a psychic negative potential of all human beings. There are "Aryans who are more Jewish than many Jews, and actual Jews who are more Aryan than certain Aryans," he wrote in his famous *Sex and Character* (1903).[51] Weininger was well aware of the projective nature of this phenomenon. Whoever hated Jews, he commented, hated the Jewish part within himself. But because it was an idea, a spiritual predisposition, he argued that Jewishness could be overcome.

49. Houston Stewart Chamberlain, *Die Grundlagen des neunzehnten Jahrhunderts* (Munich, 1906), 1:544–45, 574.

50. Conrad Alberti, "Judentum und Antisemitismus: Eine zeitgenössische Studie," *Die Gesellschaft* 4 (1889): 1730.

51. Otto Weininger, *Geschlecht und Charakter: Eine Prinzipielle Untersuchung,* reprint ed. (Berlin, 1932), p. 403.

This could never be done on a collective basis. The only satisfactory solution to the Jewish Question would take place on the individual level, where after a profound, inner struggle Jewishness could be transcended.

Like the antisemites, Weininger claimed that he was not attacking "individual Jews, to so many of whom I would have incurred highly unwillingly harm, to whom a great and bitter injustice would occur, if what I have said were to be turned against them." Yet whenever this kind of distinction was drawn—and this was very often the case—there was inevitable and alarming correspondence between the "Jewish spirit" and real, everyday Jews. As Weininger put it, although Judaism was a universal human *possibility,* its "overwhelming *realization* had occurred within historical Jewry."[52] Weininger's attempt to "spiritualize" the Jewish Problem relied upon the early Wagner and left out the more explicitly racist writings of the 1880s.[53] But even in the early Wagner the ethnic ingredient was present no matter how elevated the metaphysical discourse appeared. The distinction between person and principle, "spirit" and ethnicity, was an overwhelmingly fine one.[54] And although in his "Judaism in Music," Wagner allowed for Jewish redemption in principle, in practice this was an almost impossible task. For the German, redemption entailed regeneration through self-destruction; in the case of the ethnic Jew a double self-destruction was required, an almost superhuman act of will.

After Wagner introduced the neologism in 1850, *Verjudung* rapidly became an indispensable part of the linguistic currency of anti-Jewish discourse. The term summed up a fear that went beyond explicitly antisemitic circles. The perception of disproportionate Jewish power was certainly not limited to radical and fringe groups. The concern that public opinion was being controlled by the "Jewish press" was especially prevalent. For those who elaborated on the "Judaization" of Germany, this was particularly important, for in an age of increasingly impersonal mass communications the press was regarded as the major agent of ideological infiltration, the vehicle through which the "Jewish spirit" entered the German psyche. The Jewish press, one critic commented in 1865, had become so powerful "that it does not need to be directed by Jews

52. Ibid., pp. 413, 401.
53. See Wagner's "Erkenne dich selbst" and "Heldentum und Christentum," in *Wagners Gesammelte Schriften,* 14:182–93, 193–203.
54. See Cosima Wagner's diary entry for December 27, 1878: "Richard says: 'Personally, I have always had the best friends among the Jews, but their emancipation and civil equality before we had become (true) Germans has been destructive. I regard Germany as annihilated.'" Quoted in Rose, "Anti-Semitism of Wagner," p. 759.

anymore; the Christian has become so Judaized that no significant differences can any longer be recognized."[55]

Anti-Jewish circles concurred that the infection had spread; what differed were the diagnoses of, and proposed cures for, the disease. Clericals and conservatives agreed with radical antisemites that the "Jewish spirit" was based on the principle of Mammon (a conviction with which, as we have seen, both socialists and liberals did not really take issue). Such worldliness, conservatives argued, threatened to destroy the organic basis of society, to trample on traditional values of honest labor and authentic community. For such circles the process of "Judaization" was the consequence of the decline of religion. The triumph of the Enlightenment, of the French Revolution and liberalism, had destroyed the Christian state and the old social order and prepared the way for the rule of Judaism. This age of Jewish materialism and liberal permissiveness had tempted and overcome the believing Christian. Only with the financial crash of the 1870s, Christian polemicists proclaimed, did they begin to regret their actions: "You have made into your own God the calf that the Jews worship. You have helped the Jews," Paul Köhler wrote in his pamphlet *The Judaization of Germany: The Path to Deliverance,* "to destroy in the people the ideals of our Christian faith. Now do you wonder if Christian morality has disappeared? that Judaization has penetrated? that Germanism, which only flourished under the domination of Christian thought, was now declining? You are yourself Judaized!"[56]

If *Verjudung* followed the breakdown of the Christian *Weltanschauung,* the ideological antidote was obvious: "Whoever keeps his Christian faith high does not sink into Judaization. . . . Become Christian again and you will be freed of your *Verjudung.* . . . As long as the evangelical faith lives in the German people, to that degree it will not be Judaized. No real Protestant has become a *Judengenosse.*"[57] This was a fairly widespread sentiment. Still, most clericals and conservatives combined this hostility with a solution that was becoming increasingly antithetical to the radicals: total assimilation of the Jews through conversion to Christianity. De-Judaization of the Christian and Christianization of the Jew were their solution to the problem of *Verjudung.*

55. See the anonymous *Die Verjudung des Christlichen Staates: Ein Wort zur Zeit* (Leipzig, 1865), p. 30.

56. Paul Köhler, *Die Verjudung Deutschlands und der Weg zur Rettung* (Stettin, 1880), p. 25.

57. Ibid., pp. 30, 48.

The emerging radical antisemites took a quite different, explicitly opposed view. They self-consciously based themselves on what they designated a "nonconfessional standpoint," thus denying to the religious factor a determinative role as either an explanatory or a therapeutic factor. More important, the new antisemites combined their hostility against Jews with an attack upon Christianity itself. This was equally true for the *völkisch* prophet of a regenerated Germanic religion, Paul de Lagarde, the professional antisemite Wilhelm Marr, and the racist theoretician Eugen Dühring. This was an antisemitism avowedly radical, secular, and political in nature, although it, of course, incorporated traditional Christian strands. As such the solution to *Verjudung* could obviously not be found in Christianization, for their attack on Christianity was partly prompted by the argument that Christianity itself was the chief source, the major agent of "Judaization" in Western culture. *Verjudung* was not the product of Christian weakness but rather the result of its success. Houston Stewart Chamberlain was already an heir to an established tradition when he wrote in his *Foundations of the Nineteenth Century* (1899) that it was through Christianity that Judaism had become internalized and part of the non-Jewish soul. Were this not the case, he argued, the danger of "flesh-and-blood Jews for our culture would be far smaller."[58]

From Lagarde through Alfred Rosenberg, it became commonplace to argue that Christians had become weakened and corrupted through Judaization of the church.[59] This argument was considerably strengthened by someone who could hardly be accused of supporting political antisemitism, Friedrich Nietzsche. Yet Nietzsche's *On the Genealogy of Morals* (1887) and *The Anti-Christ* (1888) were clearly written in this idiom. A substantial part of his savage attack on Christianity was based upon the assertion of Christianity's thorough Judaization. The Jews, Nietzsche tells us, inventors of the slave revolt in morality, the revaluators of values, had been totally victorious. They had radically falsified "all nature, all naturalness, all reality, of the whole inner world as well as the outer . . . by their aftereffect they have made mankind so thoroughly false that even today the Christian can feel anti-Jewish without

58. Chamberlain, *Die Grundlagen*, 2:1115 n. 1.
59. For Paul de Lagarde, see his "Über das Verhältnis des deutschen Staates zu Theologie, Kirche und Religion: Ein Versuch Nicht-Theologen zu orientieren" (1873), in his *Deutsche Schriften* (Göttingen, 1886), pp. 56–57. For Alfred Rosenberg, see his *Race and Race History and Other Essays,* ed. Robert Pois (New York, 1970), p. 69.

realizing that he himself is the *ultimate Jewish consequence.*"[60] Of course this was meant as an attack on Christianity, but the language was quite consistent with that of the antisemites:

> This Jesus of Nazareth . . . was he not this seduction in its most un-canny and irresistible form, a seduction and bypath to precisely those Jewish values and ideals? Did Israel not attain the ultimate goal of its sublime vengefulness precisely through the bypath of this "Redeemer," this ostensible opponent and disintegrator of Israel? . . . What is certain, at least, is that *sub hoc signo,* Israel, with its vengefulness and re-valuation of all values, has hitherto triumphed again and again over all other ideals, over all *nobler* ideals.[61]

With all the important necessary qualifications, it is not surprising that, given the correct selective reading, certain antisemites could turn to Nietzsche for inspiration. The Jews, more than any other people, Nietzsche wrote, had

> a world-historic mission. The "masters" have been disposed of; the morality of the common man has won. One may conceive of this vic-tory as at the same time a blood poisoning (it has mixed the races to-gether)—I shan't contradict; but this intoxication has undoubtedly been *successful.* The "redemption" of the human race (from the "masters," that is) is going forward; everything is visibly becoming Judaized, Chris-tianized, mob-ized (what do the words matter!).[62]

There is no direct evidence that Hitler read Nietzsche, but it is certain that at least a crude version of such thinking had filtered down to him. His remarks in conversation were virtually a direct paraphrase of Nietz-sche's notions about the Jews and their overall "democratizing," weaken-ing effect in which the people, the mob, had been victorious. His com-ments to Hermann Rauschning, moreover, betray the clear influence of Nietzschean values annexed to a wholly transformed Nazi context: "But

60. Friedrich Nietzsche, *The Antichrist,* in *The Portable Nietzsche,* ed. Walter Kaufmann (New York, 1968), pp. 592–93. Nietzsche's italics here and in the follow-ing quotations.

61. Friedrich Nietzsche, *On the Genealogy of Morals,* ed. and trans. Walter Kauf-mann and R. J. Hollingdale (New York, 1969), p. 35.

62. Ibid., p. 36. Nietzsche certainly did not discourage racists reading his work with statements such as these about the Jews: "The simulation of 'holiness' which has really become genius here, never even approximated elsewhere in books or among men, this counterfeit of words and gestures as an *art,* is not the accident of some individual talent or other or of some exceptional character. This requires *race.* In Christianity all of Judaism, a several-century-old Jewish preparatory training and technique of the most serious kind, attains its ultimate mastery as the art of lying in a holy manner. The Christian, this *ultima ratio* of the lie, is the Jew once more—even *three* times more." *AntiChrist,* pp. 44, 620.

for our people it is decisive whether they acknowledge the Jewish Christ-creed with its effeminate pity-ethics, or a strong, heroic belief in Nature, God in our own people, in our destiny, in our blood."[63]

There was an irony in Conrad Alberti's choice of Paul as the model of Jewish self-overcoming, for it was precisely this Pharisee Paul who was regarded by many antisemites as the instrumental agent of "Judaization." It was he who had brought his weakening doctrines to the West and with it broken the great power of the Roman Empire. His debilitating influence was a commonplace of these circles. Paul's role was central in the pamphlet by Hitler's mentor Dietrich Eckart, which had the significant title *Das Judentum in und ausser uns* (The Judaism Within Us and Without). As a result of Paul's materialism and his literalism, the inability to understand that immortality was a spiritual not a corporeal matter, worldly Judaism had become an integral part of the non-Jewish psyche. "There is a large portion," Eckart wrote, "unbelievably much Judaism [*unglaublich viel Judentum*] that since Paul has become more and more part of our Christian being. . . . Many Germans are not true Jews only because they are not circumcised."[64] The Jew was now within.

For *völkisch* critics like Lagarde, whose life and writings span the second half of the nineteenth century, the Paulinian influence on Christianity had been so disastrous that only the creation of a regenerative *Germanic* religion would be able to stem the tide of German decline and "Judaization."[65] In Wagnerian language Lagarde wrote, "The unregenerated German, like the unregenerated Jew, is only a different species of the same genus."[66] For the Jew the choice was total assimilation or expulsion. But the German task seemed even more essential, for Lagarde's theory explained "Judaization" in terms of German national inauthenticity. Lagarde addressed "those who were not so *verjudet* that they could still recognize the illness which beset them." These people could wage the battle: "The sharper we express our character as a nation, the less place there will be in Germany for the Jews. . . . Germany must be-

---

63. On the weakening, "democratizing" effects, see Dietrich Eckart, *Der Bolschewismus von Moses bis Lenin: Zwiegespräch zwischen Adolf Hitler und mir* (Munich, 1924), esp. p. 28. For Hitler's comments to Hermann Rauschning, see Rauschning, *Hitler Speaks: A Series of Political Conversations with Adolf Hitler on His Real Aims* (London, 1939), p. 57.

64. Dietrich Eckart, *Das Judentum in und ausser uns,* in *Dietrich Eckart: Ein Vermächtnis,* ed. Alfred Rosenberg (Munich, 1928), p. 204. The whole essay is pertinent to the present theme, from which it derives its title.

65. Lagarde, "Über das Verhältnis," pp. 56–57.

66. Paul de Lagarde, "Leopold Zunz und seine Verehrer," in *Ausgewählte Schriften,* ed. Paul Fischer (Munich, 1934), pp. 223, 224.

come full of German people and German ways . . . then there will be
no room for Palestine in it. . . . To the degree that we become ourselves, the Jews will cease being Jews."[67] The return to authentic essence
was the key to redemption; *Verjudung* mirrored deviation from such
authenticity. Not all those concerned with the dangers of "Judaization"
necessarily preached Jewish self-overcoming. On the contrary, for some
it was assimilation itself that was the core of the problem. As the publicist Rudolf Pannwitz, an associate of the Stefan George circle, put it, it
was not the Jews but *Verjudung* that was so disturbing. "You," he wrote
to the Jews, "have not preserved yourselves, and we have not preserved
ourselves and this mutual neglect has led to demoralization.[68] Whether
German authenticity could be achieved through total Jewish assimilation
or its opposite was thus a matter of dispute. The fact of *Verjudung* itself
was not.

Wilhelm Marr, who coined the term *Antisemitismus,* also found that
"Judaization" was ubiquitous and that Christianity was an integral part
of the problem, not the solution. He regarded Christianity as a wild
union of Jewish religion and Platonism. Its dominion had led to nothing
short of the "Judaization of mankind" (*Verjudung der Menschheit*).
Through a process of religious superstition and mass mental indolence,
Western humanity had become totally "Judaized."[69]

Unlike Lagarde and Wagner, Marr portrayed a Germany so completely *verjudet* that no hope for redemption existed. But, as Jacob Katz
has pointed out, this pessimism was a pose, a tactic.[70] Indeed Marr believed that the Jewish Question was powerful enough to stand on its own
as an independent and unifying issue.[71] He was among the pioneers of a
self-consciously political antisemitism, convinced that this was not a
peripheral matter but rather *the* key question of German—if not world—
society. In order to make this into an issue of overriding importance, one
from which all other political issues derived, it was necessary to portray
the all-encompassing nature of "Judaization." This was the basic message

67. Paul de Lagarde, "Programm für die konservative Partei Preussens" (1884), in
Deutsche Schriften, pp. 367, 368. See, too, his "Juden und Indogermanen" (1887),
in *Ausgewählte Schriften,* pp. 239, 242–46.

68. Rudolf Pannwitz, *An das Jüdische Volk,* Flugblätter 5 (Nuremberg, 1919),
p. 3.

69. See Wilhelm Marr's rather Feuerbachian *Religioese Streitzüge eines Philoso-
phischen Touristen* (Berlin, 1876), pp. 38, 144.

70. Katz, *From Prejudice to Destruction,* pp. 260–61.

71. See Hannah Arendt's analysis of this transformation in the chapter on "Antisemitism as an Outrage to Common Sense" in her *The Origins of Totalitarianism*
(Cleveland, 1963), pp. 3–10.

of Marr's unambiguously entitled *The Victory of Judaism over Germanism: Considered from a Nonconfessional Standpoint* (1879). *Verjudung,* he stressed, was not merely a matter of individual Jewish influence but "the Jewish spirit that has conquered the world." It had penetrated the entire cultural and conceptual German domain: its ruling concept *Freiheit* was in reality *Frechheit*. The very innards, the thoughts of Germans were no longer their own.[72] Germany was enslaved.

Wagner, Lagarde, and Marr enunciated their antisemitism in clearly radical, nonconfessional ways. But if there was incipient racism—at least in principle if not in practice—they left room for the possibility of Jewish self-transcendence. With the emergence of full-blown racism, this was no longer an option. The spiritual and the biological became indissolubly fused. The possibility that the doctrine of "Judaization" had always allowed—that of somehow distinguishing between the process and its agents—was now to all intents and purposes removed. Symbol and embodiment were one.

Eugen Dühring's *Die Judenfrage als Frage der Raceschädlichkeit für Existenz, Sitte und Kultur* (1880) was one of the first attempts to articulate this notion systematically. As with most radical (and certainly all racist) antisemites, the *Judenfrage* was cast into world-historical terms, into a confrontation between the forces of good and evil. Unlike Marr's work, Dühring's work radiated an activist, dynamic energy. Both the problem and solution were posed in simple terms: "Judaization of all relations and peoples is a fact," he wrote, "de-Judaization [*Entjudung*] the challenge."[73]

Apart from the vital racist framework there was only one other ingredient Dühring added to the catalog of "Judaization." This, however, was an important one, destined to be crucial in the Nationalist Socialist brand of antisemitism. Previous formulations of the myth had equated *Verjudung* with liberalism, capitalism, materialism, and godless secularism. With Dühring, himself a socialist respected by leading figures of the German labor movement, Marxism (in at least one version, the prophet and critic of the "Judaization" of bourgeois society) was itself transformed into a "Jewish" symptom, ironically labeled as the embodiment of precisely that *Verjudung* which it had lamented. Marx's Jewish origins, materialism, and cosmopolitanism were turned against Marxism

---

72. Wilhelm Marr, *Der Sieg des Judenthums über das Germanenthum: Vom nicht confessionellen Standpunkt aus betrachtet* (Bern, 1879) pp. 33, 41–45.
73. Eugen Dühring, *Die Judenfrage als Frage der Raceschädlichkeit für Existenz, Sitte und Kultur,* reprint ed. (Berlin, 1892), p. 138.

itself and easily categorized as "Jewish" principles. Hitler's later obsession with Marxism as a Jewish conspiracy is to be found already apparent in Dühring. Marxist socialism, wrote Dühring was really a *Judenallianz,* a scheme by which all nations of the world would be controlled and absorbed by a new *Judenreich.* This so-called communist *Reich* would, in reality, be the means by which the Chosen People dispense with the common treasure of the nations.[74]

It was, of course, during the Weimar Republic that the radical, and especially the racist, Right came into its own. Liberal Weimer with its skeptical, experimental culture, that system which, in Peter Gay's memorable phrase, had promoted the traditional outsider into insider,[75] was an easy target, one that was consistently, and apparently plausibly, cast as thoroughly *verjudet.* There were few additions to the anti-Jewish canon during this period. The notion of *Verjudung* simply became cruder and more extreme, able to reach a wider audience than ever before. Weimar was surely a "Jew Republic." With Walther Rathenau as foreign minister, on the one hand, and Marxist Jewish revolutionary leaders, on the other, who could have doubted this?

If there were no significant additions to the idea of *Verjudung* during the Weimar period, there was a kind of updating, fitting it into the *Zeitgeist* of an unprecedented permissiveness and placing it within the new era of technology and consumerism. This, at least, was the emphasis of racist ideologues and self-proclaimed "culture critics" like Alfred Rosenberg and others. "Judaization" now became the metaphor for the critique of mass society. The Jews, Rosenberg wrote, were undermining the nations by "spinning our thoughts and trying, with the goods of this world, with economics, trade, industry, and technology to draw us all away from our proper spiritual direction." It was the Jews who relentlessly tried to remove individual personality and "replace it with the chaos of those cosmetic leveling phrases of Humanity, Fraternity, and Equality."[76] The modern city was the creation of, and dominated by, the "Jewish spirit"; its result was mass, atomized man. The metropolis, Rosenberg stressed, constantly engaged in "race annihilating work." The major instrument of "Judaization" was mass culture. It was Jewish management that, after all, had done away with creative acting and in its stead produced "stars"; art and theater had been converted into a form of mass hypnosis and

74. Ibid., esp. p. 72.
75. See Peter Gay, *Weimar Culture: The Outsider as Insider* (New York, 1968).
76. Alfred Rosenberg, "Der Jude" (1918), in his *Schriften aus den Jahren, 1917–1921* (Munich, 1943), p. 89.

sensual excitement; the film was now the "movie industry" and "a means of infecting the *Volk*."[77] But, Rosenberg stressed, if *Verjudung* was the leveling process—the creation of an utterly atomized society—the Jews exempted themselves from such a process. They would retain their international cohesiveness, blood ties, and spiritual unity.[78] (This perception that Jews maintained their cohesiveness and sense of identity under all conceivable circumstances was a source of both fear and envy. Indeed, for many antisemites this racial perseverance and historical continuity provided a kind of mirror-image model worthy of emulation.) The process of mass leveling and Jewish dominance had gone so far, one commentator put it, that in all the newspapers, magazines, fashion pages, cinemas, and revues, the very model of "homogenization" was being fashioned in terms of Jewish expressions and body images.[79]

The early days of Nazism produced all kinds of crackpot versions of the "Judaization" idea, schemes that tried to combine the spiritual with the biological, the religious with the racist. It was only in the confused post–World War I era that grotesque works like Artur Dinter's novel *Die Sünde wider das Blut* (The Sin against the Blood, 1918) could achieve great popularity and reach a mass audience. Dinter, the leader of early Thuringian Nazism, produced an entire philosophy of "spiritual racism" in his novels and pamphlets. Spirit, he argued, was not the product of race but the reverse. Race was merely the earthly incarnation of *Geist*. Jews were the physical embodiments of deeply fallen spirits who in the Ur-time of creation had chosen egoism and materialism as their spiritual direction. Race was the vehicle through which such a spirit was transmitted. Even if Jews perceived this "racial-spiritual" truth and tried to change their ways, they had to be condemned to a tragic life, for they could not be admitted to join and thereby endanger the *Aryan Blutgemeinschaft*. The Aryan racial spirit was, of course, an idealistic one, but, given the fact that race was only a vehicle for basic spiritual orientations, one could also find egoistic-materialistic Aryan "Jews." In fact this had occurred through the total "Judaization" of both the Catholic and the Protestant churches: "It is this Jewish-Christianity that has made us so receptive to the Jewish infection."[80] The only way to save the

---

77. Alfred Rosenberg, section entitled "Kultur: The Volkish Aesthetic," in his *Race and Race History,* esp. pp. 149, 167, 173.

78. Rosenberg, "Der Jude," p. 100.

79. See Richard von Schaukal, "Grundsätzliches zur Judenfrage," in *Der Jud ist Schuld,* p. 179 n. 6.

80. Artur Dinter, "Die Rassen- und Judenfrage im Lichte des Geistchristentums," in ibid., p. 97. The whole essay is instructive.

Aryan race was to "complete" the sadly Judaized original German Protestant Reformation.[81]

This attempt to combine the Nazi racial revolution with the Protestant Reformation—"The real challenge of a true Christianity," wrote Dinter, "is overcoming 'the Jew' in ourselves and around us"[82]—was too sectarian, too religiously "Christian" to find acceptance in the party that Dinter left in 1929. Non-Christian forms of "spiritual racism" did, however, penetrate Nazism. In many ways such ideas lay at the movement's center. Works like L. F. Clauss's *Die nordische Seele* (The Nordic Soul, 1930), for example, argued that external appearance was not the essential hallmark of Aryanism but rather the race-soul, fount of all creativity, which Nordic blood had produced. The popular and ostensibly "scientific" racist Hans F. K. Günther, in effect, regarded racial types as physical representations of inner nature.[83] Anthropology and metaphysical categories of beauty and soul conveniently merged. As George L. Mosse has shown, the Nazi "science" of race was integrated with a mystical, mythological version.[84]

It was left to Hitler, of course, to give the notion of *Verjudung* its toughest and most racist expression. All previous distinctions between Jews and the "Jewish idea" were utterly dismissed, race and spirit completely fused. As Hitler told Dietrich Eckart in the early 1920s: "This is the point: even if not one synagogue, not one Jewish school, the Old Testament and the Bible had not existed, the Jewish spirit would still be there and have its effect. From the beginning it has been there and no Jew, not one, that does not embody it."[85] The Jew was the physical incarnation of the very principle of evil.[86]

For all that, it is important to note that the metaphorical elements of the *Verjudung* myth were not dropped. They were simply fused with the racial. The traditional function of the overall critique of society and culture was maintained. The attack on the physical Jew was obvious and essential, but the all-encompassing process of "Judaization" was also a rationale for broader political activity, a sanction for radical measures within society itself. For *Verjudung* had so sapped the vital energies of

81. Artur Dinter, *The Completion of the Protestant Reformation* (London, 1937).
82. Dinter, "Rassen- und Judenfrage," p. 96.
83. See Hans F. K. Günther, *Rassenkunde des Deutschen Volkes* (Munich, 1923), and his *Rassenkunde des Jüdischen Volkes* (Munich, 1930).
84. George L. Mosse, *Toward the Final Solution: A History of European Racism* (New York, 1978), esp. the chapter entitled "The Mystery of Race," pp. 94–112.
85. Quoted in Eckart, *Der Bolschewismus,* p. 46.
86. See Rauschning, *Hitler Speaks,* esp. p. 231.

the people, so degenerated their basic values and instincts, that only a thorough purging, a radical reconstruction, would be able to regenerate Germany. *Mein Kampf* (1925) can, indeed, be read as a treatise on both the moral and physical "Judaization" of the world and as a ruthless dynamic program for radically solving the problem. "Judaization" had transformed the German respect for labor into a contempt for all productive physical work. It had penetrated everywhere, combining biological and mental corruption in the most intimate and primal areas,

> running parallel to the political, ethical and moral contamination of the people, there had been for many years a no less terrible poisoning of the health of the national body. Especially in the big cities, syphilis was beginning to spread more and more. . . . The cause lies primarily in our prostitution of love. Even if its result were not this frightful plague, it would nevertheless be profoundly injurious to man, since the moral devastations which accompany this degeneracy suffice to destroy a people slowly but surely. This Jewification of our spiritual life and mammonization of our mating instincts will sooner or later destroy our entire offspring.[87]

This "inner Judaization of our people," as Hitler put it,[88] was as dangerous as the tangible Jewish presence. The Jewish influence was the triumph of antinature over nature, of disease over health; *Verjudung* was the weakening of instinct and the loss of ability to resist infection.[89] This unremitting vocabulary in the mystic-naturalistic-biological mode not only sanctioned ruthless and final measures against all Jews;[90] it also provided a convenient rationale for the "positive" dynamic of the racial revolution, the "natural" regeneration of the German *Volksgemeinschaft,* and a sanction for such totalitarian renovation. The idea of "Judaization" could be pushed no further in thought—or in action.

87. Adolf Hitler, *Mein Kampf,* trans. Ralph Manheim (Boston, 1971), pp. 318, 246–47.
88. Ibid., p. 318.
89. On this point, see the chapter entitled "The Language of Nature," in J. P. Stern, *Hitler: The Führer and the People* (London, 1984), esp. p. 51. See, too, Ernst Nolte, *Three Faces of Fascism* (New York, 1969).
90. See the classic article by Alex Bein, "The Jewish Parasite: Notes on the Semantics of the Jewish Problem, with Special Reference to Germany," *LBIYB* 10 (1964): 3–40.

Sisterhood under Siege

Feminism and Antisemitism in Germany, 1904–38

In the early decades of the twentieth century, German-Jewish women suffered a dual stigmatization of gender and "race" in a society that became increasingly misogynist and antisemitic. In times of relative social peace and harmony, Jewish women fought the sexism of their own German-Jewish community. Often they combined with their German sisters in feminist solidarity to focus on common concerns. In an era of radical, racist antisemitism, however, Jewish women were forcibly divided from other feminists. They fought for Jewish survival, as feminist loyalties dissolved in the face of increasingly hideous antisemitic persecutions.

This history is divided into three parts. The first will delineate the programs of the Jüdischer Frauenbund (League of Jewish Women) within the Jewish community. The second will describe the Frauenbund's cooperation with the German feminist movement during the Weimar Republic. The third will discuss the survival strategies of Jewish women under the Nazi dictatorship. The story of the successes and defeat of the Jüdischer Frauenbund reveals a good deal about the roles of all women (regardless of "race"), the discrimination against all Jews (regardless of gender), and the political and social strengths and weaknesses of the German middle classes.

BUILDING THE JEWISH COMMUNITY AND A WOMEN'S ALLIANCE, 1904–33

German-Jewish women lived in a position of double jeopardy as a result of their ethnic-religious heritage (which the Nazis would later label "race") and their sex: as Jews and as women they endured discrimination in Germany, and as women they suffered from second-class citizenship in their own Jewish community. They were, for example, disenfranchised in the German states as Jews, and when the vote was extended to Jewish males in the German Empire, Jewish women had to await the enfranchisement of German women. Even when female suffrage was granted in 1918, the victory of Jewish women was only secular; as women, they were still denied a political voice in Jewish communal elections. Similarly, when German women began to achieve modest advances as teachers (1860s and 1870s) and civil servants (1880s), antisemitism blocked Jewish women from a share in this progress. Nevertheless, in Imperial Germany, German-Jewish women also benefited from the political and economic successes of Jewish men and from the inroads carved by German feminists into the male sanctuaries of higher education and the professions (circa 1900) and, finally, politics (after 1918). By the turn of the century Jewish middle-class women were increasingly able to move their energies beyond home and family, to volunteer in Jewish charities, to obtain higher educations and career entrance, and to become active in the German women's movement.

In 1904, on the occasion of the meeting of the International Council of Women, the more progressive members of the traditional Jewish women's religious societies as well as Jewish women who were involved in the German feminist movement formed the nucleus of the Jüdischer Frauenbund (JFB). Its founder and president was Bertha Pappenheim, a dedicated feminist and a devout Jew.[1] Her organization attracted a large following—fifty thousand women, or approximately 20 percent of all Jewish women over the age of thirty. It played a vital role within the Jewish community until 1938, while maintaining a cooperative and supportive role within the German women's movement until 1933. The Frauenbund combined feminist goals—"for women's work and the women's movement"—with a strong sense of Jewish identity. Its efforts were

---

1. Bertha Pappenheim was the first person to be treated by cathartic psychotherapy, and her case became well known as the case of "Anna O." Treated by Josef Breuer in Vienna from December 1880 until June 1882, her case was included in Freud and Breuer's *Studies in Hysteria* (1895). See Ellen Jensen, "Anna O.: A Study of Her Later Life," *Psychoanalytic Quarterly* 39 (1970): 269–93. This article includes a bibliography of psychoanalytic commentary on "Anna O." and on Pappenheim. Before founding the Jüdischer Frauenbund (JFB), Pappenheim wrote several plays and pamphlets with feminist themes and translated Mary Wollstonecraft's *Vindication of the Rights of Woman*. For further information, see Marion Kaplan, *The Jewish Feminist Movement in Germany: The Campaigns of the Jüdischer Frauenbund, 1904–1938* (Westport, Conn., 1979), pp. 29–58.

directed toward: (1) strengthening community consciousness among Jews; (2) furthering the ideals of the bourgeois women's movement; (3) expanding the participation of women in the Jewish community on the basis of equality with men; (4) providing Jewish women with career training; and (5) combatting all forms of immorality, specifically white slavery.[2] Its support of the goals of the German bourgeois women's movement distinguished the JFB from other Jewish women's organizations that preceded or paralleled it.[3] Its endorsement of the bourgeois movement separated it, as well, from the major Protestant and Catholic women's organizations. The JFB belonged to the mainstream of the nineteenth- and twentieth-century bourgeois women's movements, which tried to enlarge woman's sphere by increasing her opportunities and broadening her outlook. Its demands were essentially reformist, shaped not only by the position of women in Judaism but also by the situation of Jews and women in Germany, the omnipresence of antisemitism and the intransigence of antifeminism. The JFB engaged in traditional, liberal strategies to acquire political power. Simultaneously, it developed its own alternative to "male power" by building an organization "of women, for women."

Allegiance to the JFB was a product of class and age. Its members reflected the overwhelmingly middle-class socioeconomic position of German Jews.[4] JFB members were middle-class housewives who did not work for pay. They had neither the professional careers nor working-class allegiances that could have facilitated their entrance into professional women's organizations or working-class women's associations. The

2. "For Women's Work and the Women's Movement" was the subtitle of the JFB newsletter, *Blätter des Jüdischen Frauenbunds: Für Frauenarbeit und Frauenbewegung* (hereafter BJFB). The goals can be found in *BJFB*, January 1928, p. 1. In 1905 the founders' goals had been similar, but the emphasis was on the "need to work for women in any aspect that affects them, to educate them about the world around them, to help them find jobs and to offer them diversions from the difficulties of earning a living." *Jahrbuch der Frauenbewegung* 1 (1912).

3. Organizations that preceded the JFB are described by Jacob Segall in "Die Jüdischen Frauenvereine in Deutschland," *Zeitschrift für Demographie und Statistik der Juden* (hereafter ZDSJ) 10, no. 1 (January 1914): 2–5, and no. 2 (February 1914): 7–23. The JFB had a far more extensive program than earlier women's auxiliaries or the B'nai B'rith Sisterhoods. There were eighty B'nai B'rith Sisterhoods in the 1930s; as adjuncts to the male lodges, they did not engage in the struggle for women's rights.

4. By 1870 about 60 percent of German Jews were in the upper and middle classes, and another 25 percent could be described as lower middle class. Monika Richarz, ed., *Jüdisches Leben in Deutschland:* vol. 2, *Selbstzeugnisse zur Sozialgeschichte im Kaiserreich* (Stuttgart, 1979), p. 24. By 1933 only 8.7 percent of German Jews classified themselves as "workers," compared with 46.4 percent of non-Jewish Germans. *Volkszählung, Die Bevölkerung des Deutschen Reichs nach der Volkszählung 1933,* Verlag für Sozialpolitik, Wirtschaft, und Statistik, Heft 5 (Berlin, 1936), pp. 25, 27.

JFB offered such housewives the opportunity to associate with women who shared their primary religious and class identities. The Jewish working class was not represented in the JFB. It consisted of successive waves of Eastern European immigrants who engaged in petty trade and were employed in light industries in Germany's urban centers. These Eastern European Jews remained the objects of JFB concern and the recipients of its ministrations. Not only did the JFB fail to enroll working-class women; younger women, too, remained aloof. Organizations like the JFB were best suited to an era of middle-class prosperity such as had existed in the decade before World War I. With the war and postwar economic crises, the JFB was unable to recruit young volunteers, since few had the option of becoming leisured ladies. By the 1930s only a few young faces could be found amid the widowed and aging membership.[5]

Jewish feminists acknowledged the positive attachments of faith, culture, and destiny that they shared with Jewish men. Despite the obvious and considerable tensions involved in being both feminists and observant Jews,[6] Frauenbund members were unwilling to focus on secular feminism in Germany to the neglect of their Jewish roots. Their position reflects in microcosm a more general dilemma of modern minorities: the desire to be accepted by the majority while guarding their own distinctiveness. While the women of the JFB strongly supported German middle-class feminism, they did not desire complete absorption at the expense of their religious-ethnic identity. The loss of a strong Jewish identity was too high a price to pay for social acceptance. They welcomed acculturation, not total assimilation. This stance was not unusual among Jews in Germany. Many Jews had seen emancipation as an opportunity for the entry of "Jews *as Jews* to the ranks of humanity," not as a signal solely to imitate Gentile society.[7] In fact, the extent of Jewish organizational and communal activity indicates a strong, positive bonding that was often heightened—but not always caused—by periods of antisemitism. The very vitality of Jewish communal life, not simply the degree to

---

5. The membership profile reflected Jewish demographic trends as well, a result of an earlier decline in Jewish fertility. By the 1930s more than 50 percent of German Jews were above the age of forty. Erich Rosenthal, "Jewish Population in Germany, 1910–1939," *Jewish Social Studies* 6 (1944): 243–47.

6. Today, too, women who consider themselves to be feminists and observant Jews are demanding greater equality within the Jewish community and—unlike the JFB—a greater role in performing Jewish rituals. See, for examples, Susan Dworkin, "A Song for Women in Five Questions," *Moment,* May/June 1975, p. 44; Sally Priesand, *Judaism and the New Woman* (New York, 1975); and current issues of *Lilith* magazine.

7. Donald L. Niewyk, *The Jews in Weimar Germany* (Baton Rouge, 1980), pp. 99–100; quotation from Hannah Arendt, *The Jew as Pariah* (New York, 1978), p. 68.

which Jews were absorbed into the German milieu, provided the successes and hopes that ultimately blinded many Jews to the realities of Nazi Germany.

Jewish women also recognized the more negative bonds that they shared with Jewish men. Like their male counterparts, they were outsiders; both sexes were the objects of a lingering and persistent antisemitism that spurred them to join forces in self-defense. Thus, organizing a women's movement along religious lines was the result of legal and traditional circumstances beyond Jewish feminists' control, the result not only of positive feelings but of a lack of social integration. Despite their seeming political and economic success, Jews remained segregated in a religious and organizational subculture. Social acceptance was impeded by German attitudes ranging from a lingering Judeophobia with roots in ancient and medieval religious prejudices to a virulent, racist, political antisemitism originating in the 1870s and 1880s. Sporadic outbursts of hostility poisoned the atmosphere and wounded and confused Jews. Still, Jewish feminists were as unwilling to sacrifice women's issues for Jewish solidarity as they were to forfeit Jewishness for feminist solidarity. They persisted in demanding both, while their campaigns reflected the larger political and social forces that fettered Jews and women in Germany.

Whereas the importance of the German women's movement to the ideas and activities of the Jewish organization must be underscored, the JFB's primary efforts were directed toward the Jewish community. Thus, we turn first to the Jewish aspects of Jewish feminism and next to the broader feminist interests. The JFB's campaigns within the Jewish community included the attempt to provide career training for women, the fight against white slavery, and the pursuit of equality in Jewish communal affairs. Each of these efforts reflected feminist aspirations as well as the insecurities of Jews in Germany.

In support of the first—career training—the JFB set up employment offices, vocational guidance centers, night courses to improve job skills, and several schools (offering courses in the traditional female fields of home economics, child care, basic health care, and social work). While Jewish feminists insisted that housework be treated with the same respect as other employment, they challenged the attitude that a woman's place was *only* in the home. Jobs were seen as a means of economic, psychological, and emotional independence, and the JFB looked toward the growing collective importance of all working women. As Jews, members of the JFB were concerned that the job profile of German Jews was conspicuously different from that of all other Germans; a result of historical discrimination as well as of new opportunities open to them after their emancipation, Jews were heavily concentrated in commerce. For Jewish women this meant, for example, that in 1925, 53 percent were engaged in commerce and 3 percent in agriculture, compared to 14 percent and 43 percent, respectively, for non-Jewish women.[8] In the face of extreme antisemitism during and after World War I, Jewish organizations, including the JFB, committed themselves to a policy of vocational retraining, shifting Jewish youth away from commerce and toward vocations more typical of the general population. For boys this meant industry, crafts, and agriculture; for girls it meant home economics careers.

Despite years of propaganda in favor of training women for domestic careers, in the midst of the Weimar era only 9.3 percent of Jewish women—up from 8.8 percent in 1907—were employed as domestics.[9] And these women, to be sure, were not the daughters of bourgeois Jews. Class position determined that young middle-class women would remain immune to the lure of the "domestic service professions," using the skills they acquired in household management courses to become better housewives. In fact, while serving their own middle-class interests in a period in which a *Dienstbotenfrage* (servant shortage) preoccupied most bourgeois housewives, JFB members could congratulate themselves for helping working-class girls find jobs.

Through prevention and rescue efforts the JFB fought commercial prostitution, or white slavery, particularly among Jewish women from Eastern Europe lured abroad and sold or forced into prostitution by traffickers.[10] To thwart procurers, the JFB established railroad and harbor outposts for women traveling alone; offered food, hostels, financial aid, and information to needy young women or female travelers; and organized evening recreation for young women in Germany (to "keep them off the streets" and to inculcate a sense of Jewish community). As part of a prevention program, it supported vocational and educational institutions for Jewish girls in Eastern Europe, sent teachers and nurses to Eastern Europe, and published leaflets and warnings on the dangers of

8. Heinrich Silbergleit, *Die Bevölkerungs- und Berufsverhältnisse der Juden im Deutschen Reich* (Berlin, 1930), p. 109.

9. ZDSJ 7, no. 5 (May 1911): 79–80; ibid., 15, nos. 1/3 (January/March 1919): 2; *BJFB*, January 1934, pp. 7–8.

10. For details on the white slave traffic and the campaign to end it, see Kaplan, *Jewish Feminist Movement*, chap. 4.

white slavery. It cooperated with national and international volunteer organizations to suppress the traffic and founded the first Jewish home for delinquent girls, unwed mothers, and illegitimate children in Germany. Its defense of unwed mothers and its concern for Jewish prostitutes (its "erring young sisters") were its most radical challenges to the norms of its community. These met with the indifference or hostility of much of the Jewish community, which preferred to shun such issues or voice moral condemnation of "fallen women." Its determined campaign against white slavery also met with resistance from Jewish leaders, who feared that by recognizing that Jews took part in this vice, the JFB was adding to the arsenal of the antisemites.

Pappenheim responded that the Jewish community would be guilty of complicity if it did not act against these crimes. She was aware, moreover, that the energetic participation of Jews in the campaigns against white slavery put a damper on that antisemitism which could have arisen among reformers as a result of substantial Jewish involvement in this traffic in women. She felt the need to explain that the extreme poverty and discrimination suffered by East European Jewry were the primary causes of this crime. As Jews, members of the Frauenbund attempted to rescue Jewish girls and protect the Jewish community. JFB members were not, however, simply on a rescue mission or an antivice crusade: as feminists, they sought at all times to call attention to the sexual discrimination that lay at the root of sexual vice, to challenge traditional roles, to construct new institutions for women, and to improve the status of women within Judaism.

Of all the JFB's efforts, the fight for political power in the Jewish community was its longest and most arduous, ending well after women had attained suffrage in Germany. The Jewish community in Germany, like other religious entities, was a publicly constituted corporation embracing all Jews in any one place of residence.[11] It was vested with the power to levy taxes on its members. Thus participation and equitable representation were serious issues. Feminists hoped to gain the power to redirect more community revenues toward the needs of women. The JFB campaigned vigorously in individual Jewish communities (there were 1,611 in 1932). It lobbied and petitioned rabbis and community leaders and offered its cooperation to the major national and international Jewish welfare organizations in return for representation on their boards of

11. Kurt Wilhelm, "The Jewish Community in the Post-Emancipation Period," *Leo Baeck Institute Year Book* (hereafter *LBIYB*) 2 (1957): 47–75.

directors. It insisted on women's participation in every aspect of community life, not just as "honorary ladies" or on "entertainment commissions." When, after World War I, the German government granted German women the vote, Jewish women expected the Jewish communities to follow suit. They were sorely disappointed and had to continue their campaign—stepping it up to include public meetings, a national suffrage week, advertisements in Jewish newspapers, and legal battles—well into the 1920s.[12] By the end of the 1920s women had wrested the vote in six of the seven major German cities (containing more than half of all German Jews) and in various areas of southern and western Germany.[13] Thus the majority of Jewish women were enfranchised. While lacking the power of dominance or control, they had achieved formal, visible participation.

In this campaign, too, the JFB was motivated by feminist and Jewish concerns. The former included the equal participation in politics, which had been the demand of women's organizations since the first decade of the twentieth century. Jewish concerns were expressed in reminders to Jewish leaders that by modernizing women's status they would be revitalizing Judaism, bringing women—"the culture bearers"—back into the fold and, through them, their offspring.[14] Further, feminists played upon the desire of Jews to acculturate to German norms in an attempt to shame their opponents with the non-Western customs evident in the unequal treatment of Jewish women. They pressed, instead, for a form of male-female participation in Jewish communal affairs, similar to their Gentile counterparts, to diminish social antagonisms between Jews and other Germans.

As important as its campaigns to improve the status and conditions of women were, the Frauenbund itself provided an essential focal point for its members. It enabled them to derive a sense of solidarity and strength, to achieve self-expression, self-help, and self-respect. Through this association women were able to influence each other and to transform aspects of their own lives. Not only did they achieve a modicum of social reforms for their more needy sisters, but they themselves matured as they organized, agitated, and created in the public sphere. The boundless enthusiasm of Frauenbund members, interviewed almost forty years after its demise, speaks to the personal growth, the self-actualization, and en-

---

12. *BJFB*, August 1927, pp. 6–7, and February 1928, pp. 1–2.
13. Ibid., February 1928, p. 1.
14. Siddy Wronsky, "Zur Soziologie der Jüdischen Frauenbewegung in Deutschland," *Jahrbuch für Jüdische Geschichte und Literatur* 28 (1927): 84–92.

hancement of self-confidence experienced by women aware of and acting for themselves and other women. The Frauenbund, with more than 485 locals and 20 provincial associations, allowed Jewish women to take initiatives beyond those envisioned by the male Jewish establishment and outside areas defined by the German women's movement.

THE LIMITS OF SISTERHOOD

The Jüdischer Frauenbund joined with other women's organizations that pursued feminist or social welfare goals. Its leaders and individual JFB members attended conferences of the Deutsche Staatsbürgerinnen Verband, the international suffrage movement (Weltbund für Frauenstimmrecht), the international organizations against white slavery, and the German and international abolitionist associations.[15] It also worked in conjunction with other women's organizations, both confessional and nonsectarian.[16] Its locals joined with women's groups in towns or provinces to effect cooperative projects. The Breslau local, for example, was also a member of the Silesian Women's Association (Verband schlesischer Frauenvereine, 1913–33), participating in general events and helping out in special emergencies.[17] Further, the JFB showed strong interest in joining international Jewish women's organizations as well. In all, the Jewish feminist movement attempted to implement its (revised) goals of 1914, to promote sisterhood on three levels: between German and Jewish women's organizations, among Jewish women of all lands, and within a nondenominational, international framework. This section will focus on the first of these, the JFB's sense of female solidarity with German women, its "interconfessional" work.

Seeing itself—as others may not have—as an "important factor" in the German women's movement, the JFB accepted the Bund Deutscher Frauenvereine (Federation of German Women's Associations, or BDF),

15. BJFB, July 1929, p. 13, and August 1926, pp. 3–4; Deutsches Nationalkomitee, Bericht über die 9. Deutsche Nationalkonferenz zur internationalen Bekämpfung des Mädchenhandels zu Stettin, 13–14 November, 1912 (Stettin, 1912); Bericht über die 6. Deutsche Nationalkonferenz zur internationalen Bekämpfung des Mädchenhandels zu Breslau am 8–9 Oktober, 1908 (Breslau, 1908); Bericht über die 8. Deutsche Nationalkonferenz zur internationalen Bekämpfung des Mädchenhandels zu Karlsruhe am 10–11 Oktober, 1911 (Karlsruhe, 1911).

16. For example, the JFB cooperated with Catholic and Protestant railroad station missions (Bahnhofsmissionen) in helping traveling girls and women. See also Allgemeine Zeitung des Judentums (hereafter AZdJ) 83, no. 14 (April 4, 1919), supp., p. 4; BJFB, April 1933, p. 11.

17. Israelitisches Familienblatt, August 7, 1930, p. 11; AZdJ 77, no. 26 (June 27, 1913), supp., p. 2.

as a model. Pappenheim wrote, "The German's women's movement gave the shy, uncertain advances of Jewish women direction and confidence."[18] The BDF, founded in 1894, was Germany's largest bourgeois feminist organization, attracting a membership of approximately 200,000 in 1912 and 750,000 by 1931.[19] Its "feminism" evolved from the widening of women's narrow sphere within a framework of traditional social values. The conservatism of its credo—one that bowed to separate spheres, emphasized maternal clichés, and adhered to *standesgemäss* (class-appropriate) bourgeois respectability—was a legacy not only of the failure of German liberalism and the concomitant political and social timidity of the middle class, but also of the specific constraints that women faced. The BDF accepted the conventional notion that there were fundamental differences between the sexes which destined them to serve important but different functions. The Frauenbund, too, believed woman's instinctual maternal nature, her self-sacrificing personality, mildness, and patience would complement man's energy and initiative in the public sphere. The JFB followed the BDF in stressing duty and service and avoiding the equal-rights issues so central to Anglo-American feminism. They challenged the *status quo* indirectly, in the name of traditionally accepted values and roles. The tactics of the JFB were also similar to those of the BDF. Both renounced political agitation, opting for unobtrusive methods. They petitioned, published information, and educated women who did not belong to their respective organizations about the goals of feminism. With few exceptions, their members were proper bourgeois ladies who eschewed all radicalism in order to court public opinion and allay hostility.

The JFB belonged to and maintained friendly relations with the Bund Deutscher Frauenvereine from 1907 until 1933. In contrast, the Catholic women's organization (Katholischer Frauenbund, of about 220,000 members in 1921) never joined the BDF, and the Protestant women's association (Deutsch-evangelischer Frauenbund, of about 200,000 members in 1928) joined in 1908 and withdrew in 1918. Pappenheim served on the board of directors of the BDF from 1914 until 1924. Her participation in the federation reflected the symbiosis of her feminist and Jewish loyalties. Her feminist attitudes derived from those of German feminists. Yet she hoped to preserve the communal and religious dis-

18. *BJFB*, July 1936, p. 8.
19. See Amy Hackett, "The Politics of Feminism in Wilhelmine Germany, 1890–1918" (Ph.D. diss., Columbia University, 1976); and Richard Evans, *The Feminist Movement in Germany, 1894–1933* (Beverly Hills, 1976), pp. 194, 245.

tinctiveness of her people. In addition, she was sensitive to antisemitism. She believed that if Jewish women *as Jews* worked within the German movement, they could fight antisemitism through personal interactions. Her collaboration with German feminists was, thus, a means of combatting prejudice, but it was also proof to Pappenheim that there was a possibility for friendship among Jews and other Germans. This possibility for friendship—that is, for solidarity and cooperation as well as for disagreement regarding issues affecting all German women—will be explored first. Then I will turn to the relationship of JFB members as Jews to their non-Jewish feminist colleagues.

The JFB sent delegates to the general and executive meetings of the BDF and participated in many of its undertakings.[20] It discussed these meetings and the resolutions taken there at its own executive and general conventions and in its newsletter. Often JFB leaders were asked to participate as lecturers or workshop leaders at the general assemblies of the BDF,[21] and one of its most active members also ran for president of the BDF.[22] Generally the JFB supported the BDF stance on issues relating to women: "Above all separations of world view [*Weltanschauung*] and religion, we women are on a mutual path, heading toward mutual goals."[23]

The JFB newsletter reported approvingly on the BDF's attitudes toward women's work as a means of self-development. During the Depression, "double earners" (*Doppelverdiener*) came under attack by those who claimed women who brought "second incomes" into the family should give up their jobs for unemployed men. The BDF discouraged feminists from making "further difficulties for those who choose a double path," but hesitated to encourage wives and mothers to work. The JFB concurred, unlike the other confessional women's organizations which argued that marriage and career could never be combined. It continued to support married women who chose to pursue careers, but suggested that mothers of infants stay home. It reminded all women of the "double burden" (*Doppelbelastung*) of housework and careers.[24] The JFB understood the "double earner" issue to be particularly threatening for Jew-

20. See, for examples, *BJFB*, November 1927, p. 4; November 1929, pp. 7–9; November 1930, p. 12; and November 1932, pp. 8–9. See also Ottilie Schönewald's memoirs, Schönewald Collection, Archives of the Leo Baeck Institute, New York.
21. See, for examples, *BJFB*, June 1928, p. 7, and August 1928, pp. 4–5. See also Schönewald memoirs.
22. In 1931 Margarete Berent, a lawyer, ran for president of the BDF, but lost.
23. *BJFB*, November 1929, pp. 7–9.
24. Ibid., June 1931, pp. 9–10.

ish women, since a large percentage of Jewish professional women worked in declining sectors (academia was referred to as "the waiting room of the unemployed"), where women's participation was under special attack.[25] In addition, many Jewish professional women were among those women bearing the brunt of a vigorous campaign against the "big" double earner—a professional woman married to a professional man.

The Frauenbund also shared many of the prevailing social attitudes toward the reproductive sphere, though with some significant differences. Most Germans before the war praised marriage, extolled motherhood, and held sexuality to be inextricably linked with reproduction. Even the more progressive socialists refused to accept birth control or abortion. Clara Zetkin, for example, had argued that the solution to working-class women's oppression was a redistribution of wealth, not family limitation. The latter was an "easy answer for egotists."[26] After the war socialists, more radical feminists, and communists openly supported birth control and abortion, the latter insisting, "Your body belongs to you."[27] The mainstream of German feminism, however (as well as some leading socialist feminists), remained aloof from or hostile to the proabortion forces. Many bourgeois feminists, in fact, considered birth control to be only the lesser of two evils. As late as 1928 the answer to unwanted pregnancies was still, according to Agnes von Zahn-Harnack, president of the BDF, "the education of our people to a restrained sexuality."[28]

From its founding, the Frauenbund exhorted Jewish women to raise larger families. The JFB objected to birth control as further hastening an already drastic decline in the Jewish birth rate as well as on religious grounds. However, it clearly recognized its widespread use among Jews both before and after World War I. Describing such family limitation as "a sickness of the *Volk* soul [*Volksseele*] caused by economic and emotional needs," the Frauenbund still preferred it to abortion. On abortion, a major social issue of the Weimar Republic, the JFB held to a complex position. Its spokespersons viewed the law in general as

25. Ibid., November 1931, pp. 4–6.

26. Quoted in Karen Honeycutt, "Clara Zetkin: A Socialist Approach to the Problem of Women's Oppression," *Feminist Studies* 3, no. 4 (Spring-Summer 1976): 131–44. See also Robert Neuman, "The Sexual Question and Social Democracy in Imperial Germany," *Journal of Social History* 7 (1974): 272.

27. See Atina Grossmann, "Abortion and Economic Crisis: The 1931 Campaign against No. 218," in *When Biology Became Destiny: Women in Weimar and Nazi Germany*, ed. Renate Bridenthal, Atina Grossmann, and Marion Kaplan (New York, 1984), pp. 66–86.

28. Agnes von Zahn-Harnack, *Die Frauenbewegung: Geschichte, Probleme, Ziele* (Berlin, 1928), p. 105.

having "educational meaning for the German people" and insisted on seeing "respect for life" firmly anchored in the German legal code. Thus, in 1920 the JFB initiated and led the attack of religious women's organizations against bills introduced by Independent Socialists (USPD) and Social Democrats (SPD) that would have, respectively, abolished and modified the antiabortion law, Paragraph 218 of the Criminal Code. Its leaders were, however, acutely aware of the "irreconcilable contradiction between moral principles and reality, between what should be and what is."[29]

Thus the JFB accepted abortion for "valid" reasons—medical and social—even though it warned that abortion had "serious physical dangers for women."[30] In 1925 it supported the BDF position, which urged that punishment for women who had abortions be reduced, that they not be sent to prison (*Zuchthaus*), and that the law specifically state that doctors were empowered to end pregnancies in the event of danger to the mother's health, social conditions being taken into consideration in any medical assessment.[31] Even as it firmly maintained a moral and religious stance against abortion—the JFB argued that the problem could not be solved by "living an unbridled life and then unscrupulously eliminating the undesired consequences" and that abortion was a "cheap manner of self-determination of women over their bodies, an unethical resolution of a social problem"[32]—the JFB's acceptance of social conditions was a major modification, a major liberalizing stance. Acknowledging the reality of social conditions also led to demands for social reforms. JFB leaders called for better care for pregnant women, infants, and children; housing reforms; tax incentives for large families; care for unwed mothers and illegitimate children; and job security for unmarried, pregnant women (a more progressive stand than that of the BDF, which was more punitive toward the unmarried mother).[33]

The JFB did not, however, agree with the BDF on the acceptance of

29. *BJFB*, January 1926, pp. 4, 2.

30. Ibid., p. 3. In this respect the JFB was not so far from the position of the Social Democrats. For many in the SPD, opposition to Paragraph 218 meant the acceptance of valid indications, not abolition of the law. See Grossmann, "Abortion and Economic Crisis."

31. Ibid., p. 2. There was a difference in severity between a prison (*Zuchthaus*) and a jail (*Gefängnis*).

32. Ibid., p. 3.

33. Helen Boak, " 'Die Frau gehört ins Haus': Traditional Attitudes among Middle-Class Women in the Weimar Republic" (Paper delivered at Social Science Research Council Research Seminar on Modern German Social History, England, Summer 1981), pp. 12–13.

eugenic indications as a valid reason for abortion. This was an important break not only with German feminism but with a general consensus on the issue. Arguing that there was "no scientific proof with which one could with certainty analyze the value [*Wertigkeit*] of the newborn,"[34] the JFB rejection grew out of its grudging acceptance of valid causes rather than out of an absolute position against abortion. The mistrust of eugenic indications for abortion seems prescient given the uses that the Nazis later made of control over reproduction.[35] Yet its argument, based on scientific proof, obscured other issues that would become piercingly relevant after 1933. Issues of power and control, of *who* would define what was eugenically "positive" or "negative" and *who* would have decision-making power over abortions, were left unexamined. But here the JFB's myopia was fully shared by the BDF.

Over the issues of peace and pacifism—major issues of international feminism—there was early cooperation and later disagreement with the BDF. During the First World War the JFB, like the German women's movement, supported the "Fatherland." It joined the Nationaler Frauendienst (National Women's Service), an organization set up by the BDF to aid in the war effort.[36] This national association looked after the families of men at the front, helped women find work, and set up soup kitchens, hospital wards, knitting circles, and the like. After the war the Jewish organization quickly supported the peace movement, whereas the BDF maintained a more nationalistic stance. Leading members of the JFB were pacifists, and the JFB newsletter regularly printed reports and announcements of peace conferences or of the Women's International League for Peace and Freedom (WILPF), a pacifist organization founded in 1915 and led by Jane Addams.[37] In 1927 the JFB formally urged its members to join the WILPF, a radical step given the internationalism of the latter and the atmosphere of wounded German nationalism that surrounded the JFB and was found to no small extent in the BDF.[38] The Frauenbund also sent unofficial observers to disarmament conferences and circulated petitions in favor of disarmament. It argued that a women's movement (*Frauenbewegung*) had to be a peace movement (*Frie-*

34. *BJFB*, January 1926, p. 4.

35. See Gisela Bock, "Racism and Sexism in Nazi Germany," in *When Biology Became Destiny*, pp. 271–96.

36. *AZdJ* 79, no. 22 (May 28, 1915), supp., p. 2, and no. 20 (May 14, 1915), supp., p. 1; *BJFB*, April 1936, pp. 9–10.

37. *BJFB*, August 1926, p. 4.

38. *Israelitisches Familienblatt*, December 15, 1927, supp., p. 8.

densbewegung) or it was useless; there was a "natural connection between motherhood and peace."[39]

The JFB also maintained ties with the peace movement from a sense of Jewish consciousness. It sustained ties with the League of Jewish Women (Liga der jüdischen Frauen, a section of the WILPF), which combatted "antisemitism as an enemy of world peace."[40] In 1920 the German branch of the WILPF wrote an open protest against German antisemitism to the International League. Its members saw a "symptom of sickness" in the antisemitism resulting from the war. As pacifists they condemned it from a religious, patriotic, and women's standpoint.[41] In 1926 the WILPF adopted a resolution against antisemitism. Thus the JFB felt justified not only in its "women's" position but also as Jews, in supporting the International League and the peace movement.

Beyond the various issues upon which the JFB and the BDF agreed or disagreed, it is clear that the BDF played a fundamental role in the education of JFB leaders. Some of its most important activists had their earliest education in the ranks of the BDF.[42] This was the case for all its presidents as well as for many of its prominent figures. In fact its last president, Ottilie Schönewald, recognized that "for political or, perhaps, psychological reasons the German element [in the history of the JFB] has been played down. . . . The JFB was a part of the German women's movement and has to be understood in that context."[43]

It is important that the JFB considered the BDF an ally in its fight against antisemitism. When, for example, it noticed an initiative to form an antisemitic women's organization in Leipzig, it turned to the BDF for assistance.[44] As antisemitism in Germany dramatically increased during the Depression, the newly elected leader of the BDF, Agnes von Zahn-Harnack, immediately visited the JFB and declared that neither she nor the BDF would tolerate attacks on Jews or Judaism.[45] By 1930 the BDF became an integral part of the "enlightenment work" (*Aufklärungsarbeit*) that the JFB, like other German-Jewish organizations, pursued in

39. *BJFB*, November 1931, pp. 4–6.
40. Ibid., August 1926, p. 4; also Dora Edinger, former member of the JFB, interview with author, New York, 1975.
41. *Israelitisches Familienblatt*, October 28, 1920, p. 3.
42. See Schönewald memoirs; also interviews with former JFB leaders Lilli Liegner and Klara Caro, Palisades, N.Y., December 9, 1974, and Dora Edinger, New York, N.Y., 1974–79.
43. Schönewald collection, 4:14 (written in 1957 or 1958).
44. *AZdJ* 83, no. 52 (December 26, 1919), supp., p. 1.
45. *BJFB*, November 1931, pp. 4–6.

order to stem bigotry. The JFB invited non-Jewish women's and youth organizations to Frauenbund lectures, social evenings, and tours of synagogues. Agnes von Zahn-Harnack led one of these "enlightenment" meetings. Representatives of the Catholic women's organization, women theologians, and feminist leaders attended. Zahn-Harnack asked the JFB to invite Christian women to holiday festivals, synagogue services, and discussions, noting "the fight against antisemitism must originate with Christian women."[46] The JFB prepared and distributed literature that explained Jewish history, ethics, and customs to its Gentile guests.[47] It often compared the emancipation of Jews with that of women, asserting that while each group hoped to fit into the dominant society, each had acquired a consciousness of its unique qualities, which it deserved to retain. Recognizing that race and gender discrimination were mutually reinforcing and deeply oppressive, the JFB argued that German and Jewish women should fight antisemitism because Jews and feminists shared the same struggle for emancipation. Both groups required an open, liberal, pluralistic society. It appealed to the women's movement to fight antisemitism, "not *for us,* but for the idea of a German spirit in which we all believed."[48] With the growth of the Nazi party, the BDF published "Yellow Leaves" (*Gelbe Blätter*), pamphlets aimed mainly against the Nazis. The BDF was seeking to protect women's rights, rather than Jewish ones, and too often believed its own interests to be more important than those of Jews, not recognizing a mutual danger.[49] Nevertheless the JFB could take satisfaction from the BDF's official hostility to the Nazis. The BDF's final appeal of March 1933 to German women to vote only for parties that accepted the rights of women and the state of law was printed in large headings across the front page of the JFB newsletter.[50]

Yet JFB leaders were also sensitive to what they felt to be slights of the BDF to Jewish needs, as well as to a lack of respect for Jewish particularism and a certain amount of antisemitism. While the JFB and BDF shared similar gender and class concerns, the latter organization's

46. Ibid., December 1931, pp. 7–8.
47. Ibid., December 1930, p. 7.
48. Ibid., pp. 5–7, and September 1932, pp. 4–5.
49. This was the case as late as June 1932, when members of the BDF executive committee, including Agnes von Zahn-Harnack, insisted on challenging Nazi attacks only on women. The majority, however, agreed with Emma Ender that "National Socialism has grown big in its fight against Jews and women." See Evans, *Feminist Movement in Germany,* p. 255.
50. *BJFB,* March 1933, p. 1.

large membership reflected some of the more negative attitudes toward Jews of the surrounding society. These ranged from liberal impatience with Jewish distinctiveness[51] to covert or overt antisemitism. As a historian of Weimar Germany has recently stated: "More common and widespread than outright hatred or sympathy for the Jews was what we have called moderate anti-Semitism, that vague sense of unease about Jews that stopped far short of wanting to harm them but that may have helped to neutralize whatever aversion Germans might otherwise have felt for the Nazis."[52] Whereas few Jews had been the targets of personal attacks, virtually all knew antisemites and viewed antisemitism as a fact of life. This was certainly the case to varying degrees in the universities, among rightist political parties, in the churches, and in certain echelons of the civil service and army.[53] Nevertheless, even with manifestations of social and governmentally tolerated antisemitism as well as the growth of right-wing antisemitic organizations (numbering more than two hundred thousand people by 1922[54]), most German Jews believed that Jews had a place in Germany and that a German-Jewish symbiosis was possible.

Frauenbund members, too, were convinced of this. Yet they were aware of the distance that separated them and their BDF sisters. Even those non-Jewish women who volunteered to assist the JFB to fight racism remained remote. As one JFB member noted:

> We lived among each other, sat together in the same school room, attended university together, met each other at social events—and were complete strangers. Was it their fault? Ours? Hard to say but also meaningless. It was a fact, of portentous consequence for the time, that those who wanted to stand up for us knew nothing about us.[55]

Members of the JFB felt that they were accepted by their liberal feminist sisters only when they "closeted" their Jewishness. As one JFB leader stated, "Those who do not call attention to their Jewishness are valued."[56] Their perceptions were correct: the BDF avoided what it considered to be "sectarianism." Mirroring German liberalism, it invited Jewish inte-

51. Reinhard Rürup, "Jewish Emancipation and Bourgeois Society," *LBIYB* 14 (1969): 80.
52. Niewyk, *Jews in Weimar Germany*, p. 80.
53. Ibid., pp. 86, 112, 55.
54. Ibid., p. 46.
55. Rahel Straus, *Wir Lebten in Deutschland: Erinnerungen einer deutschen Jüdin, 1880–1933* (Stuttgart, 1962), p. 266.
56. *BJFB*, December 1930, pp. 5–6.

gration at the price of Jewish identity and was decidedly uncomfortable in the face of Jews who resisted homogenization. Pappenheim referred to those Jewish women who joined the BDF directly (thus subsuming their Jewish identity) as *Halbe* (half-Jews).

On occasion the BDF also reflected the insensitivity or antisemitism of some of its members.[57] In 1908 leaders of the JFB attended the BDF general assembly. The JFB was already a BDF member, and the Protestant women's association had just joined. In an attempt to win the adherence of the Catholic women's organization, the BDF leadership invited, consulted, and encouraged leaders of the Catholic women to participate in the general debates. Feeling slighted—the JFB had brought 120 affiliated clubs into the BDF to the Protestants' 43—Pappenheim took the floor during one debate "not because she had been asked to respond, like the representative of the Catholic women's groups, but because she had not been asked to speak at all."[58] A similar slight, which provoked a public outcry, occurred in 1915. Pappenheim was furious with Helene Lange, one of the founders of German feminism, when the latter in a speech omitted the JFB while naming several Catholic and Protestant women's associations that belonged to the BDF. Gertrud Bäumer, the president of the BDF, told Pappenheim that the president could not censure a private member of the BDF (although Lange was well known and therefore not simply a private member). Pappenheim angrily withdrew from the National Women's Service, which supported the war effort on the home front, accusing Lange and Bäumer of "hatefulness toward Jewish women and Judaism." Lange responded to a Jewish colleague: "It is a terrible pity that just now, suddenly, Jewish women, too, stress their religion, something from which they judiciously restrained themselves in the past."[59] The problem was not solved, but the disagreement ended when Bäumer sent an apologetic letter to Pappenheim.

Insensitivity could turn to a more overt manifestation of hostility as in the case of the Bavarian Provincial Association for Women's Suffrage. In 1913 this organization agreed to condemn kosher butchering, a rather well-known antisemitic stance. The JFB protested and was assured by the

---

57. Hackett, "Politics of Feminism," pp. 176–87; Evans, *Feminist Movement in Germany,* pp. 200, 243–44. Evans suggests (pp. 254–55) that many BDF members voted Nazi even though the organization officially opposed the party.

58. *Israelitisches Familienblatt,* November 5, 1908, p. 11.

59. Archives of the Bund Deutscher Frauenvereine, 3 Abt. Nr. 5, Berlin, West Germany.

Prussian Association for Women's Suffrage that it rejected the position of the Bavarian group.[60] In the postwar era antisemitism seemed to play a role in the denial of the BDF's top position to Alice Salomon. Despite her conversion to Protestantism, the leadership decided that in order to preserve the movement, a woman with a Jewish last name could not be president.[61]

The exaggerated "neutrality" of the BDF's political endorsements also hurt its Jewish supporters. In general, the political leanings of the majority of JFB members reflected those of the Jewish community. Most Jews supported the middle-class German Democratic party. Founded in 1918, it was a liberal party of business and professional people that supported the Weimar Constitution and opposed antisemitism as incompatible with reason, tolerance, and individual freedom. After 1930, with the increasing polarization of politics, most of the Jewish vote split between the Social Democratic party and the Catholic Center party (the latter as a defender of minority religious rights and an opponent of racism). In the early Weimar years the JFB was comfortable with the pro-Democratic party leanings of the BDF leadership, but found itself more isolated by the mid-1920s as the Right began to enter leadership positions. Claiming the need to remain "above parties" in order to hold on to its rank and file, many of whom were to the right even of the leaders, the BDF invited conservative and right-wing representatives, whose parties were often officially antisemitic, to its political debates. In fact, this alleged need to be "fair"—and possible antisemitic intentions—caused the Deutsche Staatsbürgerinnen Verband, an affiliate of the BDF, to invite Nazis to present a lecture on "What should women expect from the Nazis?" along with speakers from other parties. The Deutsche Staatsbürgerinnen Verband leadership sent a note of apology to the JFB hoping that "you will understand we came to this decision after serious discussion."[62] By the early 1930s even the staunchest supporters of Jewish involvement in the German feminist movement had to admit that "quiet, subterranean currents" could be felt in affiliates of the BDF. While these were purportedly not antisemitic tones, they were "mystical, irrational currents" that also began to dismiss the feminist movement as too rational. Jewish feminist observers experienced these currents as directed

60. *AZdJ* 77, no. 14 (April 4, 1913), supp., p. 5.
61. Dora Peyser, biographical section, in *Alice Salomon,* ed. Hans Muthesius (Cologne, 1958), p. 85.
62. For Deutsche Staatsbürgerinnen Verband, see *BJFB,* February 1931, p. 13. On Jewish political allegiances, see Niewyk, *Jews in Weimar Germany.*

against Jews and the women's movement. They feared not only for their own collaboration in the "unbiased" feminist movement, but for feminism itself.[63]

The JFB seemed to recognize—and in some ways epitomize—the ambivalent position of Jews in German society. On the one hand, it attempted to achieve a working relationship with the BDF in order to support the goals of feminism, be accepted as part of a German movement, and stem the growth of antisemitism. On the other hand, the JFB provided a congenial atmosphere for Jewish women who, while making the proper obeisances to their German heritage and to German feminism, enjoyed a feeling of ethnic community and a consciousness of kind, and reacted to a feeling of exclusion. Thus the Frauenbund provided a separatist alternative for Jewish women, independent of male Jewish leadership and independent of the German women's movement. Allied with both, its members felt truly comfortable with neither.

THE JEWISH FEMINIST STRUGGLE FOR SURVIVAL

The choices of whether to work within the German women's movement or in the Jewish community were vitiated by the maelstrom following the Nazi seizure of power. Strategies of sheer survival were forced upon Jewish women. In June 1933 the Bund Deutscher Frauenvereine disbanded itself rather than face *Gleichschaltung*—the process by which all leaders were replaced by Nazi activists and all organizations were forced to participate in Nazi programs. The JFB had resigned from the German feminist organization a few days earlier, and the BDF had accepted the Frauenbund's withdrawal with "deepest regret."[64]

If Jewish feminists expected their German counterparts to maintain a sense of sisterhood and loyalty, they were to be sorely disappointed. Paula Ollendorff, a JFB leader, became very depressed at the behavior of former friends in the German movement. Right after Hitler's accession to power, colleagues with whom she had worked for many years had "stupid excuses" so that they "would not be caught with Jews." One "old fighter" for women's careers, a well-known member of the Democratic party, asked Ollendorff and another Jewish colleague, Martha

---

63. *BJFB*, July 1933, pp. 1–2, quoting *Central-Verein Zeitung*, October 1931. By understanding criticisms of the feminist movement as also aimed against Jews, Jewish women were not being overly sensitive. The Nazis had always drawn a connection between feminism and the "Jewish Bolshevik conspiracy."

64. *BJFB*, June 1933, pp. 11–12. Despite its "regret," the BDF, insisting on its "national" and "social" character, "did not dissolve itself as an act of ideological defiance." Evans, *Feminist Movement in Germany*, p. 257.

Parker, to help her prove that she had always been nationalistic (*na-tional*). Parker reports: "I laughed and said sure, I can get signatures for you but they won't help. Paula could not laugh—she said 'everything is completely bankrupt.' I said it was Germany's bankruptcy and she responded it was also hers."[65]

Of course there were exceptions, but Ottilie Schönewald, the last president of the JFB, also suffered from the absence of female solidarity among her bourgeois sisters:

> Where were German women then? If shortly after the 9th of November 1938 they had found the same words for me that are in their letters today [1955] they would have meant so much to me. Hardly one of our German, so-called friends . . . found their way to us. This was, unfortunately, not a personal, isolated phenomenon. Yes, employees . . . workmen, the people who received poor relief in my constituency were not too shy to show their affection . . . they knew where to find us in broad daylight. And, as far as I know, it caused no harm to any of them.

This lack of soldiarity did not stop Schönewald from writing a letter of protest in 1935 to the head of the new Nazi women's organization, Gertrud Scholtz-Klink, against a speech of the *Gauleiter* of Cologne to thousands of children in which he stated that "if humanity wants to live in peace, Jews must die." Needless to say, Schönewald did not receive a response. Her effort was a courageous, if futile, attempt at female solidarity as mothers.[66]

Between 1933 and 1938 the Jüdischer Frauenbund joined other Jewish organizations in a struggle for survival. This endeavor took several forms: fighting antisemitism, preventing the disintegration of communal organizations, ensuring the continuation of Jewish practices, helping needy Jews, and preparing people for emigration. During the Hitler years the feminism of the JFB became less pronounced, and the organization concentrated instead on social work. While it continued to demand equality for women within the Jewish community, maintained its services and institutions for women, and represented the needs and views of women to the newly established Jewish central organization—the Reichsvertretung der deutschen Juden (Central Association of German Jews)—the needs of German Jews took precedence over purely feminist goals.

65. Paula Ollendorff Collection, Archives of the Leo Baeck Institute, New York, 3060, no. 15.
66. Schönewald collection, 4:8.

Furthermore, antisemitism aside, the impossibly misogynist nature of the Third Reich made feminism both futile and dangerous.

The JFB's "enlightenment efforts," like those of the rest of German Jewry, had been less than successful, since those who heard JFB pleas for a liberal, pluralistic society were not the same people who promoted racial hatred. After 1933 Jews were unable to meet with Christian groups; their social, legal, political, and, ultimately, physical ostracism commenced. In a defensive gesture the JFB concentrated its attempt to lessen antisemitism on its "self-discipline" (*Selbstzucht*) campaign. Begun in 1915 and continued throughout the 1930s this attempt to encourage "simplicity in the appearance of women and girls" was the JFB's second answer to the hostility of other Germans. As in previous JFB campaigns against white slavery or an "unrepresentative" job profile, it reflected the defensive posture of those who saw self-discipline as a key to acceptance and self-defense: an attitude that "stepchildren had to be doubly good."[67] It also mirrored a century-old reflex of Jews who had learned to be inconspicuous for fear of reprisals from their enemies. All Jews, particularly women, were cautioned to avoid the envy and resentment of antisemites by maintaining a simple standard of living. Jewish newspapers and organizations urged Jewish women to avoid any dress or action that could lead to embarrassment and warned "women who drape themselves in glittering jewelry" that they were abetting the enemy.[68] By combatting the negative images of Jewish women that were shared by Jewish men and antisemites alike, the JFB inadvertently propagated them. In doing so, it conveyed two false impressions: an exaggeration of the number of Jewish women bending under the weight of gold (particularly in a period of increasing unemployment and a boycott of Jewish businesses) and a delusion about modesty mitigating antisemitism. Under double jeopardy as Jews and as women, members of the Frauenbund demonstrated a common characteristic of oppressed minorities—blaming themselves for their victimization.

The Frauenbund was modestly successful in helping to sustain the Jewish community. It cooperated with Jewish central welfare organiza-

67. Ludwig Holländer, executive director of a German-Jewish defense organization, as quoted by Peter Gay in "Encounter with Modernism: German Jews in German Culture, 1888–1914," *Midstream* 21, no. 2 (February 1975): 60.

68. *Israelitisches Familienblatt*, February 7, 1918, p. 10; *AZdJ* 85, no. 19 (September 16, 1921), supp., p. 2; Adolph Asch, memoirs, p. 3, Archives of the Leo Baeck Institute, New York.

tions, providing volunteers for some of the social welfare offices and sharing responsibility for the divisions in charge of Jewish schools and institutions.[69] It also added its own new local chapters, attracted new members (many of whom came from the dissolved German women's movement and professional women's organizations), and initiated closer ties with other national and international Jewish women's associations. Its newsletter and cultural activities concentrated on teaching Jewish customs, history, and religion. The JFB had always promoted Jewishness, but its efforts took on a new, psychological dimension in these years. In Nazi Germany, Jews were depicted as evil and inferior. Cultural and religious activities gave a sense of perspective and an *élan vital* to a group facing rejection and hopelessness.

The JFB was as conscious of the need to provide material assistance to people whose social and economic conditions were deteriorating as it was of the need for psychological encouragement. The Frauenbund aided other Jewish groups in the collection of money, clothing, and fuel. As Jews continued to lose their livelihoods, the JFB was active in helping Jewish middle-class women and their families to adjust to a lower standard of living. It increased its housewife assistance programs, set up cooking, darning, sewing, nursing, and home repair courses, and wrote its own cookbook for Jews who had difficulty buying kosher meat after Hitler forbade ritual slaughtering. Mutual aid was encouraged, and in various cities the JFB organized communal kitchens, children's "play circles," communal maid services, and dialogue afternoons, where women could discuss their problems and receive advice as well as moral support. The Frauenbund repeatedly emphasized the pivotal role of women in maintaining the equilibrium of the home. In turn, it attempted to offer women practical, intellectual, and spiritual support.

The final major area of JFB concern was the preparation of women for emigration. In 1935 the Nuremberg Laws deprived Jews of the rights of citizens and forbade marriages as well as extramarital intercourse between Jews and "Aryans." Convinced by this "Law for the Protection of German Blood and Honor" that emigration was necessary, the JFB increased its efforts to retrain girls for vocations suited to places of refuge. The JFB newsletter devoted issues to the process and problems of female emigration, and members also accompanied children to safety in foreign lands, returning to Germany to continue their work.

After the Nazi-led pogrom of November 1938, known as *Kristall-*

69. Schönewald collection, 2:11.

nacht, the Frauenbund was ordered to be dissolved. Its treasury and institutions were absorbed by the Reichsvertretung, and its leaders joined the staff of that organization. Although these women had many opportunities to emigrate, they continued to work for the Jewish community. Those who were not in the national leadership continued to perform social work along with other Jews from their community. Most of the JFB leaders were deported in 1942 and became victims of Hitler's "final solution to the Jewish problem." Hannah Karminski, the former executive secretary of the JFB, wrote a friend of her last visit with Cora Berliner, the organization's former vice-president, on the day of the latter's deportation: "C. and our other friends took books along. They agreed on the selection. To my knowledge C. took *Faust I* and an anthology. When I went to visit them on the last day, shortly before their departure, they were sitting in the courtyard in the sun reading Goethe."[70]

The chronicle of the Jüdischer Frauenbund presents us with the complexities of the gender and ethnic (or, as the Nazis would have it, "racial") determinants of women's history. Within a specific middle-class context, it allows us to identify a particular case in which both gender and "race" struggles occurred and how they related to each other. Jewish feminists suffered from the double burden of being women in a sexist society and Jews in a racist one. They shared common experiences as women across ethnic-religious lines and yet suffered divisions created by these same identities. In the liberal, pluralistic framework of the Weimar Republic, Jewish feminists attempted to combine ethnic pride with feminist aspirations by working for women's interests within their own Jewish community and allying with German feminism. Often, however, their fears of or reactions to antisemitism forced them into an alignment with their male coreligionists, where they faced the need to subsume feminist demands to the good of the whole. Ultimately, in a period of crisis, "racial" identity as imposed from without prevailed over female solidarity.*

70. "Letters from Berlin," *LBIYB* 2 (1957): 312.
* Copyright © 1984 by Bridenthal, Grossman, and Kaplan from their book *Women in Weimar and Nazi Germany,* by permission of Monthly Review Press, New York.

The Zionist Response to Antisemitism
in the Weimar Republic

Much has been written on the Zionist response to antisemitism in the period before World War I. The interwar period has been less thoroughly researched, though this has not prevented a number of scholars from passing summary judgments on the reaction of German Zionists to the phenomenon of antisemitism during the Weimar Republic. The consensus that has emerged states that "except for the anti-Semitic outbreaks of 1923, the *Jüdische Rundschau* did not begin to take systematic, detailed notice of anti-Jewish agitation and violence until 1931. . . . Zionism's very overview of anti-Semitism operated to mute the specific awareness of particular events whose implications could easily be fit to theory."[1]

These conclusions have been reached for the most part on the basis of reading the Zionist press, which maintained a certain public stance toward the question of Jewish self-defense (*Abwehr*). Yet an examination of primary sources, which have thus far been overlooked, yields a more balanced view of the Zionist attitude toward antisemitism in the Weimar Republic.

1. Stephen M. Poppel, *Zionism in Germany, 1897–1933: The Shaping of a Jewish Identity* (Philadelphia, 1977), pp. 119–26. See also Peter M. Baldwin, "Zionist and Non-Zionist Jews in the Last Years before the Nazi Regime," *Leo Baeck Institute Year Book* 27 (1982): 90–91, 101, and passim; Eckhard Wieman, "Abwehrkämpfe und Reaktionen der deutschen Juden auf den Antisemitismus von 1924 bis zur nationalsozialistischen Machtübernahme," Staatsexamenarbeit (Hamburg, n.d.), p. 84.

THE AFTERMATH OF THE FIRST WORLD WAR

The end of the war found the Zionistische Vereinigung für Deutschland (ZVfD) confident about its future. The headquarters of the World Zionist Organization (WZO) had moved from Berlin to London—a fact that had weakened the ZVfD organizationally, financially, and even psychologically. On the other hand, German Zionists could point to the Balfour Declaration and the new international respectability of Zionism as signs of progress. The persistence of antisemitism was further proof that it was endemic and that the only solution lay in building up the Jewish national home. The German Revolution of 1918 emboldened the Zionists to demand of the new government more understanding for Zionist aspirations through a public proclamation and support for intensive Zionist activities in Germany. The antisemitic danger lurking even among the revolutionary circles seemed to the Zionists to be threatening other members of the Jewish community rather than themselves. Postwar antisemitism caught the non-Zionists and anti-Zionists at a moment when they were most vulnerable, when their hopes for a true *Burgfrieden* lay in ashes. The non-Zionist youth, especially, badly shaken by the experiences of the war, was groping for a new sense of identity. This was the opportune moment to capture these confused and wandering souls for the Zionist cause. The Zionist ideal would provide them with the moral and psychological fiber they so badly needed.[2]

Though taking note of the increase in antisemitism, the executive of the ZVfD decided in August 1919 merely to devote more space to the phenomenon in the *Jüdische Rundschau* and to reject all demands for Jewish self-defense.[3] A month later the executive empowered Siegfried Moses to prepare an outline and directives for the ZVfD's official position on antisemitism.[4] If Moses indeed prepared such a blueprint, it does not seem to have been seriously discussed by the ZVfD executive in the early years of the Weimar Republic, though the phenomenon of antisemitism and possible countermeasures did occupy the Zionists and were occasionally on the agenda of the Delegiertentage.[5] Indeed, in his far-

2. Zionistische Vereinigung für Deutschland (hereafter ZVfD), "An die Ortsgruppen und Vertrauensmänner," November [24], 1918, Central Zionist Archives, Jerusalem (hereafter CZA), A15/VII/29.

3. Protokoll der Sitzung des Geschäftsführenden Ausschusses der ZVfD vom 21. August 1919, Schocken Archives, Jerusalem, 531/61. See also Ernst Simon, "Antisemitismus und Zionismus," *Jüdische Rundschau*, October 24, 1919, no. 74, p. 580.

4. Protokoll der XIV. Sitzung vom 21. September 1919, Schocken Archives, 531/61.

5. See, e.g., Kurt Blumenfeld's speech at the Sixteenth Delegiertentag, "Notwendig-

ranging speech, entitled "Zionistische Arbeit in Deutschland," before the
Seventeenth Delegiertentag in Hanover in 1921, Felix Rosenblüth, then
joint-president of the ZVfD, did not once mention defense against antisemitism as a Zionist task. He was much more concerned with Zionist
defense against the newly formed Verband nationaldeutscher Juden,
headed by Max Naumann.[6] In the early 1920s the ZVfD saw its main
task not in defense of German Jews but in attempting to protect the
Ostjuden in Germany against antisemitic measures.[7]

1923–24: VIOLENCE AND ZIONIST REASSESSMENT

Yet, despite their claim that "our conception of Judaism is much too
positive, and the tasks before us much too urgent to permit ourselves to
devote our time to the sick fantasies of antisemitism,"[8] the Zionists could
hardly ignore the social, economic, and political upheaval in Germany in
1918–23, which affected them like all other German Jews.

The Zionists viewed with alarm the increasing strength of the various
antisemitic parties and the steadily mounting excesses against Jews. A
noticeable change in the Zionist attitude to and concern over antisemitism
came in the wake of Walther Rathenau's murder in the late spring of
1922.[9] Like most German Jews, the Zionists, too, were confused and
helpless at the onslaught against them and unable to provide sure guidance for Jewish self-defense. They called Judeophobia a sickness against
which no defense was effective except the settlement of the Jews in their
own territory.[10] At the same time they suggested support of those political parties that would take up the cudgels on behalf of Jews.[11] In a confidential report to its members in 1923, the ZVfD allowed that when
Jewish life itself was at stake, as was the case in Bavaria, a common front
was possible even with the Centralverein deutscher Staatsbürger jüdischen

keit einer Bekämpfung des Antisemitismus in Deutschland," reprinted in *Jüdische
Rundschau*, July 6, 1920, no. 44, p. 353; and "Antisemitismus in Swinemünde," ibid.,
August 20, 1920, no. 57, p. 57.

6. Felix Rosenblüth's speech was printed in full as a separate pamphlet; see CZA,
Z4/795. See also F[ritz] L[oebenstein], "Der Weg des deutschen Judentums," *Jüdische
Rundschau*, June 20, 1922, no. 49, pp. 320–22.

7. See "Deutschland: Die Ostjüdischen Verfolgungen," *Jüdische Rundschau*, April
16, 1920, no. 24, p. 182; "Neue Razzia auf Ostjuden in Berlin," ibid., May 4, 1920,
no. 29, p. 218; and "Umschau," ibid., April 7, 1922, no. 28, pp. 151–53.

8. "Umschau," ibid., April 7, 1922, no. 28, p. 151.

9. Ibid. July 14, 1922, nos. 53/54, p. 355; July 28, 1922, no. 59, p. 384; and
December 8, 1922, no. 97, p. 635.

10. "Zum Rathenau Prozess," ibid., October 13, 1922, no. 81, p. 541.

11. Ibid., October 10, 1922, no. 80, p. 1.

Glaubens (CV), provided the CV was willing to give up its accustomed rhetoric. In the same memorandum the ZVfD declared for the first time that the Zionists themselves had a stake in the battle against antisemitism for two reasons: to protect the honor of the Jewish people, whose guardians they were, and because the ideological debate with the antisemites provided the Zionists with a convenient springboard for Zionist propaganda.[12]

The debate over whether Zionists ought to participate in defense activities occupied Zionist circles throughout 1923–24 and intensified as the antisemitic excesses became more frequent. In a discussion in April 1923 within the Kartell jüdischer Verbindungen, Moritz Bileski argued that the time had come for more active Zionist measures against antisemitism, and he rejected Kurt Loewenstein's counterargument that such a position would hamper Zionist work for Palestine.[13] A lead article in the *Jüdische Rundschau* called for Zionist participation in the CV's *Abwehr,* provided this could be done without compromising Zionist ideology.[14] The Nineteenth Delegiertentag in Dresden, in June 1923, devoted an entire session to a discussion of "Die Bekämpfung des Antisemitismus."[15] In October 1923 the *Jüdische Rundschau* publicly asserted what it had confidentially shared with its *Vertrauensmänner:* that in cases of physical violence, all Jews must band together for defense. It went one step further and declared that the ZVfD would actively seek to coordinate its *Abwehr* activities with other Jewish organizations. Its rationale for this new departure was that defense activities could not be left in the hands of other organizations and that the Zionists needed to take the lead immediately since time was of the essence.[16]

The ZVfD's more activist approach to the problem of antisemitism was fueled not only by the attacks on Jews in 1923 and 1924. To no lesser degree it was due to the fact that during these two years Alfred Landsberg was its president. Unlike Felix Rosenblüth before him and

12. See Erich Cohn on behalf of the ZVfD, "An die Mitglieder des Landesvorstandes und des Zentralkomitees, an die zionistischen Ortsgruppen und Vertrauensleute," Schocken Archives, 531/241.

13. "Antisemitismus und Nationales Judentum," *Jüdische Rundschau,* April 13, 1923, no. 30, p. 179.

14. "Die Bekämpfung des Antisemitismus," ibid., May 29, 1923, no. 43, pp. 251–52. See also a letter from a reader, ibid., June 8, 1923, no. 46, p. 276.

15. Ibid., June 19, 1923, no. 49, pp. 298–99, 306. See also ibid., October 5, 1923, nos. 85/86, p. 506.

16. "Antisemitismus und Einheitsfront," ibid., October 23, 1923, no. 91, pp. 535–36. See also "Zusammenfassung der Kräfte," ibid., October 26, 1923, no. 92, pp. 539–40.

Kurt Blumenfeld who succeeded him, Landsberg was keenly interested in the question of *Abwehr* and throughout the 1920s tried to steer the ZVfD in that direction. In preparation for the Reichstag elections of May 4, 1924, he circulated a confidential memorandum urging Zionists to exercise their rights as voters. Landsberg pointed out in his opening paragraph that he was aware that such a request stood in contradiction to the Zionist policy of neutrality and distance from German politics—*Abgrenzung* and *Distanz* in Blumenfeld's terms. But times had changed, and since the Jewish Question was part and parcel of the election campaign, it was the duty of Zionists to defend their rights as Jews. It was important to vote for those parties that upheld the rights of Jews. Landsberg went further and implied that Jews ought not to vote for the Deutsche Demokratische Partei, which had not taken a stand on the Jewish Question during the last party caucus. But he also acknowledged that among those parties not openly hostile to Jews, it was difficult to find one to which the ZVfD could give its wholehearted support. Zionists, therefore, ought to vote for parties according to their own local conditions.[17] In a further departure from its erstwhile policies, the ZVfD executive protested publicly against an epilogue written by Theodor Fritsch to a new printing of the *Protocols of the Elders of Zion*, which was titled "Die Zionistischen Protokolle." In it Fritsch argued that the *Protocols* were based on Zionist ideology. The ZVfD even filed a formal complaint against Fritsch.[18] This was the kind of activity for which the ZVfD normally derided the CV.

During 1923–24, then, a practical—if not ideological—rapprochement seemed possible between the ZVfD and the CV, but a number of factors militated against this process. For one, after some initial setbacks to the democratic spirit of the republic, the external pressure on German Jewry was soon easing. At the elections to the Reichstag in May 1924 the Nationalsozialistische Deutsche Arbeiterpartei (NSDAP), together with the Deutschvölkische Freiheitspartei, succeeded in capturing thirty-two seats in the Reichstag—or 6.6 percent of the votes. But their initial success was short lived. Following the Dawes Plan of August 1924, Ger-

17. Alfred Landsberg, "An die zionistischen Ortsgruppen und Vertrauensleute! Vertraulich!" April 18, 1924, CZA A102/12/14. See also Georg Bernhard, "Die deutschen Juden und die Reichstagswahlen," *Jüdische Rundschau*, April 4, 1928, no. 27, p. 196.

18. See "Erklärung des Landesvorstandes der ZVfD," *Jüdische Rundschau*, May 23, 1924, no. 41, p. 299.

many began an accelerated economic recovery. In the Reichstag elections of December 7, 1924, the NSDAP received only fourteen seats. At the time of the elections of May 20, 1928, Germany was at the height of its economic development, and the NSDAP was elected to only twelve seats.[19] Thus, until 1930 the radical antisemites could claim few successes, and the Jewish Question ceased from occupying the center stage in the political debate, though it by no means disappeared.

BLUMENFELD'S IDEOLOGICAL STANCE

Alfred Landsberg's tenure as president of the ZVfD had pointed to a departure in policy, but it proved short lived when Kurt Blumenfeld took over as president in 1924. It is impossible to underestimate the influence of Blumenfeld on the Zionist attitude toward both the CV and the question of *Abwehr,* which for him was bound with the policy of assimilation. Under Blumenfeld's direction, the ZVfD, which never numbered more than twenty thousand during the Weimar Republic,[20] resumed its pre–World War I ideological stance toward the CV and questions of *Abwehr.* The *Zionistisches Handbuch,* published in 1923, reprinted an article written by Blumenfeld during the war as the ZVfD's credo on the subject of antisemitism. In it Blumenfeld clearly stated:

> Antisemitism is a sign that we are still a productive community. Our uniqueness is perceived by others. Therefore there is only one way to combat antisemitism: to oppose those who hate and despise us with our Jewish uniqueness. . . . There is only one weapon against antisemitism, Judaism itself. . . . Uniting all Jewish energies for the great task of building a Jewish life in Palestine . . . will mean overcoming the terrible degradation of millennia.[21]

When he was elected president of the ZVfD at the Wiesbaden Delegiertentag in 1924—a position he held until Siegfried Moses took over in 1933—Blumenfeld was no longer the young radical of the pre–World

---

19. See Richard F. Hamilton, *Who Voted for Hitler?* (Princeton, 1982), pp. 77–78.

20. This is the upper limit of possible Zionist membership, based on *shekel* contributions to the ZVfD—a highly unreliable measure. See Poppel, *Zionism in Germany,* table 3. A much more accurate estimate is that of Ludwig Pinner, who calculated the number of Zionists in Germany to be 2 percent of the total German-Jewish population. This means that, at most, the Zionists in Germany numbered somewhere between eleven and twelve thousand. See Ludwig Pinner, "Vermögenstransfer nach Palaestina, 1933–1939," *In Zwei Welten: Siegfried Moses zum Fünfundsiebzigsten Geburtstag,* ed. Hans Tramer (Tel Aviv, 1962), p. 134.

21. Blumenfeld, "Antisemitismus," *Zionistisches Handbuch,* ed. Gerhard Holdheim (Berlin, 1923), pp. 32–33.

War I period. He had become a member of the ZVfD establishment.[22] Being a member of the establishment had done nothing, however, to alter the two major premises of his Zionist ideology: to keep away from German politics—practicing *Distanz* as he called it—and to conduct an exclusively Palestino-centric policy. It is clear then that he and his like-minded peers had little use for the CV's *Abwehr* strategies. In his memoirs Blumenfeld stated clearly that upon his election to the presidency of the ZVfD he saw as his most urgent task a thorough and uncompromising debate with the CV about the nature of German antisemitism.[23] In speech after speech Blumenfeld and the *Jüdische Rundschau* castigated the misguided CV policies and strategies and reiterated that the only defense against antisemitism consisted in fostering Jewish pride largely through active participation in the upbuilding of Palestine.[24] The ZVfD also—unjustifiably—accused the CV of defending the rights of German Jews only and abandoning the *Ostjuden* in Germany to the merciless harassment of the police and various antisemitic groups.[25] For its part, the ZVfD executive in the mid-1920s seemed unconcerned about the subject of antisemitism. The ZVfD Delegiertentag in Erfurt in August 1926 did not devote a single session to the subject.[26] At most, the Zionists suggested, one could have a frank confrontation between Jews and Germans.[27] But this seems to have been a fleeting thought and was not taken up seriously.[28]

22. In fact, not a single member of the first generation of German Zionists held any important office within the ZVfD leadership during the Weimar period, although some of them distinguished themselves within the World Zionist Organization.

23. Blumenfeld, *Erlebte Judenfrage: Ein Vierteljahrhundert deutscher Zionismus,* ed. Hans Tramer (Stuttgart, 1962), p. 180.

24. See, e.g., "Vor den Wahlen zum Landesvorstand: Das Echo der CV-Parole," *Jüdische Rundschau,* November 4, 1924, no. 88, p. 623; "Der XX. Delegiertentag," ibid., January 2, 1925, no. 1, pp. 3–4; "Das Programm der Jüdischen Volkspartei," ibid., January 20, 1925, no. 6, p. 49; "Lessing und CV," ibid., June 25, 1926, no. 49, p. 357; "Die Ritualmordhetze in Breslau," ibid., June 29, 1926, no. 50, p. 372; "Der Fall Haas," ibid., August 13, 1926, no. 63, p. 456.

25. This charge had been made during Landsberg's presidency, but it was repeated throughout the 1920s. See, e.g., "Müncherer Brief," ibid., January 5, 1923, nos. 1/2, p. 4; "Wahrheit und Aufrichtigkeit," ibid., December 18, 1923, no. 105, p. 607; "Ein erstaunlicher Bericht," ibid., August 23, 1927, no. 67, pp. 479–80.

26. See "XXI. Delegiertentag der ZVfD, . . . Tagesordnung," ibid., July 20, 1926, no. 56, p. 413.

27. See ibid., November 16, 1926, no. 90, pp. 643–44.

28. See "Die Judenfrage," ibid., December 23, 1926, nos. 100/101, p. 100.

THE THIRD GENERATION OF GERMAN ZIONISTS

Blumenfeld's ideological stance found resonance not only among his cohort from the prewar period but also among the so-called third generation of German Zionists who had embraced Zionism during and after World War I.[29] Throughout the Weimar Republic new trends appeared among the young Zionists with regard to the issues of personal fulfillment and immigration to Palestine that were in tandem with Blumenfeld's ideology. Among the results of these trends was the founding of the Jungjüdischer Wanderbund, the Hechaluz movement, and, among the religiously oriented Zionists, the Zeirei Misrachi and Brith Chaluzim Datiim. All groups included in their platform, and prepared themselves for, emigration to Palestine. The questions of antisemitism and the defense against it were either of no concern to them or, at best, relegated to a place of low priority.

Thus the most dynamic elements within the ZVfD were concerned almost exclusively with Palestine,[30] leaving it to Blumenfeld and his handpicked executive to determine Zionist policy in Germany. While only a few of them actually emigrated to Palestine in the 1920s, it is clear that they were often more aware of and interested in conditions in Palestine than in their own *Gemeinden.*

THE JÜDISCHE VOLKSPARTEI

One exception to the Zionists' lack of interest in what was called *Gegenwartsarbeit* and *Gemeindepolitik* was the Jüdische Volkspartei (JVP), founded in 1919.[31] Its center of activities was Berlin, and its most prominent members—Max Kollenscher, Alfred Klee, Georg Kareski, Hans Goslar, and Ahron Sandler—were men who disagreed with Blumenfeld's exclusively Palestino-centric orientation. In turn, they were prevented by him from attaining positions of power within the ZVfD. In fact one could make the argument that most of the leaders of the JVP whose Zionist activity predated World War I had had personal or ideological conflicts with Blumenfeld in the past and found in the JVP an alternative

29. See Jehuda Reinharz, "Three Generations of German Zionism," *Jerusalem Quarterly*, no. 9 (Fall 1978): 95–110. Concerning the first two generations of German Zionism, see Reinharz, *Fatherland or Promised Land: The Dilemma of the German Jew, 1893–1914* (Ann Arbor, 1975), chaps. 3, 4.

30. See "Unsere Lage," *Der Junge Jude*, November 1927, no. 1, pp. 2–3.

31. See Protokoll der Sitzung des Geschäftsführenden Ausschusses der ZVfD vom 21. August 1919, Schocken Archives, 531/61; Programm der Jüdischen Volkspartei, [June 1920], CZA, Z142/53/2.

through which to express their Zionism. Since the members of the JVP did not reject life in the Diaspora, they believed that their work within the communities would have permanent value for future generations. It was natural that those Zionists involved in *Gemeindepolitik*[32] and *Gegenwartsarbeit* would also be more concerned with the problem of antisemitism than either Blumenfeld's group or members of the Hechaluz or Bachad. Thus men like Alfred Klee—who had been involved in the work of the CV as early as the turn of the century—cooperated from time to time with the Reichsbund jüdischer Frontsoldaten or the CV in various *Abwehr* activities.[33]

The opposition of Blumenfeld and his peers to the activities of the JVP was not solely grounded in ideology. Another source for the conflict was rooted in the fact that the leadership of the ZVfD in those years was in the hands of academics who themselves were representatives of the postassimilationist Zionism about which Blumenfeld often talked and wrote. Fully integrated in German culture, they were searching for their ties to Judaism and found them in Zionism and an affinity to the renewed Jewish national home in Palestine. They felt estranged, however, from the Jewish community as it existed in Germany. *Gemeindepolitik* did not interest them, and they often viewed such work with a measure of condescension.[34] On the other hand, it seems that, on the whole, the leaders of the JVP were Zionists who had been closer to Jewish tradition and did not arrive at Zionism through a process of assimilation; they were less absorbed by German culture and closer to the Jewish community. Thus there were sociological as well as ideological differences between the two groups.[35]

32. Max Kollenscher, *Aufgaben Jüdischer Gemeindepolitik* (Berlin, 1905). See also *Jüdische Rundschau*, June 2, 1908, no. 24, pp. 220–21; Kollenscher, "Unsere Stellung zur Gemeindepolitik," [May 1908], CZA, A142/47/5; and Kollenscher, "Memoiren," MS in the Archives of the Leo Baeck Institute, Jerusalem. See also Gustav Witkowsky, "Ein Gemeindeprogramm," *Jüdisches Gemeinde Jahrbuch, 1913/1914* (Berlin, 1914), pp. 7–11; and Programm der Jüdischen Volkspartei, CZA, A142/53/2, which gives the most detailed blueprint of Jüdische Volkspartei activities in the 1920s.

33. See, e.g., "Die Rechtsnot der Juden in Deutschland," *Jüdische Rundschau*, February 22, 1927, no. 15, p. 105.

34. Of course there were exceptions to this more common type of leader within the ZVfD—e.g., Felix Rosenblüth. It ought to be mentioned that there were quite a few young German Zionists whose *Gegenwartsarbeit* was in the field of social work rather than politics.

35. The fact that the foremost leader of the JVP during the last phases of the Weimar Republic was the Revisionist Georg Kareski certainly contributed to the antipathy that Blumenfeld felt toward this group, but his opposition predates the period of Kareski's preeminent role as chairman of the Berlin Jewish community. On Kareski,

DISSENSION WITHIN ZIONIST RANKS

Despite the claims made by some who have written on the subject, that the ZVfD "did not begin to take systematic, detailed notice of anti-Jewish agitation and violence until 1931,"[36] it is quite clear that the ZVfD membership—if not always the leadership—was deeply concerned with the phenomenon of antisemitism throughout the 1920s, though more intensely after 1929.

Rank-and-file Zionists, especially those residing outside Berlin, were becoming increasingly worried by the spread of antisemitism and less interested in the difference in ideology between the CV and the ZVfD. They demanded from the ZVfD leadership a much more aggressive approach to the problem even if it meant that the Zionists would have to cooperate with the CV. For example, in anticipation of the *Landtagswahlen* in April 1928, and *Reichstagswahlen* of May, a leading member of the ZVfD in Nuremberg demanded that the ZVfD be involved in influencing various candidates as well as the Bayerische Volkspartei, the Sozialdemokratische Partei Deutschlands (SPD), and the Demokratische Partei, each of which had Jewish members. Not waiting for the nod of approval from the executive in Berlin, the leading members of the ZVfD and the CV in Nuremberg coordinated their activities in order to help elect candidates friendly to Jews.[37] In a similar vein, a leading Zionist in Breslau urged that the Zionists contribute funds to the SPD so that the party recognize that the Zionists were as interested in promoting its pro-Jewish sentiments as were other Jewish organizations—that is, the CV.[38]

An interesting and by no means atypical exchange of letters between Kurt Blumenfeld and Max Markreich, a Zionist who was president of the Jewish community in Bremen, illustrates the difference in approach between the ZVfD leadership in Berlin and other Zionists in the Reich. On April 18, 1929, Blumenfeld wrote that he was shocked to read in the

---

see Hans Klee, "Georg Kareski and the Jüdische Volkspartei," Yad Vashem Archives, Jerusalem, 01/217.

36. See Poppel, *Zionism in Germany*, p. 119.

37. See letter from J. Bamberger, of Nuremberg, to the ZVfD, February 7, 1928, in Zur Sitzung des Geschäftsführenden Ausschusses am 13. II. 1928, Schocken Archives, 531/61.

38. See letter from Regierungsrat Dr. Marcus, May 3, 1928, CZA, A102/14/161. On early ties of the ZVfD to the SPD, see Jehuda Eloni, "Die Zionistische Bewegung in Deutschland und die SPD, 1897–1918," *Jahrbuch des Instituts für deutsche Geschichte*, Beiheft 2 (Tel Aviv, 1977), pp. 85–112.

Gemeindeblatt of Bremen that Markreich had demanded that members of the community join the CV. Did Markreich not know of the anti-Zionist attitude of the CV?[39] Markreich's reply, which came by return mail, is instructive:

> In my opinion, there is no question that every *Gemeinde*-administration in Germany supports—whether publicly or privately—the *Abwehr* activities of the CV. *Abwehr* is a necessity, and since the *Gemeinde* has no similar functioning defense organization at its disposal, such as the voluntary CV, it is the self-evident duty of a [*Gemeinde*] president to accept this aid gladly and to ensure its continuation through subventions. . . .
>
> Please view my demand in the new *Jüdisches Gemeindeblatt Bremen* [to join the CV] not through the particular tunnel vision of the [Zionist] party in Berlin, but in light of the facts in Bremen, where we have excellent relations with the CV. . . . I am even of the (perhaps heretical) opinion that the *Abwehr* against antisemitism in Germany ought to be the joint work of the CV and the Zionists much as Jews throughout the world are united within the Jewish Agency.[40]

Blumenfeld was not convinced by this forceful and frank letter,[41] but the pressure from local Zionist groups and individuals[42] throughout the Reich for ZVfD-CV cooperation in defense activities increased after the world economic crisis of 1929 and the ensuing unemployment, which in Germany in February 1932 reached 6.1 million. The crisis led to renewed antisemitic outbreaks[43] and to increased strength of the radical antisemites, foremost among them the NSDAP. In fact, the ZVfD was well aware of the rising tide of hostility toward the Jews even before the crisis. It secretly monitored election results in the Reich beginning in May 1928. The figures available to the ZVfD were alarming. The evidence was detailed and shows intimate knowledge of Nazi activities throughout Germany with accurate breakdowns of the increase in Nazi votes, membership figures, number of meetings, military units, publishing houses and their circulation figures, and the addresses of the NSDAP's offices throughout the Reich.[44]

39. Blumenfeld to Max Markreich, April 18, 1929, Schocken Archives, 531/61.

40. Markreich to Blumenfeld, April 19, 1929, ibid.

41. See Blumenfeld to Markreich, April 30, 1929, ibid.

42. See Werner J. Cahnman, "The Nazi Threat and the Central Verein: A Recollection," *Conference on Anti-Semitism,* ed. Herbert A. Strauss (New York, 1969), pp. 27–36. Cahnman recounts how a leading Zionist from Munich helped raise funds for CV defense activities in 1930.

43. See, e.g., *Central-Verein Zeitung,* May 3, 1929, no. 18, p. 323, and following issues.

44. This detailed information for 1928 and 1929 is housed in the Schocken Archives,

DEPARTURE FROM TRADITIONAL ATTITUDES

Thus when Zionist representatives from Dresden, Bautzen, Oberhausen, and elsewhere requested, toward the end of 1929, that the ZVfD approve their cooperation with the CV in forming a joint, neutral committee for defense against National Socialists, the executive had little choice but to acquiesce. The ZVfD did add a proviso that Zionists join the CV in such efforts as individuals, not as a group, but this distinction was meaningless in any case.[45] At a meeting of the executive of the ZVfD in December 1929, Blumenfeld declared that in light of the increasing onslaught of antisemitism it had become practical and necessary for the ZVfD, too, to begin a propaganda and educational campaign against these attacks. He suggested that the campaign commence with a large public gathering in which the theme of Jew-hate would be discussed. He planned, moreover, to bring this decision to the attention of Ludwig Holländer, the executive director of the CV.[46] This session of the executive, then, can be seen as a first *official* departure in the ZVfD's tactics in dealing with antisemitism. After years of ignoring, belittling, and quietly observing the growth of antisemitism, the ZVfD was now willing to adopt—if reluctantly—a public stance on the issue.[47] At a meeting of the executive in February 1930, Blumenfeld suggested that Jews apply their considerable political and economic power in all countries to stop antisemites. Since the *Abwehr* methods of the CV had proven futile, the Zionists must consider whether

---

518/9. It is not clear who collected the information, but the fact that it was available to Salman Schocken would seem to suggest that if the material was not collected by the ZVfD, it was at least shared with its leadership. On the gathering and analysis of such material by the CV, see Arnold Paucker, *Der jüdische Abwehrkampf gegen Antisemitismus und Nationalsozialismus in den letzten Jahren der Weimarer Republik*, 2d ed. (Hamburg, 1969), pp. 20–21.

45. The initiative for the proviso came from the CV. See Protokoll der 49. Sitzung des Geschäftsführenden Ausschusses vom 13.12. 1929, and Protokoll der 3. Sitzung des Geschäftsführenden Ausschusses vom 20.1. 1930, Schocken Archives, 531/61.

46. Protokoll der 50. Sitzung des Geschäftsführenden Ausschusses vom 13.12. 1929, ibid. At this time the CV had already undertaken other, more aggressive, *Abwehr* measures. Younger CV functionaries had begun to reject the methods that had been in effect for four decades and established in late summer 1929 the Büro Wilhelmstrasse, which undertook large-scale antifascist propaganda. Blumenfeld must have been aware of the existence of this propaganda arm of the CV, since Salman Schocken was one of the largest contributors to its coffers. See Paucker, *Der jüdische Abwehrkampf*, pp. 110–28; also a letter from Paucker to the author, November 8, 1983.

47. See also *Jüdische Rundschau*, November 19, 1929, no. 91, p. 609; November 26, 1929, no. 93, p. 624; and "Zwangsläufige Entwicklung zur Lage der Juden in Deutschland," ibid., January 24, 1930, no. 7, pp. 45–46: "Was sollen wir tun? Alles unternehmen, was mit Abwehr und Aufklärung verbunden ist."

they could permit it to continue to monopolize this work. For the first time the ZVfD suggested that perhaps the *Gemeinden* were better suited for the task.[48] All the members of the executive agreed that the ZVfD needed to be more active in the fight against antisemitism but that the fight ought not to be conducted in cooperation with the CV or along its line of defense. The Zionists needed to strengthen the inner conviction of Jews as Jews and to establish projects for economic self-help.[49]

Thus the executive of the ZVfD established in its meeting of February 23, 1930, an ad hoc Kommission zur Behandlung der Fragen: Zionismus und antisemitische Bewegung in Deutschland und der Wirtschaftslage der deutschen Juden.[50] Early in May 1930 Siegfried Moses presented the members of the executive of the ZVfD with a blueprint outlining the current economic and political difficulties of German Jewry with a number of suggestions for future action.[51] Moses's suggestions formed the basis for discussion within the ZVfD Landesvorstand, which confirmed that while Zionists needed to do something to halt the spread of antisemitism, they had to do it outside the framework of the CV even if that organization were to delete from its program the anti-Zionist Mecklenburg Resolution of February 1928.[52] Georg Landauer pointed out to those

48. On this issue, see also "Im Kampf um die Selbstbehauptung: Dringende Aufgaben der Gemeinde," ibid., February 25, 1930, no. 16, p. 107; and "Berliner Jüdische Gemeinde: Sitzung der Repräsentantenversammlung," ibid., May 6, 1930, no. 35, p. 244.

49. Protokoll der 6. Sitzung des Geschäftsführenden Ausschusses vom 19.2. 1930: "Unsere Haltung und unsere Massnahmen gegenüber der antisemitischen Bewegung in Deutschland," CZA, Z4/3567/VI, and Schocken Archives, 531/61.

50. See Protokoll der Sitzung Des Landesvorstandes der ZVfD vom 23. February 1930, CZA, Z4/3567/VI. The members of the commission included Alfred Berger, Dr. Epstein, Georg Gerson, Max Kreutzberger, Alfred Landsberg, Siegfried Moses, Fritz Naphtali, and Salman Schocken. See letter from Betty Frankenstein to members of the commission, May 5, 1930, Schocken Archives, 531/66. The membership of the commission was expanded in May 1930. See Protokoll der 15. Sitzung des Geschäftsführenden Ausschusses vom 30.5. 1930, ibid., 531/61.

51. See letter from Frankenstein to members of the executive, May 16, 1930, and Moses's outline, entitled "Zu Punkt 1) in der Tagesordnung: Fortsetzung der grundsätzlichen Debatte zum Antisemitismus und zur Wirtschaftslage der deutschen Juden," Schocken Archives, 531/66.

52. The resolution had been proposed by Georg Mecklenburg and was adopted by the CV, with very few changes, in February 1928. It states:

Die von den Zionisten in der Öffentlichkeit betriebene Propaganda hat es dahin gebracht, dass die früher nur von den Judengegnern betonte Trennung von 'Deutschen' und 'Juden' in der öffentlichen Meinung mehr und mehr an Boden gewinnt. . . .

Der CV muss daher wirksamer als bisher der zionistischen Anschauung entgegentreten, nach welcher das Judentum die Volks- und Kulturgemeinschaft aller Juden und Palästina ihr nationales und kulturelles Zentrum sein soll. Das von den Zionisten behauptete oder angestrebte jüdische Volk ist nicht das der auf dem CV-Standpunkte stehenden deutschen Juden, da diese in nationaler und kultureller Hinsicht

present that the ZVfD was ill-prepared for any effective *Abwehr* work. In any case, that was the task of an organization representing all German Jews. Moses then suggested that the ideal situation would be to take over the organization built by the CV, strip it of all ideology, and use it on behalf of all German Jews. Though Robert Weltsch argued forcefully that it was impossible for Zionists to fight antisemitism on any but the ideological plane,[53] the Landesverband adopted the following resolutions:

> The battle against antisemitism and the economic distress of the Jews in Germany must be viewed as a Zionist duty and requires setting up a permanent commission within the ZVfD that would devote its time to these problems. . . .
>
> The ZVfD . . . will need to be active [in defense] only insofar as Zionist interests are threatened. . . . For the rest, the various problems can only be handled by a representative Jewish institution [*gesamt-jüdische Stelle*]. . . .
>
> Since the composition, structure, and history of the CV make it impossible in the foreseeable future for Zionists to join its ranks, and since the attempt to shut out the CV from *Abwehr* activities is doomed to failure and would not even be justified, our aim must be to force the CV into the role of carrying out directives. Its technique and apparatus must be available, while the spirit guiding the *Abwehr* must be determined as much as possible by a representative neutral Jewish organization.[54]

COOPERATION WITH THE CV

But events overtook any plans the ZVfD may have had for a neutral umbrella organization to combat antisemitism. In preparation for the *Reichstagswahlen* of September 1930, the CV, supported by the Reichsbund jüdischer Frontsoldaten, initiated a neutral *Reichstagswahlausschuss 1930*,[55] which was also to include representatives of the *Gemeinde* in Berlin, the *Grossloge* of B'nai B'rith, and the Zionists. The ZVfD was

---

ausschliesslich dem deutschen Volke angehören. Das Vorhandensein einer nationalen Einheit der Juden aller Länder wird schon durch diese Tatsache widerlegt.

Gegenüber der Wirkungen der zionistischen Propaganda sieht der CV seine Aufgabe darin *seiner* Auffassung von Deutschtum und Judentum in der Öffentlichkeit Geltung zu verschaffen.

See Jehuda Reinharz, ed., *Dokumente zur Geschichte des deutschen Zionismus, 1882–1933*, Schriftenreihe wissenschaftlicher Abhandlungen des Leo Baeck Instituts, vol. 37 (Tübingen, 1981), p. 405 n. 5.

53. Protokoll der Sitzung des Landesvorstandes vom 18. Mai 1930 in Berlin, Archives of the Leo Baeck Institute, Jerusalem.

54. Allgemeine Grundlinien für ein Arbeitsprogramm der ZVfD, [May 1930], Schocken Archives, 531/66. See also "Landesvorstand der ZVfD tagt," *Jüdische Rundschau*, May 20, 1930, no. 39, p. 269.

55. See Paucker, *Der jüdische Abwehrkampf*, pp. 180–81.

reluctant to join the *Wahlausschuss*,[56] but there was great pressure from the Zionist rank and file to participate in this common effort.[57] Moreover the *Landtagswahlen* in Saxony on June 22, 1930, which increased the NSDAP votes by 250,000 over the previous year, served as a dire warning against complacency and inaction. Thus on August 12, 1930, Blumenfeld notified Alfred Wiener of the CV of the ZVfD's consent, not without making it clear that the arrangement was only to last through the elections. The Zionist participation was to be channeled through the Jewish community in Berlin, where the Zionists were in control at the time. Moritz Bileski and Nachum Goldmann were elected as the Zionist representatives to the Reichstagswahlausschuss.[58] As agreed, this arrangement terminated two days after the elections of September 14, 1930.[59]

The election of 107 Nazis, making the NSDAP into the second strongest party in the 541-member Reichstag, represented an almost ninefold increase over the elections of 1928. To these, one must add the 41 Deutschnationale Volkspartei (DNVP) members elected to the Reichstag, who together formed an extreme right-wing bloc of 148 Reichstag members.[60] This election result proved a terrible shock for the Zionists, as it was for all German Jews.[61] The violence in Berlin that accompanied the opening of the Reichstag on October 13 served as dire warning for even worse excesses, yet it did nothing to contain the internal Jewish conflict.[62] The dissolution of the Wahlausschuss took place amid mutual

56. See Protokoll der 22. Sitzung des Geschäftsführenden Ausschusses vom 11. August 1930, Schocken Archives, 531/61.

57. See Protokoll der Sitzung des Landesvorstandes vom 12. Oktober 1930, CZA, Z4/3567/VI. See also "Es geht um die Juden," *Jüdische Rundschau*, June 20, 1930, no. 48, p. 325; "Erscheinungsformen des Antisemitismus," ibid., p. 329; and "Zionistische Kooperation mit dem CV?" ibid., July 25, 1930, no. 58, pp. 385–86.

58. See Protokoll der 22. Sitzung des Geschäftsführenden Ausschusses vom 11. August 1930, Schocken Archives, 531/61.

59. See Protokoll der 27. Sitzung des Geschäftsführenden Ausschusses vom 14. September 1930, ibid. The executive passed the following resolution: "Das Mandat unserer Vertreter zur Führung der Abwehrarbeit innerhalb des Ausschusses 1930 ist mit dem 14. September erloschen. Sie können einem Weiterbestehen des Ausschusses nur zustimmen, um unsere Forderungen nach Umgestaltung der Abwehrarbeit im Ausschuss zu diskutieren." See also Protokoll der 28. Sitzung des Geschäftsführenden Ausschusses vom 24. September 1930, ibid.

60. For a breakdown of the election results, see Abraham Seligman, "Die Reichstagswahlen des 14. September 1930 in der jüdischen Presse in Deutschland," unpublished MS. For greater detail, see Alfred Milatz, *Wähler und Wahlen in der Weimarer Republik* (Bonn, 1966).

61. See, e.g., "6,400,000 NS Wähler: Niederlage der bürgerlichen Demokratie," *Jüdische Rundschau*, September 16, 1930, no. 73, p. 479; "Was weiter?" ibid., September 19, 1930, nos. 74/75, p. 485.

62. See *Central-Verein Zeitung*, October 17, 1930, no. 42, p. 545.

recriminations. The CV accused the Zionists of lack of experience, initiative, and financial contributions to the election effort, while at the same time attempting to undermine the *Abwehr* activities of the CV. The Zionists, on the other hand, accused the CV of using the election committee to fill their own coffers without affording the Zionists an opportunity to participate meaningfully in the elections.[63] Thus, when at the initiative of Max Kollenscher, the *Gemeinde* in Berlin suggested the formation of an independent "action committee" with unlimited powers, composed of representatives of the *Gemeinde,* the CV, the Preussischer Landesverband, and the ZVfD, the ZVfD accepted only on condition that the Zionists have the same number of representatives as the CV,[64] in order to ensure Zionist ability to influence the decision-making process.

THE ANTISEMITISMUS-KOMMISSION

Clearly the cooperation of the ZVfD and CV during the 1930 election campaign—the only instance of formal collaboration between them since they were founded in the last decade of the nineteenth century—did nothing to improve their relations. On the contrary, it left both organizations embittered and suspicious of one another. The Zionists came out of this collaboration convinced that the CV's anti-Zionist stance had not changed and that its methods of defense were useless.[65] On October 12, 1930, some four weeks after the Reichstag elections, the Landesvorstand of the ZVfD met for a daylong discussion assessing its activities in the past few months and attempting to map out new directions for the future.[66] Most of the speakers recognized the fact that it was almost impossible to replace the CV, which had four decades of experience in fighting antisemitism. Not that the fight against the CV's methods and ideology was to be given up altogether, but it ought to be done in a more moderate tone, with recognition of its achievements in *Rechtsschutz* and *Kleinarbeit.* A more promising avenue was to try to attract to Zionism those members of the CV who stood on the periphery of its activities.[67] The Zionist

63. Paucker, *Der jüdische Abwehrkampf*, pp. 42–44, 253–54.

64. Blumenfeld was the only member of the executive who voted against a Zionist participation. See Protokoll der 29. Sitzung des Geschäftsführenden Ausschusses vom 5. Oktober 1930, Schocken Archives, 531/61.

65. ". . . dass ihre Methode der Abwehrarbeit Schiffbruch erlitten hat." Protokoll der Sitzung des Landesvorstandes vom 12. Oktober 1930, CZA, Z4/3567/VI.

66. Ibid.

67. "Den CV können wir nicht ändern, aber CV-er können wir in den Bannkreis des Zionistischen Gedankens bringen." Ibid.

leadership was not in a mood for compromises. The time seemed opportune for conducting a vigorous propaganda campaign. Those German Jews who were thrown off balance by the Nazi triumphs would find solace and strength in the Zionist message calling for the rebuilding of Palestine.

At the same time the Zionists seemed at a loss what to do. The demand to participate in *Abwehr* had been repeated for some two years in Zionist circles with ever greater insistence. Yet in their inner counsels they admitted that they did not have effective methods for combatting the antisemites, and the ZVfD leadership was criticized time and again for its lack of imagination and initiative on the issue of defense. A number of Zionist leaders—Blumenfeld included—demanded that the Zionists admit frankly that they had no radical and immediate solutions for the problems of German Jewry. Thus all they could offer was psychological and moral sustenance while trying to improve the Jews' economic opportunities. To the degree that *Abwehr* was within the province of the ZVfD activities, it had to be conducted through the *Gemeinde* in Berlin or some other neutral and representative organization. Not a few of the participants in the October meeting of the Landesvorstand demanded that the Zionists leave *Abwehr* to the CV and concentrate all their efforts on Palestine. Blumenfeld asserted that *Abwehr* could not, by its very nature, be a neutral activity, because the concept of *Abwehr* rested on an assimilationist German-Jewish *Weltanschauung,* which was anathema to Zionists. The debate ended with an agreement to call Zionist representatives from throughout the Reich for a conference that would determine Zionist practical work (i.e., economic and social work) in the *Gemeinden.*[68]

Following the October 12, 1930, meeting of the executive, the ZVfD grappled with ways in which to combat antisemitism. That same month it confirmed the *Allgemeine Grundlinien* proposed by Siegfried Moses in May 1930, which conformed with the more general resolutions arrived at on October 12. The ZVfD also created a permanent Antisemitismus-

---

68. For the resolution and the entire discussion, see Protokoll der Sitzung des Landesvorstandes vom 12. Oktober 1930, CZA, Z4/3567/VI. For Zionist demands for the Reichsverband, see also "Verbandstag der Preussischen Juden: Die Situation der Juden in Deutschland," *Jüdische Rundschau,* March 20, 1931, no. 22, p. 137; and "Unsere Forderung: Der Reichsverband," ibid., October 1, 1930, nos. 77/78, p. 503. The ZVfD protocol of October 1930 fell somehow into the possession of the *Völkischer Beobachter.* See "Zum Thema: Abwehrarbeit," *Jüdische Rundschau,* April 17, 1931, no. 29, p. 183.

Kommission in October 1930, under the chairmanship of Alfred Berger.[69]

The task of providing the ZVfD with an intellectual framework for the battle against antisemitism fell naturally to the Antisemitismus-Kommission, which met for this purpose on April 22, 1931. Georg Landauer opened the debate[70] and shortly thereafter sent the members of the commission an outline of his speech for approval.[71] A final version seems to have been adopted by the commission for presentation to the executive of the ZVfD at the end of May 1931.[72] Given the stature of the members of the commission and the fact that some of them were also members of the executive, it is safe to assume that the final version of May 29, 1931, was accepted by the ZVfD. The *Grundlinien* proposed by Landauer, the debate that followed, and the final version give us a good idea of the transformation that the ZVfD had undergone during 1929–31 on the question of *Abwehr*.

Landauer began his speech with an unequivocal assertion that "We engage in the battle against antisemitism because our colleagues [*Gesinnungsgenossen*] are disoriented and without proper leadership in all questions relating to antisemitism. The uncertainty leads to doubts in the Zionist position, especially in our battle against the CV and its methods."[73] But at the same time Landauer also suggested that the *Abwehr* methods and educational programs (*Aufklärungs-Tätigkeit*) of the CV could no longer be discredited. Instead one ought to infuse them with a Zionist point of view. Further, he suggested that the Zionists admit that their predictions for the Jewish future had not come true. It was because they believed that Palestine would solve the *Judennot* that they neglected *Abwehr*. Now they have come to realize that Palestine would not solve the Jewish Problem in the near future, and therefore they must turn to a Zionist-oriented *Abwehr*. Though this point elicited a heated discussion in the commission by those who opposed a public admission of failure,[74] Landauer's suggestion was incorporated into the final version.[75]

69. See letter from Frankenstein to Blumenfeld, Berger, Gerson, Kreutzberger, Moses, Naphtali, Schocken, and Moses Waldmann, October 23, 1930, Schocken Archives, 531/66.

70. See letter from Berger to members of the Antisemitismus-Kommission, April 13, 1913, ibid.

71. See Grundlinien des Referates in der Antisemitismus-Kommission, May 4, 1931, ibid.

72. Thesen für den Bericht der Antisemitismus-Kommission, May 29, 1931, ibid.

73. Grundlinien des Referates, ibid.

74. Protokoll . . . vom 12. Oktober 1930, ibid.

75. See Thesen für den Bericht, ibid.

It is clear that by the spring of 1931 the ZVfD abandoned its attempts of October 1930 to dislodge the CV from *Abwehr* activities and indeed acknowledged that the CV's *Kleinarbeit*—as it had been derisively called in the past—was important and indeed necessary. What the Zionists wished for was that Zionist ideology serve as a basis for *Abwehr*. Fully aware that the Antisemitismus-Kommission could not possibly replace the CV's *Abwehr* activities, the Zionists were willing to settle for a neutral organization to handle such matters. Moreover some within the ZVfD, such as Alfred Landsberg of the Antisemitismus-Kommission, even suggested that the CV itself might become a neutral defense organization that the Zionists could then join.[76] This point of view was too radical for the members of the executive of the ZVfD, but there is a clear difference in the tone in which the ZVfD treated the CV's efforts henceforth; indeed some of the arguments employed by the ZVfD began to resemble CV pronouncements, even while attacking the CV methods.[77] The *Jüdische Rundschau* even occasionally engaged in debates with antisemites,[78] something it had shied away from in the past. While blaming the CV for its bankrupt policies,[79] the official ZVfD organ publicly praised the work done by the CV, especially as the economic and political situation of German Jewry continued to deteriorate in 1932.[80] Moreover, as the violence against Jews mounted, the Zionists became increasingly more pessimistic about the future of German Jewry.[81] How close the ZVfD was moving to the CV in its *Weltanschauung* and methods of *Abwehr* can be gauged from its respective petitions to the government in the spring of 1931.

INTERCESSION WITH THE GOVERNMENT

On March 30, 1931, Kurt Blumenfeld met with Staatssekretär der Reichskanzlei Hermann Pünder and pointed out that the increase in

76. See the debate, "Zionismus und antisemitische Bewegung in Deutschland, [late 1930 or early 1931], ibid.
77. See, e.g., "Die Lage in Deutschland," *Jüdische Rundschau*, July 28, 1931, no. 58, p. 357; "Der Alltag," ibid., July 31, 1931, no. 59, p. 362; and "Die Ausschreitungen in Berlin," ibid., September 18, 1931, no. 73, pp. 445–46.
78. See, e.g., "Unsere Auseinandersetzung mit Wilhelm Stapel," ibid., December 18, 1931, no. 98, p. 574; Gustav Krojanker, "Die antisemitische Idee," ibid., February 24, 1928, no. 16, p. 111.
79. See, e.g., "Nachklang zu den Preussenwahlen," ibid., May 3, 1932, no. 35, p. 165; and "Wer ist Kleinmütig?" ibid., July 5, 1932, no. 53, p. 253.
80. See, e.g., "Seelische Abwehr," ibid., August 2, 1932, no. 61, p. 293; "Unter dem Namen 'Anti-Anti,' " ibid., August 23, 1932, no. 67, p. 323.
81. See, e.g., ibid., September 15, 1931, no. 72, pp. 441–42.

antisemitism since the elections of September 14, 1930, had given Germany the reputation as the center of antisemitism. It was necessary to declare to the world at large that the perception of the German nation as antisemitic was wrong.[82] Blumenfeld's intention was to insert a passage he would prepare into a public declaration to be made by Reichskanzler Heinrich Brüning, condemning the antisemitic excesses against German Jews and assuring them of their civil and political rights.[83] Independent of Blumenfeld's petition, Alfred Wiener of the CV also turned to Pünder on April 27, 1931, with two alternative texts that he requested be included in a public address by Brüning.[84] The two separate petitions were almost identical, the major difference being that Blumenfeld spoke of a *Volksstaat* in which the Jews asked to be recognized as citizens with equal rights, whereas Wiener had spoken of a *Volksgemeinschaft* to which the Jews wanted to belong. The intentions of both organizations were, however, the same. So were their tactics and their line of argument as to why it was necessary to include such a passage into a speech by the Reichskanzler.[85] It was left to the German officials to suggest that the two Jewish organizations act in concert.[86] Yet these officials may have been unaware of the heated battle just then unfolding between the ZVfD and CV over elections to the Preussischer Landesverband, which precluded any meaningful cooperation between them. In the event, only a delegation led by the CV was received by Reichsinnenminister Wilhelm Groener in February 1932.[87]

RAPPROCHEMENT WITH NATIONAL SOCIALISTS

There were some within the ZVfD who wanted to go further than the intercession attempts of Blumenfeld. They wished to gain a basic understanding of National Socialism and to examine whether there were points of contact between National Socialism and Zionism that would permit a *modus vivendi,* if not a rapprochement, between them. Among those involved in this discussion were none other than Robert Weltsch, editor of

82. See Paucker, *Der jüdische Abwehrkampf,* pp. 217–19.

83. Three weeks later, on April 17, 1931, Blumenfeld again impressed upon Hermann Pünder the importance of such a declaration for allaying Zionist fears. See ibid., p. 220.

84. Ibid., pp. 223–24.

85. See Leni Yahil, "Jewish Assimilation *vis-à-vis* German Nationalism in the Weimar Republic," in *Jewish Assimilation in Modern Times,* ed. Bela Vago (Boulder, Colo., 1981), p. 46.

86. Paucker, *Der jüdische Abwehrkampf,* pp. 222 and passim.

87. See *Central-Verein Zeitung,* February 12, 1932, no. 7, pp. 53–54.

the *Jüdische Rundschau* since 1919, and Gustav Krojanker, a leading member of the ZVfD.[88] Krojanker and his like-minded colleagues made a distinction between the public manifestations of National Socialism and its basic sources and *Weltanschauung*. The party and even Adolf Hitler, with their crude, noisy demonstrations were—they asserted—transitory, whereas the movement itself stemmed from authentic, living forces (*romantisches Erneuerungsstreben*), which would eventually gain the upper hand and determine its future.[89] Krojanker and Weltsch called the movement *Neuer Nationalismus, Volkstumsbewegung,* and *Jungdeutsche Nationalbewegung,* not "National Socialist," in order to emphasize its positive goals of renewal and renaissance rather than focus on the excesses of its bureaucratic and organizational arms, which they condemned. They therefore ascribed to some members of the elite in the German Right—who in truth were marginal—the power to shape the new radical forces in Germany. They felt that these circles were not only sympathetic to Zionism but that there existed between them and the Zionists an intellectual affinity.[90] Though Krojanker was careful to emphasize the humanitarian element in Zionism and its revulsion from violence,[91] he and his colleagues felt that the mutual elements which did exist between Zionists and some segments of the National Socialists (*Edelnazismus*) permitted the Zionists an insight into the psychological and historical forces that were operating in Germany. Moreover, the new manifestations of antisemitism simply proved the validity of the Zionist doctrine that had been preached for some four decades. Their basic premise that the fate of German Jewry was part and parcel of the world Jewish Problem, that it could and should simply be understood in the context of the abnormal situation inherent in the Jewish Diaspora, was not shaken by events around them.[92]

88. For a detailed examination of this question, see Abraham Margaliot, "Ha-Tguvah ha-Politit shel ha-Mosadot veha-Irgunim ha-Yehudiyim be-Germanyah le-Nokhah ha-Mediniyut ha-anti-Yehudit shel ha-National-Sozialistim bashanim 1932–1935" (Ph.D. diss., Hebrew University, Jerusalem, 1971), pp. 104–10, 250. For a more general discussion, see Eva G. Reichmann, "Diskussionen über die Judenfrage, 1930–1932," *Entscheidungsjahr 1932: Zur Judenfrage in der Endphase der Weimarer Republik,* ed. Werner E. Mosse and Arnold Paucker (Tübingen, 1965), pp. 503–31.
89. See Gustav Krojanker, *Zum Problem des neuen deutschen Nationalismus* (Berlin, 1932), pp. 30–31.
90. See Margaliot, "Ha-Tguvah ha-Politit," pp. 105–6.
91. See Krojanker, *Zum Problem des neuen deutschen Nationalismus,* p. 43.
92. See Margaliot, "Ha-Tguvah ha-Politit," pp. 107–8. See also Uriel Tal, *Law and Theology: On the Status of German Jewry at the Outset of the Third Reich (1933/4),* Third Annual Lecture of the Schreiber Chair of Contemporary Jewish History (Tel Aviv, 1982), pp. 22–23 n. 29.

Despite their organizational and intellectual stature, it is quite clear that the views expressed by Weltsch and Krojanker reflected those of a small minority within the ZVfD.[93] Though Krojanker's booklet on the subject was published in the Schriftenreihe der *Jüdischen Rundschau,* its first page includes an official disclaimer by the ZVfD making it clear that the author's thesis had been rejected by many Zionists.[94] Referring to him by name, Georg Landauer refuted Krojanker's thesis in the *Grundlinien* he prepared for the Antisemitismus-Kommission. Landauer made the flat assertion that

> we all accept the premise that it is wrong to place Jewish and German nationalism on the same plane. . . . The question may be asked, whether the national interpretation of Judaism reflects a reactionary stance much like that of the *völkisch* National Socialism. We must declare two things: a. that Jewish nationalism is not expansionist, imperialist, aggressive, but rather preservative and constructive . . . b. the *völkisch* elements strike for a dispossession of Judaism. . . . The nationalist belief of the others is the instrument of reaction, Zionism is the arena for a progressive new order in Jewish affairs.[95]

Kurt Blumenfeld, too, emphatically denied that there was any parallel to be drawn between the *völkisch* nationalist movement and Zionism. Jewish nationalism, he made clear, developed in the context of Jewish history and in its modern guise was influenced by the national ideology of the nineteenth century. These influences led Jewish nationalism to an internationalism embracing all national outlooks and accorded with those espousing the freedom and progress of other nations. The exclusionary German nationalism, on the other hand, which divided the nation along racial lines, had no room for people who are different and sought to impose uniformity throughout the state. There was no intellectual or even political affinity, Blumenfeld concluded, between Jewish nationalism and German *völkisch* nationalism, which must be viewed as its worst opponent.[96]

As the power of National Socialism swelled unhindered throughout

93. See, e.g., David Schlossberg, "Zum Problem des Neudeutschen Nationalismus: Einige Anmerkungen zur gleichnamigen Broschüre von Bbr. Krojanker," *Der Jüdische Student,* June 1932, no. 5, pp. 134–38; and the reply by Krojanker, "Die unangenehme Parallele," in the same issue, pp. 138–40. See also *Jüdische Rundschau,* June 14, 1932, no. 47, p. 222.

94. See foreword to Krojanker, *Zum Problem des neuen deutschen Nationalismus.*

95. See Grundlinien des Referates in der Antisemitismus-Kommission, May 4, 1931, Schocken Archives, 531/66.

96. Blumenfeld, "Die Zionistische Situation im Wandel der Generationen," *Jüdische Rundschau,* January 15, 1932, no. 4, p. 15.

1932, the ZVfD was aware—albeit much too late—that severe material and physical dangers awaited German Jewry, and it accelerated efforts to promote and facilitate emigration to Palestine.[97] As it did in 1924, the executive of the ZVfD once again turned to the WZO headquarters in London asking the WZO to ensure its property against wanton destruction. Once again it fell to Kurt Blumenfeld at the 24th Delegiertentag, which took place in Frankfurt am Main in September 1932, to articulate what many tried wishfully to deny. Blumenfeld stated unequivocally that one of the major aims of National Socialism was nothing less than the destruction of Judaism. He clearly saw that the hate toward Jews permeated German life. Murder of Jews was being glorified. National Socialism was being dressed up as a messianic movement and had indeed become an *Ersatz*-religion for those who had lost authentic religious ideals. The state had superseded God.[98] The Delegiertentag thereupon passed a resolution affirming Blumenfeld's exhortation for renewed Jewish pride, Zionist education, and steadfast support of Palestine. It declared—as Zionists have always done—the intention of German Zionists to fight for their rights as German citizens. The most remarkable part of the resolution was the Zionists' assumption that the Nazis would accept a form of nationalist pluralism and would make a distinction between adherence to *Staat* and *Volk*. Thus the Zionists declared their intention to do battle for a recognition in Germany of Jewish nationalism as a legitimate expression.[99] Yet the fact that soon after the Delegiertentag the ZVfD established a fund to support its political activities[100] indicates that it also recognized the need to bolster its assumptions with concerted political activity.

CONCLUSION

In retrospect it seems clear that the German Zionist ideological stance on the subject of antisemitism cannot be taken at face value—at least not

97. See Georg Landauer to Hugo Schachtel, January 7, 1932, and February 18, 1932, CZA, A102/12/16.
98. Blumenfeld, "Die Zionistische Aufgabe im heutigen Deutschland," *Jüdische Rundschau*, September 16, 1932, nos. 73/74, pp. 351–56. For a sharp polemic against Blumenfeld's speech at the Delegiertentag, see A. Kupferberg, "Bemerkungen zum politischen Referat des Vorsitzenden der ZVfD auf dem Frankfurter Delegiertentag," Schocken Archives, 531/61.
99. See "Resolution zur Lage in Deutschland," *Jüdische Rundschau*, September 16, 1932, nos. 73/74, p. 35. See also Moses, "Die innerdeutsche politische Tätigkeit der ZVfD auf dem Frankfurter Delegiertentag," Schocken Archives, 531/61.
100. See "Zionisten!" *Jüdische Rundschau*, October 21, 1932, no. 84, p. 407; and "Politische Arbeit," ibid., October 25, 1932, no. 85, p. 411.

during the Weimar Republic. Though German Zionists continued to maintain to the very end of the republic's life that antisemitism was an inevitable by-product of life in the Diaspora,[101] they were far from complacent in the face of the antisemitic danger. Like all German Jews, the Zionists, too, were shocked and dismayed by the *Judenzählung*,[102] though they hoped that the end of World War I would produce new opportunities for intensive Zionist work in Germany, unencumbered by either popular or government interference. And like most German Jews, they hailed the Weimar Constitution as a new era for German Jewry. The Zionist position throughout the Weimar period continued to be essentially Palestino-centric, but it became clear that the Posen Resolution of the pre–World War I period was not about to be implemented in the near future, that German Zionists would continue to live in Germany even if they adhered to an ideological position of *Distanz* or *Abgrenzung*. Simultaneously there was a subtle change in orientation within certain segments of the ZVfD, which no longer called for *Galuthverneinung* and instead proclaimed Zionist interest in Jewish life in the Diaspora. The Zionists began to emphasize that they saw a role for themselves in the Diaspora, though they were careful to point out the difference between themselves and other German-Jewish organizations.

Yet the Zionists never clearly defined what their role in the general Jewish community was to be. They could not make up their mind, for example, as to how involved they ought to be in *Gemeinden* elections. Similarly, they had not adhered to a clear-cut policy on the question of antisemitism. Zionist theoretical formulations aside, attitudes on this issue fluctuated in the early 1920s between the point of view of Alfred Landsberg, who wanted to see the ZVfD involved in the battle against antisemitism, and Kurt Blumenfeld, who did not consider *Abwehr* a Zionist task. During the first half of his tenure as president of the ZVfD, from 1924 to about 1928–29, Blumenfeld's position won the day, aided no doubt by the relative economic and political calm prevailing in the country. It was during this period that the ZVfD and CV fought their most determined battles and struggled to define and redefine their positions on *Deutschtum* and *Judentum* not only externally but also in relation to each other. Indeed at times it seems that the two organizations considered the internal opponent more dangerous to their respective existence than

101. See, e.g., Blumenfeld, "Die Zionistische Situation im Wandel der Generationen," ibid., January 15, 1932, no. 4, p. 19.
102. See, e.g., Bericht über die Plenar-Sitzung des Zentralkomitees vom 12. November 1916, CZA, A15/111/28.

the attacks of the antisemites. It can be clearly seen from all the available documentation that the ZVfD's position toward antisemitism was from the start circumscribed and limited by the position of the CV on *Abwehr*. The ZVfD realized that it could not compete with the CV in this field, nor did it want—even in the face of great danger from the outside—to adopt positions that could be interpreted as emulating its rival's methods. Instead the Zionists alternately called for a communitywide representation in questions of *Abwehr* or tried to dislodge the CV from its preeminent role in this field by discrediting its ideological motivations.

Blumenfeld's position must be understood in terms of his own pre-1914 Zionist evolution into a radical position from which he was unwilling, or perhaps unable, to retreat when he became part of the ZVfD establishment. It was further consolidated by the CV's own inflexible attitude toward Zionism, determined by hardliners like Ludwig Holländer and Julius Brodnitz, who were on the defensive from attacks by Max Naumann and the Verband nationaldeutscher Juden, which seemed to push them to ever more insistent protestations of German patriotism and consequently a more radical anti-Zionist attitude. In general neither the CV nor the ZVfD progressed or developed much ideologically after World War I. Despite the lack of uniformity in position, especially among the Zionist periphery and the young CV functionaries, this is largely true for the majority in each of the two organizations. Both often employed concepts and ideas that did not take account of the changing political and economic circumstances prevailing in the Weimar Republic. They were thus locked into a position of hostility that was dictated by ideological, institutional, and personal motivations. Saddled by set attitudes and behavior patterns, there was little chance for meaningful cooperation between them.

Blumenfeld's unyielding stance on the question of antisemitism was further hardened by events within the World Zionist Organization that had always influenced German Zionist ideology. A new generation of German Zionists shaped by the experience of World War I, the Balfour Declaration, and the Yishuv came to the fore in the 1920s. They made up for their small numbers by their vitality, and their battle cry was from the start "Nach Palästina!"[103] They were more concerned with pioneer life or the riots in Palestine in 1929 than they were with the development

103. See Berthold Cohn and Walter Preuss, "Nach Palästina," *Der Jüdische Student,* January 26, 1916, no. 5, pp. 134–35. See also the subsequent discussion in documents contained in Reinharz, *Dokumente zur Geschichte des deutschen Zionismus,* pp. 175ff.

of their own *Gemeinden,* antisemitism, or German economic and political affairs. It is not surprising that the *Jüdische Rundschau* devoted more
space in 1929–30 to the Arab Question in Palestine than to the rise of
National Socialism. This question and its interpretation within Germany
certainly consumed a good deal of the time and energy of the ZVfD
leadership.

And yet, as I have shown, the ZVfD position on antisemitism was by
no means uniform. One has to recognize that Zionist politics in Germany
were determined in Berlin and for the most part took into consideration
only conditions in Prussia. It is not surprising that Alfred Landsberg, who
resided in Wiesbaden, had a different perspective on the question of antisemitism than did Blumenfeld. Outside of Berlin, and especially in small
localities, Zionists had different needs and a more pragmatic approach to
antisemitism. They saw no contradiction between their Zionist *Weltanschauung* and *Abwehr* or cooperation with the CV. There was a good deal
of tension and conflict, therefore, between the Zionist periphery and its
center in Berlin. Nor were members of the Jüdische Volkspartei as un-
perturbed by antisemitism as was the ZVfD executive. The internal
memorandums of the ZVfD executive and the minutes of the Landesvorstand constantly reiterate the need for keeping the Jüdische Volkspartei—its official arm in *Gemeinde* politics—in check, lest it strike out
on its own and forge alliances with other Jewish organizations on questions of *Abwehr.*[104]

Thus, when the ZVfD began to reformulate its policy toward antisemitism in 1928–29, it did so reluctantly and because of pressure from
the Zionist rank and file.[105] The ZVfD leadership was therefore caught
in a dilemma. It had scant chance to undertake *Abwehr* on its own and
needed to cooperate with the CV, despite its many years of criticism of
CV methods. Thus, while on the ideological level the ZVfD criticized
and deprecated the CV, it had no better solutions at hand. Its only alternative was to offer German Jews psychological and moral sustenance, but
the CV claimed that it, too, contributed toward Jewish self-esteem and
pride, if in a different context and with different goals in mind. While
the short period of cooperation between the organizations in 1930 served
only to intensify the antipathy between them, one may say that the ZVfD
moved closer to adopting the CV techniques of *Abwehr,* as evidenced by
Blumenfeld's intercession in 1931 with Staatssekretär Hermann Pünder.

104. See, e.g., Moses to ZVfD, February 4, 1933, Schocken Archives, 531/66.
105. This is most clearly articulated in Protokoll der Sitzung des Landesvorstandes
vom 12. Oktober 1930, CZA, Z4/3567/VI.

At the same time it must also be stated that the Antisemitismus-Kommission—though composed of front-rank leaders of the ZVfD—never fully became a top priority of the Zionist executive.

One can only arrive at the conclusion that the Zionist attitude toward antisemitism during the Weimar Republic was far from clear cut, both on the ideological and the practical level, and among the rank and file and the ZVfD hierarchy. Attitudes and positions shifted in response to internal and external conditions and were determined no less by personalities than by political and economic conditions. Yet, though ambivalent and uncertain in their *Weltanschauung* toward antisemitism, all Zionist groups agreed that their guiding principle must be first and foremost the welfare of the Zionist movement, however one interpreted it. Both the Jüdische Volkspartei, which favored involvement in *Gemeinde* politics, and the ZVfD leadership, which maintained the primacy of Palestine, agreed that the crises of 1924 and 1930 afforded the Zionists an opportunity to advance their cause and to strengthen their influence within German Jewry. It is in this context, too, that one must understand the attempts to find a *modus vivendi* with the quasi-progressive element of the German nationalists. Quite apart from the fact that those who advocated discussions with National Socialists represented a small minority within the ZVfD, it must also be kept in mind that in the period prior to 1933 their theories and formulations did not yet have the associations attached to them after the Nazi rise to power. Nor were the Zionists the only ones within the German-Jewish community to attempt such a dialogue.[106] One can perhaps fault these Zionists for their naïveté in evaluating the National Socialist phenomenon, but one must keep in mind that even their fiercest enemies did not believe until the last moment that the Nazis would be able to seize control. The Zionists, of course, had always been less optimistic than others about the phenomenon and consequences of antisemitism and should, perhaps, have been better prepared for what was to come. But the lack of ideological homogeneity within their own ranks prevented them from preparing themselves ideologically and organizationally for a proper defense in case of a radical shift in the

106. See, e.g., Uriel Tal, "Aspects of Consecration of Politics in the Nazi Era," in *Judaism and Christianity under the Impact of National Socialism (1919–1945)* (Jerusalem, 1982), pp. 55–56. Many years later, in a ceremony marking his ninetieth birthday, Robert Weltsch referred to the reasons that moved Zionists to conduct discussions with the "respectable Right." See Weltsch, "Looking Back over Sixty Years," *Leo Baeck Institute Year Book* 27 (1982): 383–84. In the period after World War II, Weltsch bitterly regretted his contacts with the Right, calling his actions "naïve" and "misguided." Letter from Paucker to the author, November 8, 1983.

German political constellation. In addition, they were hampered from active defense work by their own ideological stance of some four decades. It would have taken more time and effort than they had to educate their members toward a new orientation. If there is one failure common to all German-Jewish organizations, it is the failure to abandon particularistic ideologies and organize internally as a united front. Given the ideological gulf between them, this was perhaps too much to expect. It was just as impossible—indeed unthinkable—for them to abandon either liberal ideology or those parties that upheld a left-of-center position.[107]

A recent study of the Jews in Weimar Germany has arrived at the unfounded conclusion that by their policies and ideology during the Weimar Republic, the Zionists may well have damaged German Jewry more than they benefited it.[108] Another has gone so far as to say that the ZVfD along with the SPD and Kommunistische Partei Deutschlands "must bear their full measure of guilt for Hitler's triumph."[109] Even if one could in hindsight venture to criticize the Zionists for failing to assess the contemporary scene realistically, this cannot stand as a final judgment. Given the objective conditions in Weimar Germany, especially toward the end of the period—the Zionists' lack of allies, the irrational hatred facing them, their almost total isolation, and their particular ideology—it is difficult to see what more they could have done to defend themselves. Indeed this evaluation holds for both the CV and the ZVfD. The former did what it knew best—*Abwehr*. The Zionists concentrated on fortifying the Jewish spirit through a dignified reassertion of Jewish identity and cohesion in Germany and the promise of a better future in Palestine.

107. See Ernest Hamburger, *Jews, Democracy and Weimar Germany,* Leo Baeck Memorial Lecture 16 (New York, 1973).

108. Donald L. Niewyk, *The Jews in Weimar Germany* (Baton Rouge, 1980), p. 164; see also p. 139.

109. Lenni Brenner, *Zionism in the Age of the Dictators* (London, 1983), p. 29.

KURT DÜWELL

Jewish Cultural Centers in Nazi Germany
Expectations and Accomplishments

We want to give bread to Jewish artists and performers, thereby enabling them by physical and spiritual support to work as artists again. We want to give to the masters of the word the opportunity to speak to us. Jewish artists should show their work. For ourselves, however, we are preparing a path that we need now more than ever before: to elevate ourselves by enjoying artistic creations in a time that depresses us so deeply. . . . We have no wish to restrict our activities to Jewish art, but the authorities require that all the practicing artists be Jewish.

No one who becomes a member of our Kulturbund should believe himself to be making a charitable gesture. All of us should know that the good we are doing is for ourselves!

Dr. Paul Moses, chairman of the Jüdischer Kulturbund
Rhein-Ruhr, *Mitteilungsblätter*, November 1933

In view of the brutal monstrosities of National Socialist policies toward Jews, it could seem almost a diversion from the main problems to consider the cultural life of the Jews in Germany after 1933. The danger in looking at organized Jewish cultural life in Nazi Germany is that it might seem to confirm the Nazis' assertion that Jews were granted, at least for a while, both a freedom of action and the status of a protected minority. This potential misunderstanding must be cleared up first, and then I shall examine how it was possible for contemporaries to have this impression, at least for a time.

After a short period of complete emancipation under the Weimar Republic,[1] the Jews in Germany faced—seemingly without preparation—the National Socialist take-over in 1933. With their relatively small numbers, their loose community organization, and soon also as a consequence of their shrinking social contacts with the non-Jewish population, Jews were more deeply affected by the Nazis' extraordinary restrictions than were other social groups. Support from non-Jews was not the rule but the exception. The psychological oppression of this increasingly isolated minority led, however, to a new consciousness of the religious and moral roots of Jewish existence and awakened spiritual counterforces that, operating in this time of injustice and terror, emerged in one of the most impressive of all cultural movements.

When on April 1, 1933, the Nazi policy of boycott against the Jewish minority was officially sanctioned, the work of Jewish writers and artists was naturally affected. They were no longer allowed to be members of public orchestras or opera or theater companies, to have concert agents, or to join artists' clubs or similar organizations. The great age of Elisabeth Bergner, Leo Blech, Ernst Deutsch, Alexander Granach, Leopold Jessner, Otto Klemperer, Fritz Kortner, Fritz Lang, Max Liebermann, Peter Lorre, Ernst Lubitsch, Lucie Mannheim, Grete Mosheim, Max Pallenberg, Max Reinhardt, Joseph Schmidt, Richard Tauber, Ignaz Waghalter, Bruno Walter, Jakob Wassermann, Franz Werfel, and many other fine writers, artists, and performers of Jewish origin seemed to have come to an end.

On the other hand, one of the most remarkable effects of the Nazis' policies of boycott and terror was the founding, that very same year, of

1. For discrimination existing in the time of the Weimar Republic, see, as standard literature: Fritz Marburg, *Der Antisemitismus in der Deutschen Republik* (Vienna, 1931); Werner E. Mosse and Arnold Paucker, eds., *Entscheidungsjahr 1932: Zur Judenfrage in der Endphase der Weimarer Republik*, 2d ed. (Tübingen, 1966); Arnold Paucker, *Der jüdische Abwehrkampf gegen Antisemitismus und Nationalsozialismus in den letzten Jahren der Weimarer Republik*, Hamburger Beiträge zur Zeitgeschichte, vol. 4 (Hamburg, 1968); George L. Mosse, *Germans and Jews: The Right, the Left, and the Search for a "Third Force" in Pre-Nazi Germany* (New York, 1970); Hans-Helmut Knütter, *Die Juden und die deutsche Linke in der Weimarer Republik, 1918–1933* (Düsseldorf, 1971); Werner E. Mosse, ed., *Deutsches Judentum in Krieg und Revolution, 1916–1923*, Schriftenreihe wissenschaftlicher Abhandlungen des Leo Baeck Instituts, vol. 25 (Tübingen, 1971); Hans-Joachim Bieber, "Anti-Semitism as a Reflection of Social, Economic and Political Tension in Germany, 1880–1933," in *Jews and Germans from 1860 to 1933*, ed. David Bronson (Heidelberg, 1979), pp. 33–77. For the increasing importance of Zionism at the end of the Weimar Republic, see also Jehuda Reinharz, ed., *Dokumente zur Geschichte des deutschen Zionismus, 1882–1933*, Schriftenreihe wissenschaftlicher Abhandlungen des Leo Baeck Instituts, vol. 37 (Tübingen, 1981).

the Kulturbund Deutscher Juden. In a way this organization was a response to the Reichskulturkammer, which had excluded all Jews. Public
activity by Jewish artists—though there were still some exceptions—no
longer seemed possible. The option of emigration, even for the sake of
intellectual opposition to National Socialism alone, was open only to a
few, on account of the cost and the difficulties of obtaining a visa from
the country of destination. For those Jewish artists, writers, and performers who remained in Nazi Germany, the only option seemed to be to
work within the framework of a cultural self-help organization.

The Kulturbund Deutscher Juden was founded in Berlin by Dr. Kurt
Singer, an intendant of the opera in Berlin-Charlottenburg until he was
expelled from this position by Nazi boycott legislation. Very prudently
did he plan the new organization. A few months later he recalled:

> During those days at the beginning of April when we Jews feared
> the severe loss of the freedom of movement we were used to, the young
> director Kurt Baumann came to me with a plan for establishing a thea-
> ter and a membership organization. I had worked out a similar plan
> and submitted both of them to Rabbi Dr. [Leo] Baeck as a competent
> judge. After getting his recommendation, I consulted the leading men
> from Jewish organizations. . . . One committee formulated the consti-
> tution; another committee made arrangements for publicity evenings; a
> third prepared them from the artistic point of view. I submitted the of-
> ficial applications for a license for a Kulturbund Deutscher Juden to
> various governmental authorities. The decision about the license was
> delegated by the minister president of Prussia to the Ministry of Edu-
> cation, within which the president of the Prussian Theater Commission,
> Staatskommissar [Hans] Hinkel, or his deputy, was to lead the nego-
> tiations. Simultaneously I gave reports to the chief of police and to the
> ministry of Propaganda (here the president of the theater commission,
> Ministerialrat [Otto] Laubinger).[2]

Plans for the cultural center were supported by the leading representatives of Jewish cultural life, and the board of honorary chairmen included
Leo Baeck, Martin Buber, Arthur Eloesser, Leonid Kreutzer, Max Liebermann, Max Osborn, Franz Oppenheimer, and Jakob Wassermann.

This new organization to aid Jewish artists in Berlin soon served as a
model for similar cultural centers in other parts of the Reich. In autumn
1933 the Jüdischer Kulturbund Rhein-Ruhr (Freunde des Theaters und

2. Kurt Singer, "Vor der Premiere des Kulturbundes," *Central-Verein Zeitung,*
September 28, 1933, no. 37, Beilage 2. See also the recollections of Kurt Baumann in
Jüdisches Leben in Deutschland, ed. Monika Richarz, vol. 3, *Selbstzeugnisse zur So-
zialgeschichte, 1918–1945* (Stuttgart, 1982), pp. 313–22.

der Musik e.V.), was founded in the great industrial Rhenish-Westfalian area, where fifty thousand Jews still lived in the administrative districts of Cologne, Düsseldorf, and Arnsberg. Its first chairman was Dr. Paul Moses, and next to the Berlin Kulturbund, it was the most important cultural center in Germany.[3] In addition the Kulturbund Rhein-Main in Frankfurt maintained its own philharmonic orchestra of about fifty members, and the Hamburg Kulturbund had its own theater and traveling company.[4] By 1935 Jewish cultural centers had been founded in Breslau and other towns. In this time of increasing economic and social troubles, they became important economic factors. Together they maintained three theater ensembles (Berlin, Hamburg, Cologne), one opera (Berlin), two philharmonic orchestras (Berlin, Frankfurt), one cabaret stage, one school theater, and a few choirs and ensembles in which a total of twenty-five hundred artists made a modest living. Until 1938 nearly six hundred artists and almost the same number of support staff, plus three hundred artisans, mechanics, and additional assistants, were permanently engaged by the Jewish cultural centers in Germany, and they were "the greatest single factor in the provision of work for Jewish people in Germany under Nazi rule."[5] Almost seventy thousand Jewish people in about a hundred towns attended Kulturbund performances.[6] Along with the Jewish communities and the sixty Jewish weekly newspapers, journals, and other periodicals still published in 1935, which had a total circulation of 350,000, the cultural centers were among the greatest intellectual and economic forces in Jewish life in Germany.

The Berlin Kulturbund was the largest, employing, up to 1938, more than two hundred people—soloists and supernumeraries as well as technical and supplementary personnel and an administrative staff of ten. In 1933–34 its annual expenses reached six hundred thousand *Reichsmark*.[7]

The Jüdischer Kulturbund Rhein-Ruhr, which grew out of efforts of

---

3. Herbert Freeden, *Jüdisches Theater in Nazideutschland,* Schriftenreihe wissenschaftlicher Abhandlungen des Leo Baeck Instituts, vol. 12 (Tübingen, 1964), pp. 53ff. For the Jüdischer Kulturbund Rhein-Ruhr, see also Kurt Düwell, *Die Rheingebiete in der Judenpolitik des Nationalsozialismus vor 1942: Beitrag zu einer vergleichenden zeitgeschichtlichen Landeskunde* (Bonn, 1968), pp. 132–40. Another regional example was treated by Erwin Lichtenstein, "Der Kulturbund der Juden in Danzig, 1933–1938," *Zeitschrift für die Geschichte der Juden* 10 (Tel Aviv, 1973): 181–90. For figures about the whole Kulturbund organization in Germany, see Herbert Freeden, "A Jewish Theatre under the Swastika," in *Leo Baeck Institute Year Book* 1 (1956): 159–60. I am grateful to Dr. Ernst Lustig, Wolfenbüttel, for a large number of references to the work of the Jewish cultural centers.

4. Freeden, *Jüdisches Theater,* p. 25.

5. Ibid., pp. 25–26.   6. Ibid., p. 4.   7. Ibid., pp. 22–23.

the Kölner Zentralstelle für jüdische Wirtschaftshilfe to include support for artists among its activities,[8] had five thousand members by the summer of 1935. Monthly dues were only *Reichsmark* 2.50. During the first six months of its performances, 1934–35, it employed more than three hundred people, a great number of whom had regular appointments, reported the center's *Mitteilungsblätter*.[9] In the 1935–36 season, thirty-five artists were engaged for appointments of six months or a year, and forty-six others had appointments for less than six months, mostly in connection with the traveling theater. Seventeen clerical workers and five manual workers had regular appointments, and ninety additional assistants were hired for shorter periods in the towns the theater company toured. Altogether 191 people were employed. At the center of the Kulturbund's activities were the theater performances in Cologne and in ten other towns in the Rhenish-Westfalian area where it had local affiliations: Aachen, Bochum, Bonn, Duisburg, Essen, Gelsenkirchen, Krefeld, Wuppertal, and, from 1934–35 onwards, also Dortmund and Düren.

The emphasis of the Kulturbund Rhein-Ruhr's activities lay in the theater, the director of which was Willibald Fränkel-Froon. In November 1933 he opened the Kulturbund stage with a performance of the tragicomedy *Sonkin und der Haupttreffer* by Semen Juschkewitsch, a play that had already had great success in Max Reinhardt's staging. In the November/December 1933 issue of the *Mitteilungsblätter,* Fränkel-Froon described the aims of his efforts:

> The goal of our stage is to bring joy and the courage to face life to all by letting them participate in the eternal values of poetry or by discussing the problems of our time, but also by showing lighthearted pieces and not rejecting them. We intend to keep up the connection with the German *Heimat* and to form, at the same time, a connecting link with our great Jewish past and with a future that is worth living.[10]

After *Sonkin,* the plays performed in 1933 and 1934 included Johann Wolfgang von Goethe's *Stella* and Carlo Goldoni's *Mirandolina,* Henry Bernstein's *Der Dieb,* James Briedie's comedy *Tobias und der Erzengel,* Hugo von Hofmannsthal's *Dame Kobold,* Raoul Auernheimer's *Die*

---

8. *Jüdische Rundschau,* October 17, 1933, cited in ibid., p. 53.

9. "Zusammenschluss der jüdischen Kulturbünde Deutschlands," *Mitteilungsblätter des jüdischen Kulturbundes Rhein-Ruhr* (hereafter *Mitteilungsblätter*), June 1935, p. 4, and October 1936, p. 4. See also materials in the Archives of the Leo Baeck Institute, New York, esp. the Julius Bab Collections.

10. Willibald Fränkel-Froon," Das Theater entsteht," *Mitteilungsblätter,* November/December 1933, unpaginated.

grosse Leidenschaft, Arthur Schnitzler's *Der einsame Weg,* and a drama by a young writer from Cologne, Julius Wolffsohn, entitled *Joseph Ben Matthias.*[11] Besides the plays, there were poetry evenings with Ludwig Hardt, Otto Bernstein, and other distinguished masters of recitation, and lectures by Leo Baeck, Kurt Blumenfeld, and Martin Buber. David Carlebach, Joseph Carlebach, Adolf Kober, Benedikt Wolf, and other rabbis also gave talks, mostly through cooperative arrangements with the Vereinigung jüdisches Lehrhaus in Cologne.[12] In addition there were concerts of chamber music and piano and vocal recitals by soloists of the first rank. In 1935 the so-called Kleinkunst performances included the star performance of the famous diseuse Dela Lipinskaja. But the theater dominated the activities of the Kulturbund Rhein-Ruhr up to its dissolution in 1938.

On the principles that should guide a Jewish theater program, the Kulturbund Rhein-Ruhr largely supported the position of Julius Bab, the highly esteemed dramaturge in Berlin, who expressed his opinion in the *Israelitisches Familienblatt* that a repertory exclusively Jewish as a matter of principle (*grundsätzlich nur jüdisches*) would be neither desirable nor possible.

> We do not want to set up a new ghetto. Through our work we want to keep the German Jews in vital contact with the great life of Western culture in which they have become so deeply rooted over one and a half centuries! And therefore: Lessing, Mozart, and Shakespeare! But there is another side that is just as right and proper: because we exist within this Western sphere of culture as a community in which the performances are given only by Jews and for Jews, there are also duties of a special kind, and we have to pay special regard to the work of Jewish writers who today have no place elsewhere (even if their works have no special Jewish content). We have to pay regard to them as much as to all creative works of intellectual worth that deal with sub-

---

11. The program for the following years contained: Franz Grillparzer's *Esther,* Heinrich Heine's *Almansor,* Pedro Calderón's *Absalons Locken,* Jean Baptist Molière's *Streiche des Scapin,* George Bernard Shaw's *Der Arzt am Scheidewege, The Importance of Being Earnest* by Oscar Wilde, Johann Nestroy's *Titus Feuerfuchs,* and two lighter entertainment numbers—Adler's *Drei Herren im Frack* and Garais's *Der Fall Jadin Grandais.* For later, *Miss Selby* by Ervine, Johann Wolfgang von Goethe's *Clavigo,* William Shakespeare's *Twelfth Night,* Gerhart Hauptmann's *Michael Kramer,* Georg Hirschfeld's *Hosea,* and Israel Zangwill's comedy *Der König der Schnorrer* were planned. Some were not performed, however, for reasons that cannot be precisely determined.

12. See also Ernst Simon, *Aufbau im Untergang: Jüdische Erwachsenenbildung im nationalsozialistischen Deutschland als geistiger Widerstand,* Schriftenreihe wissenschaftlicher Abhandlungen des Leo Baeck Instituts, vol. 2 (Tübingen, 1959).

jects of special Jewish interest. . . . Therefore it will not cease to be a
German theater, a stage within the Western cultural tradition.[13]

Some months previous, despite the oppression of Nazi censorship under
the direction of Staatskommissar Hinkel, there had been a sharp discussion
within the Jewish community about the work of the Berlin Kulturbund—
some even called it an internal Jewish *Kulturkampf*. The *Kulturkampf*
was fought much more vigorously over the repertory of the theater than
over the program of operas and concerts.[14] The preliminary result of the
discussion was the acceptance of the line of reasoning Bab later formulated. But this line of reasoning was only a compromise, and it was questioned, from time to time, by the *Jüdische Rundschau* and other Zionist
publications.[15]

Moreover, the Nazis in 1934 prohibited the Jewish cultural centers
from performing the works of Friedrich von Schiller and the German romantics, and in 1936 they also banned performances of Goethe's works
and those of other classical German writers. These restrictions were next
extended to the performance of music; in 1937 Beethoven was forbidden,
and immediately after the *Anschluss* with Austria, Mozart, too, was no
longer allowed to be played in the cultural centers.

It had long been clear, however, that the Nazi policy of restriction
would render performances of "German music" increasingly difficult.[16]
In May 1934 the head cantor of Wuppertal, Hermann Zivi, had tried to
come to terms with the question of whether there was such a thing as
"Jewish music." In the *Mitteilungsblätter* of the Kulturbund Rhein-Ruhr
he pointed to the amalgamation of the musical tradition of the synagogue with the traditions of music in the different host countries in which
Jewish communities had emerged:

> In the East they sing in a melancholy manner, as do the Slavic and
> oriental people; in the West they sing in another way, and this is also

13. Julius Bab, "Warum *Nathan der Weise?*" *Israelitisches Familienblatt* 36, no. 2
(1934): 12, as quoted in *Mitteilungsblätter*, February 1934, p. 3.
14. Freeden, *Jüdisches Theater*, p. 4.
15. For Bab's considerations and for the opening performance of *Nathan the Wise*
by the Berliner Kulturbund theater, 150 years after Gotthold Ephraim Lessing wrote
the play, see *Jüdische Rundschau*, July 25, 1933, no. 59; and October 4, 1933, nos.
79/80.
16. Freeden, *Jüdisches Theater*, p. 46, quotes a letter of November 19, 1934, from
the NSDAP-Gauleitung Berlin, in which performances of Beethoven's music by the
local Jewish Kulturbund were sharply criticized: "to see our magnificent Beethoven in
such dubious company" was intolerable and even "more tactless" if "the Jewish Kulturbund performed 'Fidelio' with an all-Jewish cast"—whereas there was no alternative
open to the Kulturbund according to the regulations.

true in the synagogue. The question as to whether there is such a thing as "Jewish music" must be answered in the negative. If the Jews one day become permanently established, and live in compact communities unmolested by oppression and compulsion, then, with spiritual peace, they might also gain the strength to develop in this native country a music of their own that has grown up in the soil of Jewry.[17]

But in the following number of the *Mitteilungsblätter* Joachim Stutschewsky, a Viennese cellist and collector of music, contradicted Zivi's claims. Stutschewsky asserted that twenty-five years before no one would have talked of "Jewish music," but an important change had taken place. He mentioned the names of Joseph Achron, Ernest Bloch, Alexander Krein, Levin Milner, Brandmann, Michail Gnessin, and Lazare Ssaminsky, and included his own name, too. "For a long time we had many Jewish musicians, concert artists, composers of operas and symphonies, but no Jewish music. Today we have Jewish musicians who also compose music of their own kind out of their deepest personal being and who, striving for a new inner center, are creating a Jewish art of music."[18] Here again there are two diametrically opposed opinions, and a new *Kulturkampf* seemed to be getting under way.

The editors of the *Mitteilungsblätter,* therefore, in August 1934 asked Oskar Guttmann, a connoisseur and academic teacher of music, for a final opinion. Guttmann altered the basic question a little: did there or does there exist a Jewish music? He gave an affirmative reply to the first part of this question, but to the second he asserted:

Today there no longer exists a Jewish music. Stutschewsky has totally confused the music Jews have composed with Jewish music. Certainly we have great Jewish composers, and indeed many of them have broken through the "latent Orientalism" [Heinrich] Berl described in his suggestive book *Das Judentum in der Musik.* Here the Jewish sentiment is strong and genuine. But it will not develop so quickly. Perhaps a new Jewish music will come from a new permanent culture. Let us hope and wish so. And, for the time being, above all let us hear what Jewish musicians play and compose, though they may not yet create things as "Jewish" as we might dream of.[19]

To the editors of the *Mitteilungsblätter* it seemed obvious that with this answer the discussion was not yet over. But it was also clear that they

17. Hermann Zivi, "Gibt es eine jüdische Musik?" pt. 1, *Mitteilungsblätter,* May 1934, p. 4.
18. Joachim Stutschewsky, "Gibt es eine jüdische Musik?" pt. 2, ibid., June 1934, p. 4.
19. Oskar Guttmann, "Gibt es eine jüdische Musik?" pt. 3, ibid., August 1934, p. 7.

did not want to prolong controversial debate on this problem because the daily, basic difficulties of the Kulturbund's cultural work were so urgent as to require all their effort. Therefore, the editors restricted themselves to a short concluding remark:

> The answers of the three commentators are widely divergent and differ so much that one can see how difficult it is to comply with the request for concerts of Jewish music. Without defining our attitude regarding this subject, we share Dr. Guttmann's opinion in demanding that for the time being Jewish composers, especially, should be given a hearing. But beyond this we believe that with concerts by orchestras which consist of Jewish musicians we are serving in the best way the interests, if not of Jewish music, at least of Jewish performance of music.[20]

This was the principle according to which in 1934 the Jüdischer Kulturbund Rhein-Main in Frankfurt founded its orchestra, which had great success in the Rhenish-Westfalian towns as well.

The theater, however, remained the chief work of the Kulturbund Rhein-Ruhr. In regard to the future shaping of its program, the artistic director Gerhard Walter-Rosenbaum wrote in the summer of 1934:

> The process of assimilation during the last decade destroyed the old community of German Jews. The only acknowledged tie remained the religious faith, and in view of a general turning away from religion, it was no longer strong enough to mold Jewish community life. But the pressure of recent events has forced a new common cause into being. To transform this cause into a real community by creating a mental bond is a vital task for German Jewry. The principle task of the Kulturbund theater is to participate in the renewal of the cultural life of German Jews by depicting Jewish destinies and Jewish people and by disseminating the works of Jewish poets and writers.
>
> The new Jewish community in Germany cannot and must not tear itself away from the German culture to which all are tied by language and education and most of us also by history and *Heimatliebe*. Another and equally important task of the Kulturbund theater is to maintain and strengthen links with German culture.
>
> By putting on the stage artistically important dramatic entertainment, the theater of the Kulturbund should free its audiences from their everyday sorrows and thereby fulfill its third task.[21]

Quite rightly Walter-Rosenbaum pointed again and again to the psychological difficulties of the Jewish theater work: the everyday life of the German Jews was oppressed by such a heavy psychological burden and

20. Editors' comments, ibid.
21. Gerhard Walter-Rosenbaum, "Aufgaben der Kulturbundbühne Rhein-Ruhr, ein Wort zur Künftigen Spielplangestaltung," ibid., p. 3.

by such severe troubles which "for many reasons could not be represented on the stage" that a return to "the individualistic dramas of the last years" would be unthinkable:

> Nothing would be more senseless than to show problems that, by reason of the personal oppression of the spectators, have become inconsequential. It may be remarked, moreover, that in the new Germany there is no longer room for the problematic plays of yesterday. The new task of creating works for the cultural centers, which fortunately has already started, will not be in full operation for some time.[22]

From this it is clear that the Kulturbund Rhein-Ruhr sought suitable Jewish plays but did not renounce links with general German theatrical tradition. The same is clear also from Walter-Rosenbaum's final appeal: "The Kulturbund theater has set high aims for the coming months. It will reach these goals if every Jew stands by the Kulturbund, showing thereby that he is willing to work with heart and soul for the cultural support and strengthening of German Jewry."[23] But it was precisely this intention of retaining contact with the German theatrical tradition that was opposed by Nazi authorities. The performances were under the permanent control of Gestapo officials—the *Herren mit der Aktentasche* as Herbert Freeden has called them. The *Mitteilungsblätter* could not report on this matter explicitly, lest it run the risk of itself being prohibited.

In the fall of 1934 Dr. Heinrich Levinger, a man experienced in theatrical profession, took over the management of the Kulturbund Rhein-Ruhr in Cologne. In October he wrote in the *Mitteilungsblätter* about his plans and hopes: "We want to deal with our task deliberately as Jews to whom their Jewishness is not only an innate fact but also the means of cultivating a proud tradition. But we want to deal with it also as Jewish citizens of Germany and the world, Jews who do not want to lose touch with the cultural heritage that has become a vital possession for them."[24] Practical and social aims had to be combined with cultural and artistic objectives. So the theater performed during the summer as well as the regular season, and the management turned directly to the audience of the Kulturbund with urgent appeals:

> Remain members of the *Kulturbund!* It's your work created by yourselves at a time of greatest crisis. Help to safeguard its existence, to complete its structure, because our artistic performances must be enhanced, more and more unemployed artists must earn a living in it; the

22. Ibid., p. 4.   23. Ibid.
24. Heinrich Levinger, "Unser zweites Arbeitsjahr beginnt! Pläne und Hoffnungen," ibid., October 1934, p. 3.

youth shall be drawn in. It is necessary to achieve these objectives!
Bear in mind that it was always a most dignified Jewish duty to help
creative people and to support the arts.[25]

The mostly assimilated Jews in the Rhineland and Westfalia found it
very difficult, however, to follow Hans Hinkel's insistent demands that
the Kulturbund stick to Jewish themes and authors. As early as June
1934 the Kulturbund Rhein-Ruhr had to organize a competition in order
to find new plays with specifically Jewish contents. Within three months
fifty plays were submitted for the judges to examine. This was no doubt a
sign of the Kulturbund Rhein-Ruhr's vitality, but it was also a sure sign
that Jews well understood how necessary it was for them to shed light on
the central question of their cultural task at this time.

On this matter the *Mitteilungsblätter* in the fall of 1934 published a
series of essays on "Das jüdische Element in der Kulturbundarbeit."
Rabbi Hugo Hahn from Essen stated his opinion that as long as, for
cultural or technical reasons, Jews had not yet succeeded in articulating
the Jewish existence as an expression of the general human situation, they
could make this an objective of their artistic work: "It could also be a
legitimate task of a Jewish Kulturbund to defend the Jews' own cause by
pleading the general one: to let the cultural creations of the world flow
through a Jewish heart, through a Jewish temperament. By this the Jewish cause would be rendered a good service in these times."[26]

This critical analysis of the Jewish point of view was continued in the
successive numbers of the *Mitteilungsblätter*. Kurt Alexander of Krefeld,
a member of the managing committee of the Centralverein deutscher
Staatsbürger jüdischen Glaubens (CV) and of the board of the Kulturbund Rhein-Ruhr, expressed his opinion in the November issue:

> At the founding of the Kulturbund it was clear to me that without
> establishing a theater it would not be of long duration. Concerts and
> lectures capture the attention of only a small circle of people. But the
> theater exists for all. . . . The theater must under no circumstances
> fail to take an active part in the cultural work of our German *Heimat;*
> next to this it has to cultivate the sublime and imperishable heritage of
> the Jewish cultural community. We are on the right road. Let us pro-
> ceed onward.[27]

25. "Bleibe Mitglied des Kulturbundes!" ibid., June 1934, p. 4.
26. Hugo Hahn, "Das jüdische Element in der Kulturbundarbeit," ibid., October
1934, p. 6.
27. Kurt Alexander, "Kulturbund-Theater—warum und wie," ibid., November 1934,
p. 6.

So here again was mention of the double task: to intensify the consciousness of the Jewish existence as well as to pay regard to the historical fact
that Jewish culture had struck roots in German language and civilization.
In spite of Nazi policies, this approach continued to be characteristic of
the Jews in the West of Germany.

In December 1934 Dr. Auerbach, rabbi of the district of Recklinghausen, pointed to the special service the Kulturbund would render to the
small communities:

> The National Revolution[28] resulted in the exclusion of Jews from al-
> most all non-Jewish associations and forced them, especially the Jews
> in the countryside and in the small communities, into total mental,
> social, and psychological isolation. At that point the Kulturbund rees-
> tablished ties. Of course we would not fail to recognize that its found-
> ing originated to a great extent in philanthropic motives, since Jewish
> artists, expelled and therefore suffering, could earn a living only
> through this organization. But more important than the ridiculously
> small amount of money that we pay to the Kulturbund as our monthly
> dues, are the great ideals and values that the Kulturbund presents to us,
> and this especially again to the small communities. . . . By the Kultur-
> bund's not restricting its performances to the large communities but
> coming also to the medium-sized and small communities, there serving
> in addition the surrounding tiny communities, we all are united by a
> great bond. . . . It is precisely the individual Jew in the small com-
> munities who feels in a double way the heavy economic and psychologi-
> cal struggle for existence and who is dependent on the work of the
> Kulturbund and owes to it a debt of gratitude for its efforts.[29]

The Kulturbund Rhein-Ruhr, unlike the Kulturbund in Berlin, made
a specific effort to reach out into the rural communities and play a role
in the cultural consolidation of Jews in small towns. Of course there were
also risks in this—the risks incurred by Jews staying too long in these
communities—but they were only realized later. In 1934–35 the work of
the Kulturbund was primarily seen as helpful. Nevertheless it was precisely in these small and medium-sized communities that as early as 1935
it became increasingly difficult for the Kulturbund even to find halls for
performances.

In spite of all external hardships, the discussion about Jewish values

28. The term *nationale Revolution* was like *Machtergreifung,* a catchphrase of Nazi
propaganda and had been first used by the conservative Right. Its use at this time in
the *Mitteilungsblätter* must be seen in part as a tactical concession to Nazi censorship.
29. Dr. Auerbach, "Was bedeutet der Kulturbund für die kleinen Gemeinden?"
Mitteilungsblätter, December 1934, p. 6.

continued, and it also determined the decision of the jury in March 1935 on the fifty plays on Jewish themes that had been submitted. What had been called for was "the best play, but particularly with a Jewish content." But the jury could not agree on the awarding of a first prize, which might seem surprising in view of the large number of works submitted. The judges gave their reasons as follows:

> The Kulturbund had hoped that the competition would provide it with mature dramatic works which, when performed on the stage, would transmit Jewish values and a Jewish consciousness to a broad section of the public. But in addition it was also hoped that the competition would advance and foster the work of Jewish dramatists. Unfortunately these hopes have been realized to only a small extent. Almost all the plays submitted were imitative of other styles, and there was no work suitable for performance that satisfied the particular demands of the Kulturbund theater.[30]

So only a second prize was awarded, to the play *Channa,* by Martha Wertheimer of Frankfurt am Main, which was performed the following fall. Seven more plays received commendations. Among them was *Benjamin oder die Überwindung* by Heinrich Infeld from Tel Aviv, which in the opinion of the jury was "the only play in the competition to achieve a form appropriate to the outlook of our times." It depicted the career of a *chaluz.*[31]

The Kulturbund Rhein-Ruhr's intensive efforts on behalf of the Jewish theater redounded to its own benefit when on April 27–28, 1935 (no doubt also as a result of Nazi pressure), thirty-six regional and local Jewish cultural centers joined together in Berlin to form the Reichsverband der jüdischen Kulturbünde in Deutschland. Later a few additional groups joined them. Singer of Berlin was elected chairman of a small steering committee, and Levinger, the head of the Kulturbund Rhein-Ruhr, was elected senior deputy chairman. Since the purpose of this umbrella organization was to facilitate the exchange of events among the various cultural centers, the *Mitteilungsblätter* of the Kulturbund Rhein-Ruhr thought it had good potential: "Within this framework, our Kulturbund

30. Walter-Rosenbaum, "Unser Preisausschreiben! Die Entscheidung des Preisgerichts," ibid., March 1935, p. 7.
31. Ibid. In addition, the area from which this competition attracted entries shows the considerable circulation of the *Mitteilungsblätter* of the Jüdischer Kulturbund Rhein-Ruhr, for none of the other six authors who received commendations lived in the Rhineland or Westphalia either. They were Fritz Rosenthal of Munich (*Das Messiasspiel*); Maurice Rübner (*Pax eterna*) and Oswald Pander (*Man türmt*), both of Hamburg; Herbert Schönlank of Amsterdam (*Kalenner fährt Auto*); Martin Mansbacher of Lübeck (*Chanukkafestspiel*); and Sylvia Cohn-Oberbrunner of Offenburg/Baden (*Esther*).

theater, as the only Jewish traveling theater company, should find a larger sphere of activity opened up to it." It concluded its report about the confederation of Jewish cultural centers by asserting: "Every individual must be fully aware what an important brick his membership represents in the overall structure of Jewish cultural work in Germany! Then no one will lightly neglect something that is among the most important obligations of Jews in Germany: to extend on a cultural level the Jewish *Lebensraum* in Germany and to help provide work for Jewish artists!"[32]

Through the confederation of Jewish cultural centers in the Reichsverband der jüdischen Kulturbünde in Deutschland, every member of an individual Kulturbund was automatically a member of the Reichsverband. In return for a small addition to their monthly dues, individual members thereby had the right to attend the events of other local and regional centers. In addition all the centers had improved opportunities for cooperation. But these advantages were offset by the possibility of tighter controls by Staatskommissar Hinkel and the Gestapo. This opportunity was not fully exploited by the Nazi regime during 1935–36, since the Hitler government temporarily held back from antisemitic measures in view of the approaching Olympic Games, but the Reichsverband was an avenue for facilitating more restrictive policies at a later time.

Meanwhile the cultural and social work of the Jewish cultural centers continued undismayed. Friedrich Brodnitz, the former chairman of the CV and now a committee member of the Reichsvertretung der deutschen Juden, encouraged the centers' activities in a lecture in Cologne in November 1935: "Your recent confederation has formed the basis for united, effective work. Now it is a matter of giving life to the organizational framework. From being individual audience groups, you must become real centers of strength in the cultural life of the German Jews." Brodnitz thought that, just as new paths were being developed in all areas of German-Jewish community life, artistic work must also be built anew "right down to the smallest details." Each of the many questions that arose in this regard would have to be examined afresh:

> The meaning of artistic creation and enjoyment for a new age and a new generation, the relationship of specifically Jewish art to the art of Germany and to the art of the whole world, the tasks of the new individual areas in the overall plan for a new cultural life, all these prob-

---

32. "Zusammenschluss der jüdischen Kulturbünde Deutschlands," *Mitteilungsblätter*, June 1935, p. 4. The term *Lebensraum*, so overused by the Nazis, turns up here most likely, again, as a tactical concession to Nazi censorship.

lems must be thought out and shaped anew from the ground up. It must be our leading principle that there cannot be a place in our Jewish cultural centers for art that no longer has anything essential to say to the people of our time. . . . The particular cultural needs of German Jews of today, recognized and formulated in an undogmatic way independent of party views, must give our work its stamp.

In Brodnitz's opinion the Jewish cultural centers would have to "draw all sectors of German Jewry around themselves" and prove that they were determined to be the cradle of an art that would "stand up to the serious situation of our days" and to demonstrate that they were not just "emergency shelters" but valid forms of cultural life.[33] The difficulty lay in turning theory into practice, and that could be done only by the centers themselves.

In January 1936 Singer spoke in Cologne, Dortmund, Essen, and Krefeld on "The Foundation and Extension of Jewish Cultural Work in Germany."[34] But already the future of programs for extending cultural work was uncertain. In March 1936 Dr. Paul Moses, senior chairman of the Jewish Kulturbund Rhein-Ruhr, left Germany; the second wave of emigrations since 1933 was on its way. Although the membership of the Kulturbund Rhein-Ruhr had now declined from its high of five thousand, its work continued. But major theatrical performances gradually gave way to poetry evenings and Kleinkunst, while art exhibitions and solo musical recitals increased in number. At the exhibition of the Jewish cultural centers in Berlin in May 1936, at which Jewish artists from all over the country were represented, Rhenish painters such as Flora Jöhlinger, Lisel Wetzlar, Lotte Prechner, Hans Eltzbacher, and Otto Schloss had considerable success.

The Kulturbund Rhein-Ruhr found it increasingly difficult to stick to the original performance schedules of its theater,[35] as it had serious problems maintaining a large staff. Nevertheless the company managed to perform Somerset Maugham's *Sacred Flame* in May 1936 and Rudolf Kurtz's comedy *Hut ab vor Onkel Eddie* in June. For November 1936 Marcel Pagnol's comedy *Zum goldenen Anker* was scheduled, and for 1937 two premieres—Gerhard Hirschfeld's *Der Pojaz* and Willi Buschhoff's *Hachscharah*—and three additional plays—George Bernard Shaw's

33. Friedrich Brodnitz, "Kulturbünde und jüdische Öffentlichkeit," ibid., November 1935, p. 3.
34. Kurt Singer, "Die Grundlage und Erweiterung jüdischer Kulturarbeit in Deutschland," ibid., January 1936, p. 9.
35. For the original performance schedule, see n. 11, above.

Candida or Ferenc Molnár's *Die grosse Liebe,* Georg Düren's *Der Stär-kere,* and *The Importance of Being Earnest* by Oscar Wilde. It proved impossible to perform the plays by Buschhoff and Düren. Other performances included the Hungarian comedy *Jean* by Ladislaus Bus-Fekete and *The Man Who Changed His Name* by Edgar Wallace.

From 1937 onwards, light plays and comedies came to dominate the Kulturbund Rhein-Ruhr's theater program. Among these were *Bob macht sich gesund* by Axel Ivers, *Achtung, frisch gestrichen!* by René Fauchois, Molnár's comedy *Delila,* evenings of light entertainment with the irrepressible Max Ehrlich, Offenbach evenings, and the like. The audience needed diversion and temporary respite from cares in a time of increasing psychological oppression, and the management no doubt conceded to the wishes of the public on whom the continued existence of the theater so heavily depended. In view of this, the premiere in Cologne of Franz Werfel's most recent play, *In einer Nacht,* as late as January 1938 must be regarded as a considerable achievement.

In May 1937 the Kulturbund Rhein-Ruhr had to raise a one-time "theater subsidy" in the form of an additional contribution from its members.[36] The new tightening of anti-Jewish policies by the regime after the Olympic Games in Berlin was already making itself felt. But even before that the cultural expression of Jews in Germany had been limited. In spring 1936 there had been a six-week ban on all Kulturbund events, and in March, Jews had been prohibited from using stage names.[37] Yet the Reichsverband der jüdischen Kulturbünde, primarily a central organization forced on the centers by the Nazis as a means of control, had brought certain benefits to the Jews that Hinkel had certainly not intended. This was due above all to Singer, Levinger, and Werner Levie, the Reichsverband's general secretary in Berlin, who had thereby improved cooperation between Berlin and Cologne, as well as among other Kulturbund centers. But the overall situation had changed. Levie acknowledged this in September 1936 in the *Mitteilungsblätter* of the Kulturbund Rhein-Ruhr as he discussed the aims of Jewish cultural work in Germany:

> The problems of Jewish cultural work in Germany are clear for all to see. The discussion has long since left the deep waters of the false

36. "Members of the Jewish Kulturbund Rhein-Ruhr, keep your theater going, your place for rest and relaxation! Show yourselves to be true Jews who recognize and help others to understand the pressing need of the moment!" "Theaterhilfe!" *Mitteilungsblätter,* May 1937, p. 3.
37. Freeden, *Jüdisches Theater,* p. 175. See also Düwell, *Die Rheingebiete,* p. 136.

opposition of "Jewish" and "non-Jewish," the doctrinaire and theoretical preoccupations with technique and people talking straight past one another. Today we must focus on practical considerations. We are all struggling together to discover how, given the present circumstances, we can create a Jewish theater, Jewish concerts, in short, artistic work by Jews for Jews in Germany. To be practical here, to move toward a conclusion, is the task I have taken upon myself.

We all know that neither Yiddish theater nor theater in Hebrew can be the basis of our work. Such an attempt would certainly founder (at least at the beginning), if for no other reason than that the Jewish public are not intellectually ready for it. But we all know that in many ways Yiddish and Hebrew theater can hold out values to us that can be useful in our efforts. To establish intellectual links with Jewish theater, wherever in the world it manifests itself, to make the Jewish artists in Germany who are called upon to present their art before Jewish audiences familiar with Jewish material and Jewish knowledge, these are the tasks in both content and organization that represent the beginning of cultural work in a truly Jewish sense.

I consider it one of the most lofty tasks of the Reichsverband to realize this essential Jewish atmosphere, to achieve this incredibly difficult educational aim.[38]

Levie was pleading for a closer attachment between practicing artists and the representatives of Jewish culture abroad. It seemed possible to break through the spiritual isolation of the Jews in Germany in this way, at least in part. But he also stressed that, however obvious the Jews' connection with all manifestations of European culture might seem to be, ties with their own culture must be considered basic:

It is not a matter of different doctrines, the question of Zionism or assimilation (in the nonpolitical sense this can no longer be considered a matter for discussion), it concerns a positive response to our own culture, a mental break with habit in the direction of an enrichment, . . . so that the Jewish cultural centers can develop from being a social organization today into a cultural institution that has achieved an intellectual foundation.

Applied to the theatrical work that was so central to the Kulturbund Rhein-Ruhr, this meant the theater company should grow from a social into a "moral institution," according to Schiller's conception. Levie spoke about *"working on ourselves,* those of us whose job it is to carry out the cultural work." He believed that this was the most important task in cultural education; it had to be kept in the foreground, not because the pub-

38. Werner Levie, "Ziele jüdischer Kulturarbeit in Deutschland," *Mitteilungsblätter,* September 1936, pp. 3–4.

lic had to be made ready for something new, but "because the presenters must first be made ready for their presentation."[39]

Levie attempted to stimulate thought about the problems of presenting a specifically Jewish culture by lecturing in Cologne, Aachen, Dortmund, Duisburg, Essen, Gelsenkirchen, Krefeld, Recklinghausen, and Wuppertal. He proposed a study visit to Palestine, as he had an idea about transferring the Jewish Kulturbund organization there, but it subsequently came to nothing.[40] By this time the Nazis' anti-Jewish policies had become even more severe, and there were sporadic outbursts of antisemitism even in the Rhineland. In September 1936 the *Mitteilungsblätter* of the Kulturbund Rhein-Ruhr warned its members, for the first time, to travel in groups both to and from Kulturbund events.[41] As emigration increased, so the number of members fell, especially in the small communities, although at first Jews in these communities moved only into the larger towns.

Nevertheless, in 1936 the theater of the Kulturbund Rhein-Ruhr reached the height of its activities. The company had successfully produced Max Brod's *Reubeni, Fürst der Juden* in an adaptation by Walter-Rosenbaum. This Cologne dramatization was also taken up by Jewish theaters in Berlin, Warsaw, Basle, Bratislava, Vienna, and even the Habimah in Tel Aviv, as Levinger pointed out with justified pride in his annual report for 1935–36.[42] But the same report made it quite clear that the labor-intensive and relatively costly theater work in Cologne and the ten affiliated towns in the Rhineland and Westphalia, with occasional guest performances in addition, was in the long run incurring increasing financial difficulties. It seems that Levinger tried to counteract the expense of theater by presenting more frequent musical events. The violinist Boris Schwarz and his father, the pianist Joseph Schwarz, together with Godfried Zeelander, the former solo cellist of the Berlin Philharmonic, the tenor Alexander Kipnis, the contralto Ruth Kisch-Arndt, the pianist Michael Wittels, violinists Annie Steiger-Betzak and Ernst Drucker, the pianist Kurt Heinemann, and not least Emanuel Feuermann on the violin and cello were among those who gave special recitals in Cologne. Levinger

39. Ibid., p. 4.

40. See E. G. Lowenthal, ed., *Bewährung im Untergang, ein Gedenkbuch* (Stuttgart, 1965), pp. 114–15.

41. "Werden unsere Mitglieder dringend ersucht, vor und nach den Veranstaltungen Ansammlungen vor den Veranstaltungslokalitäten zu vermeiden!" *Mitteilungsblätter*, September 1936, p. 11.

42. Levinger, "Rückblick und Vorschau," ibid., October 1936, p. 3.

also established contact with the orchestra of the Kulturbund Rhein-Main, founded in 1934 by the Cologne conductor Hans Wilhelm Steinberg, and arranged for it to give a number of guest performances for the Kulturbund Rhein-Ruhr. When by August 1937 the Kulturbund Rhein-Main had run into considerable financial difficulty and the future of its highly respected orchestra seemed threatened, Levinger took over the direction of this neighboring Kulturbund as well.[43] He reorganized it and increased cooperation between it and the Kulturbund Rhein-Ruhr. One of the cultural highlights of this collaboration in the West of Germany was the recital tour in autumn 1937 of the string quartet of the Kulturbund Rhein-Main (Ernst Drucker and Theo Ratner, violin; Richard Karp, viola; Heinz Edelstein, cello), which presented, among others, compositions by Ernst Toch.

In all, during the 1936–37 season the Kulturbund Rhein-Ruhr had put on 318 events in nine towns. Nevertheless, Levinger complained in his annual report for 1937 of a distinct fall in the number of members "connected with a considerable amount of emigration." He announced for the new season the performance, among others, of Henrik Ibsen's *John Gabriel Borkmann* and Shaw's *Candida,* and the premiere of Georg Hirschland's *Solms, der Ungeratene,* and stated a further objective: "If finances will permit it, we wish to undertake the performance of a great classical work with Shakespeare's *Hamlet.*"[44] The 140th anniversary of the birth of Heinrich Heine, on December 13, 1937, was also to be celebrated with the premiere of an arrangement by Walter-Rosenbaum entitled *Heinrich Heine, ein Märchen vom verlorenen Sohn.* But there were more and more appeals for voluntary contributions to make the programs possible. Special passes were introduced for patrons, and campaigns to recruit new members were launched. Additional guest performances were scheduled for the Kulturbund in Düsseldorf, which was independent of the Rhenish-Westphalian cultural center. But all these efforts were rendered useless by the events of November 9, 1938; all Jewish cultural centers in Germany were banned.

But then the incredible happened: even while the fires were still smoking in the ruins of the synagogues, on November 12, 1938, the propaganda minister decreed that the Reichsverband der jüdischen Kulturbünde was to continue its work.[45] But that work changed radically. In the first

43. "Dr. Heinrich Levinger," ibid., September 1937, p. 4.
44. Levinger, "Wege und Ziele unserer Arbeit," ibid., October 1937, pp. 3, 4.
45. Freeden describes the macabre situation in Berlin in which this enforced rebirth of the theater took place. *Jüdisches Theater,* pp. 147–49.

place, the Reichsverband was to be in firm control, and regional activities, particularly those developed by the Kulturbund Rhein-Ruhr, were forced into the background. In addition, the economic and social rights of Jews were steadily removed as they were arbitrarily placed in "protective custody" and subjected to other instruments of terror. Kulturbund performances were like playing with fire.

The compulsory centralization of the work of the Jewish cultural centers drew off most of the artists of the Kulturbund Rhein-Ruhr to Berlin by the end of 1938. The Reichsverband, which had left considerable freedom of action to the regional cultural centers, was replaced on January 1, 1939, by an organization called the Jüdischer Kulturbund in Deutschland e.V. Its headquarters were in Berlin; the Cologne center was defined as a subsidiary or local branch. Up to the final banning of this last Kulturbund on September 11, 1941, there were still occasional theatrical performances, but lectures and the performance of works by non-Jewish German writers and composers remained forbidden. Films were shown in their place, but these were selected more by the Ministry of Propaganda than by any Jewish body. In the area formerly served by the Jewish Kulturbund Rhein-Ruhr, cultural life withered away. Yet in spite of everything people occasionally got together for cultural evenings.

Most of the founders and the moving forces behind the Jewish cultural movement in Germany—including Kurt Singer and Werner Levie—paid for their courageous involvement with their lives. A very few—one of them, Alfred Balthoff, who had helped to stage many performances for the Kulturbund Rhein-Ruhr—were able to escape with the help of friends. It might be suggested that, if it had not been for the adventure of founding these cultural centers, many more human lives would have been saved. But twenty years ago Herbert Freeden countered that argument:

> Was there any alternative for the German Jews in this matter? Of course, they need never have initiated such a cultural organization. Then hundreds of artists would have gone hungry and tens of thousands of Jewish people would have had no chance for years on end to forget their hostile surroundings for a few hours at a concert or at the theater. But that was not a flight from reality in the sense of escapism: no Jew delayed his emigration for even a single day because he wanted to go to the theater, but many received strength from Shakespeare and Beethoven.[46]

This was true, especially, for the West of Germany.

46. Ibid., p. 47.

But why, up to 1937–38, did the Nazis remain relatively willing to make concessions in what they were prepared to allow? Above all we must consider here Freeden's "showcase" thesis: "The Kulturbund was to be the showcase whereby the Nazis could demonstrate to the world how much 'freedom' they allowed the Jews, and how much 'tolerance' they showed them so long as they remained within their own sphere." In addition, the Nazis probably intended, possibly even as early as 1933, to centralize the Jewish Kulturbund organizations—as they did in 1936—in order to gain total control over Jewish cultural activities. "What could at first be taken for a gesture toward cultural self-determination," wrote Freeden,

> was exposed as a means of restricting more and more the intellectual basis of Jewish existence and forcing the Jews into a cultural ghetto—in Hinkel's words, the "crowding together of intellectual and artistic Jewry": that was to be the effect of the straitjacket measures and the ever-tightening censorship, which was devised as an instrument of demoralization.[47]

But this Nazi calculation was only partly successful, since for several years the work of the Jewish cultural centers turned out to be a source of reflection and inner consolidation among Jews and an agent for building a Jewish sense of community. Herein lies its fascination. As Freeden has summarized:

> Today, when we look back to that time, the activities of the Kulturbund seem like a dance on a volcano. Like that ghostly premiere after the November pogrom . . . that is what the whole of the eight years of the Kulturbund were like: seeing the abyss, but going on playing. And the whole of its work was like that, too: knowing, but still doing. Its people could not stand up against the regime; but that they played *in spite* of it, that was the great thing. Night after night, in Berlin and in the Rhineland, in Hamburg, in Frankfurt, and on tours, they made liars out of those who maintained that Jews could not be interpreters of music or poetry; night after night they proved, if any proof were necessary, that art did not cease to fulfill and move Jews, even under the whips of persecution. There was something unique in this attempt to go in search of Jewish forms and contents while the ground fell away beneath their feet.[48]

Time and time again this phenomenon arouses wonder and amazement, and admiration, too. A few years ago it compelled Elisabeth Ples-

47. Ibid., pp. 51, 52.
48. Ibid., p. 168.

sen to interview surviving members of the Jewish cultural centers. In the course of her investigations it became clear just how much these Jews had been attached to both the German language and its intellectual tradition that had provided a fertile soil for the Kulturbund experiment. Standing opposed to this fundamental intellectual need were the interests of Nazi politics:

> Here the reigning fascists used an elementary human need—the desire of a boycotted minority to create and enjoy art—for their own propaganda ends, both at home and abroad. Systematically they applied increasing restrictions of a spurious legality finally to destroy the minority. Seen in this way, the Kulturbund appears as the object of an encircling motion drawing in ever tighter, functioning flawlessly in the pedantic German manner; a bureaucratic registration, centralization, and dispatching—in all senses of the word.[49]

The dignity of the Jewish Kulturbund work remains essentially untouched by the Gestapo's purposes, even though the Gestapo was present—like Banquo's ghost—at almost every Kulturbund event; in Cologne the Gestapo even had a place in the same Disch-Haus where the Kulturbund administration worked. But as a result of the Nazis' forcing even those artists who no longer felt particularly strong Jewish ties into a Jewish role, something remarkable happened, which Freeden as a witness of these events has described:

> With a twist of genius that gave a new spirit to modern German Jews, the artists discovered the daring, the *avant garde,* in Jewish themes. Those proclaimers of words and performers of music on German stages and platforms had strayed away from Jewishness; they had swum out too far into the sea of Western art to take any pleasure in the Jewish tradition. And suddenly the unexpected happened: excluded from public theaters, thrown out of the concert halls, banished from the art galleries, they sought to find their artistic expression in things Jewish, and to arrive at final definitions and an ultimate analysis. That happened, not in a time of leisurely reflection, but in that period of pressure and persecution.[50]

As Freeden so aptly put it, the Kulturbund was "still tinged by the rays of the setting sun of the Jewish cultural achievement in Germany: the last evening light of the great days of European Jewry still lay on its

---

49. Elisabeth Plessen, "Jüdische Kunst im faschistischen, rassistischen Deutschland: Die Geschichte des 'Kulturbunds Deutscher Juden,' " pt. 1, *"Nathan der Weise* im Staate der Nazis: Gespräche mit Augenzeugen," *Die Zeit,* October 7, 1977, no. 42; pt. 2, "Flamme des Geistes in der Zeit der Not," ibid., October 14, 1977, no. 43.

50. Freeden, *Jüdisches Theater,* p. 3.

work, the last light—and the first shadow!"[51] The work of the Kulturbund Rhein-Ruhr, which broke off abruptly in 1938, was a testimony to
both. For a few years its activities made possible, in spite of difficult conditions, the continuation and revitalization of a community of people
whose spiritual home was Germany, but who at the same time had begun
to rediscover and strengthen the Jewish roots of their own religious and
cultural traditions. The pogrom of 1938 put a brutal end to this experiment. If the Nazis considered the Jewish cultural centers as a showcase
for their propaganda, we must ask whether these centers were rather a
bell jar, under which very different plans were prepared.

51. Ibid.

Lost, Stolen, and Strayed

The Archival Heritage of Modern German-Jewish History

Current archival practices are determined largely by historical methodology, but the task of selecting and preserving those records that characterize and document an ethnic or religious group within a host country is inherently subjective. Certain problems are common to all types of contemporary records from the Enlightenment to the Holocaust; others are unique to German Judaica. Until recently, the standards of historical significance have been frankly elitist, concerned with the careers of prominent personalities, with the role of political, economic, and cultural elites and organizations, and, for German Judaica, with the history of autonomous Jewish communities in Germany. The newer perspectives of social, quantitative, and women's history as well as the study of the Holocaust, have placed increasing demands on the surviving fragmentary archival record.

The most striking characteristic of modern records is that they are fractured or fragmented, despite their initial creation by a single organization, common agency, or person (called "provenance"). Thus the personal literary estates of most major twentieth-century figures reflect the migratory patterns of careers split between government service, university employment, and private business. This has resulted in the scattering of official and personal papers of one individual among several archival depositories, assuming that the records do not altogether disappear with the emigration or demise of their creators. The several archival agencies holding different fragments of one figure seldom correlate bibliographic data about their common subject holdings in joint finding aids or even exchange data on more than an informal and sporadic basis. This neglect has contributed to the recent international discussion about subject retrieval and problems of scholarly access to records and manuscripts.[1]

Access is also determined by other variables, and conditions range from virtually open door with minimal restrictions (usually about copyright and privacy) in Western Europe and North America to restrictive legislation and arbitrary access in Eastern Europe and the Third World.[2] For German Judaica, Jewish separateness in Christian-German society has resulted in the administrative division of extant Jewish records between two parallel types of agencies: state repositories with jurisdiction over files about Jews within their geographic boundaries and private institutions under Jewish auspices. The first central depository for the records of German-Jewish communities and organizations, the Gesamtarchiv der deutschen Juden, was established in 1905 in Berlin. In the mid-1930s its archival holdings were seized by the Reichsstelle für Sippenforschung (State Office for Ancestral Research), and, despite losses, many Jewish communal birth, marriage, and death registers were saved from destruction as an ironic by-product of the Nazi pseudoscientific obsession with racial biology. In 1945 the U.S. Army recovered many of these files and subsequently transported them from the Offenbach archival depot for captured documents to Jewish successor institutions in the United States and Israel. Noncaptured remnants of the Gesamtarchiv still remain in both East and West Germany.[3] The Gesamtarchiv was never as comprehensive as the name implied, and Jewish records often remained *in situ* in the offices, seminaries, and synagogues that created them. The complex pattern of migration of records and manuscripts alienated from their geographical or administrative points of origin has been further complicated by the existence of private Judaica archives, bibliophiles, and collectors. In 1924, for example, the librarian of the Jewish Theological Seminary

1. Richard H. Lytle, "Intellectual Access to Archives: Provenance and Content Indexing Methods of Subject Retrieval," *American Archivist* 43 (1980): 64–75, 191–207.

2. Michel Duchein, *Obstacles to the Access, Use and Transfer of Information from Archives* (Paris, 1983). This 79-page study was prepared as "A RAMP study of UNESCO," PGI–83/WS/20.

3. Information provided by Elisabeth Kinder of the Bundesarchiv in Koblenz, March 1981, and Dr. Hermann Simon of the East Berlin Jewish Community, June 1983. See also the inventory to the Jacob Jacobson Papers, Archives of the Leo Baeck Institute, New York (hereafter LBI, NY), AR 7002. The statement of purpose of the Gesamtarchiv is published in Eugen Täubler, "Zur Einführung," *Mitteilungen des Gesamtarchivs der deutschen Juden* 1, no. 1 (1908): 1–8.

in New York, Alexander Marx, purchased 39.6 pounds of documents for $293 from the Berlin bookdealer Louis Lamm. The materials included communal records from fifty-nine German–Jewish and Polish–Jewish communities in the province of Posen.[4] In the late 1930s, Jewish emigrants fleeing Nazi Germany often carried family papers and other archival files to localities scattered throughout the world. One emigrant carried the memorial book of late nineteenth-century Zerkow, Upper Silesia, to her new home in Montevideo; after her death, the volume was inherited by distant American relatives who donated it to the Leo Baeck Institute in 1983.[5] This illustration is not atypical.

The idiosyncrasies of German geography and political history are also reflected in surviving German-Jewish records. The amalgam of more than three hundred sovereign entities that existed prior to the unification of Germany further increased the fragmentation and decentralization of German and Jewish records alike. Thus the papers of Jewish communities on the west bank of the Rhine were already split between France and Germany at the time of the French Revolution and Napoleon. Similarly the files of the Jewish consistories in Alsace and Lorraine have been repeatedly transferred between France and Germany throughout the last hundred years: from France to Germany in 1871, back to France in 1919, reconquered by Germany in 1940, and only partly retrieved by France in 1945. In fact, some of the materials recovered by the U.S. Army in 1945 were eventually shipped to several American-Jewish depositories (the YIVO Institute for Jewish Research, the Leo Baeck Institute, and the Jewish Theological Seminary) and to Israel (Central Archives for the History of the Jewish People).[6] Analogous shifts in the citizenship of both German and Jewish archival holdings also occurred in Breslau (today Wrocław in Poland) and Königsberg (today Kaliningrad in the Soviet Union).[7] Non-German records captured by German soldiers dur-

4. List of communal records, Rare Books and Manuscript Division, Library of the Jewish Theological Seminary, New York, no. 8683. See also Michael Moses Zarchin, *Jews in the Province of Posen: Studies in Communal Records of the Eighteenth and Nineteenth Centuries* (Philadelphia, 1939).

5. LBI, NY, AR 5165, includes the records of the Hevrah Kadisha of Zerkow, 1865–1914.

6. For a discussion of French Judaica, see Bernhard Blumenkranz, ed., *Documents modernes sur les Juifs xvie–xxe siècles réunis par l'Équipe de recherche 208 "Nouvelle Gallia Judaica"* (Toulouse, 1979); and Phyllis Cohen Albert, *The Modernization of French Jewry* (Hanover, N.H., 1977), pp. 387–402.

7. The records of the Breslau Jewish Theological Seminary and the Breslau Jewish community are today located at the Zidovske Institute in Warsaw and the Wrocław University Archives. The records of the Jewish community of Königsberg are dispersed

ing the invasion of Russia were eventually captured in turn by the U.S. Army, as for example, the Communist party archives of the Smolensk region.[8] The result of these repeated changes of sovereignty is a gigantic jigsaw puzzle with numerous torn and missing pieces.

Neglect and the ravages of time have also influenced the quantity and quality of the surviving historical record. Thus most records of the Sephardic community of Berlin had been lost before the 1930s.[9] It is clear that Jewish communal records, kept intermittently since the seventeenth century, became more systematic as the administrative organization of the modern German state evolved during the nineteenth century. But Jewish records prior to the nineteeenth century were not always complete, accurate, or even systematic, especially during periods of tension and persecution. Occasionally the absence of some records was deliberate, a stratagem to evade harassment, military conscription, residence restrictions, or discriminatory taxation in the preemancipation period. Often problems resulted from the nature of the record itself. *Mohelbücher* (circumcision registers) were not records of all male children born in a specific town or region but the private record of the individual circumciser. Circumcision registers did not, of course, contain data about Jewish female children.[10]

World War II and the Holocaust intensified the dispersion and destruction of Jewish documentation and artifacts. Although the Security

---

among the Prussian State Archives in West Berlin, the East German State Archives in Potsdam and Merseburg, and Polish archives.

8. Smolensk Archives, records of the All-Union Communist Party, T 87, 64 rolls (inventory located on T 87, roll 1); and Miscellaneous Russian Records Collection, T 88, 3 rolls (inventory located on T 87, roll 1), National Archives, Washington, D.C. (hereafter NARS, DC). For a general discussion of captured German records, see Robert Wolfe, ed., *Captured German and Related Records: A National Archives Conference* (Athens, Ohio, 1974). Among the captured German records were also a collection of Hungarian political and military records, 1909–45 (T 973, 21 rolls); a collection of Italian military records, 1935–43 (T 821, 506 rolls); the papers of Count Galeazzo Ciano [Lisbon Papers] (T 816, 3 rolls); and the personal papers of Benito Mussolini together with some official records of the Italian Foreign Office and the Ministry of Culture, 1922–44 (T 586, 318 rolls). The story of captured Italian records is told in Howard McGaw Smyth, *Secrets of the Fascist Era: How Uncle Sam Obtained Some of the Top-Level Documents of Mussolini's Period* (Carbondale and Edwardsville, Ill., 1975).

9. Herman Simon, *Das Berliner Jüdische Museum in der Oranienburger Strasse* (Berlin, 1983), pp. 63–66; Rahel Wischnitzer-Bernstein and Josef Fried, *Gedenkausstellung Don Jizchaq Abrabanel: Seine Welt, sein Werk* (Berlin, 1937).

10. Sybil Milton, "German-Jewish Genealogical Research: Selected Resources at the Leo Baeck Institute, New York," *Toledot: The Journal of Jewish Genealogy* 2, no. 4 (Spring 1979): 13–18; L. G. Pine, *The Genealogist's Encyclopedia* (New York, 1969), pp. 155–70.

Police Chief Reinhard Heydrich stipulated in his directives during the pogrom of November 9, 1938, that "the archives of Jewish communities are to be confiscated by the police, so that they will not be destroyed," there was nevertheless widespread Nazi looting and records stored in synagogues were often destroyed.[11] The pattern established inside Nazi Germany soon spread to all of occupied Europe from the Pyrenees to the Urals. Often German military and police units saved rare Judaica volumes and manuscripts as curiosities for their own collections, for use in potential antisemitic exhibitions organized by German museums, for deposit in the Institut zur Erforschung der Judenfrage in Frankfurt, and for resale in foreign auctions to obtain hard currency. In April 1943, Cecil Roth stated that he had received offers to buy rare Judaica from Nazi individuals and organizations transmitted via Switzerland.[12] For the most part, conditions that threatened human life also endangered the preservation of documents. Nazi lootings and confiscations were compounded by the fire storms and resultant damage during Allied bombing raids, the vulnerability of most storage places, the deliberate burning of incriminating records by retreating German soldiers and the SS to hide their complicity in mass murder, and the taking of souvenirs by both Allied liberators and civilian noncombatants. Whether records were destroyed or not was often only a matter of chance.

One anecdote, possibly apocryphal, about the disarray of Joseph Goebbels' diary in liberated Berlin, is typical for the fate of all records at the time. In a publisher's note to Louis P. Lochner's edition of Goebbels' diary, Hugh Gibson wrote:

> When the Russians occupied Berlin in 1945, they went through the German official archives with more vigor than discrimination; shipped some materials to Russia, destroyed some, and left the rest scattered underfoot. They often followed a system that is difficult to understand—emptying papers on the floor and shipping to Russia the filing cabinets that contained them.
>
> Considerable fragments of Goebbels's diaries . . . were found in the courtyard of his ministry, where they had evidently narrowly es-

11. *Trial of the Major War Criminals before the International Military Tribunal, Nuremberg, 14 November 1945–1 October 1946* (Nuremberg, 1947–49), 31:515–519 (Nuremberg document PS 3051).

12. Cecil Roth, opening address, April 11, 1943, *Conference on Restoration of Continental Jewish Museums, Libraries, and Archives* (London, 1943), unpaginated; Philip Friedman, "The Fate of the Jewish Book," in his *Roads to Extinction: Essays on the Holocaust* (New York and Philadelphia, 1980), pp. 88–99.

caped burning, many of the pages being singed and all smelling of
smoke. Apparently they were originally bound in the German type of
office folder. Thin metal strips in the salmon-colored binders were run
through holes punched in the paper, bent over, and locked into place.

At that time all Berlin was one great junk yard, with desperate
people laying hands on anything tangible and movable that could be
used for barter. The unburned papers were taken away by one of these
amateur junk dealers, who carefully salvaged the binders and discarded
the contents—leaving more than 7,000 sheets of loose paper. A few
binders had not been removed but most of the pages were tied up in
bundles as wastepaper. It later proved a considerable task to put them
together again in the right sequence, as they were not numbered.[13]

Several characteristics are common to all German Judaica records, irrespective of date: the multiplicity of languages (German, Judeo-German,
Hebrew, and occasionally also Ladino or Aramaic) and extensive damage
through neglect or deliberate destruction. The fragmentation of textual
and visual records in widely scattered government and private archives
has unfortunately limited the systematic reappraisal of criteria for archival
retention of documents, artifacts, and audiovisual materials. Although
there were mandatory religious and secular legal requirements for certain
types of genealogical records before the twentieth century, the pervasive
pattern of destruction and dispersal has led to the practice that everything
that survived is considered intrinsically valuable. This has, in effect, limited the archivists' role as "prophet" in deciding what new records might
give us a better understanding of the past and be usable in planning for
the future. Potential duplication and overlap of collections for pre–
World War II records are not viewed as serious problems, despite the
increasingly prohibitive costs of scholarly travel. But the practice of al-
lowing duplication and overlap is far more debatable for textual and audiovisual records created after 1945. The paper and film heritage of the
Nazi period, the Second World War, and the Holocaust (1933–45) have
several distinctive problems that must be discussed separately.

Many early Judaica records were saved virtually intact, as for example,
the records of the Jewish community of Worms shipped to the Jewish
Historical General Archives in Jerusalem in 1939 and subsequently incorporated into the holdings consolidated in the Central Archives for the

13. Hugh Gibson, publisher's note to *The Goebbels Diaries, 1942–1943,* ed. and
trans. Louis P. Lochner (Garden City, N.Y., 1948), p. v. These diaries are today located
in the Hoover Institution Archives, Stanford, California. The "rules" of Allied looting
are described in Margaret Bourke-White, *Portrait of Myself* (New York, 1963), pp.
261–63.

History of the Jewish People.[14] Other documents about the Jews of Worms remained in the Worms Municipal Archives, and substantial numbers of original and transcribed records were carried by immigrants to the United States. During the 1960s and 1970s the literary estates of three refugees who died in the United States—Berthold Rosenthal, Isidor Kiefer, and Fritz Nathan, all containing significant fragments of documentation about Worms—were deposited in the Leo Baeck Institute in New York.[15] Alongside his research notes about the Jews of Baden and Mannheim, Berthold Rosenthal packed in his luggage a complete transcript of the Green Book of Worms, 1560–1812. Isidor Kiefer, former president of the Worms Jewish community, who emigrated to the United States via Belgium in 1934, took eighteenth- and nineteenth-century administrative and correspondence files from the Worms Jewish communal offices; a copy of the Worms *Judenregister,* 1739–1814; an inventory of the Worms Jewish Museum, whose contents were later impounded and partly vandalized during the pogrom of November 1938; and photographs of the Rashi synagogue and ritual objects. The architect Fritz Nathan brought to the United States forty-two rare glass positive slides with detailed structural images of the Raschi synagogue prior to renovations completed at the beginning of the twentieth century.[16] These slides and photographs provided essential data for the reconstruction of the Worms synagogue and museum during the 1970s.[17]

The records of the demise of the Worms Jewish community under Nazi persecutions were located in depositories other than those holding earlier archival material. Deportation lists for Jews residing within the city and district of Worms were found in the municipal and police ar-

14. "Jüdische Kulturschätze von Worms nach Israel," *Wormser Zeitung,* December 21, 1956; "Worms jüdisches Archiv in Jerusalem übergeben," *New Yorker Staatszeitung und Herold,* November 5, 1957, p. 6. These clippings are located in the Worms Jewish Community Files, LBI, NY, AR 145/2 and AR 145/16.

15. Unpublished inventories available at the LBI, NY. See manuscript of the forthcoming *Leo Baeck Institute Catalog: Archives.*

16. The Berthold Rosenthal Papers, LBI, NY, AR 638/II 13, contains the Green Book of Worms (349 pages transcribed) and the Worms *Judenschaftsverzeichnis,* 1515–1760 (128 pages transcribed). The Isidor Kiefer Papers, LBI, NY, AR 1895/II 1, contains the *Judenregister,* 1739–1814; AR 1894/III 1–26, contains administrative files of the Worms Jewish community; AR 1897/IV 1–76, contains records and photos of the Worms synagogue from the nineteenth and twentieth centuries; and AR 1899/VI 1–8, contains files of the Worms Jewish Museum. The Kiefer literary estate also includes 220 historic photos from Worms. The Fritz Nathan Papers, LBI, NY, AR 7197/IV, contains forty-two glass positive slides of the Worms synagogue.

17. Otto Böcher, *Die alte Synagogue in Worms* (Berlin, 1982). The Worms Jewish Community Files, LBI, NY, AR 145, contains clippings from March and October 1974 about the reconstruction of the *Judengasse,* the synagogue, and the museum.

chives of Worms, the Hessen State Archives, the International Tracing
Service at Arolsen, Yad Vashem in Jerusalem, and the Leo Baeck Institute in New York.[18] Furthermore, the YIVO Institute in New York acquired several hundred identity cards for Worms Jewish inhabitants as
part of the record group of captured German documents containing the
files of the Institut zur Erforschung der Judenfrage.[19] The records of
Worms from the Nazi period were thus fragmented among more than
six institutions in three countries on three continents.

The first contact between unassimilated *Ostjuden* and the Prussian bureaucracy occurred during the Napoleonic era, when the regions of Bialystok and Plock were annexed to New East Prussia with the Third Parti-
tion of Poland in 1795 until the creation of the Napoleonic duchy of
Warsaw in 1807. The newly annexed territories were administered from
Königsberg by Gustav Schrötter and became the testing ground for many
of the later Stein-Hardenberg reforms that led to the emancipation of
Prussian Jews. Initially, all historical records from this period were deposited in the Prussian State Archives in Königsberg. After the Second
World War, the files of the Kriegs- und Domänenkammer of Bialystok
and the Generaldirektion Neuostpreussen were separated; the former
were returned to Poland in 1947 and the latter dispersed between the
East German State Archives in both Potsdam and Merseburg and the
temporary storage depot for Prussian cultural property in Göttingen in
West Germany. The records center in Göttingen was dissolved in 1978,
and all East Prussian records subsequently transferred to the State Archives in West Berlin.[20] Independently, a partial parallel and duplicate

18. Henry R. Huttenbach, *The Destruction of the Jewish Community of Worms,
1933–1945* (New York, 1981), pp. 217–19. See also deportation lists from Jewish
communities in the Palatinate, LBI, NY, AR 2039/1–3.

19. The record group, "Das Institut zur Erforschung der Judenfrage," YIVO Institute for Jewish Research, New York (hereafter YIVO) contains a file entitled
"Kennkarten: Worms and Bezirk Worms."

20. For wartime reports about the German transport and evacuation of the Königsberg State Archives, see NARS, DC, *German Records Microfilmed at Alexandria, Va.,*
Records of the Office of the Reich Commissioner for the Baltic States (Reichskommissar
für das Ostland), 1941–45, microfilm publication T 459, especially rolls 3, 11, and 12;
and Records of the Reich Ministry for Occupied Eastern Territories (Reichsministerium
für die besetzten Ostgebiete), microfilm publication T 454, roll 2, frames 4907953–4,
and roll 107, frames 1236–38. See also Kurt Forstreuter, *Das Preussische Staatsarchiv
in Königsberg: Ein geschichtlicher Rückblick mit einer Übersicht über seine Bestände*
(Göttingen, 1955); Bernhart Jähnig, "Militärgeschichtliche Quellen des Staatsarchivs
Königsberg (Archivbestände Preussischer Kulturbesitz) im Staatlichen Archivlager in
Göttingen," *Militärgeschichtliche Mitteilungen* 16, no. 2 (1974): 173–214; and Hans
Branig, Winfried Bliss, and Werner Petermann, *Übersicht über die Bestände des
Geheimen Staatsarchivs in Berlin-Dahlem* (Berlin and Cologne, 1966–67).

record existed; during the 1920s, Jacob Jacobson visited the State Archives in Königsberg and took copious extracts and research copies from Schrötter's reports. These notes survived with the remnants of the Gesamtarchiv and were eventually deposited along with Jacobson's literary estate at the Leo Baeck Institute.[21]

Often artifacts from the past have been rediscovered by chance. In 1978 the Jagellonian Library in Cracow renovated an almost forgotten subbasement and accidentally unearthed the original correspondence of Rahel Varnhagen, scores by Wolfgang Amadeus Mozart and Franz Schubert, and several manuscripts about ichthyology from the early nineteenth century.[22] Such spectacular finds are admittedly rare.

Nonliterary evidence and older printed literature often make possible the reconstruction of a past otherwise lost. Thus the history of the Danzig Jewish community was written because its ritual objects are extant, having been shipped intact in 1939 to the Jewish Theological Seminary in New York.[23] Similarly the history of eighteenth-century Jewish communities in Mecklenburg can be found in late nineteenth-century publications available in major Judaica libraries.[24] The use of art, artifacts, and older secondary literature makes scholarship about the early period of German-Jewish history possible.

Nazi and Jewish records about the Holocaust, however, present distinctive problems that rarely occur in the archival heritage of earlier epochs. First is the problem of the colossal size of even the incomplete record. More than sixteen hundred tons of paper (many millions of pages, often torn out of context) were captured by the Western Allies in 1945 and shipped to the United States and England for microfilming.[25] Known to-

21. Jacob Jacobson Papers, LBI, NY, AR 7002/IV.
22. Deborah Hertz, "The Varnhagen Collection Is in Krakow," *American Archivist* 44 (1981): 223–28.
23. Jewish Museum, New York, *Danzig 1939: Treasures of a Destroyed Community* (Detroit, 1980), p. 34.
24. For example, see Leopold Donath, *Geschichte der Juden in Mecklenburg von den ältesten Zeiten (1266) bis auf die Gegenwart (1874)* (Leipzig, 1874).
25. War Documentation Project Study, no. 1, *Guide to Captured German Documents*, prepared by Gerhard L. Weinberg and the WDP Staff under the direction of Fritz T. Epstein (Maxwell Air Force Base, Ala., 1952); and *Supplement to the Guide to Captured German Documents* (Washington, D.C., 1959). See also the seventy-six *National Archives Guides to German Records Microfilmed at Alexandria, Va.* (Washington, D.C., 1958–84); and George O. Kent, ed. and comp., *A Catalog of Files and Microfilms of the German Foreign Archives, 1920–1945* (Stanford, Calif., 1962–72). A concise list of the more than thirty thousand rolls of microfilm of these captured records is found in Wolfe, *Captured German and Related Records*, pp. 267–76. Further data are found in John A. Bernbaum, "The Captured German Records: A Bibliographical Survey," *Historian* 32 (1970): 564–75.

day as captured German documents, they contain a great variety of material: the records of German government agencies; the records of Nazi party organizations; the records of private business enterprises (e.g., I. G. Farben); the papers, art, and artifacts of other nations and Jewish individuals looted by the German army; and many personal German and non-German literary estates.[26] These records were barely intact even in 1945. Documents from an intact common provenance were often dispersed at the end of the war. American, French, British, and Russian troops seized those papers left behind by the Germans for tactical and intelligence information, the needs of occupation government, the preparation of war crimes trials, historical study, and as souvenirs.

By 1960, many of the original records had been returned from the Captured Records Section of the Federal Records Center at Alexandria, Virginia, to successor institutions in West Germany, and from the Soviet Union to depositories in East Germany.[27] In addition to the more than thirty thousand microfilms at the National Archives in Washington, D.C., many original records in a multiplicity of languages (French, German, Italian, Polish, Russian, Hungarian, and Yiddish) were dispersed to specialized subject research centers like the Library of Congress, the Hoover Institution, the YIVO Institute, and the Leo Baeck Institute.[28] Similar records were also deposited in analogous foreign research centers, as, for example, the Centre Documentation Juive Contemporaine in Paris, the Netherlands State Institute for War Documentation in Amsterdam, the Wiener Library in London, the Institut für Zeitgeschichte in Munich, and Yad Vashem in Jerusalem.[29] Other German government, corporate, and

26. Wolfe, *Captured German and Related Records,* pp. 267–73.

27. Friedrich P. Kahlenberg, *Deutsche Archive in West und Ost: Zur Entwicklung des staatlichen Archivwesens seit 1945* (Düsseldorf, 1972); Josef Henke, "Das Schicksal deutscher zeitgeschichtlicher Quellen in Kriegs- und Nachkriegszeiten: Beschlagnahme, Rückführung, Verblieb," *Vierteljahrshefte für Zeitgeschichte* 30 (1982): 557–620; Helmut Lötzke, "Bericht über die von der UdSSR an die DDR seit 1957 übergebenen Archivbestände," *Archivmitteilungen* 10 (1960): 12–15; George O. Kent, "Research Opportunities in West and East German Archives for the Weimar Period and the Third Reich," *Central European History* 12 (1979): 38–67.

28. Henke, "Das Schicksal deutscher zeitgeschichtlicher Quellen," passim; *Guide to Captured Documents* and 1959 *Supplement,* passim; Agnes Peterson, comp., *Archival and Manuscript Materials at the Hoover Institution on War, Revolution, and Peace: A Checklist of Major Collections* (Stanford, 1978); "The YIVO Institute for Jewish Research and Its Holdings on the Holocaust," *American Committee on the History of the Second World War Newsletter,* no. 19 (April 1978): 22–24; Sybil Milton, "The Leo Baeck Institute in New York and Its Holdings on the Second World War," ibid., no. 20 (Fall 1978): pp. 7–11.

29. Henry Friedlander, "Publications on the Holocaust," in *The German Church Struggle and the Holocaust,* ed. Franklin Littell and Hubert Locke (Detroit, 1974),

personal papers were pulled from filing cabinets and torn out of context for use in the International Military Tribunal in Nuremberg and other subsequent U.S. Army trials. The surviving files were not historical archives arranged for scholarly use; they were usually current office files from the Weimar and Nazi years captured *in situ*. The Nuremberg documentation alone amounted to thousands of pages in twenty-five series. Often the newly created record series were purely arbitrary; the famous PS designation, for example, stood for Paris-Storey, or the documents collected by Col. Robert G. Storey in Paris.[30] It is important to remember, moreover, that traditional distinctions between private and public records did *not* apply to documents created under totalitarian rule. Thus, the Gestapo (a government agency) and the Sicherheitsdienst (a party agency) functioned in reality as a single unit. It is also important to remember that denunciation and reprisals meant that some types of documentation remained unwritten and unrecorded in order to evade state censorship and police control. Fortunately, the German bureaucracy used duplicating and mimeograph machines with abandon, and even if the original of a letter or report was lost, one of the many copies often survived—as, for example, did a copy of the Wannsee protocol.

In the world of official Nazi documents and captured German records, the filmed copy rather than the original document is the norm. This has led to certain problems of bibliographical control for both the scholar and the archivist. Despite the relatively large number of guides and published inventories to American, German, and Israeli depositories, there is colossal confusion about the location and nature of the records.[31] In the United States, the National Archives used RG (record group) numbers, T numbers, and microfilm roll and frame numbers; in Britain, the Foreign Office used multiple digit serial numbers with letter tags like EAP, although naval records filmed in England have PG or TA labels. "At times," Henry Friedlander has observed, "this profusion of letters and

---

pp. 69–94; Friedlander, "The Historian and the Documents" (Paper presented at the annual meeting of the Society of American Archivists, Chicago, September 27, 1979).

30. John Mendelsohn, "Trial by Document: The Uses of Seized Records in United States Proceedings at Nuernberg" (Ph.D. diss., University of Maryland, 1974); Jacob Robinson and Henry Sachs, *The Holocaust: The Nuremberg Evidence—Documents, Digest, Index, and Chronological Tables* (Jerusalem, 1976).

31. Sybil Milton, review of *Guide to Unpublished Materials of the Holocaust Period*, by Yehuda Bauer, vols. 1–5, *American Archivist* 40 (1977): 349–51; Wolfgang Scheffler, "Der Beitrag der Zeitgeschichte zur Erforschung der NS-Verbrechen: Versäumnisse, Schwierigkeiten, und Aufgaben," in *Vergangenheitsbewältigung durch Strafverfahren?* ed. Jürgen Weber and Peter Steinbach (Munich, 1984), pp. 121–22.

symbols resembles the secret designations of the ancient cabala."[32] This complexity and confusion is repeated in the footnotes and citations of published scholarship. The same document can be, and often is, cited in different books as a Nuremberg document, a National Archives microfilm, and an item from the Bundesarchiv. Because there are few, if any, concordances, the citation depends on when and where the research was done. Compounding the confusion, many depositories have subsequently acquired original captured document collections and then imposed their own classification systems without reference to identical documents in parallel microfilm collections. Thus the Berlin Collection at YIVO lists one document as Occ E 2–84, in fact identical with Nuremberg document PS 1472, a report dated December 16, 1942, about the shipment of forty-five thousand Jews from Bialystok, Theresienstadt, the Netherlands, and Berlin to Auschwitz.[33] All of the institutions have also purchased microfilms from the National Archives, the Berlin Document Center (BDC), or the Bundesarchiv in Koblenz.

The liberalization of reprography rules has led to an increase in the number of microforms and photocopies purchased by American scholars in foreign archives and subsequently deposited as part of their literary papers in American repositories.[34] Although there are no common standards for cataloging archival microfilms, three distinctive patterns can be identified. The first practice is to classify foreign microfilms containing archival records as if they were books, assigning them Library of Congress classification numbers. The Hoover Institution on War, Revolution, and Peace, in Stanford, California, has adopted this practice, and its card catalog integrates microfilms of captured German documents from the British Public Record Office and the Berlin Document Center with published literature.[35] The second practice is to use the archive accession or record group number of the depository, meanwhile retaining the original inven-

32. Friedlander, "Historian and the Documents." See also Scheffler, "Der Beitrag der Zeitgeschichte."

33. Berlin Collection, YIVO, Record Group 215; this document is also listed as PS 1472 in Robinson and Sachs, *Holocaust*, p. 140 (item 2074).

34. Walter Rundell, Jr., *In Pursuit of American History: Research and Training in the United States* (Norman, Okla., 1970), pp. 202–59; International Council on Archives, Microfilm Committee, "Recommended Practices for the Titling of Microfilm (Microfiche and Roll Microfilm) of Archives and Manuscripts," *Bulletin* (Madrid) 6 (1977): 28–33; Ernst Posner, "Effects of Changes of Sovereignty on Archives" and "Public Records under Military Occupation," in his *Archives and the Public Interest* (Washington, D.C., 1967), pp. 168–81, 182–97.

35. Card catalog of the Hoover Institution on War, Revolution, and Peace, Stanford, California.

tory or collection identification of the primary depository. This is the practice of the Institut für Zeitgeschichte in Munich and the Leo Baeck Institute in New York.[36] The third usage is to give archival microforms new numbers without connection or reference to the originals, a practice similar to laundering out the identity of the primary depository; this is occasionally followed by Yad Vashem.[37] All three patterns coexist in the United States, Europe, and Israel, creating additional bibliographical confusions. Consequently identical materials available on film and as originals are given different citations if located in two repositories. Furthermore, this freedom to cite the same material in a multiplicity of ways makes it virtually impossible for scholars to identify duplicative and unique materials; it also hampers any possibility of correlating or linking segments of a fractured record group between repositories.

The residual archival papers of Julius Streicher form an archival maze through the different cataloging styles of four American and two West German depositories. The surviving fragmentary records consist of Streicher's correspondence and manuscripts about the early history of the Nazi party in Franconia and the Nuremberg police files about his journalistic and party activities, 1920–40. These records were transferred from the BDC to the Bundesarchiv in Koblenz and also duplicated as a segment of the microfilmed NSDAP Hauptarchiv at the Hoover Institution.[38] A second part of the Streicher papers is the partial editorial files of *Der Stürmer,* which include Streicher's correspondence with contributors, illustrators, photographers, and readers. The letters to the editors between 1933 and 1945 come from all of occupied Europe and often contain illustrations or photographs submitted for potential use in the paper. These fragments are located at both the Leo Baeck Institute and the YIVO Institute in New York. They originate, however, from differ-

---

36. Card catalogs of the Institut für Zeitgeschichte, Munich, and the Leo Baeck Institute, New York, which cite the repository where microfilm was purchased. For example, the 260 archival and press clipping rolls of the Wiener Library Microfilm (LBI, NY, AR 7187) use the original inventory of the Wiener Library in London, including all its roll numbers. See also "The Press Archives of the Wiener Library," *LBI Library and Archives News,* no. 16 (June 1982): 6.

37. Yehuda Bauer, ed., *Guide to Unpublished Materials of the Holocaust Period* (Jerusalem, 1975), vols. 3–5, and the footnotes in all Yad Vashem publications. See particularly Chana Byers Abells, ed., *Archives of the Destruction: A Photographic Record of the Holocaust* (Jerusalem, 1981), which never cites the institution that provided Yad Vashem with its photographic duplicates.

38. Gerhard Granier, Josef Henke, and Klaus Oldenhage, eds., *Das Bundesarchiv und seine Bestände,* 3d ed. (Boppard a.R., 1977), p. 661; Grete Heinz and Agnes Peterson, eds., *NSDAP Hauptarchiv: Guide to the Hoover Institution Microfilm Collection* (Stanford, 1964), pp. 129–31, 143–44.

ent sources: the files at the Leo Baeck were "liberated" from the larger *Stürmer* archive and library in Nuremberg; the YIVO records came via the U.S. Army and the Offenbach records depot in the immediate aftermath of the war. These two fragments are the missing files of the larger editorial archives of *Der Stürmer* that are today deposited in the Nuremberg Municipal Archives (Stadtarchiv Nürnberg). An additional splinter of seventy-seven microfilm frames of *Der Stürmer* correspondence with authors and illustrators is found on captured German documents films deposited in the National Archives in Washington, D.C.[39] The fifth and last set of Streicher files includes his interrogation, trial, and sentencing by the International Military Tribunal in Nuremberg. These official records resulting from the American presence in postwar Germany are American administrative records and deposited at the National Archives.[40] Currently available institutional guides and national catalogs do not unravel this maze of duplicative and unique Streicher materials, nor can these dispersed records stemming from a common or similar provenance be currently linked by subject retrieval. The result is surely not cost effective, nor does it prevent the blind passages of research, since scholars must visit or contact at least four institutions.

The German looting of rare Judaica artifacts, manuscripts, and books occasionally—unwittingly—led to their survival. Alfred Rosenberg created the half-million-volume Judaica library at the Institut zur Erfor-

39. Bernard Kolb Papers, LBI, NY, AR 3959/V. Kolb was the business manager of the Jewish community of Nuremberg from 1923 until his deportation to Theresienstadt in 1941. He returned to Nuremberg in 1945 to testify before the International Military Tribunal and "liberated" more than one thousand pages of original files from the editorial offices of *Der Stürmer*. He brought these papers with him to the United States, and they were deposited as part of his literary estate at the Leo Baeck Institute. Substantial excerpts from these records have been published in Fred Hahn, ed., *"Lieber Stürmer": Leserbriefe an das NS Kampfblatt, 1925–1945* (Stuttgart, 1978). The LBI, NY, inventory is organized by locality and name of the *Stürmer* column. A similar organization is clear in the holdings of the *Stürmer* library and editorial archive deposited in the Stadtarchiv Nürnberg (Nuremberg Municipal Archives). See Arnd Müller, "Das Stürmer-Archiv im Stadtarchiv Nürnberg," *Vierteljahrshefte für Zeitgeschichte* 32 (1984): 326–29. See also Berlin Collection, YIVO, NY, Record Group 215; and *German Records Microfilmed at Alexandria,* guide 39, which includes a seventy-seven-page fragment of Streicher and *Stürmer* correspondence with authors and illustrators during the mid-1930s, NARS, DC, microfilm publication T 174, roll 415, frames 1941149–225.

40. See *Trial of the Major War Criminals. National Archives Microfilm Publications,* Pamphlet M-1019, lists an interrogation report about Streicher, dated July 2, 1945, p. 85. See also Sybil Milton, "The Archival Jigsaw Puzzle: Fragmentation and Foreign Language Records of the Holocaust" (Paper presented at the annual meeting of the Society of American Archivists, Chicago, September 27, 1979).

schung der Judenfrage in Frankfurt am Main, which incorporated more than seven hundred crates from the holdings of the International Institute for Social History (Amsterdam), the Rosenthaliana Library (Amsterdam), the YIVO Institute (Vilna), and other private collections (such as the Warburg Library in Hamburg, the Rothschild archives in Paris and Vienna, and the holdings of the rabbinical seminary in Berlin).[41] Eight Jewish scholars were employed as library catalogers in this bizarre Nazi enterprise, and the Reichsvereinigung der Juden in Deutschland eventually acceded to the requests of the Reich Security Office and appointed an additional twenty-five Jewish librarians, professors, and scholars to administer this collection. These books and papers eventually were transferred to Theresienstadt, where they formed the core of the Ghetto Central Library. Even the 1944 propaganda film *Der Führer schenkt den Juden eine Stadt* included one scene in the ghetto library.[42] Although many of the original libraries were destroyed initially by Nazi vandalism and later by Allied bombings of German cities, the U.S. Army captured many items in 1945 and restored them to either the original owners or designated successor institutions around the world via the Offenbach depot.[43]

It is important to remember that there is also a Jewish record of the Holocaust created at the time or in the immediate postwar period. The secret archives of the Warsaw ghetto, *Oneg Shabbat,* were buried in milk cans under the supervision of Emanuel Ringelblum and recovered from the rubble in 1946 for deposit in the Jewish Historical Institute of Warsaw.[44] Similar ghetto archives and historical projects recording the fate of the Jews of Nazi-occupied Europe existed in Kovno, Bialystok, and Lodz; memoirs, chronicles, diaries, and art works were buried by their creators in windowsills, in the ground, in walls, and in attics, and only partly relocated and retrieved after the war.[45] In the DP camps and centers, Jewish historical commissions sought to record the experiences of

41. Council of Jewish Communities in the Czech Lands, *Terezin* (Prague, 1965), pp. 170–77.
42. Ibid. See also H. G. Adler, *Theresienstadt, 1941–1945: Das Antlitz einer Zwangsgemeinschaft,* 2d rev. ed. (Tübingen, 1960); Adler, *Die verheimlichte Wahrheit: Theresienstädter Dokumente* (Tübingen, 1958). A videotape copy of the *Der Führer schenkt den Juden eine Stadt* is available in the LBI, NY.
43. Seymour J. Pomrenze, "Protection, Use, and Return of Captured German Records," in Wolfe, *Captured German and Related Records,* p. 13.
44. Friedman, "Fate of the Jewish Book," pp. 88–99.
45. Janet Blatter and Sybil Milton, *Art of the Holocaust* (New York, 1981), pp. 36–43.

the survivors.[46] These well-defined postwar projects have had few successors in more recent oral history ventures.

Many German-Jewish refugees sought to reconstruct the history of their former communities. Rudolph Apt, for example, residing in London, corresponded with fellow emigrants and survivors from Dresden in order to compile a card and manuscript file about the fate of Dresden Jews between 1933 and 1947.[47] Morris Vierfelder took his chronicle of family and Jewish life in Buchau, a village in southern Württemberg, with him to the United States. His daughter was subsequently stationed as an army nurse near Buchau shortly after the war. She was able to retrieve a rare series of lantern slides showing the unique village synagogue with steeple and bell. The building had been destroyed during the pogrom of November 1938.[48]

Historical records were often saved by accident. Two instances drawn from the experience of the Leo Baeck Institute are probably typical. The case files of the Gildemeester rescue effort to aid the emigration of Austrian Jews after 1938 were found together with the papers of the group's secretary, Hermann Fuernberg, by an attentive neighbor in Fuernberg's New York apartment house. After Fuernberg's death, his landlord had stored his papers and possessions in the trash room, where they were found virtually intact though filthy, as they had been dumped near a coal furnace.[49] A similar incident occurred when a Long Island garbage hauler retrieved rare Berlin Jewish communal photo albums inscribed with dedications to Heinrich Stahl, chairman of the Berlin Jewish community from 1938 to 1942. The albums contained several hundred illustrations showing the concerts and other cultural programs of the Jüdischer Kulturbund, the offices and activities of the Jewish *Winterhilfe* campaign, life in a suburban old age home of the Berlin Jewish community, and other Ber-

---

46. Yad Vashem holds the records of several of these Jewish historical commissions. See also David P. Boder, *I Did Not Interview the Dead* (Urbana, Ill., 1949); and Boder, "Topical Autobiographies of Displaced People" (1950–57), transcripts of seventy interviews completed between 1946 and 1949 in the DP camps. The interviews were recorded on a model-50 wire recorder and two hundred spools of carbon steel wire and are transcribed verbatim in sixteen volumes (3,162 pages), including a detailed subject and geographical index. Boder's interviews were financed by grants from the U.S. Public Health Service and the National Institute of Mental Health. They contain detailed narratives about experiences in concentration and labor camps throughout Europe. The volumes are available in the library of the Simon Wiesenthal Center in Los Angeles and the Neurological Medical Library at UCLA, Los Angeles.

47. Rudolf Apt Papers, LBI, NY, AR 7180/II–IV.

48. Morris Vierfelder Papers, ibid., AR 7180/I–VIII.

49. Hermann Fuernberg Papers, including case files of the Gildemeester-Hilfskomitee, ibid., AR 7194.

lin Jewish organizations at work between 1936 and 1940.[50] Most lost records went unrecorded and consequently unknown. Only in the rarest instances could the written record be reconstructed through the use of oral history. The papers of the Verein der Ostjuden and the Reichsverband polnischer Juden in Deutschland from 1933 to 1939 have vanished, and two slender postwar oral histories amounting to about sixty pages are insufficient to tell us much about these self-defense organizations before the expulsion of Polish Jews from Germany in late October 1938 and their relationship with other German-Jewish organizations.[51]

The uses of oral history to recover lost fragments of the German-Jewish experience have several troubling features when applied to the period of the Holocaust. Although the value of oral history to fill historical lacunae is clear, it is important to remember that oral testimony is subjective for both the interviewer and interviewee. The usual criteria for selecting interview subjects are either topical or biographical and may focus on either prominent figures or the average person.[52] The constraints of time and money in audio- or videotaping and transcribing interviews require selectivity in project design, so that those subjects for which aggregate data are needed or unclear events (where, perhaps, only a handful of survivors are available) receive priority. Instead, American oral history projects about the Holocaust have had little focus and often elicit vague, repetitive, emotional, and often factually erroneous testimony from all survivors residing in any given community who volunteer to be taped, simply because funding was available for these interviews. The resulting mishmash trivializes the events and exploits the individual survivor, who must recall emotionally charged events at a distance of forty years and whose evidence may be useless for future historical scholarship. Few recent programs have aided scholarship, although they do produce impressive results for classroom use in the public schools.

One of the best-designed postwar interview series was completed by

50. Heinrich Stahl Papers, ibid., AR 7171.

51. Sybil Milton, scholars' query column, *LBI Library and Archives News*, no. 19 (December 1983): 8; Milton, "The Expulsion of Polish Jews from Germany, October 1938–July 1939: A Documentation," *Leo Baeck Institute Year Book* 29 (1984): 169–99. The oral histories are an interview with Zygmund Glicksohn, September 1944 (3 pp.), Ball-Kaduri Collection, Yad Vashem, Jerusalem, O 1/7; and Dr. Shaul Esch's interview of Moshe Ortner, former head of the Reichsverband polnischer Juden (56 pp.), Oral History Division, Institute of Contemporary Jewry, Hebrew University, Jerusalem, no. 00332–00388.

52. The Oral History Program at Columbia University interviews only prominent personalities; the publications of Studs Terkel exemplify interviews with average people around certain themes, such as the Depression or the Second World War.

the Wiener Library with participants in the women's demonstration in Berlin during March 1943, the so-called *Fabrikaktion,* protesting the roundups of Jewish relatives living in protected mixed marriages.[53] This demonstration was a unique instance of mass popular resistance that did not bring Gestapo reprisals upon the demonstrators; it certainly requires further analysis and study. A second project that would have value for scholarship is the collection of aggregate data about Jews who survived by passing or in hiding between 1941 and 1945. Since altruism was not normative behavior during the Third Reich, this type of oral history project would allow systematic analysis of the profiles and motivations of individuals and groups who aided Jews in hiding without profit or reward.[54] Oral testimonies could also be used to elicit data about Jewish folklore and popular culture under Nazi terror, the role of religion, humor, family life, and the gender-specific experiences of women.[55] Such subjects would add to our historical knowledge and understanding of this tragic epoch, whereas random interviews of survivors are probably useless for historians and social scientists.

Film and photographic records are important historical artifacts; the absence of formal academic training in the interpretation of visual communication, however, has led to abuses tantamount to visual illiteracy.[56] Historical use and interpretation of visual images, whether art or photography, depends on the quality of supplementary written data. Dating or

53. Wiener Library Microfilm, LBI, NY, AR 7187, roll 600. See also LBI Microfilm Collection, roll 239: Anklageschrift in der Strafsache gegen Otto Bovensiepen et al., 1969, the indictment of the Berlin Gestapo for the deportation of the Jews of Berlin. See also, transcript of an interview by Bernd H. Stappert, "Zu denen halten, die verfolgt sind!: Zeitgeschichtliches in der Lebensgeschichte der Mieke Monjau" (28 pp.), transcribing an interview broadcast on Südwestfunk, Stuttgart, 1982; typescript available through Südwestfunk.

54. Aggregate data on survival in hiding have been gathered by interviews with Berlin survivors and published in Jochen Köhler, *Klettern in der Grossstadt: Volkstümliche Geschichten vom Überleben in Berlin, 1933–1945* (Berlin, 1979); Leonard Gross, *Last Jews in Berlin* (New York, 1982); and Eva Fogelman and Valerie Lewis Wiener, "From Bystander to Rescuer: A Social-Psychological Study of Altruism in Wartime" (Social-Personality Psychology Department, Graduate Center of the City University of New York, January 1983, photocopy).

55. See Esther Katz and Joan Miriam Ringelheim, eds., *Women Surviving the Holocaust: Conference Proceedings,* Institute for Research in History, Occasional Papers (New York, 1983).

56. For an introduction to serious studies in photographic and visual communication, see Gisele Freund, *Photography and Society* (Boston, 1980); Roland Günter, *Fotografie als Waffe: Geschichte der sozialdokumentarischen Fotografie* (Hamburg and Berlin, 1977); Jean Berger and Jean Mohr, *Another Way of Telling* (New York, 1982); and Dino Brugioni, "Aerial Photography: Reading the past, Revealing the Future," *Smithsonian,* March 1984, pp. 150–60.

assigning authorship to unlabeled photographs is difficult in any epoch; even dated photographs present difficult interpretive problems. The huge number of photos (approximately one million images) available as part of the captured German documents from the Second World War present some of the same problems as parallel written and textual records. Multiple copies of the same photograph often are located in several repositories, frequently with completely different descriptive labels.[57] Systematic and comprehensive information rarely accompanies the original negative or file reproductions. The record includes battle scenes and aerial photography; photos showing the persecution of German Jews and liberation from the camps; social, industrial, or architectural photos; and portraits of family groups and individuals. Archival control of these images must be improved so that the historical record is not further damaged or lost by inaction and indifference.

There will never be a perfect archive, but our existing resources can be more skillfully managed if scholars and repositories find cooperative solutions to the problems of intellectual and bibliographical control of our archival heritage. It would be utopian to assume that computer-assisted indexing alone could overcome some of the problems caused by the absence of common descriptive standards for dispersed historical materials. The veritable maze of splintered and fractured collections in German Judaica and the wild array of possible scholarly citations are neither cost effective nor good scholarship. The liberalization of conditions of access and use, the growing number of theme-specialized Judaica archives and Holocaust repositories with overlapping and often duplicative collecting areas, and the international expansion of archival clientele since the Second World War have created both new problems and new opportunities for cooperative solutions. The ravages of time, the destruction caused by wars and natural catastrophes, and the almost inevitable fragmentation of materials have certainly damaged the surviving historical record. But it is just as certain that our own attitudes and actions as archivists and historians can make an important difference in the quality and availability of the historical record documenting the modern German-Jewish experience.

57. See Sybil Milton, "The Camera as Weapon: Documentary Photography and the Holocaust," *Simon Wiesenthal Center Annual* 1 (1984): 45–68; esp. pp. 61–63.

Contributors

ALEXANDER ALTMANN was born in Kassa, Hungary, in 1906. He received his Ph.D. from the University of Berlin in 1931. He served as a rabbi in Berlin and then in Manchester, England, where he founded the Institute of Jewish Studies and served as its director from 1953 to 1959. In 1959 he emigrated to the United States, where he occupied the Lown Chair at Brandeis University, Waltham, Massachusetts, until 1976 and served as Director of the Philip W. Lown Institute for Advanced Studies from 1960 to 1965. He is currently Philip W. Lown Professor of Jewish Philosophy and the History of Ideas, Emeritus, at Brandeis University, and an Associate at the Center for Jewish Studies at Harvard University. He is a Fellow of the American Academy of Arts and Sciences, the Medieval Academy of America, the American Academy for Jewish Research, and the Lessing Academy in Wolfenbüttel. He is a member of the Board of Directors of the Leo Baeck Institute, New York, and an honorary member of the Council of the World Union of Jewish Studies. He holds honorary degrees from the University of Manchester, Hebrew Union College—Jewish Institute of Religion in Cincinnati, the University of Munich, Brandeis University, the University of Trier, and the Hebrew University, Jerusalem. His publications include *Isaac Israeli: A Neoplatonic Philosopher of the Early Tenth Century* (with S. M. Stern, 1958), *Studies in Religious Philosophy and Mysticism* (1969), *Moses Mendelssohns Frühschriften zur Metaphysik* (1969), *Moses Mendelssohn: A Biographical Study* (1973), *Essays in Jewish Intellectual History* (1981), *Die trostvolle Aufklärung* (1982), and *Panim shel Yahadut* (*Selected Essays*) (in Hebrew, 1982).

STEVEN E. ASCHHEIM was born in 1942 in Johannesburg, South Africa. He received his Ph.D. in 1980 from the University of Wisconsin—Madison, and is currently Lecturer in German Cultural and Intellectual History at the Hebrew University, Jerusalem. He is the author of *Brothers and Strangers: The East European Jew in German and German Jewish Consciousness, 1800–1923* (1982).

KURT DÜWELL was born in Düsseldorf, Germany, in 1937. He studied history, German literature, philosophy, and art history at the Universities of Bonn, Munich, and Cologne, and earned his Ph.D. in 1966 from the University of Cologne. He has been a research assistant at the Institute for History at the Rheinisch-Westfälischen Technischen Hochschule in Aachen and taught in the History Department at the University of Cologne. In 1974 he completed his Habilitation. Since 1977 he has been Professor of Modern History at the University of Trier. His recent publications include *Entstehung und Entwicklung der Bundesrepublik Deutschland, 1945–1961* (1981) and the four-volume *Rheinland-Westfalen im Industrie Zeitalter* (*1815–1965*) (1983–85). He is editor of the series *Beiträge zur Geschichte der Kulturpolitik* and co-editor of *Archiv für Kulturgeschichte*.

LOTHAR KAHN was born in the Saar Territory in 1922. He emigrated to Luxembourg, and then to the United States in 1937. He received his Ph.D. from Columbia University in 1954. Since 1946 he has taught at Central Connecticut State University in New Britain, where he is now Professor of Modern Languages. He received the University Distinguished Service Award in 1974. He is the author of *Mirrors of the Jewish Mind* (1968) and *Insight and Action: The Life and Work of Lion Feuchtwanger* (1975).

MARION KAPLAN was born in New Jersey in 1946. She received her Ph.D. from Columbia University in 1977 and was Associate Director of the Leo Baeck Institute, New York. She is currently Associate Professor of History at Queens College of the City University of New York. She is the author of *The Jewish Feminist Movement in Germany: The Campaigns of the Jüdischer Frauenbund, 1904–1938* (1979), a contributing co-editor of *When Biology Became Destiny: Women in Weimar and Nazi Germany* (1984), and a contributing editor of *The Marriage Bargain: The Dowry in European History* (1984).

JACOB KATZ was born in Magyargencs, Hungary, in 1904. He received his Ph.D. from the University of Frankfurt in 1934. Since 1950 he has taught at the Hebrew University, Jerusalem, where he is currently Professor of Jewish Social History, Emeritus. He has been a visiting professor at Harvard University, UCLA, and Columbia University, and in 1983 received an honorary degree from the Hebrew University. He is a member of the Senate of the Lessing Academy in Wolfenbüttel, an Honorary Fellow of the University of Frankfurt, and an Honorary Foreign Member of the American Academy of Arts and Sciences. In 1980 he received both the Israel Prize for Jewish History and the Kaplun Prize of the Hebrew University, and in 1981 the B'nai B'rith International Award. He is the author of *Exclusiveness and Tolerance: Studies in Jewish-Gentile Relations in Medieval and Modern Times* (1961), *Tradition and Crisis: Jewish Society at the End of the Middle Ages* (1961), *Jews and Freemasons in Europe, 1723–1939* (1970), *Emancipation and Assimilation: Studies in Modern Jewish History* (1972), *Out of the Ghetto: The Social Background of Jewish Emancipation, 1770–1870* (1973), and *From Prejudice to Destruction: Anti-Semitism, 1700–1933* (1980).

MICHAEL A. MEYER was born in Berlin in 1937. He emigrated to the United States in 1941. In 1964 he received his Ph.D. from Hebrew Union College, Cincinnati, and has taught at its Jewish Institute of Religion in Los Angeles, and at UCLA, Antioch College, the University of Haifa, Ben Gurion University in Beersheba, and the Hebrew University, Jerusalem. Currently he is Professor of Jewish History at Hebrew Union College—Jewish Institute of Religion, Cincinnati. He is the author of *The Origins of the Modern Jew: Jewish Identity and European Culture in Germany, 1749–1824* (1967), which won the Jewish Book Council of America Award for the best book on Jewish thought in 1967, and *Ideas of Jewish History* (1974).

SYBIL MILTON was born in New York in 1941. She received her Ph.D. from Stanford University in 1971 and from 1974 to 1984 served as Chief Archivist of the Leo Baeck Institute, New York. She is currently consultant archivist for the U.S. Holocaust Memorial Council and co-editor of the *Simon Wiesenthal Center Annual*. She is coauthor of *Art of the Holocaust* (1981), which won the National Jewish Book Award in 1982. She translated and edited a new facsimile edition of *The Stroop Report* (1979) and served as a contributing co-editor to *Ideology,*

Bureaucracy, and Genocide (1981), *The Musy and Saly Mayer Affairs* (1982), and *Genocide* (1983).

GEORGE L. MOSSE was born in Berlin in 1918. He received his Ph.D. from Harvard University in 1946. He is currently Weinstein-Bascom Professor of Jewish Studies at the University of Wisconsin–Madison, where he has taught since 1955, and Koebner Professor of History at the Hebrew University, Jerusalem. He has held appointments at Stanford University, the Jewish Theological Seminary of America, the Australian National University, the University of Capetown, and the University of Munich. He has been a member of the Board of Governors of the Wiener Library since 1968, of the Leo Baeck Institute, New York, since 1974, and of the Tauber Institute for the Study of European Jewry at Brandeis University since 1979. He is co-editor of the *Journal of Contemporary History*. His recent publications include *Towards the Final Solution* (1978), *Nationalism and Sexuality: Respectability and Abnormal Sexuality in Modern Europe* (1985), and *German Jews beyond Judaism* (1985).

WERNER E. MOSSE was born in Berlin in 1918. He received his Ph.D. from Cambridge University in 1952. He is currently Professor Emeritus of the University of East Anglia, Norwich, a Fellow of the Royal Historical Society, and chairman of the London Board of the Leo Baeck Institute. He is the author of *The European Powers and the German Question, 1848–1871* (1958), *Alexander II and the Modernization of Russia, 1855–1881* (1959), *The Rise and Fall of the Crimean System, 1855–1871* (1963), and *Liberal Europe: The Age of Bourgeois Realism, 1848–1875* (1974), and co-editor of *Entscheidungsjahr 1932: Zur Judenfrage in der Endphase der Weimarer Republik* (1965; 2d ed., 1966), *Deutsches Judentum in Krieg und Revolution, 1916–1923* (1971), and *Juden im Wilhelminischen Deutschland, 1890–1914* (1976).

JEHUDA REINHARZ was born in Haifa, Israel, in 1944. He received his Ph.D. from Brandeis University in 1972. He has taught at the University of Michigan, Ann Arbor, and is currently Richard Koret Professor of Modern Jewish History and Director of the Tauber Institute for the Study of European Jewry at Brandeis University in Waltham, Massachusetts. He is also a Fellow of the Leo Baeck Institute, New York, and general editor of a series in modern Jewish history for Oxford University Press. He is the author of *Fatherland or Promised Land: The Dilemma of the German Jew, 1893–1914* (1975) and *Chaim Weizmann: The Making of a Zionist Leader* (1985), editor of *Dokumente zur Geschichte des deutschen Zionismus, 1882–1933* (1981), and co-editor of *The Jew in the Modern World: A Documentary History* (1980) and *Israel in the Middle East* (1984).

WALTER RÖLL was born in Berlin in 1937. He studied at the University of Hamburg, where he completed his doctorate in 1964 and his Habilitation in 1969. Since 1970 he has been Professor of Medieval German Philology at the University of Trier. His publications include *Kommentar zu 20 Liedern Oswalds von Wolkenstein* (1968) and *Oswald von Wolkenstein* (1981). He is the editor of *Fragen des ältern Jiddisch: Kolloquium in Trier, 1976* (1977) and *Jiddisch: Beiträge zur Sprach- und Literaturwissenschaft* (1981).

NATHAN ROTENSTREICH was born in Sambor, Poland, in 1914. He emigrated to Palestine in 1932. In 1938 he received his Ph.D. from the Hebrew University, Jerusalem, where he is Ahad Ha'am Professor of Philosophy, Emeritus. He has been a visiting professor at the City College of New York and at Harvard University and holds honorary degrees from the Jewish Theological Seminary in New York and Hebrew Union College in Cincinnati. In 1963 he received the Israel Prize for Humanities. He is the author of *Jewish Philosophy in Modern Times: From Mendelssohn to Rosenzweig* (1968) and *Jews and German Philosophy* (1984). He has also translated (with S. H. Bergman) Kant's *Three Critiques* and *On Eternal Peace* into Hebrew.

DAVID SORKIN was born in Chicago in 1953. He received his Ph.D. in 1983 from the University of California, Berkeley. He is currently an Assistant Professor of Judaic Studies at Brown University, Providence, Rhode Island. His article "Wilhelm von Humboldt: The Theory and Practice of Self-Formation, 1791–1810," appeared in the *Journal of the History of Ideas* in 1983.

GUY STERN was born in Hildesheim, Germany, in 1922. He received his Ph.D. from Columbia University in 1953 and has taught at Denison University, Columbia University, the University of Cincinnati, and the

University of Maryland. He is currently Distinguished Professor of Romance and Germanic Languages and Literatures at Wayne State University in Detroit. He has been a member and officer of the Leo Baeck Institute in New York, the American Association of Teachers of German, the Lessing Academy, the Kurt Weil Foundation, and the Society for Exile Studies. His publications include *War, Weimar, and Literature: The Story of the "Neue Merkur," 1914–1925* (1971) and *Alfred Neumann* (1979).

SHULAMIT VOLKOV was born in Tel Aviv, Israel, in 1942. She received her Ph.D. from the University of California, Berkeley, in 1972. She has been a Fellow at St. Anthony's College, Oxford, and at the Wissenschaftskolleg zu Berlin and is currently Associate Professor of History at Tel Aviv University in Israel. Her publications include *The Rise of Popular Antimodernism in Germany: The Urban Master Artisans, 1873–1893* (1978).

HARRY ZOHN was born in Vienna in 1923. He emigrated to the United States in 1940 and received his Ph.D. from Harvard University in 1952. He has been on the faculty of Brandeis University, Waltham, Massachusetts, since 1951 and is currently Professor of German. He holds an honorary degree from Suffolk University and has been a member and officer of the International Arthur Schnitzler Research Association, the International Stefan Zweig Society, the Austro-American Association of Boston, and the American Translators Association. He has translated works by Theodor Herzl, Jacob Burckhardt, Walter Benjamin, Marianne Weber, Karl Kraus, Kurt Tucholsky, Gershom Scholem, and Martin Buber. His publications also include *Wiener Juden in der deutschen Literatur* (1964), *Karl Kraus* (1971), and *Der Farbenvolle Untergang* (1971).

Index

Titles of works are indexed under author's name only.